Real Talk: Reality Television and Discourse Analysis in Action

Edited by

Nuria Lorenzo-Dus
Swansea University, UK

and

Pilar Garcés-Conejos Blitvich
University of North Carolina at Charlotte, USA

palgrave
macmillan

First published 2013 by
PALGRAVE MACMILLAN

Palgrave Macmillan in the UK is an imprint of Macmillan Publishers Limited,
registered in England, company number 785998, of Houndmills, Basingstoke,
Hampshire RG21 6XS.

Palgrave Macmillan in the US is a division of St Martin's Press LLC,
175 Fifth Avenue, New York, NY 10010.

Palgrave Macmillan is the global academic imprint of the above companies
and has companies and representatives throughout the world.

Palgrave® and Macmillan® are registered trademarks in the United States,
the United Kingdom, Europe and other countries.

ISBN 978–0–230–36871–2   hardback
ISBN 978–0–230–36872–9   paperback

This book is printed on paper suitable for recycling and made from fully
managed and sustained forest sources. Logging, pulping and manufacturing
processes are expected to conform to the environmental regulations of the
country of origin.

A catalogue record for this book is available from the British Library.

A catalog record for this book is available from the Library of Congress.

Typeset by MPS Limited, Chennai, India.

Contents

Part III   Reality Television and Aggression

Real Talk: Reality Television and Discourse
Analysis in Action

List of Tables

List of Figures

Acknowledgments

We would like to thank a number of people for their support in the preparation of this book. We are grateful to Olivia Middleton at Palgrave Macmillan for her diligence throughout, and to Jill Lake for her professionalism and advice during the editing process. We are also grateful to Joaquin Primo Pacheco for his work on the index, to the anonymous referees, who most constructively reported on first drafts of the different contributions included in this book, and of course to each and every one of our authors. Our warmest thanks, finally, go to our families.

Notes on Contributors

Monika Bednarek is Senior Lecturer in Linguistics at the University of Sydney. Her books include *Evaluation in Media Discourse* (about evaluative language use in British newspapers), *Emotion Talk across Corpora* (about the use of emotion words in different varieties of English) and *The Language of Fictional Television: Drama and Identity* (about the linguistic characteristics of television series). While she currently identifies most with the label 'corpus-based discourse analyst' she occasionally dabbles in other methodologies, including qualitative multimodal discourse analysis. Monika's current research focuses on the discursive construal of news values as well as the discourse in and around television series.

José Luis Blas Arroyo is Professor of Spanish Linguistics at the Universitat Jaume I (Castellón, Spain), where he teaches Sociolinguistics and Pragmatics in the Faculty of Arts. His main research areas are concerned with variationist and sociopragmatic topics (political discourse, (im)politeness, and so on), as well as bilingual issues related to Spanish in contact with other languages. He has published a number of books (*Políticos en conflicto, Sociolingüística del español, Lenguas en contacto, Discurso y sociedad*) and many articles on these subjects in international journals and research monographs. Since 1998 he has headed the 'Sociolinguistic Laboratory' at the Universitat Jaume I, and is currently co-editor of the academic journal *Culture, Language and Representation*.

Patricia Bou-Franch is Associate Professor at the University of Valencia, Spain. Her research interests include television / computer-mediated communication, gender and discourse, interpersonal and cross-cultural communication. She has published in international journals such as *Intercultural Pragmatics, Journal of Pragmatics, Journal of Computer-Mediated Communication, Journal of Politeness Research, Journal of Language and Politics, Gender and Language* and *Pragmatics and Society*. She is editor of *Ways into Discourse* (2006), and co-editor of *Discurso, Pragmática y Sociedad / Discourse, Pragmatics and Society* (2007) and *Gender and Sexual Identities in Transition: International Perspectives* (2008).

Jonathan Culpeper is Professor of English Language and Linguistics in the Department of Linguistics and English Language at Lancaster

University, UK. His work spans pragmatics, stylistics and the history of English. His major publications include *Language and Characterisation in Plays and Other Texts* (2001), *Early Modern English Dialogues: Spoken Interaction as Writing* (2010; co-authored with Merja Kytö), and *Impoliteness: Using Language to Cause Offence* (2011). He recently completed a three-year ESRC Fellowship investigating impoliteness. He is co-editor-in-chief of the *Journal of Pragmatics*.

Pilar Garcés-Conejos Blitvich is Professor of English at the University of North Carolina at Charlotte. She is interested in im/politeness models, genre and identity theories, and traditional and new media. Recent publications have appeared in international journals such as *Intercultural Pragmatics, Journal of Pragmatics, Journal of Politeness Research, International Review of Pragmatics, Journal of Computer Mediated Communication*, and *Journal of Language and Politics*. She recently co-edited *Pragmatics and Context* (2012) and guest edited special issues for *Intercultural Pragmatics* (2010) *and Journal of Politeness Research* (2013). She is co-editor of the series "Advances in Pragmatics and Discourse Analysis" (CSP) and editor of the *Journal of Language of Aggression and Conflict*.

Cynthia Gordon is Associate Professor of Communication and Rhetorical Studies at Syracuse University. She is author of *Making Meanings, Creating Family: Intertextuality and Framing in Family Interaction* (2009) and co-editor (with Deborah Tannen and Shari Kendall) of *Family Talk: Discourse and Identity in Four American Families* (2007). Her research interests include family discourse, health communication, and language and identity.

Michal Hamo is a lecturer at the School of Communication, Netanya Academic College, Israel. Her research interests include discourse analysis, children's peer talk and broadcast talk, with a focus on the relations between the discursive patterns of popular television texts, particularly talk shows, reality television and broadcast television news, and their cultural, social and institutional contexts. Her publications have appeared in journals such as *Discourse & Society* and *Media, Culture & Society*.

Oliver Holmes was an undergraduate in the Department of Linguistics and English Language at Lancaster University. In 2010, under the supervision of Jonathan Culpeper, he produced a dissertation entitled 'Ways of performing (im)politeness: A comparison of X-Factor and American Idol'. Data from that dissertation form the foundation of his chapter. He is now pursuing a career in secondary/high school education.

Nuria Lorenzo-Dus is Professor in English Language and Linguistics in the Department of English Language and Linguistics at Swansea University, where she also directs the Language Research Centre http://www.swansea.ac.uk/riah/researchgroups/lrc/. Her research expertise lies in the fields of media discourse analysis and pragmatics. She is author of *Television Discourse* (2009) and editor and chapter author of *Spanish at Work: Analysing Institutional Discourse across the Spanish-speaking World* (2010). Nuria Lorenzo-Dus has recently completed a collaborative AHRC project on mediated memory and the 2005 London bombings. She has published extensively on the discourse of citizens in the media, in journals such as *Discourse & Communication, Journal of Pragmatics* and *Journal of Politeness Research*.

María Laura Pardo is Professor of Media Discourse Analysis at the University of Buenos Aires and researcher at the Argentinean CONICET. She is also founding Director of the Latin American Discourse Analysis Network for the Study of Poverty (REDLAD), Director of the Linguistics Department of the CIAFIC-CONICET, and author of numerous research monographs. Her most recent book is *Metodología de la investigación lingüística. Método de análisis lingüístico sincrónico-diacrónico de textos* (2011).

Chris Shei has an MA in Linguistics, a PhD in TESOL from National Taiwan Normal University (1996), an MPhil in English and Applied Linguistics from the University of Cambridge, and a PhD in Informatics from the University of Edinburgh (2003). He has worked in Swansea University since 2003, teaching subjects in applied linguistics and translating between Chinese and English. His research interests include translation studies, computers and language, corpus linguistics, psycholinguistics, discourse analysis and Chinese and English language teaching.

Philippa K. Smith is based at AUT University in Auckland, New Zealand where she is research manager at the Institute of Culture, Discourse and Communication and a lecturer in the School of Language and Culture. Her research interests are media, communication and discourse analysis and her doctoral thesis investigated the discursive construction of New Zealand national identity in online environments. Philippa has written about animated sit-coms and documentary series and she has co-authored a number of book chapters with Allan Bell, Professor of Language and Communication at AUT, covering topics such as news discourse, the language of journalism, and English in mass communication.

Andrew Tolson is Professor of Media and Communication at De Montfort University, Leicester. He is also a founder member of the international Ross Priory Broadcast Talk Seminar. His publications include *Media Talk: Spoken Discourse on TV and Radio* (2006) and *Media Talk and Political Elections in Europe and America* (co-edited with Mats Ekström, 2013). He has published articles on celebrity talk and reality television but most of his recent work focuses on media talk (extended interviews and debates) in political communication.

Introduction

Planning for this book started in 2011, as we organized a specialist panel at the 12th *International Pragmatics Association Conference* on 'The discourse of reality television: Multidisciplinary and cross-cultural approaches'. The rationale behind this panel was our belief that, although reality television (RTV) has been under considerable scrutiny within the broad academic fields of sociology and cultural and media studies (e.g. Bonner 2003; Hill 2005, 2007), considerably less work has been conducted on its discourse features. The same rationale – and need for linguistic scholarship into RTV – has inspired this book. To our knowledge, *Real Talk: Reality Television and Discourse Analysis in Action* provides the first systematic attempt at bringing together key debates, challenges and opportunities in the analysis of the discourse – indeed the discourse practices – of RTV. Our aim is thus to shed fresh light on current understanding of this important media phenomenon through close examination of its multiple discourse realizations.

The scope and structure of *Real Talk: Reality Television and Discourse Analysis in Action*

To achieve our aim, we have set ourselves an ambitious though, we feel, achievable target: to interrogate RTV from within a diversity of discourse-analytic frameworks, and from multiple cultural/linguistic and generic contexts. For clarity of presentation, we have structured the book around three main parts. In Part I: *The Reality of Discourse and Discourse Analysis: Theory, Approaches, Practices*, we contextualize conceptually (Chapter 1) and methodologically (Chapter 2) the various empirical case studies that follow. These, in turn, are grouped into the next two parts, each bringing together empirical chapters around a uniting theme: identity

(Part II – Chapters 3 to 7) and aggression (Part III – Chapters 8 to 12). Both themes are commonplace in non-linguistic scholarship about RTV but the discourse-analytic perspective adopted in the five chapters that are devoted to each theme in the book provides new insights into how different identities are constructed (promoted or otherwise), and how relationships are routinely forged in ways that favour (non)verbal conflict and aggression, across genres of RTV.

In Chapter 3, titled 'How "real" is reality television in China? On the success of a Chinese dating programme', **Chris Shei** examines a reality dating show called *Feichengwurao* (FCWR, or 'do not disturb if you are not sincere') broadcast by China's Jiangsu Satellite TV. This is an adaptation from the British ITV dating show *Take Me Out* (TMO), effecting a change from a joyful and light-hearted atmosphere to serious courting sessions where formal partnership is contemplated. The launch of FCWR produced unprecedented viewing figures and overwhelming viewer responses. Many more reality shows followed. Shei's analysis shows the range of discourse structures through which different identities relating to, especially, the sphere of marriage for men and women are constructed in FCWR, as well as how the success of the show has contributed to RTV playing an important role in China for attracting people's attention and offering a site for social discussions on various topics (except political ones).

In 'The (inter)play of nationality, religiosity and gender: Textual mechanisms for the rich representation of Israeli identity on a reality gamedoc' (Chapter 4), **Michal Hamo** examines the tension between pluralistic and stereotypical identity representation on RTV in a unique case study – an Israeli race gamedoc explicitly dedicated to promoting secular–religious dialogue and tolerance within Jewish-Israeli society. Hamo's analysis reveals three mechanisms for rich identity representation: emphasizing diversity among religious contestants, thus demonstrating the flexibility of religious identity; a recurrent narrative structure of growing complexity; and highlighting the multidimensionality of identity. The use of these mechanisms involves tensions and balances between simplistic and complex perceptions of identity, the reaffirmation and challenge of stereotypes, and entertainment value and social responsibility. Hamo's analysis also demonstrates that self-reflection, humour, expectation reversal and playful performance are significant contemporary practices for identity construction and for its representation in popular culture texts.

'"There's no harm, is there, in letting your emotions out", a multimodal perspective on language, emotion and identity' (Chapter 5) offers an in-depth multimodal analysis of two extracts from the Australian RTV programme *MasterChef Australia* – one from *Junior MasterChef Australia* (with child contestants), and one from the 'classic' adult version. In this chapter, **Monika Bednarek**'s analysis focuses on strategies used in the Australian *MasterChef* franchise for projecting an image of *MasterChef Australia* as being 'uplifting' and 'supportive'. Her analysis identifies 'emotional identity construction' as a salient aspect of the discourse of RTV.

The aim of **Laura Pardo**'s chapter – 'The aesthetics of poverty and crime in Argentinean reality television' (Chapter 6) is to analyse the discourse in the Argentinean show *Police in Action* (PIA) about people who live in extreme poverty. Using a linguistic analysis framework developed by Pardo, the synchronic-diachronic method – this author shows how PIA uses discourse fragmentation in order to construct particular identities for those who live in extreme poverty. Discourse fragmentation manifests itself in the written presentation on the television screen of the speech of PIA's characters, which marks the transition from orality to literacy and is limited by the number of characters that can be shown on the screen. A double (oral-written) discourse arises as a result, in which utterance rheme and foci are disrupted, speakers' foci often disappearing in the edited version. Even semantic and (mandatory) grammaticalized categories change from a focal to a non-focal position and vice-versa, depending on whether the speaker's utterances are heard or read.

In the final chapter in Part II, titled 'Heroic endeavours: flying high in New Zealand reality television' (Chapter 7), **Philippa Smith** applies Norman Fairclough's (1995) Critical Discourse Analysis framework to explore nation-building processes at work in *Rescue 1* – a reality programme that follows the dramatic missions of the helicopter rescue service in Auckland, New Zealand. Through detailed examination of text, discursive and social practices, Smith's work demonstrates the programme's construction of ordinary New Zealanders as heroes and how this contributes to reinforcing a historically dominant discourse about New Zealanders that instils a sense of national pride about who they are as a people and where they stand in the world.

The first two chapters in Part III of the book examine, from complementary angles, language used to cause offence – impoliteness – in the US and UK versions of the talent reality show *Idol*. In '(Im)politeness and exploitative TV in Britain and North America: *The X Factor* and *American Idol*' (Chapter 8) **Jonathan Culpeper and Oliver Holmes** argue that linguistic impoliteness contains the apparatus to explain what makes RTV 'tick'. Using a sizeable corpus of *Idol* shows on both sides of the Atlantic, their analysis of impoliteness demonstrates how participants use language and non-verbal behaviours exploitatively, causing humiliation and hurt, in part for the entertainment of the audience. Culpeper and Holmes also explore whether the impoliteness, and politeness, interactions that constitute these two shows suggest differences between them. Moreover, Culpeper and Holmes deploy the notion of 'activity type' to help understand the context, and of cultural 'rich point' to help understand moments of cultural difference that may lead to puzzlement.

Chapter 9, 'Impoliteness in US/UK talent shows: a diachronic study of the evolution of a genre' tests the hypothesis that impoliteness has progressively come to characterize 'exploitative' RTV. **Nuria Lorenzo-Dus, Patricia Bou-Franch and Pilar Garcés-Conejos Blitvich** undertake a diachronic case study of the actual use of impoliteness strategies in the talent show genre over an eight-year period (2002–2009). Their analysis of a corpus comprising c. 100,000 words, extracted from 80 live *Idol* audition sequences from the UK and 80 from the US, reveals a statistically significant increase in the use of, especially, positive impoliteness strategies over time. This 'boost' in the use of impoliteness, the authors argue, reflects the evolution of the talent show genre, which is converging with other RTV genres in an emphasis on features (impoliteness) that contrast with wider cultural norms regarding civility in public discourse.

José Luis Blas Arroyo, in '"No eres inteligente ni para tener amigos... Pues anda que tú" ["You are not even clever enough to have any friends... Look who's talking!"]: a quantitative analysis of the production and reception of impoliteness in present-day Spanish reality television' (Chapter 10), analyses the factors conditioning both the production and the reception of impoliteness in the Spanish dating show *Mujeres, hombres y viceversa* (MHYV). Unlike other reality shows with which MHYV is compared, impoliteness is not concentrated in counter moves, where those who have been previously offended inflict all sorts of attacks upon those who criticized them, with an almost total disregard for other defensive responses. As far as the study of its reception by the audience is concerned, Blas Arroyo's analysis reveals some contradictions between earlier and subsequent opinions of those who rated impoliteness in the show.

The idea that frames can be 'laminated' or 'layered' in discourse is used by **Cynthia Gordon** in Chapter 11, '"You are killing your kids": framing and impoliteness in a health makeover reality TV show', to explain the impoliteness present in a recurring scene on the family health makeover RTV show, *Honey We're Killing the Kids*. In this scene, Gordon's analysis reveals, the show's expert nutritionist negatively assesses, and directly confronts parents about, their children's poor health practices. The encounter is linguistically and visually framed as a health consultation, in which the nutritionist's behaviour is conventionally 'impolite'; however, it is also framed as a life-saving intervention, rendering possibly – for the at-home audience, if not the parents – an 'appropriate' or 'politic' interpretation. Uncovering the layered nature of frames highlights the complexity of 'impoliteness' on RTV.

In the final chapter of the book, 'Moments of truth: telling it like it is on the *Jeremy Kyle Show*' (Chapter 12), **Andrew Tolson** examines segments of the *The Jeremy Kyle Show*, a leading mid-morning talk show currently on British commercial television. Typically the programme deals in problematic family scenarios (infidelities, paternity disputes, dysfunctional parenting etc.) through an investigative discourse of disclosing the 'truth' (often supported by quasi-scientific DNA and lie detector tests). Segments then culminate in scenes where the host delivers aggressive moral judgments in a speech genre defined here as the 'harangue'. Tolson's detailed discourse analysis reveals how this involves the host delivering unmitigated face-threatening statements directly towards the guilty parties on his show, who are cast as degenerate members of the 'moral underclass'. In this way *Jeremy Kyle* reproduces a populist, 'neoliberal' approach to social exclusion which has similarities with other forms of 'belligerent broadcasting'.

Together, the ten case studies that comprise Parts II and III of the book have significant global reach, both in geographical and linguistic terms. As we have just outlined, the discourse structures and practices of RTV shows from China, Israel, Australia, Argentina, New Zealand, Great Britain, the United States of America and Spain are all examined. This cross-cultural/linguistic dimension is in clear recognition not only of a veritable tradition of discourse-analytic research that has warned against analytic ethnocentrism but also, and specifically, of the little attention thus far paid within the 'global phenomenon' of RTV to the national / cultural characteristics that may emerge in its localized variations. As we have also outlined above, the range of programmes is diverse: from dating and talent shows to health makeover shows and police docudramas. Across generic and cultural/linguistic varieties, it is our hope that readers will be able to identify and reflect upon similarities and differences. In doing this, they will be aided by the commonality of purpose that micro-linguistic analysis of language-in-use (discourse) can uniquely provide.

Nuria Lorenzo-Dus and Pilar Garcés-Conejos Blitvich

References

Bonner, Frances (2003) *Ordinary Television* (London: Sage).

Fairclough, Norman (1995) *Media Discourse* (London and Mahwah, NJ: Lawrence Erlbaum Associates, 1995).

Hill, Annette (2005) *Reality TV: Audiences and Popular Factual Television* (London: Routledge).

Hill, Annette (2007) *Restyling Factual TV* (London: Routledge).

Part I
The Reality of Discourse and Discourse Analysis: Theory, Approaches, Practices

1

Reality television: a discourse-analytical perspective

Pilar Garcés-Conejos Blitvich and Nuria Lorenzo-Dus

Introduction

The empirical chapters of this book offer original studies of reality television (RTV henceforth) in a wide range of cultural contexts. Importantly, they all share a discourse-analytical approach even though they employ different discourse-analytic frameworks in order to address specific research questions, from multimodality and interactional sociolinguistics to Critical Discourse Analysis. The aim of this chapter is to explain the need, at this point in time, for a discourse-analytical approach within RTV scholarship. Doing so requires explaining our conceptualization of RTV as a *discourse,* one comprised of various *genres.* It also requires reviewing, albeit briefly, the two broad areas on which the empirical studies of RTV included in this book focus: identity and impoliteness.

RTV and discourse analysis

RTV has become a widespread phenomenon, from its modest beginnings in 'actuality programming' in the America of the 1940s. Forerunners include *Candid Camera, Real People, The Gong Show* (Siegel 2003), and the Chinese version of *Pop Idol, Super Girl,* which drew an audience of 400 million people and 8 million text votes in 2005, only to be outright banned by the government in 2006. As expected, with the proliferation of show formats that fall loosely under the RTV label and the globalization of some of those formats (e.g. *Big Brother, Idol* franchise), RTV has come under considerable (non)academic scrutiny. Non-academic commentary has often focused on the seeming ills of RTV, which have been said to include a debasing of cultural and even moral standards in society (Genzlinger 2011; Sanneh 2011). Some academic commentary has voiced similar criticism (Turner 2010). Yet, RTV is also recognized as a phenomenon well worthy of academic enquiry (Lorenzo-Dus 2006, 2009b; Tolson 2006). Opinion on its having contributed to an egalitarian, democratization agenda in the media is however mixed, with some scholars crediting RTV with empowering of citizens through facilitating their access to the public domain of the media (e.g. White 2002) and others seeing in this manifestation of the 'demotic turn' (Turner 2010) only superficial democratization (e.g. Lorenzo-Dus 2008, 2009b) and, in some cases, open exploitation of 'ordinary folk' (e.g. Culpeper 2005).

Scholarship has also sought to circumscribe the phenomenon, specifically trying to provide definitions of what 'counts' or otherwise as RTV. Whereas some include talk shows and game shows under that label, others limit their selections to the *Survivor* or *Big Brother* formats (Collins 2009). For Holmes and Jermyn (2004, p. 3), what we consider RTV has moved from 'crime and emergency service-based texts, the docusoap trend, to what might be conceived as a "docu-show" or possible "game-doc" phase, in which factual-entertainment programming has increasingly incorporated elements of the game show.' To date, though, no agreement seems to have been reached as regards definition.

A separate, though related, matter of academic concern is the label 'reality' itself, which many regard as suspiciously essentialist and pre-modern. Today, most scholars would agree that what we perceive as 'reality' is in fact cultural, constructed fiction. It has also been argued that the label 'RTV' is too general to be helpful (Barnfield 2002). We will return to these two issues – categorization and the constructed nature of 'reality' in RTV – later in our discussion.

In the same way that it is quite obvious by now that, far from being an ephemeral fad, RTV is here to stay, academic interest in RTV has continued to grow, especially post-2000 (see Collins 2009 for an excellent review). However, this interest has mostly come from academic fields such as media and cultural studies, philosophy, or ethics. With few exceptions (e.g. Bousfield 2007, 2008; Culpeper, Bousfield & Wichmann 2003; Culpeper 2005; Garcés-Conejos Blitvich, Lorenzo-Dus & Bou-Franch 2013; Lorenzo-Dus, 2005, 2006, 2008, 2009a, 2009b; Thornborrow & Morris 2004; Tolson 2006), scholars have not looked closely at the 'language' of RTV – at its discourse, in a micro-analytical sense. Even when scholarly works have claimed either to take a discursive approach or to refer to matters related to 'language' (Friedman 2002; Kavka 2008; Lemi & Park 2011; Reid 2007), they have often done so from a macro-analytical perspective, rarely descending to the textual level. And in those cases in which the latter is explicitly cited, textual samples are generally provided in support of the writers' claims but no analysis based on linguistic theory is carried out. Yet, work based on micro analysis of media texts, we would argue, has contributed significantly to our understanding of the media in general and broadcasting in particular (see Corner 2000, for example, for a defence of textual (discourse) analysis in the study of the media). Within the latter, work within the 'broadcast talk' tradition has yielded – and continues to yield – novel, rigorous analyses of a range of television and radio formats, contributing fresh insights to issues regarded also as key in the cognate fields of political, media and cultural studies, such as media authenticity and bias/neutralism. It is therefore the overarching goal of this book to advance this work within the context of RTV by providing systematic, close analysis of its textual practices. It is our contention that the kind of systematic, theory-grounded examination of actual textual practices that characterizes discourse analysis as a field can provide both the theoretical and analytical tools that scholarship on RTV needs.

Discourse versus genre

To be properly understood, we also contend, RTV should be tackled as a discourse (*à la* Fairclough 2003; Gee 2005; or Scollon & Scollon 2001), rather than a genre. As a matter of fact, it seems to us that the difficulties found by many scholars in conceptualizing RTV come from their trying to fit under the genre rubric its multiplicity of formats (Penzhorn & Pitout 2007, p. 65). Reality TV may have started out as a genre, but it has certainly evolved into a discourse.

Other scholars have raised similar concerns regarding the notion of genre and its applicability to TV in general. Caughie notes, for example, that while 'assumptions of genre permeate television studies' (1991, p. 127), these have been less theorized, interrogated and historicized than studies of film genre. For her part, Stempel-Mumford describes how 'a profound theoretical uncertainty' underlies most discussions of television form: 'a lack of an adequate theory of genre as a whole' (1995, p. 19). Holmes and Jermyn (2004, p. 6) relate this to the ambiguity surrounding whether the concept is in fact 'directly applicable to the medium'. Moreover, although the notion of genre is pervasive in the discussion of TV, notions of genre are often taken as a given and not overly theorized. One of the obvious pitfalls, even in very rigorous approaches to RTV such as Holmes and Jermyn's (2004), is the lack of a definition of what is understood as 'genre'.

The notion of genre is far from being uniformly understood in the literature. Within linguistics and related disciplines, for example, there are different schools of thought regarding how the analysis of genre should be tackled. A sound theory of genre could solve some of the problems that scholars face when trying to conceptualize RTV, namely its inherent hybridity and the constructive nature of discursive categorizations (Holmes & Jermyn 2004). A sound theory of genre needs, in turn, to be embedded within a sound theory of discourse, as we will argue below. In his insightful essay on film and genre, Neale (1990) claims that genres need to be coalesced into discourses in order to be properly studied. His discursive approach to genre, however, sees the study of texts going beyond the text itself to encompass the contexts in which they are produced, marketed and assessed: 'the mass-produced, popular genres have to be understood within an economic context, as conditioned by specific economic contradictions – in particular, of course, those that operate within specific institutions and industries... it is also important to stress the peculiar nature of films as aesthetic commodities, commodities demanding at least a degree of novelty and difference from one another...' (p. 64). Neale, then, sees genres as part of discourses, but with the latter being understood *à la* Foucault or Bourdieu, that is, as high-level social structures, rather than with a focus on the linguistic realization of those structures, i.e., in Gee's (2005) terms, as discourses with a little 'd'.

Understanding genre and discourse

Our view of discourse is that it is always situated, anchored in social practices or genres. Therefore, a discussion of the language of any social practice, such as that of many formats of RTV to be carried out in this book, needs to be preceded by a discussion of genres, as understood from a linguistic perspective, and how these relate to discourse, especially because genre and discourse are multidisciplinary terms which may mean different things to different people.

Our understanding of genre and discourse draws from Swales (1990), Fairclough (2003), Pennycook (2010), Scollon and Scollon (2001) and Gee (2005). Within many subfields of linguistics, Swales's approach and definition of genre has been widely influential. Swales (1990) defines genre as:

A class of communicative events, the members of which share some set of communicative purposes. These purposes are recognized by the expert members of the parent discourse community, and thereby constitute the rationale for the genre. This rationale shapes

the schematic structure of the discourse and influences and con-
strains choice of content and style... exemplars of a genre exhibit
various patterns of similarity in terms of structure, style, content and
intended audience.

Accordingly, a given communicative purpose triggers a particular genre,
which is realized by a specific move structure or functionally distinct
stages along which the genre unfolds. The move structure, in turn, is
realized by rhetorical strategies or formal choices of content and style.
In his discussion of genre, Swales draws upon a trend initiated in the
1980s that saw genre not as text or text type, but as social action (Miller
1984).

This view of genre as social action or social practice is at the core
of Fairclough's (2003) discourse model as well as Pennycook's (2010)
elaboration of it. In Fairclough's model, social practices are equated
with 'orders of discourse' (a network of social practices in its language
aspect). The elements of orders of discourse are discourses (ways of
representing, i.e., two different discourses may represent the same area
of the world from different perspectives), genres (ways of (inter)acting
discursively) and styles (ways of being, ways of constructing particular
social or personal identities). These elements are dialectically related
in a top-down/bottom-up fashion: Discourses (representational meanings, e.g. political discourse) are enacted in genres (actional meanings,
e.g. presidential speech) and inculcated in styles (identification meanings, Obama's presidential speech). Actions and identities (including
genres and styles) are, in turn, represented in discourse (Fairclough 2003,
p. 29). Discourses, genres and styles are durable and stable, but they are
also in constant flux. At the style level, agents are carriers, as it were, of
discourse/genres. However, they do not merely reproduce them, by constructing recognizable identities, but can reinterpret/reinvent them in a
way that, if constant and shared, may significantly alter the genre and,
in turn, the discourse.

Fairclough's level of discourse corresponds broadly to Scollon and
Scollon's (2001) concept of discourse systems. Scollon and Scollon
define discourse as systems of communication shared by certain communities, such as corporations, public (state) school teachers, fashion
experts or those involved as producers, participants and audiences of
RTV programmes. According to Scollon and Scollon (2001, p. 107):
'Such broad systems of discourse form a kind of self-contained system
of communication with a shared language or jargon, with particular ways in which people learn what they need to know to become

members, with a particular ideological position and with quite specific forms of interpersonal relationships among members of these groups.' One becomes a member of a discourse system, is socialized into it, by mastering a series of preferred forms of discourse (genres) used by the community to carry out their business.

We see RTV as a discourse system, rather than a genre. The socialization of members into the system is manifold and depends on whether they belong to the producing, participant or audience sides. In the case of participants, for instance, it occurs through exposure to RTV shows and through selection processes prior to the filming of programmes. It can be argued that the broad ideology of RTV is egalitarian, democratic (but see Turner 2010), and this egalitarian ideology is reflected in an apparent lack of power that blurs the differences between experts and lay participants, or fosters strong parasocial relationships between viewers and participants, which some have called 'intimate' (Penzhorn & Pitout 2007, p. 67).

Interpersonal relationships among members, as they relate to the linguistic notion of face, tie back to the general ideology of the RTV discourse system, but are nonetheless genre-specific, i.e. the norms regulating interpersonal relationships vary from genre to genre. RTV takes place within an institution, that of broadcasting, and can therefore be regarded as public discourse. The expectations of civility that guide public manifestations of discourse (Sellers 2004) are hence also expected to apply to RTV. At the same time, though, RTV often – though not always – claims to give viewers unprecedented access to the 'private realm' of participants. The result is a conscious, on the part of the producers at least, blurring between public and private discourses – one of the many blurrings brought about by RTV. Aspects of the private realm of participants relating to private, be it sexual, family or friendship, relationships are routinely publicly displayed – *performed* – in ways that assign primacy to emotions in general and conflict-based ones, such as anger or jealousy, in particular. This accounts, at least in part, for the high levels of incivility, linguistic aggression and confrontation that can be found in many genres of RTV. Below, we discuss the role that impoliteness, linguistic aggression and conflict, play in the success of RTV.

Penzhorn and Pitout (2007) attribute four characteristics to, in their terminology, the genre of RTV: (i) a focus on ordinary people, (ii) voyeurism, (iii) audience participation, and (iv) an attempt to simulate real life. These easily apply to our description of the RTV discourse system: the focus on ordinary people and the attempt to simulate real life tie back to the use of language that seeks to resemble 'ordinary', 'casual' talk and to the democratic ideology that seemingly underlies the system. Audience participation can also be related to this ideology, in as much as RTV seems to foster egalitarian types of relationships among its members.

The different format types of RTV have evolved into different genres (among others, health makeover shows, dating shows, talent shows, gamedocs, docudramas), which have different communicative purposes, although sharing the overarching goal of entertaining the audience, and different move structures which are, in turn, realized by different sets of rhetorical strategies. What is more, although fluctuating and exhibiting a high degree of hybridity, they are now recognizable and categorized as members of different format types, or genres in our terminology. Understanding RTV as a discourse realized in a variety of related genres helps solve the problems in scholarly discussion associated with hybridity. As Fairclough (2003, pp. 30–1) argues, modern societies often involve the networking of different social practices across different domains of social life. This results in the creation of genre chains, genres that are linked together and have a transformative influence on one another. Genre chains and mixing also occur within discourse systems: the preferred forms of discourse (genres) of a given system become linked and influence each other by sharing recognizable features of the system. This is clearly the case among the very different genres of the RTV discourse system.

Reality television, identity and impoliteness

According to Gee (2005), the main function of discourse systems, or 'big D' discourses, is to facilitate the performance of social activities and social identities. Identity construction is then at the core of Discourse systems. This coincides with Turner's view of current media, especially in their frantic production of RTV programmes, as no longer the mediators but the *creators* of cultural identities:

> The identities constructed by the media networks I am referring to here are … not merely 'mediated'…, sometimes they are created from whole cloth. Although I would accept the possibility that this observation might apply to public or national identities as well, my primary focus here is on the media's construction of the private identity: the personal, the ordinary and the everyday… In its most vivid location, the hybrid reality TV/game-show franchise, the production of celebrity promises a spectacular form of personal validation. (Turner 2010, p. 23)

The manufacturing of personal identities, the main goal of which is to generate commercial returns, is then also the main function of the RTV Discourse system. In this system, personal rather than social or ego identities (Goffman 1963) are given preeminence. Goffman (1963, p. 57) argued that personal identities are based on 'the assumption that the individual can be differentiated from all others and that around this means of differentiation a single continuous record of social facts can be attached'. Usually, personal identities are those that are co-constructed with intimates with whom we share those 'sets of facts' that make us unique and different. This focus on personal identities contributes, in part, to the blurring of the public and private spheres which is a trademark of RTV.

Another important point that needs to be made with regard to the personal identities constructed within the Discourse system of RTV is that they are expendable by nature and can be easily replaced. Rojek (2001) referred to the turning of ordinary people into celebrity commodities as *celetoids*. In a way, the personal identity of the celetoid has become a new social identity – there is a reiterative performance of different (but equally constructed and media-manufactured) personal identities that enjoy enormous exposure and fame for a while, to be soon forgotten and replaced by the next celetoid.

Identity construction, be it social or personal, is, in our view mostly carried out discursively. From a discursive perspective, identities are not contained within the self, 'but in a series of representations mediated by semiotic systems such as language' (Benwell & Stokoe 2006, p. 31). Therefore, coming to grips with the new identities that the RTV Discourse system creates involves a micro analysis of how these are discursively constructed (de Fina, Schiffrin & Bamberg 2006). The centrality of discourse to the construction of identity is another reason why we believe it is crucial to approach RTV from a discourse-analytic perspective. Identities are not constructed in a vacuum but through the display of culturally recognizable acts and stances (Ochs 1993) as individuals engage in social practice. Thus, genres/discourses are central to the construction and recognition of identities, which following Fairclough's model, we see as integral to the level of style.

The culture/genre-bound nature of identity construction/recognition poses an important obstacle to the globalization of RTV formats. If, according to Turner (2010, p. 53), the main product of RTV is the construction of cultural identities to the point that RTV's 'preferred identities have colonized the expectations of everyday life in contemporary western societies', adaptations of the original format to different cultures need to 'translate' those identities usually constructed within a Western cultural milieu. Different models that delve into how identity is constructed in discourse will provide the necessary tools to carry out analysis that will unveil how identities have been relocated and can also provide the basis for a comparison with the original model.

The focus on ordinary people is one of the main characteristics of RTV (Penzhorn & Pitout 2007). However, some scholars, like Bonner (2003), have argued that RTV contestants are not as ordinary as the rest of us: shows go through a process of selection that ensures participants have the ability to perform spectacular ordinariness. The key moments in RTV are those when participants display their 'real', 'authentic' selves (Turner 2010). Often, those moments are associated with the display of raw emotions (Grindstaff 2003). Not surprisingly, 'negative' emotions – such as anger, frustration, etc. – related to conflict and linguistic aggression have become a staple of RTV (Lorenzo-Dus 2008, 2009b).

Linguistic aggressiveness has been linked to both the construction and maintenance of identities (Garcés-Conejos Blitvich 2009, 2010; Garcés-Conejos *et al.* 2013; Turner 2010) and to the overall success of RTV (e.g. Lorenzo-Dus 2009b). This, we believe, is another key feature of RTV that can be better understood through the tools offered by those approaches that focus on interactional issues such as linguistic politeness and impoliteness (Brown & Levinson 1987; Culpeper 1996 2005, 2011; Garcés-Conejos Blitvich 2010; Locher & Watts 2005). Both politeness and impoliteness have proven very difficult to define (Garcés-Conejos Blitvich 2010). Research on impoliteness, despite the pervasiveness of the phenomenon in human interaction, is still in its infancy. However, 'spectacular impoliteness', that is, impoliteness as spectacle in reality programmes (Lorenzo-Dus 2009b), has received its share of attention. The constructed nature of the broadcasts means that specific interactional moments fraught with emotion, especially conflict-based ones that result in (non)verbal aggressiveness, are routinely selected – and perhaps instigated – by the shows' producers for public consumption.

The issue of whether or not these manifestations of (non)verbal aggressiveness constitute *real* impoliteness has been debated (Culpeper 2005; Lorenzo-Dus 2009a). Since impoliteness and conflict have become a staple of RTV, they could be interpreted as part of the expectations of the interaction within the genres of the discourse system, and hence as not *really* impolite. The general agreement borne out by both theoretical and empirical analyses of impoliteness in RTV, nevertheless, seems to be that though expected, impoliteness is not 'neutralized' in such programmes.

Rather, it is interpreted as 'real' by both participants and the audience (Culpeper 2005; Garcés-Conejos Blitvich 2009, 2010; Garcés-Conejos Blitvich, Lorenzo-Dus & Bou-Franch 2010; Garcés-Conejos Blitvich, Bou-Franch & Lorenzo-Dus 2013). If that is the case, and we believe it is, RTV offers impoliteness scholars unprecedented access to the *backstages* (Goffman 1959) where impoliteness manifestations are more prone to occur: 'the backstage conduct is one which allows minor acts which might easily be taken as symbolic of intimacy and disrespect for others present and for the region, while front region conduct is one which disallows such potentially offensive behavior' (Goffman 1959, p. 128). Analysis of the anatomy of conflictive and aggressive language use in RTV shows through the application of the extant models of impoliteness will, no doubt, help us better understand the nature of the phenomenon by providing insights into the multifunctionality of impoliteness (Garcés-Conejos Blitvich 2009, 2010) as well as into the typology of conflicts and the kinds of impoliteness manifestations associated with them.

Furthermore, RTV acts a trigger of everyday talk about shows, participants and their behaviour in the net public sphere. Very much in the way that Graham and Hajru (2011) describe for political discourse, in the forums and other online communicative spaces dedicated to RTV, people often engage in discussions about the participants' linguistic behaviour and the social norms that (should) guide it. These unsolicited comments provide unparalleled access to audiences' assessments of im/politeness, which are the focus of the new scholarly approaches to the field (Eelen 2001; Garcés-Conejos Blitvich, 2010, 2013; Locher & Watts 2005). Net-based public sphere research, as it relates to the RTV phenomenon, has much to contribute to our understanding of impoliteness.

By closely analysing audiences' assessments of RTV, we may also get a better grasp of the reasons behind the widely successful use of conflict and impoliteness in its many genres. Both social and cognitive explanations have thus far been advanced to account for this success. For example, while discussing generic and social and cultural verisimilitude in RTV, Neale (1990, p. 48) argues that audiences often derive their pleaure and enjoyment from those genre-sactioned elements that are least compatible with regimes of cultural verisimilitude. This would make sense in the case of im/politeness, as politeness is socially sanctioned – i.e., the default term – in public discourse (the language of the frontstage, in terms of Goffman 1959). Thus, the use of impoliteness, a common occurrence in the discourse of RTV, would be verisimilitudinous within its many genres, but in sharp contrast to daily societal usages, and in that contrast would lie the pleasure derived by audiences.

Nabi *et al.* (2006 applied a 'uses and gratifications' approach to ascertain why people continue to watch RTV. This approach posits that viewers make an active choice of what media to consume and this choice is based on certain viewers' needs that are fulfilled by the programme chosen. They found that one of the reasons viewers watch some reality programmes is to satiate feelings of voyeurism. Viewers also reported that viewing those programmes increased feelings of happiness, parasocial relationships, negative outcomes and feelings of dramatic challenge. Reiss and Wiltz (2004) added vengeance as a very important reason, after status, why people are drawn to RTV. Since these programmes contain a large amount of competition and interpersonal conflict, viewers can satiate their need for vindication through viewing such programming. Crook *et al.* (2004) found that not necessarily voyeurism but morbid curiosity was the personality characteristic more strongly associated with watching RTV. They concluded that since individuals are morbidly curious, it is not surprising that the networks and cable stations come up with more extreme shows each season. As most violence enacted in RTV is verbal (Coyne, Robinson & Nelson 2010), that would entail an increase in the level of conflict and rudeness found in the shows. Also, it has been shown that (non-verbal) aggression heightens arousal, which is closely tied to levels of attention (Mutz & Reeves 2005), and that our brain cannot distinguish between – that is, it does not react differently to – non-mediated and mediated violence (Reeves and Nass 1996).

Mediated verbal aggression is therefore a good attention-grabbing device (Mutz & Reeves 2005). Moreover, since impoliteness is associated with raw emotions (Kienpointner 2008) and the latter are an important aspect of the performance of authenticity in media discourse (see e.g. Montgomery 2001), impoliteness may be seen to contribute to the impression of reality sought after in a number of these programmes (but see Lunt & Stenner 2007 for a discussion of the explicit performance of raw emotions in *The Jerry Springer Show*). Impoliteness, including cases in which raw emotions lie at its heart, can of course also be used strategically (Beebe 1995; Kientpoiner 2008; Garcés-Conejos Blitvich 2009). In a number of RTV shows, this is certainly the case (see. e.g. Lorenzo-Dus 2008, 2009a).

Conclusion

Reality television, we have argued, is in need of *systematic* investigation from a micro-analytic, discourse perspective. In addition to yielding rigorous examinations of the manifold, constantly evolving genres of

RTV – we have also argued – such a perspective can contribute significantly to theorizing RTV as a discourse system. Taking this as our starting point, in the next chapter we provide an overview of the different
discourse-analytic frameworks that are deployed in the empirical studies
of this book, and explain how these frameworks may address specific
questions relating to the central issues in RTV scholarship that we have
already introduced: identity construction and aggression.

References

Barnfield, Graham (2002) From direct cinema to car-wreck video: Reality TV and
the crisis of content. In Dolan Cummings (ed.), *Reality TV: How Real is Real?*
(London: Hodder Arnold), pp. 47–66.

Baruh, Lemi & Ji Hoon Park (eds.) (2011) *Reel Politics: Reality Television as a
Platform for Political Discourse* (Newcastle, UK: Cambridge Scholars Publishing).

Beebe, Leslie M. (1995) Polite fictions: Instrumental rudeness and pragmatic
competence. In James E. Alatis, Carolyn A. Straehele, Maggie Ronkin &
Brent Gallenberger (eds.), *Georgetown University Round Table on Languages and
Linguistics* (Washington, DC: Georgetown University Press), pp. 154–68.

Benwell, Bethan & Elizabeth Stokoe (2006) *Discourse and Identity* (Edinburgh:
Edinburgh University Press).

Bonner, Frances (2003) *Ordinary Television: Analyzing Popular TV* (London:
Sage).

Bousfield, Derek (2008) *Impoliteness in Interaction* (Amsterdam and Philadelphia:
John Benjamins).

Brown, Penelope & Steven Levinson (1987) *Politeness: Some Universals of Language
Usage* (Cambridge: Cambridge University Press).

Caughie, John (1991) Adorno's reproach: Repetition, difference and television
genre. *Screen*, 32(2): 127–53.

Collins, Kathleen (2009) Reality television: Scholarly treatments since 2000.
CBQ, 40(1): 2–12.

Corner, John (2000) What can we say about 'documentary'? *Media, Culture and
Society*, 22(5): 681–8.

Coyne, Sarah M., Simon L. Robinson & David A. Nelson (2010) Does reality back-
bite? Physical, verbal, and relational aggression in reality television programs.
Journal of Broadcasting and Electronic Media, 54(2): 282–98.

Crook, Sarah F., Tracy R. Worrell, David Westerman, Jeffrey S. Davis, Emily
J. Moyer & S. H. Clarke (2004). Personality characteristics associated with
watching reality programming. Paper presented at the annual meeting of the
International Communication Association, New Orleans, LA (April).

Culpeper, Jonathan (1996) Towards an anatomy of impoliteness. *Journal of
Pragmatics*, 25: 349–67.

Culpeper, Jonathan (2005) Impoliteness and entertainment in the television quiz
show: *The Weakest Link*. *Journal of Politeness Research*, 1: 35–72.

Culpeper, Jonathan (2011) *Impoliteness. Using Language to Create Offence*
(Cambridge: Cambridge University Press).

Culpeper, Jonathan, Derek Bousfield & Anne Wichmann (2003) Impoliteness revisited: With special reference to dynamic and prosodic aspects. *Journal of Pragmatics*, 35 (10/11): 1545–79.

de Fina, Anna, Deborah Schiffrin & Michael Bamberg (eds.) (2006) *Discourse and Identity* (Cambridge: Cambridge University Press).

Eelen, Gino (2001) *A Critique of Politeness Theories* (Manchester: St. Jerome Publishing).

Fairclough, Norman (2003) *Analysing Discourse: Textual Analysis for Social Research* (London: Routledge).

Friedman, James (ed.) (2002) *Reality Squared: Televisual Discourse on the Real* (New Brunswick, NJ: Rutgers University Press).

Garcés-Conejos Blitvich, Pilar (2009) Impoliteness and identity in the American news media: The 'Culture Wars'. *Journal of Politeness Research*, 5(2): 273–304.

Garcés-Conejos Blitvich, Pilar (2010) A genre approach to the study of impoliteness. *International Review of Pragmatics*, 2: 46–94.

Garcés-Conejos Blitvich, Pilar (2013) El modelo del género y la des/cortesía clasificatoria en las evaluaciones de Sálvame por parte de la audiencia. In Catalina Fuentes (ed.), *(Des)cortesía para el espectáculo: Estudios de pragmática variacionista* (Madrid: Arco Libros), pp. 167–96.

Garcés-Conejos Blitvich, Pilar, Nuria Lorenzo-Dus & Patricia Bou-Franch (2010). A genre-approach to im-politeness in a Spanish TV talk show: Evidence from corpus-based analysis, questionnaires and focus groups. *Intercultural Pragmatics* 7(4): 689–723.

Garcés-Conejos Blitvich, Pilar, Nuria Lorenzo-Dus & Patricia Bou-Franch (2013) Identity and impoliteness: The expert in the talent show *Idol*. *Journal of Politeness Research*, 9(1): 97–120.

Gee, James P. (2005) *An Introduction to Discourse Analysis Theory and Method*, 2nd edn. (New York: Routledge).

Genzlinger, Neil (2011) An old-fashioned date can't beat a night out debating reality TV. *The New York Times* (October 7). Available at http://www.nytimes.com/2011/10/08/arts/television/reality-tv-debate-critics-notebook.html

Goffman, Erving (1959) *The Presentation of Self in Everyday Life* (Garden City, NY: Doubleday Anchor Books).

Goffman, Erving (1963) *Stigma. Notes on the Management of the Spoiled Identity* (New York: Simon & Schuster).

Graham, Todd & Auli Hajru (2011) Reality TV as a trigger of everyday political talk in the net-based public sphere. *European Journal of Communication*, 26(18): 18–32.

Grindstaff, Laura (2003) Daytime talk shows: Ethics and ordinary people on television. In Larry Gross, John Katz & Jay Ruby (eds.), *Image Ethics in the Digital Age* (Minneapolis: University of Minnesota Press), pp. 115–41.

Holmes, Su & Deborah Jermyn (2004) Introduction. Understanding reality TV. In Sue Holmes & Deborah Jermyn (eds.), *Understanding Reality TV* (London: Routledge).

Kavka, Misha (2008) *Reality Television, Affect and Intimacy: Reality Matters* (Language, Discourse, Society series) (Basingstoke and New York: Palgrave Macmillan).

Kienpointner, Manfred (1997) Varieties of rudeness: Types and functions of impolite utterances. *Functions of Language*, 4: 251–87.

Kienpointner, Manfred (2008) Impoliteness and emotional arguments. *Journal of Politeness Research*, 4: 243–65.

Locher, Miriam A. & Richard J. Watts (2005) Politeness theory and relational work. *Journal of Politeness Research*, 1: 9–33.

Lorenzo-Dus, Nuria (2005) A rapport and impression management approach to public figures' performance of talk. *Journal of Pragmatics*, 37: 611–31.

Lorenzo-Dus, Nuria (2006) Buying and selling: Mediating persuasion in British property shows. *Media, Culture & Society*, 28: 739–61.

Lorenzo-Dus, Nuria (2008) Real disorder in the court: An investigation of conflict talk in US courtroom shows. *Media, Culture & Society*, 30: 81–107.

Lorenzo-Dus, Nuria (2009a) *Television Discourse. Analysing Language in the Media* (Basingstoke and New York: Palgrave Macmillan).

Lorenzo-Dus, Nuria (2009b) 'You're barking mad – I'm out': Impoliteness and broadcast talk. *Journal of Politeness Research*, 5: 159–87.

Lunt, Peter & Paul Stenner (2005) *The Jerry Springer Show* as an emotional public sphere. *Media, Culture & Society*, 27: 59–82.

Miller, Carolyn (1984) Genre as social action. *Quarterly Journal of Speech*, 70: 151–67.

Montgomery, Martin (2001) Defining 'authentic talk'. *Discourse Studies*, 3: 397–405.

Mutz, Diana & Byron Reeves (2005) The new videomalaise: Effects of televised incivility on political trust. *American Political Science Review*, 99: 1–15.

Nabi, Robin L., Carmen S. Stitt, Jeff Halford & Keli L. Finnerty (2006) Emotional and cognitive predictors of the enjoyment of reality based and fictional television programming: An elaboration of the uses and gratifications perspective. *Media Psychology*, 8(4): 421–47.

Neale, Stephen (1990) Questions of genre. *Screen*, 31(1): 45–66.

Ochs, Elinor (1993) Constructing social identity: A language socialization perspective. *Research on Language and Social Interaction*, 26: 287–306.

Pennycook, Alastair (2010) *Language as Local Practice*. (London: Routledge).

Penzhorn, Heidi & Magriet Pitout (2007) A critical-historical genre analysis of reality television. *Communication*, 33(1): 62–76.

Reeves, Byron & Clifford Nass (1996). *The Media Equation: How People Treat Computers, Television, and New Media Like Real People and Places* (Cambridge: Cambridge University Press).

Reid, Gwendolynne (2007) *The Rhetoric of Reality Television – A Narrative Analysis of the Structure of Illusion* (London: Routledge).

Reiss, Steven & James Wiltz (2011) Why people watch Reality TV. *Media Psychology*, 6: 363–78.

Rojek, Chris (2001) *Celebrity* (London: Reaktion).

Sanneh, Kelefa (2011) The reality principle. The rise and rise of a television genre. *The New Yorker* (May). Available at http://www.newyorker.com/arts/critics/atlarge/2011/05/09/110509crat_atlarge_sanneh.

Scollon, Ron & Suzanne W. Scollon (2001[1995]) *Intercultural Communication*, 2nd edn. (Oxford: Blackwell).

Sellers, Mortimer (2004) Ideals of public discourse. In Christine T. Sistare (ed.), *Civility and its Discontents* (Lawrence, KS: University Press of Kansas), pp. 15–24.

Siegel, Lee (2003) *Reality in America*. Available at http://www.tnr.com/article/reality-america (Accessed November 29, 2010).

Stempel-Mumford, Laura (1995) *Love and Ideology in the Afternoon: Soap Opera, Women and Television Genre* (Bloomington, IN: Indiana University Press).

Swales, John (1990) *Genre Analysis. English in Academic and Research Settings.* (Cambridge: Cambridge University Press).

Thornborrow, Joanna & Deborah Morris (2004) Gossip as strategy: The management of talk about others on reality TV show 'Big Brother'. *Journal of Sociolinguistics*, 8(2): 246–71.

Tolson, Andrew (2006) *Media Talk: Spoken Discourse on TV and Radio* (Edinburgh: Edinburgh University Press).

Turner, Graeme (2010) *Ordinary People and the Media. The Demotic Turn* (London: Sage).

White, M. (2002) 'Television, therapy and the social subject; Or, the TV therapy machine'. In J. Friedman (ed.), *Reality Squared. Televisual Discourse on the Real* (New Brunswick, NJ: Rutgers University Press), pp. 313–21.

2
Discourse approaches to the study of reality television

Nuria Lorenzo-Dus and Pilar Garcés-Conejos Blitvich

Introduction

In the previous chapter we discussed why the study of reality television (RTV) can benefit much from adopting a discourse-analytical approach. We also noted that, even within this approach, different theoretical and methodological frameworks can be fruitfully drawn upon in order to examine the two key themes covered in this book: identity and aggression. This chapter is thus intended to equip readers whose background is not in discourse analysis – and those who are not perhaps equally familiar with the different frameworks in discourse analysis used therein – with the necessary conceptual and methodological 'toolkit' to understand the detailed analyses that are offered in the case studies that follow. For the part of the book dealing with identity in RTV, this chapter provides a brief overview of relevant aspects of Critical Discourse Analysis and Multimodality. And for the part of the book devoted to aggression in RTV, it reviews two key approaches: broadcast talk and linguistic im/politeness. It is important to clarify at this early juncture that this chapter is not intended as a 'how to do discourse analysis' manual – a number of excellent book-length works exist for that purpose. Instead, our remit is to describe key methods and issues though which the various discourse analysis frameworks used by the book authors have contributed – and continue to contribute – to our understanding of the discourse of RTV, as well as to how, in the process of doing so, the various frameworks under consideration may have been theoretically and methodologically refined.

Discourse analysis, identity and reality television

Identity, as we outlined in Chapter 1, is central to the discourse of RTV. Its study, in turn, is premised on the belief that identity is fluid and co-constructed by interactants in and through semiotic systems that centrally – though not exclusively – include language. Two key discourse analysis frameworks that share this premise, and upon which the case studies in Part II of this book draw, are Critical Discourse Analysis and Multimodality. Let us consider each in turn, focusing on those aspects that are most relevant to the analysis of the discourse of RTV.

Critical Discourse Analysis and reality television

Critical Discourse Analysis – also referred to as Critical Discourse Studies – is not a methodology but a type of research 'that primarily studies the way social power abuse, dominance and inequality are enacted, reproduced and resisted by text and talk in the social and political context.' (van Dijk 2001, p. 352). Some scholars actually describe it as 'an academic movement' (Baker *et al.* 2008, p. 273). The reluctance to describe Critical Discourse Analysis as a methodology is simply due to the fact that there is no unitary theoretical framework for those working on critical studies of language use – no one way of doing Critical Discourse Analysis. Instead, Critical Discourse Analysis adopts any method that is adequate to realize the aims of specific Critical Discourse Analysis-inspired research. Across methods, however, there is a strong emphasis on the role assigned to the analysis of context and the need for interdisciplinarity, as well as a tendency to use qualitative techniques – at times combined with quantitative ones, such as in corpus-assisted (critical) discourse analysis, see, for example, Baker *et al.* (2008). Critical Discourse Analysis research, too, is united in its emancipatory goal. In other words, it adopts an overt political stance in respect of the topics that it examines, and the role that the results of research need to play outside academia.

While diverse methods are drawn upon, there are three, largely compatible, key approaches in Critical Discourse Analysis: the socio-cognitive approach, the 'discourse-practice' approach; and the historical approach.

The *socio-cognitive approach* has been developed principally by Teun Van Dijk and encompasses three analytic components: social functions, cognitive structures and discursive expression and reproduction. A key research aim in this approach is to unveil the relationships between societal and discourse structures. These structures are indirectly related to one another through social actors and their minds. Ideologies, understood as mental representations shared by the members of a social group (van Dijk 1998), are therefore central to this approach. They are regarded as the basic principles governing social judgment and, hence, as essential to our being able to make sense of how inequalities in society inform specific discursive or interpretative acts.

The *discourse-practice approach*, developed by Norman Fairclough, provides a broadly Marxist perspective on social conflict in which the means of production play a paramount role. The aim of research within this approach is thus to identify the specific means through which inequalities and conflicts, which are seen to arise from the capitalist mode of production, become manifest in discourse. There are three dimensions of analysis to achieve this aim: textual (involving the micro level of, for example, vocabulary and syntax, and the macro levels of, for instance, text structure and interpersonal elements), discourse practice and sociocultural practice (see Smith, Chapter 7, for further description of these dimensions). Within the textual practice level, the analysis is abductive – that is, there is no pre-determined set of linguistic strategies (nor of the linguistic realizations of these strategies) one should look for in advance. The textual practice level, crucially, can draw upon particular linguistic theories. In Chapter 6, on police reality shows in Argentina, Pardo's textual practice analysis is conducted via a 'synchronic /diachronic' method. In Chapter 3, it is identification of locally instantiated textual features that drives Shei's linguistic analysis of Chinese-language dating shows and enables it to be linked to the other levels. There are also both socio-cognitive aspects of discourse processing and intertextual aspects that need to be examined within each of these dimensions. The latter are assigned primacy in Fairclough's approach, for they are regarded as crucial to our being able to understand 'how in the production and interpretation [...] of a text people draw upon other texts and text types which are culturally available to them' (Fairclough 1998, p. 145).

As for the *historical approach*, this originated as a case study by Ruth Wodak and associates of the emergence of an anti-Semitic stereotyped image ('*Feinbild*') in public discourse (press reporting) during the 1986 Austrian presidential campaign of Kurt Waldheim. It subsequently developed as a fully fledged methodological approach that combines theoretical discourse studies with ethnographic work, and that places great emphasis on interdisciplinarity. In this approach, the wider context of discourse is seen as a *sine qua non* of analysis. Four levels of context are examined in order to unveil how power and dominance operate in discourse, from most to least text-bound: the actual use of language; the relationship between utterances, texts, discourse, and genres; the extra-linguistic sociological and institutional context of discourse; and the socio-political and historical context.

As is evident from the brief overview of key approaches in Critical Discourse Analysis, a common denominator in this research is to unveil the workings of dominance and power within a range of – for the main part – institutional contexts. And it is here that we begin to see how the media in general have become a staple institution to which Critical Discourse Analysis has been applied. Work in this field has often adopted a 'hermeneutics of suspicion', which assumes that language and the media are 'systems of representations that, in ordinary practice and use, misrepresent the reality which they re-present' (Scannell 1989, p. 156). This critical dimension, however, is not about 'intolerant fault-finding' but about 'acknowledging the artificial quality of the categories concerned' (Fowler 1991, p. 25). The object of study is often media representations that are seen to favour one or another aspect of reality and, in so doing, to link to higher-order levels of analysis in order to construct certain identities in particular ways within specific cultural and contextual settings.

In the television medium, examples of this kind of work abound which interrogate – and denounce – ideologically biased representations of race and immigration in, often, the news. As for RTV, this is generally viewed – and analysed – as factual media output, that is, as a set of genres and programmes that work according to the conventions of what is known as 'the assertive stance to reality' (Plantiga 1997, p. 40). Essentially, the assertive stance to reality claims that a number of documentaries and other forms of factual television – including a range of RTV genres – are premised on viewer acceptance of there being strong connections between recording and reality. A full gamut of built-in signals encourage viewers to accept this stance, including pro-filmic and filmic conventions that seek to increase the viewers' impression of being in the socio-historical world shown on their television screens, such as location shooting, presenters addressing the camera directly, and use of 'natural lighting' and of hand-held or shoulder-mounted cameras to generate jagged movements. It is important to stress that this does not automatically mean that viewers treat (R)TV as reality, and the identities on screen as real. Rather, the concept of an assertive stance to reality simply, though not unproblematically, seeks to capture (R)TV's work on producing outputs that seem to give viewers direct access to aspects of reality and to a range of 'real' identities. We say 'not unproblematically' because of the explicitly performed – rather than 'real' – feel of some genres of RTV, such as some highly-scripted quiz shows. However, and as pointed out by Lunt and Stenner (2005) in their investigation of *The Jerry Springer Show*, it is the overtly performed, and at times exaggeratedly dramatic, nature of some of these broadcasts that paradoxically continues to hold their 'reality status' within the parameters of RTV. The emotional excesses and theatricality that characterize several RTV genres, especially those that are most confrontational, are thus still 'real' within their respective genres. This is also perhaps why, as we pointed out in Chapter 1, the kind of 'spectacular impoliteness' or 'impolitainment' (Lorenzo-Dus 2009a) that characterizes a number of RTV genres is interpreted as 'really impolite' by a number of viewers.

The representation and construction of a range of aspects of reality and identities in RTV is thus of manifest interest to scholars working within Critical Discourse Analysis frameworks. And a key discursive practice regularly examined concerns the naturalization of certain identities, and the ideologies that underlie such naturalization practices. Naturalization refers to the fact that the way things are presented to us is not inevitable or unchangeable. Instead, it is the result of specific actions and it is intended to serve specific interests. Speaker choices are, therefore, ideologically patterned and through them particular social arrangements – serving particular interests – are made to appear as the only possible or rational ones.

In short, without denying the performed and pre-/post-broadcast editing of RTV, analysis of identity in such shows from within Critical Discourse Analysis approaches works on the assumption that the different genres of RTV are influential in supporting and constructing particular identities and ideologies. Through rigorous Critical Discourse Analysis one is able to recognize naturalization practices at work within the shows and, in turn, unveil their constructed nature. In the case studies included in Part II of this book, constructions of poverty (and hence of 'the poor') as morally deviant permeate the narrative arc of Argentinean police shows (Chapter 6). Also, constructions of 'Kiwis' as national heroes drive the narrative structure and forms of talk of the rescue show examined in the New Zealand context (Chapter 7). Particular gender constructions, especially surrounding the institution of marriage, in contemporary China are unveiled through Critical Discourse Analysis of Chinese-language dating game shows (Chapter 3). And a specific interplay of gender, national and religion-based identity is constructed in reality race gamedocs in Israel (Chapter 4).

Multimodality and identity in RTV

In Multimodal Discourse Analysis, or Multimodality, meaning is seen as 'made in many different ways, in the many different modes and media which are co-present in a communicational ensemble.' (Kress & Van Leeuwen 2001, p. 111). This framework was developed to highlight the importance of taking into account semiotic modes other than language, such as image, music, gesture, and so on, with a view to generating comprehensive and powerful analyses of discourse. Two conditions prepared the ground, as it were, for the emergence of Multimodality as an influential framework for the analysis of a range of communicative events, and especially of those of a mass-mediated nature. One was the de-centring of language as favourite meaning-making mode in Western cultures in the late twentieth century. The other was a 're-visiting and blurring of the traditional boundaries between the roles allocated to language, image, page layout, document design, background music, and so on' (Kress & van Leeuwen 2001, p. 2). This change from monomodality to multimodality in the analysis of communication was triggered by the so-called digital era, in which different communicative modes have technically merged at some representational level. They can nowadays 'be operated by one multi-skilled person, using one interface, one mode of physical manipulation, so that he or she can ask, at every point: "Shall I express this with sound or music?", "Shall I say this visually or verbally?" and so on.' (Kress & van Leeuwen 2001, p. 2).

The relevance of examining (R)TV in this vein is obvious, given that the television medium is intrinsically multimodal. Within this approach, camera work, background music, screen graphics, language, paralanguage, and so forth are all treated as significant meaning-making modes. Multimodality has been successfully applied to the study of factual programming of a 'serious' nature, such as news coverage of life events. Examination of sound files in the live coverage of both the New York (Jaworski, Fitzgerald & Constantinou 2005) and London (Lorenzo-Dus & Bryan 2011a, 2011b) terrorist attacks has revealed the implementation of what we may term 'sonic sanitization' principles of news reporting, whereby certain media materials that likely included distressing sounds were muted and / or broadcast over poignant music. But it is in the analysis of recorded, highly edited, RTV genres that Multimodality has been shown to be capable of generating particularly powerful analyses. In UK-produced property shows, for example, filming tends to last between three days and a week. The actual episodes, however, last between 30 and 60 minutes, inclusive of commercial breaks. Viewers are thus presented with a concatenation of scenes that carry the plot forward. This narrative chain is the result of careful choices regarding which scenes to select and in which order to present them, which scenes to omit, and which modes of communication (visual, aural, verbal) to use in order to persuasively communicate different messages, from empathy with the viewer through to melodramatic climax (Lorenzo-Dus 2006a, 2006b, 2008).

But what about any particular benefits of Multimodality to the study of *identity* in RTV? A key one is the actual salience of identity features that are not conveyed (exclusively) through language but through, for instance, body language and a whole range of non-verbal communication cues. These are incredibly influential. Non-verbal signs of communication are generally seen as more believable than co-occurring verbal ones, though – admittedly – they are also much more indeterminate and ambiguous. This is because verbal signs draw on a series of fixed and rather complex devices to indicate a number of connections, such as causality, similarity, difference and so forth, whereas non-verbal signs are considerably less explicit about such relationships. Even those non-verbal signs normally associated with lying (e.g. fidgeting and averting one's gaze) cannot be unequivocally related to deception. The strong point of non-verbal signs such as images is precisely their implicitness. This is why, for example, soft-sell advertising techniques, which work through implicitness (verbal and visual), are generally regarded as more persuasive than their hard-sell counterparts (Cook 2001).

The value of non-verbal signs is far from taken for granted in RTV. RTV shows place great emphasis on ensuring that viewers get their 'emotionality fix' through strategic and systematic use of camera angles, amongst other things, in order to maximize moments of 'raw' emotion – what Grindstaff (2002), using a term from pornographic media, calls 'the money shot'. In a number of RTV genres, these are packaged for public consumption around cleverly edited 'moments of confession' (Lorenzo-Dus 2009a) in which ordinary people are filmed often in medium-close or close-up as they engage in monologues to camera. In these, they reveal not only their struggles to achieve a certain aspired-to identity (e.g. being a thin man/woman, being a 'better spouse', and so forth), but also their determination to overcome their difficulties. Whilst initially performed as private moments of self-evaluation, post-production editing techniques in many of these shows ensure that the thus constructed identities of ordinary people become public and accountable through the discourse of a range of shows' experts and/or presenters. And in doing this, once again, use of non-verbal signs is not only crucial but maximally exploited by the shows, as integrated analyses of images, sound and verbal interactions have revealed.

In the UK version of the health makeover show *You Are What You Eat*, for example, ordinary people's confessional monologues are sandwiched between narrative voice-overs in which presenter Gill McKeith relays in no uncertain terms how little she thinks of their 'identity work' at becoming thinner selves. These voice-overs are combined with her own on-screen appearances in which her expressions of shock and disappointment are maximized for the viewers through strategic camera close-ups (Lorenzo-Dus 2009a). Another example is the systematic use of close-up shots in reality game shows to emphasize the emotional disappointment of successful experts/entrepreneurs in relation to ordinary citizens aspiring to become 'better selves' (successful entrepreneurs) (Lorenzo-Dus 2009b), which is an effective visual mechanism for controlling how identities claimed by ordinary members of the public participating in these shows are meant to be interpreted by audiences.

Camera work is also strategically combined with music and sophisticated graphics to construct a range of 'aspirational' identities and associated lifestyles in property shows, where identity categorization, or a rather explicit form of pigeonholing, is a common practice. For example, the 'affluent young professional' identity – explicitly labelled as such in the shows – is multimodally constructed by means of, amongst other things, a quick succession of close-ups of stainless steel kitchen appliances, power showers and other 'modern' furniture, being synched with up-beat music against the verbal description of what such material signs represent in identity and lifestyle terms (Lorenzo-Dus 2006a). Along the same lines, in Chapter 5 Bednarek shows how 'positive emotions' are foregrounded through strategic use of camera angles that highlight the value of certain emotions in attaining a particular identity.

Discourse analysis, aggression and RTV

Linguistic aggression has been associated not only with the construction of identity in, but also with the success of, RTV. Its examination has been fruitfully conducted within an influential framework in interactional sociolinguistics, known as linguistic im/politeness. It has also been examined within a tradition of interdisciplinary research that integrates methods in discourse analysis with those developed in, especially, Media Studies and is known as the 'broadcast talk' approach. Both are drawn upon in the various case studies included in Part III of this book.

Broadcast talk, aggression and reality television

As with other approaches, there is a wide range of methodological tools used by scholars working within the broadcast talk tradition. Yet, these cohere around a shared premise, namely that analysis of 'linguistic form, discursive practice or interactional order' is fundamentally shaped by the 'technological and interactional frameworks within which broadcast talk is produced' (http://ross-priory-broadcast-talk.com/). There is, it is argued within the broadcast talk approach, one aspect of television (and radio) discourse that makes its analysis distinctive vis-à-vis that of other, unmediated, spoken discourse contexts: its 'double articulation'. As Scannell (1991, p. 1) first put it, broadcast talk is 'a communicative interaction between those participating in discussion, interview, game show or whatever and, at the same time, is designed to be heard by absent audiences.' Television discourse is indeed explicitly designed and produced to be heard and seen (as we discussed earlier in relation to Multimodality) by these absent audiences.

The double articulation of television talk also makes its analysis challenging within speaker-hearer models of communication, such as Ferdinand de Saussure's (1916) 'speaking circuit'. More sophisticated models have been developed since, including those by Shannon and Weaver (1949), Sebeok (1991), Sperber and Wilson (1995) and Goffman. The last-mentioned author has been especially influential in subsequent work on broadcast talk. Erving Goffman did not set out to model spoken communication *per se*. However, a considerable part of this work examined in detail how we talk to each other in given social encounters, included mass-mediated ones. Goffman replaced the traditional notions of speaker and hearer with those of the 'production format' and the 'participation framework' (for the reception of talk), respectively. He divided the production format into three roles: 'animator', 'author' and 'principal'. These respectively designate 'the sounding box from which utterances come'; 'the agent who puts together, composes, or scripts the lines that are uttered'; and 'the party to whose position, stand, and belief the words attest' (Goffman 1981, p. 226). As for the reception of talk, Goffman also identified further roles, namely those of 'ratified' and 'unratified' recipient. The former refers to the 'official' or intended receivers of a message, who can be either 'addressed' or 'unaddressed'. Addressed receivers are those 'to whom the speaker addresses his visual attention and to whom, incidentally, he expects to turn over his speaking role' (1981, p. 132). Unaddressed receivers are any other of the 'official hearers' in a given communicative exchange, even those who may not be actually listening' (1981, p. 133). Unratified recipients, for their part, are those non-official, unintended recipients of talk and can be either 'overhearers' ('inadvertent', 'non-official' listeners or bystanders) or 'eavesdroppers' ('engineered', 'non-official' followers of talk) (1981, p. 132). Goffman stressed that production and reception roles are interactionally fluid. Interactants can – and do regularly – shift between them, engaging on each occasion in what he called a 'shift of footing': 'a change in the alignment we take up to ourselves and the others present as expressed in the way we manage the production or reception of an utterance.' (1981, p. 128).

In the wake of Goffman's research, studies of broadcast talk have explicitly sought to better understand the complexity of how the different roles that comprise given participation frameworks are actually enacted. Goffman's disaggregation of the traditional speaker role, for example, has led to a fuller conceptualization of how those 'doing speaking' on television may accomplish specific interactional tasks. In terms of conflict talk, for instance, interviewers have been found to be able to escape accusations of bias by formulating challenging questions in formally neutral ways. These often include shifts of footing, whereby interviewers retain, for instance, the role of talk animators but attribute talk authorship to a third party (Clayman 1992; Clayman & Heritage 2002). Goffman's disaggregation of the traditional hearer role has also led to more nuanced analyses of television interaction in which his roles of the 'overhearer' or 'eavesdropper' have been applied to the various parts played by television's non-co-present audiences – its viewers – in the performance of television talk (see, for example, Heritage & Roth 1995; Illie 1999). Goffman-influenced work on establishing 'who stands in which when' in the talk of television has consistently upheld the need to include all those 'who happen to be in the perceptual range of [a television communication] event' (1981, p. 3). Recent research on aggression in RTV, as we will see later, has indeed sought to ascertain how these viewers interpret such aggression from their non-directly involved position – from the so-called overhearing audience position.

On this particular notion, Goffman's legacy has also prompted further conceptual refinement. Lorenzo-Dus (2009a) argues that treating viewers either as overhearers or as eavesdroppers on grounds of their physical non-co-presence is misleading, even if somehow understandable. This is because in Goffman's participation framework, the roles of overhearer and eavesdropper are placed within the position of unratified (unofficial, unintended) reception of talk. Yet, the nature and function of television is to broad-cast, which means that these viewers are by definition ratified (official, intended) receivers of television talk. They can therefore never be overhearers/eavesdroppers, even if the current television climate of 'closeness' and voyeurism oftentimes seeks to make them feel so. Hutchby's (2006, p. 167) suggestion to replace the standard term in much media discourse research – 'overhearing audience' – with the term 'distributed recipients' makes perfect sense.

The above brief overview of Goffman's notion of the participation framework, and its subsequent application to the study of broadcast talk, has special import in the context of RTV, particularly as regards the performance of conflict talk. The detailed analysis of participation frames and participatory structures and roles – including shifts of footing – in a British reality talk show (Tolson, Chapter 12) and an American health makeover show (Gordon, Chapter 11) are two cases in point. Further evidence comes from the links between persuasion and conflict talk in makeover property shows (Lorenzo-Dus 2006a). These shows seek to convince viewers that the lifestyles – and associated identities around the sphere of domesticity – that they showcase are worth emulating: that is, they are clearly persuasive texts. Detailed analysis of persuasion strategies reveals that this is crucially framed via two participatory frameworks, skilfully interwoven within and across individual episodes. One of them is characterized by overt didactics: viewers are directly addressed, and placed as intended beneficiaries of the advice provided by the shows' presenters / experts about how to sell their homes. The other framework entails covert didactics. Here experts/presenters and show participants are shown engaging in 'naturally occurring' interactions about the 'dos and don'ts' of property transactions for the benefit of viewers, who can 'learn' vicariously through the experiences – good and bad – of those with whom they may be expected to identify as members of the same discursive category, namely, being 'ordinary folk'. Conflict talk is performed within many of these shows as part of their narrative arc, and the requirement to provide an entertainment hook. Crucially, conflict talk is only embedded within the covert didactics framework, and entails participants in the show either challenging the expert's/presenter's advice and, no surprise here, failing either to find their ideal property or to sell their current one. Conflict talk, in other words, is made to serve not only a dramatic/entertainment function but also an educational one.

Im/politeness, aggression and RTV

As we noted in Chapter 1, a number of RTV genres make systematic and strategic use of verbal – and occasionally physical – aggression as a means to pander to the assumed preferences of their viewers for entertainment – what has been termed 'confrontainment'. We also discussed in Chapter 1 that the status of (non-)verbal aggression in RTV as 'really impolite' has been a hotly debated academic issue (e.g. Culpeper 2005; Mills 2003; Garcés-Conejos Blitvich 2009; Garcés-Conejos Blitvich *et al.* 2010; Lorenzo-Dus 2009a; Lorenzo-Dus *et al.* 2011; Blas-Arroyo, Chapter 10 in this volume; Culpeper & Holmes, Chapter 8 in this volume). Research into this aspect of impoliteness in television contexts has been conducted on a range of RTV genres, from quiz to dating shows. First things first: what is impoliteness?

Though not a particularly helpful start, it is necessary to preface any definition of impoliteness with what has become a truism in the field, namely that impoliteness – as was the case with politeness – is notoriously difficult to define. A range of definitions have been proposed since the notion was first coined by Jonathan Culpeper in an article published in 1996. Despite their differences, these tend to place 'face' – or face-related concepts such as self-image or social identity – centre stage. They also consider the role played by intentionality in determining whether certain communicative behaviour may get categorized as impolite (Culpeper 2011, pp. 19–21).

Broadly speaking, research on im/politeness has adopted either bottom-up (known as first-order or im/politeness1) or top-down (known as second-order or im/politeness2) models. The former target participants' assessments of discourse as im/polite (e.g. Locher & Watts 2005). The latter rely on the analyst's assessments of discourse as polite, politic or impolite (e.g. Bousfield 2008; Culpeper 1996, 2005). Such assessments are grounded in pragmatic theories, often in Brown and Levinson's (1987) politeness model. Recently, other models have emerged. One of them, by Garcés-Conejos Blitvich (2010), conceptualizes impoliteness by drawing centrally upon Swales's (1990) and Fairclough's (2003) notions of genre and hence incorporates 'a top-down – predictive – approach with a bottom-up co-constructed, emergent, discursive approach, instantiated at the level of style'. Garcés-Conejos Blitvich distinguishes between impoliteness in genres in which face-threatening behaviour is and is not sanctioned:

> For those genres in which face-threatening behaviour is not the norm, i.e. where it is not sanctioned or expected, impoliteness can be defined as (i) the use of lexico-grammatical strategies or realizations of prosodic features not typically associated, i.e. not recurrent, with a specific (pre)genre and/or (ii) a disregard for the established, (per)genre-sanctioned, norm and interactional parameters regulating

the rights and obligations associated therein with a given individual/ social identity which can thus be interpreted as face threatening. For those genres in which face-threatening behaviour is the norm, i.e. where it is sanctioned and expected, impoliteness interpretations may still ensue, i.e. they may not be neutralized, (i) when there is a mismatch between the social, generic, norms of the interaction and the participants' background and expectations, i.e. experiential norms; (ii) when the face-threatening behaviour goes beyond the genre-established limits of what is acceptable as the normal course of events. (Garcés-Conejos Blitvich 2010, p. 63)

Culpeper, too, has recently revised his definition of impoliteness in ways that move beyond the impoliteness1 or impoliteness2 dichotomy, stressing instead that:

Impoliteness is a negative attitude towards specific behaviours occurring in specific contexts. It is sustained by expectations, desires and/ or beliefs about social organisation, including, in particular, how one person's or a group's identities are mediated by others in interaction. Situated behaviours are viewed negatively – considered 'impolite' – when they conflict with how one expects them to be, how one wants them to be and/or one thinks they ought to be. Such behaviours always have or are presumed to have emotional consequences for at least one participant, that is, they cause or are presumed to cause offence. Various factors can exacerbate how offensive an impolite behaviour is taken to be, including for example whether one understands a behaviour to be strongly intentional or not. (Culpeper 2011, p. 23).

An important aspect that both definitions share is the role of genre/ context in determining whether certain behaviour is considered 'impolite'. In the case of broadcasting, this means taking on board the double articulation of its talk, and hence integrating the views of a selection of viewers. Methodologically this was tested in a study of the production and interpretation of impoliteness in the UK version of the international franchise *Dragons' Den* (Lorenzo-Dus 2009b). The results of an impoliteness2 analysis of impoliteness-containing sequences of interactions between the show's experts ('the dragons') and participants aspiring to become successful entrepreneurs were contrasted with the assessment of representative samples of such interactions by a demographically controlled group of viewers obtained via a multimodal questionnaire. Other studies have adapted this two-pronged (production and interpretation) methodological design as a way to investigate audience interpretation of impoliteness in the context of Spanish RTV (Garcés-Conejos Blitvich *et al.* 2010; Blas Arroyo, Chapter 10 in this volume).

Conclusion

The brief overview of methodologies for the study of the discourse of RTV presented in this chapter reflects the rich and sophisticated analyses that their respective analytic 'toolkits' enable, as well as their complementariness. Several chapters in Part II of the book, for instance, include both a multimodal and a Critical Discourse Analysis angle (especially Chapters 3, 5, 6 and 7). Similarly, chapters in Part III integrate identity construction issues within their examination of aggression in RTV (e.g. Chapters 10, 11 and 12). Now that the conceptual and methodological foundations for the study of the discourse of RTV have been laid out, these may be fully developed through situated, empirical case studies that span a diverse range of cultural, linguistic and generic contexts.

References

Baker, Paul, Gabrielatos, Costas, Khosravinik, Majid, Krzyzanowski, Michal, McEnery, Tony and Wodak, Ruth (2008) A useful methodological synergy? Combining critical discourse analysis and corpus linguistics to examine discourses of refugees and asylum seekers in the UK press. *Discourse & Society*, 19(3): 273–306.

Bousfield, Derek (2008) *Impoliteness in Interaction* (Amsterdam and Philadelphia: John Benjamins).

Brown, Penelope & Stephen Levinson (1987) *Politeness: Some Universals in Language Usage* (Cambridge: Cambridge University Press).

Clayman, Stephen (1992) Footing in the achievement of neutrality: The case of news-interview discourse. In Paul Drew & John Heritage (eds.), *Talk at Work: Interaction in Institutional Settings* (Cambridge: Cambridge University Press), pp. 163–98.

Clayman, Stephen & John Heritage (2002) *The News Interview* (Cambridge: Cambridge University Press).

Cook, Guy (2001) *The Discourse of Advertising*, 2nd edn. (London: Routledge).

Culpeper, Jonathan (1996) 'Towards an anatomy of impoliteness', *Journal of Pragmatics*, 29: 173 – 191.

Culpeper, Jonathan (2005) Impoliteness and entertainment in the television quiz show: *The Weakest Link. Journal of Politeness Research*, 1: 35–72.

Culpeper, Jonathan (2011) *Impoliteness. Language to Cause Offence* (Cambridge: Cambridge University Press).

Fairclough, Norman (1998) Political discourse in the media: An analytic framework. In Allan Bell & Peter Garrett (eds.), *Approaches to Media Discourse* (Oxford: Blackwell), pp. 142–62.

Fairclough, Norman (2003) *Analysing Discourse: Textual Analysis for Social Research* (London: Routledge).

Fowler, R. (1991) *Language in the News: Discourse and Ideology in the Press* (London: Routledge).

Garcés-Conejos Blitvich, Pilar (2009) Impoliteness and identity in the American news media: The 'Culture Wars'. *Journal of Politeness Research*, 5: 273–304.

Garcés-Conejos Blitvich (2010) A genre approach to the study of im-politeness. *International Review of Pragmatics*, 2: 46–94.

Garcés-Conejos Blitvich, Nuria Lorenzo-Dus & Patricia Bou-Franch (2010) A genre approach to impoliteness1 in a Spanish TV talk show: Evidence from corpus-based analysis, questionnaires and focus groups. *Intercultural Pragmatics*, 7: 689–724.

Goffman, Erving (1981) *Forms of Talk* (Oxford: Blackwell).

Grindstaff, Laura (2002) *The Money Shot. Trash, Class, and the Making of TV Talk Shows* (Chicago and London: The University of Chicago Press).

Heritage, John & A. L. Roth (1995) Grammar and institution: Questions and questioning in broadcast news interviews. *Research on Language and Social Interaction*, 28: 1–60.

Hutchby, Ian (2006) *Media Talk. Conversation Analysis and the Study of Broadcasting* (Maidenhead: Open University Press).

Jaworski, Adam, Richard Fitzgerald & O. Constantinou (2005) Busy saying nothing new: Live silence in TV reporting of 9/11. *Multilingua*, 24: 121–44.

Kress, Gunther & Teun van Leeuwen (2001) *Multimodal Discourse* (London: Arnold).

Locher, Miriam & Richard Watts (2005) Politeness theory and relational work, *Journal of Politeness Research*, 1: 9–33.

Lorenzo-Dus, Nuria (2006a) Buying and selling: Mediating persuasion in British property Shows. *Media, Culture & Society*, 28: 739–61.

Lorenzo-Dus, Nuria (2006b) The discourse of lifestyles in the broadcast media. In Patricia Bou-Franch (ed.), *Ways into Discourse* (Granada: Comares), pp. 135–48.

Lorenzo-Dus, Nuria (2008) Real disorder in the court: An investigation of conflict talk in US courtroom shows. *Media, Culture & Society*, 30: 81–107.

Lorenzo-Dus, Nuria. (2009a) *Television Discourse: Analysing Language in the Media* (Basingstoke and New York: Palgrave Macmillan).

Lorenzo-Dus, Nuria (2009b) 'You're barking mad – I'm out': Impoliteness and broadcast talk. *Journal of Politeness Research*, 5: 159–87.

Lorenzo-Dus, Nuria & Annie Bryan (2011a) Recontextualising participatory journalists' mobile media in British television news: A case study of the live coverage and commemorations of the 2005 London bombing. *Discourse and Communication*, 5: 23–40.

Lorenzo-Dus, Nuria & Annie Bryan (2011b) Dynamics of memory: Commemorating 7/7 in British television news discourse. *Memory Studies*, 4: 281–97.

Lorenzo-Dus, Nuria, Pilar Garcés-Conejos Blitvich & Patricia Bou-Franch (2011) On-line polylogues and impoliteness: The case of postings sent in response to the Obama reggaeton YouTube video. *Journal of Pragmatics*, 43: 2578–93.

Lunt, Peter & Paul Stenner (2005) *The Jerry Springer Show* as an emotional public sphere. *Media, Culture & Society*, 27: 59–82.

Mills, Sara (2003) *Gender and Politeness* (Cambridge: Cambridge University Press).

Plantiga, Carl R. (1997) *Rhetoric and Representation in Nonfiction Film* (Cambridge: Cambridge University Press).

Saussure, Ferdinand de (1916) *Cours de linguistique générale*, edited by C. Bally and A. Sechehaye, in collaboration with A. Riedlinger. (Paris: Éditions Payot).

Scannell, Paddy (1989) Public service broadcasting and modern public life. *Media, Culture & Society*, 11: 134–66.

Scannell, Paddy (ed.) (1991) *Broadcast Talk* (London: Sage).

Sebeok, T.A. (1991) *A Sign is Just a Sign* (Bloomington: Indiana University Press).

Shannon, C.E. & W. Weaver (1949) *The Mathematical Theory of Communication* (Urbana, IL: University of Illinois Press).

Sperber, D. & D. Wilson (1995) *Relevance: Communication and Cognition*, 2nd edn. (Oxford: Blackwell).

Swales, John (1990) *Genre Analysis. English in Academic and Research Settings* (Cambridge: Cambridge University Press).

Van Dijk, Teun (2001) Critical Discourse Analysis. In Deborah Schiffrin, Deborah Tannen and Heidi E. Hamilton (eds.), *The Handbook of Discourse Analysis* (Oxford: Blackwell), p. 352–71.

Part II
Reality Television and Identity

3
How 'real' is reality television in China? On the success of a Chinese dating programme

Chris Shei

Introduction

Globalization has brought about similarities in world media formats, among other things. Postcolonial theory in media studies claims that the Western media productions 'are exported around the world and set the standard for local media production' (Laughey 2007, p. 122). Furthermore, according to Laughey, Theodor Adorno's theory of media and culture suggests the idea of 'standardization' whereby the 'pursuit of consumer demand generates superficial differences between mass-produced commodities based on stylistic quirks, as opposed to substantial variations in quality' (p. 124). This seems to indicate that media in non-Western cultures in the world are at a vulnerable position and stand to be colonized by the Western media.

At the other end of the scale, Turner (2010) notes 'some instances where western reality TV formats have run up against local cultural norms and values' (p. 55). As a result, modifications are often made to cater to preferences of different nations and cultures. For example, in the Chinese version of *Who Wants to be a Millionaire*, 'celebrity gossip-based quiz questions were replaced with those that drew upon more formal educational knowledge' (p. 57). Another player in this equation is government intervention. 'China is one of the few countries in the world that controls its media' (He 2008, p. 21). This amounts to saying that, in the case of China, culture and politics work together to rule out the possibility of standardization of global media. Apart from cultural modifications and censorship, some other socio-political factors may be at work to create a new profile for a TV programme adopted from another culture.

In this chapter, I examine how the Chinese version of a reality dating show modelled on a Western counterpart is dramatically different from

43

its predecessor. After establishing the differences, I ponder about the reasons for these differences and for the popularity of the show in its modified form. As a result, I propose a model of 'perspectives of reality' about reality TV, contrasting the situation of China to that of the UK.

Methodology

This project was conceived following the viewing of *Take Me Out* (TMO) for approximately a season in 2011 on UK television and more than a year's viewing of *Feichengwurao* (FCWR) from 2010 to 2012. While having some TMO shows on tapes and all FCWR episodes as video files, I started my analysis of the data by extracting relevant video sections based on impressions of earlier viewing and transcribed them using Conversation Analysis (CA) conventions. According to Wilkinson and Kitzinger (2011), CA makes use of six 'building blocks' of talk-in-interaction: turn-taking, action formation, sequence organization, repair, word selection and overall structural organization. While my analysis does not necessarily include all six variables named above, I largely follow the essence of CA and look at what people do with their talk in the shows, trying to formulate an overall structure of the match-making events. However, at a later stage of the project, when more differences appeared between TMO and FCWR, I began to notice not only the unique and extra features of FCWR in comparison to TMO, but also the non-existent features of talk (which may be prevalent in Western media) on FCWR and on Chinese TV media as a whole. This drove me to seek a broader discourse analysis framework to encompass the results of analysis so far and to help develop a theory, for which I drew upon Critical Discourse Analysis (CDA).

CDA does not have a fixed theoretical and methodological position. Wodak (2011) suggests that 'the CDA research process begins with a research topic that is a social problem' (p. 40). At some point in this investigation, a problem seemed to emerge regarding the 'discourse system' (editors' Introduction to this volume) of RTV in China, which subsumes the dating show genre FCWR, in comparison to the Western media. On the one hand, shows such as FCWR have achieved unprecedented popularity in China in recent years, bringing about an 'open atmosphere' of some sort; on the other hand, a void in the area of political discourse becomes more conspicuous (or hidden?) among the increasingly open talk shows and lively performance in non-political areas of China's RTV. As noted by Bloor and Bloor (2007, p. 5), in modern society, some 'highly structured organizations... hold most power and... control the way we live and influence the way we think'. They also note that 'language is an integral part of that control'. More interesting to me is their suggestion that 'non-existence of certain texts' is also of interest to critical discourse analysts. Fairclough's definition of *critical language study* comes to mind at this point, where '[c]ritical is used in the special sense of aiming to show up connections which may be hidden from people – such as the connections between language, power and ideology' (2001, p. 4). This chapter started from uncovering the discourse structure of a Chinese dating show and ends up with a media control theory by following the ethos of the CDA discipline.

Dating shows and reality TV

Traditionally, TV journalism mostly concentrates on the provision of information and entertainment in the form of storytelling. Ekström (2000) justifiably added 'attraction' as the third mode of communication applicable to TV journalism in addition to 'information' and 'storytelling'. For Ekström, attraction is 'intimately related to deviations from normality' (p. 478), appealing not to the audience's intellect or rational thinking 'but rather our more spontaneous emotions' (p. 479). However, Palmer (2002) notes that reality TV represents a new broadcast climate where 'sensationalism married to a fascination with surveillance is increasingly seen as acceptable' (p. 222). In other words, with the launch of RTV, surveillance, a surreptitious glimpse into others' lives and thoughts, has become a sensational offer and an attraction to twenty-first century TV viewers. Emotional DIY, a term used in Lorenzo-Dus (2003) to explain how the no-longer on air British talk show *Kilroy* advocates certain family values and social norms to serve as guidelines for people to fix their problems, is another phenomenon in contemporary TV chat shows. On *Kilroy*, the host of the show takes the guests' personal narrative as a foundation on which to present his Do-It-Yourself principles on emotional healing. On FCWR, the participants tell their personal stories to suggest how they deal with problems such as courtship, relationship, parental love, or livelihood in general. In both cases, there is a mixture of surveillance and collective learning activity which seems both entertaining and enlightening.

Dating game shows have existed on TV for some time (e.g. *Blind Date* in the UK ran from 1985 to 2003). Traditional dating shows were conducted in a more controlled environment with fewer reality elements. For example, on ITV's *Blind Date* hosted by Cilla Black, the choosing male or female contestant may only verbally interact with the three candidates of the opposite sex without seeing them (being separated by a retractable wall) before making a decision. Many of them are surprised at who they chose in the end (for example, a tall, gorgeous blonde may choose a short and unattractive lad because of his witty answers to her questions). Traditional dating shows are thus meant to make fun of participants rather than being helpful and realistic. Contemporary dating shows no longer hide male and female candidates from each other. Both the participants themselves and the activities they do now look more like the real thing – people are able to see their prospective dating partners and interact with them 'realistically'. Extra elements of reality outside the show are also introduced into the programme. For example, in the TMO series, male candidates are normally filmed at their home or work settings in the form of a condensed self-introduction, offering a glimpse of the 'reality' of their daily life so as to satisfy the likely minimum surveillance requirement of the decision-making ladies and the TV viewers.

Ward and Rivadenrya (1999) found that the viewing of primetime, comedy and drama is positively associated with the endorsement of three attitudes regarding men and women: 'men are sexually driven', 'dating is a game', and 'women are sex objects'. Ferris *et al.* (2007) investigated TV dating game shows and noted the same effect. Furthermore, according to Gray (2009), 'most dating shows operate within a frame of being just for fun' (p. 267). However, as the following analysis will show, while the Western-style dating show such as TMO may well illustrate the attitude of 'dating is a game', the Chinese version, FCWR, does not give such an impression.

Take Me Out and *Feichengwurao*

Take Me Out (TMO) is an ITV production first broadcast on 2 January 2010. Each episode of TMO includes host Paddy McGuinness, 30 single women looking for a date and four single men, each leading a segment of the show, seeking for a date. A man can take a woman out if he successfully wins at least one woman's heart after the video introduction of himself and his on-site performance. A man who does not gain the approval of any woman leaves the stage alone with the accompanying tune 'All by Myself'. Each episode of TMO attracted more than four million viewers in its first and second series from January 2010 to March 2011.

The Chinese version of TMO, called *Feichengwurao* (FCWR, or 'do not bother if you are not sincere') closely followed the ITV version and started broadcasting on 15 January 2010. There are 24 women participants instead of 30. The format of the show is largely the same as TMO but now there is a team of hosts with two specialists joining the main host, Mr Meng Fei, providing comments and help during the show. FCWR became, in less than a year, one of the most watched satellite TV programmes on the web produced by China television (Chinese Wikipedia).

Although the structure and content of FCWR is more or less the same as TMO, there are dramatic differences in the discourse and behaviour produced and the background 'dating ideology' held by participants of the show. Ideology here refers to the motivations of the female and male contestants in coming to the show and the rationale held by all participants of the show regarding the choice of prospective dating partners. While TMO largely exhibits a lively and fun-making atmosphere where male and female candidates look for a date in a pleasant and light-hearted manner, in FCWR, on the other hand, the women and men are seriously looking for life-long partners. A direct piece of evidence for this dramatic difference is the high successful match rate of TMO (between 75% and 100%) and the extremely low match rate of FCWR (often as low as 20%, or one in five male candidates successfully 'winning' a female), signifying the careful attitudes of female candidates in FCWR in picking up a date. On the 23 June 2012 show, for instance, a successful male asked the female he selected earlier whether she would move to Shenzhen to work, where he owned a company. The female answered, 'If I married you, it means following a chicken when you marry a chicken, following a dog when you marry a dog (as the Chinese saying goes)'. She even said, 'I'd like to have two kids, one boy and one girl if possible, so we can take them for a walk, each holding a child's hand'. This happened in the after-match interview and is typical of a successfully matched couple on FCWR, who not only show their excitement of the moment but also their vision of the future together as a married couple.

In the next sections, I will examine a few variables regarding the two dating game shows to illustrate how participants from both shows differ in their attitudes towards dating. I will show how this fundamental difference generates a complete array of different outlooks and outcomes between the shows.

Analysis

Programme structure

The basic structures of TMO and FCWR are largely the same, both consisting of 4–5 cycles of matching events centring around a male candidate trying to impress women and get a date. At the opening, the host of TMO greets the audience and introduces the women into the arena. After all 30 women are in place (each standing behind her own lectern), the host briefly chats with a couple of them as a warm-up activity. Upon the command of the host with a witty metaphor ('Will the goose see the gander? Single man, reveal yourself!') the first male candidate marches into the centre of the arena to join the host. The first cycle of the show begins.

The entrance of the man into the scene consists of his descent from the Love Lift, his brisk walk to the centre of the stage accompanied by the music of his choice, and his brief self-introduction (e.g. 'Good evening ladies. My name's Darren and I'm from London'). Subsequently, the host activates the first round of the light-extinguishing activity by asking the women to 'turn on or turn off' based on their first impression of the man – turning off her light (i.e. changing the brightness condition of the pedestal in front of her from bright to dark) means the female is no longer interested in the male. The host will then approach the lecterns and ask some women why they turned off the light or kept their light on. Next, a video introduction of the male candidate is shown and a second round of light manipulation follows. The host approaches the women again and has verbal exchanges with some of them. Then, the male candidate gets to perform an act to impress the women, be it singing, playing a musical instrument, or demonstrating some kind of sporting skills. Male candidates who do not perform can opt to show a second video clip where their friends or relatives speak on their behalf. A third and final round of the light-extinguishing activity then follows.

The male candidate survives (i.e. he gets a date) if after the third round there is at least one light left on. If there is only one light left, the corresponding woman is his date. If there are more than two lights, the male candidate is asked to turn off those lights whose owners he is less impressed with until there are only two lights left. When there are exactly two lights left, the man is entitled to ask a question and choose the one of the two women whose answer he likes better. If there is no light left, it is a blackout (which is rare for TMO but frequent in FCWR) and the male leaves the stage alone.

In TMO, there are normally four cycles of matching sessions (i.e. involving four single men). In FCWR, there are normally five males for each episode. Also, in FCWR there is no male skill performance session but there are normally three video clips to be shown from each male candidate (1: basic information, 2: personal statements about love and relationships, 3: friends and relatives' opinions), each triggering a light-extinguishing event. There are 30 female date-seekers on TMO per session and 24 on FCWR. A single presenter hosts the TMO show, while there are two additional co-hosting consultants for FCWR, presumably because dating is taken as a more serious matter in the Chinese version and more opinions from specialists are needed.

Contrasts in interactional patterns

In this section, I will show how the verbal interactions between participants in TMO differ dramatically from those in FCWR. In particular, I will highlight the fact that the discourse of TMO does manifest the attitude of 'dating is a game' proposed by Ferris *et al.* (2007). In contrast, the Chinese participants on FCWR seem to endorse the attitude of 'dating is a serious business' in their talk and demeanour on the show.

First of all, turn-taking is an important variable to distinguish between the talk of TMO and that of FCWR. In TMO, women do not have the right to initiate verbal interactions. They frequently make noises in the background (cheering, approving, disagreeing...) but they rarely have a chance to speak unless being addressed by the host, who asks questions to solicit their answers (mainly why they turn the lights on or off). Females on FCWR, on the other hand, can raise their hands and demand a turn of speech at almost any point when a conversation is going on between the participants of the show (i.e. the hosts, the male candidate and the female contestants). Table 3.1 is a summary of kinds of first turn in a block of conversation given to or obtained by female and male contestants of TMO or FCWR respectively in one episode. The host always self-selects and initiates conversations on both shows. The female and male contestants on TMO are normally appointed by the host to speak. The females on FCWR, on the other hand, frequently raise their hands to solicit turns.

Table 3.1 Different turn structures between TMO and FCWR

Turns	Female-appointed	Self-initiated	Male-appointed	Self-initiated
TMO (1 Jan. 2011)	46	0	10	0
FCWR (22 Jan. 2011)	15	15	16	0

A typical, appointed turn on TMO is shown in (1):

(1) Paddy: Corene, why did you turn your light off?
    Corene: Well, when he first came in, he looked so nice, but I've got
             a phobia of hair on the chest so now I'm not keen at all.

In (1), the host of TMO asks one of the women why she turned off
the light, allocating the turn to her by sounding out her name. When
females on TMO are asked questions by the host, they normally comment on the appearance or demeanour of the male candidate or reveal
their ideology about stereotyped images of the male's profession, the
social group he belongs to, his interests and hobbies, and so on. The
response is normally quick and direct, definite and without doubt.
There is no room for negotiation and no need for serious consideration.
The conversations between the host and the contestants, like (1), are
thus often shallow and brief, casual and light-hearted.

Female participants on FCWR, on the other hand, are much more
pro-active. They often raise their hands to solicit turns to make remarks
or ask questions. They ask questions to dig deeper into the personality
of the male candidates as well as their objects in life, career aspects, family and financial circumstances, and so on. They also make clear their
own ideas, circumstances and preferences about dating and marriage in
general. Some examples of female speech on FCWR follow:

(2) MF (host): *shiyi hao mie deng de yuanyin?*
    No. 11, [what is] the reason why you turn off the light?

    No.11: *wo juede ta gen wo qingkuang chabuduo…. ye shuyu nazhong
       daochu piao de.*
    I feel he is in a similar situation to me… he is also wandering about
       a lot.
    suoyi wo juede keneng jiushi butai shihe ba.
    So I feel he might not be suitable to me.
    (some verbal exchanges between MF and No.2)
    No.2: *wo jiushi xiang zhendui shiyi hao nage hua a, jiexialai zai shuo
       liang ju.*
    I just want to add a few words after what No. 11 says.
    ruguo ni yaoshi you zhege meili, ni jiu hui ba zhege nanren liuzhu.
    If you are attractive enough, your man will stay around.
    jiu buhui zai rang ta piao le.
    He will no longer have to wander about.

wo xiangxin wo you zhege meili
I believe I have this kind of charisma.
ruguo weiwo lai de nansheng , erqie wo ba deng ye liudao zuihou
If there is a man coming for me, and I keep my light to the last.
wo xiangxin women liangge zhebeizi wo jiu gending ta le.
I believe the two of us, I'll follow him to the end in our life together.
wo shi hen zhuanyi de nvren.
I am a one-man woman.

First, we note that in FCWR, the female contestants are normally identified by numbers rather than names in verbal interactions. While in (1), the host of TMO officially appoints Corene to speak by referring to her by name, in (2) the host of FCWR addresses the female participant by her allocated number. Using names to address contestants indicates the human-centred nature of TMO; while using numbers to represent people puts the females on FCWR at a distance, allowing them to enjoy some anonymity while discussing very personal matters. What happens in (2) is, after No. 11 was appointed by the host and gave her reasons for rejecting the man, No. 2 self-selected herself and made her views public – that she intended to find a partner from the show and stick to him for life. The speech of No. 2 is representative of the attitudes of most female participants on FCWR, which also form the general ethos of the show.

Returning to the data in Table 3.1, it is telling that all 45 female speakers on TMO in the episode are appointed to speak by the host. No female speakers initiate any stretch of conversation. In contrast, for the FCWR episode sampled, 14 female contestants are appointed by the host to speak, while there are also 15 occasions when these women raise their hands to initiate a conversation with other participants of the show. The fact that there are more fresh beginnings of conversations in TMO (i.e. 45 female contestants being appointed to speak) than FCWR (only 29 stretches of conversation altogether) shows that the conversations in TMO are much shorter than those in FCWR. Participants on FCWR often get into serious discussions about gender and marriage, society and country, environment and livelihood, and so on. On both TMO and FCWR, the male contestants, on the other hand, very rarely initiate a conversation, as they are fixed in a relatively passive position, undergoing a process of 'cross-examination' by the female contestants.

Contrasts in demeanour

Apart from talk, facial expressions, emotional outbursts, gestures and bodily movements also show how participants conceptualize and respond to the dating event which they jointly co-construct. Participant demeanour is quite different for the two dating programmes in question. In the case of FCWR, for example, it is not rare for female contestants to cry in front of the camera, whether in excitement, sadness, or a combination of both. This never happens to any participants on TMO in the episodes under examination. Female contestants on FCWR become emotional when they tell a personal story, sympathise with others' stories, explain a particular position, are leaving the programme, and so on. Some examples from FCWR follow which illustrate some of the occasions on which female contestants choked and sobbed on the show while giving a personal account.

(3) Kou: *ni rensheng zuigao de lixiang shi shemo?*
    What is the highest ambition of your life?
    No. 5: *wo rensheng zuigao de mubiao shi zhao yige xiangqinxiangai de ren* (chokes)
    The highest ambition of my life is to find a person who loves me and who I love.
    han ta pingdan xingfu de guo yibeizi
    I will live an ordinary and happy life with him.
(4) No. 21: *yinwei wo laidao feichengwurao zhege wutai, qishi bingbushi wo ziji baodeming*
    Because I have come to this FCWR stage, actually not as a result of my own initiation.
    wo yiqian de nanpengyou yinwei naoai bingshi
    My late boyfriend died because of brain cancer.
    ta zai bingshi zhiqian weiwo zuode zuihou yijian shiqing
    Before he passed away, he did one last thing for me
    jiushi lai – lai bang wo bao zhege ming
    which is to enroll me on this show.
    ta duiwo shuo de zuihou yijuhua jiushi (chokes with sobs)
    The last words he said to me were:
    xiaolei, wo yihou bukeyi zhaogu ni le
    Xiaolei, I can no longer take care of you in the future.
    xiwang zaizhege wutai shang , zai yihou de weilai de rizi li
    I hope you can on this stage, in future years to come
    ni neng zhaodao yige biwo genghao, bi wo gengneng kuanrong han baorong ni
    you can find someone who is better than me, who is kinder to you than me –
    qu aini de nanren
    a man who loves you very much.

The women speaking in (3) and (4), identified as numbers, both choked in their speech and continued with a sobbing tone. These emotional surges happen not only to female and male contestants, but also not infrequently to the host and the consultants, causing them to choke in their speech, wipe their eyes, unable to continue, and so on. This is by far the strongest contrast to the Western version of dating shows, where there is only fun and banter.

Participants' behaviour also differs drastically in both programmes in the 'men choose' session. This occurs when more than two women leave their lights on at the end of the 'women choose' session. The man then has to march towards the women and extinguish those lights whose owners he dislikes until there are only two left. There are two behavioural differences here. In TMO, the neighbours of a woman still having her light on often gather around to 'protect' the light so the approaching man finds it harder to extinguish it. There is no such behaviour in FCWR. This shows the playful nature of TMO and the different meaning attached to a woman being rejected. No one is playful or light-hearted in FCWR at the moment when the privileged male candidate makes a selection. Indeed, turning off a woman's light at this moment is like rejecting a marriage proposal. Consequently, it is natural for the selecting man in FCWR to feel apologetic towards the woman that he rejects. Hence, male candidates on FCWR often extend their hands to the woman to offer a handshake before turning off her light.

Behavioural aspects of show hosting also differ between TMO and FCWR. In the case of TMO, the host often makes jokes and teases the female or male contestants with funny little remarks. The hosting team of FCWR, on the other hand, consists of three members: the main host and the two advisers who are psychologists able to comment on gender and relationships. The main host of FCWR, Meng Fei, also makes light-hearted remarks from time to time, but he never jokes about the serious business of dating on his show. Likewise, the interactions between the host of FCWR and the two advisers are casual and informal, but the tone is always serious when the talk dwells upon dating and relationships. The advisers are there to help and the male and female contestants normally address them respectfully with the title 'teacher'. When a relatively 'long-surviving' woman eventually chooses a preferred man, the woman often approaches the two advisers and hugs them emotionally before leaving the stage. For instance, one of the two advisers (the female one) even said during the show that 'seeing the girl go is like sending a daughter off to her wedding'.

In summary, all the behavioural aspects examined in this chapter highlight the differences in participant intentions and motivations in joining the shows. While the women and men on TMO go to the programme literally looking for a date, the Chinese young men and women come to FCWR with a view to finding a future bride or bridegroom. Evidently, Eastern and Western audiences conceptualize TV dating game shows differently, which clearly leads to different patterns of participant behaviour on the shows.

Programme tempos

The third variable we will look at in this chapter is the tempo of the show. By tempo, I mean the speed at which discourse or activity happens in the show. The tempo of the show is normally controlled by the host. There are two aspects to the host's control of the show: their initiation of and response to discourse and actions, and their tolerance of others' interruptions. During the viewing of the two shows, I was constantly drawn to the slow tempo of FCWR, the relatively long pauses between interactions, and the frequent diversions of attention to topics relatively unrelated to dating. These aspects are in sharp contrast to the quick tempo of TMO and its water-tight turn-taking patterns and strictly controlled topics (i.e. about dating).

In the case of TMO, the tempo is relatively quick, one event following another in a speedy and seamless fashion without significant pauses. It is rarely that someone makes a voluntary verbal contribution. All conversations are initiated by the host and the male and female contestants are only in a position to answer questions or otherwise respond to comments or instructions in a brief fashion. Everyone knows the rule and follows the tempo of the show from the beginning to the end. There are no diverting remarks on philosophy of life or serious views about gender and relationships. There are only brief, witty remarks, normally comprising one utterance, and one or two exchanges per person with the host; yet the performance is not fully scripted, as the speakers and content of their speech vary depending on which women turn off their lights against which man, whom the women obviously did not see beforehand.

In the case of FCWR, the tempo is much slower with frequent pauses and 'disfluencies' and the interaction patterns are much more complex, with larger verbal exchange units and plenty of impromptu discussions having no direct bearing on the matching event (e.g. a discussion on the meaning of money and the processes of earning it, or a dispute about reactions to seeing couples taking wedding pictures at the seaside). Although it is up to the host whether or not to yield the floor to an enthusiastic speaker, some females always get extra turns to speak. Often, a question or a point raised by one of the participants will trigger a longer discussion about certain aspects of life or relationships. The host himself or the advisers also frequently depart from the routine to express their opinions about certain things, whether relevant or not to the current happenings. Most of the discussions are slow in pace and the host is very tolerant of interruptions, challenges, repairs and disfluencies, additional thoughts, and pauses while the candidate thinks of a response.

As a result of the different pace in the two programmes, there is a significant difference in the amount of time taken for each 'male contestant cycle' to complete. A male cycle with TMO, from his entering the stage via the lift to his exit with or without a date, normally lasts around 10 minutes. A male cycle for FCWR, by contrast, can last from 15 to 20 minutes, because of the extra time spent on various side sequences. The quick tempo of TMO is indicative of a more casual attitude towards dating. That is, dating can be arranged quickly and without much consideration. The slow tempo of FCWR, on the other hand, offers a calm and reflective environment where male and female candidates formulate their hypotheses about candidates of the opposite sex in a thoughtful fashion.

Criteria for selecting a date

A typical exchange between the host and the female participants in both TMO and FCWR is a question-answer pair regarding why the woman turns off the light against a certain male candidate. By examining the answers of the women, we can extract a bundle of male contestant features which the women like or dislike. We can also build a profile for a certain group of female participants in terms of their selection criteria for their ideal dates.

We will analyse female answers on TMO in the first instance. In the episode under analysis, the host asked a total of 35 questions about the reasons why the women accepted or rejected a certain male candidate. Table 3.2 offers a summary of categories of women's answers in response to the question on why they turn off or keep the lights on and the numbers of instances in a particular episode. Some women may mention more than one characteristic in a single response to an enquiry. Appearance (in terms of hair, dress, or general look and feel) accounts for 42% of all answers to the question of why a woman turns the light on or off in one episode of TMO. This is in line with Guadagno, Okdie & Kruse's (2012)

Table 3.2   Categories of female response to light manipulation enquiry

No. of mentions	Reasons for turning lights on or off						
	Appearance	Profession	Age	Skill	Interests	Other	Total
TMO (1 Jan. 2011)	15	6	1	5	4	5	36
FCWR (22 Jan. 2011)	4	0	0	0	0	2	6

finding regarding online dating, that '[f]or women, physical appearance – an indicator of fertility – garnered the most emails from potential suitors.' (p. 643). Some professions were not liked by the female contestants (e.g. school teacher, pest controller). Some skills mentioned in the men's introductory videos win a woman's heart (e.g. being able to cook or play music). Some interests (e.g. sports) coincide with the women's own interests and become positive indicators. Age should be a significant factor but it is not mentioned much in TMO even if sometimes the men are much older (e.g. they are over 50 years old) than the women, who are normally in their 20s or 30s. Some women did not give an obvious reason why they kept or turned off the light.

In the case of FCWR, it should be noted here again that the host rarely has to ask the females why they keep on or turn off the light. Most of the time, the Chinese women are eager to ask questions or express their opinions about the male candidate or about a topic currently under discussion. In the episode examined in detail for this study, only six women were specifically asked by the host why they turned off the light. Four of them mentioned the man's appearance. Compare this with the 15 women in Table 3.1 who were called on by the FCWR host to speak – it means that there were nine occasions where the host appointed a woman to speak but was not asking her why she turned her light off (or kept it on). This is an interesting contrast with TMO, where the host calls on the woman primarily for her to explain why the light is on or off 36 out of 46 times. In the case of FCWR, the host often asks a female candidate other questions, for example, her views about sociocultural affairs, environmental issues, marriage and family, and so on. In other words, FCWR provides a context where the meaning of dating is expanded to include all aspects of family life and society. Male and female contestants evaluate their prospective dating partners not only on the basis of mutual attraction, but also based on the other party's views on the wider context of the partnership. Example (5) illustrates an exchange where the issue of dating and relationship is extended into topics concerning sociocultural and socio-economic issues.

(5) No. 15: *ni zuo huanbao shiye,*
     You work in the environment protection section.
     ranhou wo xiang wen ni dui luo hun zen mo kan?
     Therefore, I would like to ask your opinion about a 'naked wedding'.

The woman in (5) wanted to find out the male candidate's opinion about 'naked weddings' – the kind of wedding where no ceremony, gifts or money are involved (unlike the traditional Chinese weddings where magnificent ceremonies are often held with large amounts of money and gifts exchanged to impress each other and outsiders). Earlier in the same episode the man had portrayed himself to be an environmental fighter in his video and talks. However, he was less certain about a marriage without any kind of ceremony and exchange of gifts. Therefore, the No. 15 female contestant extinguished her light immediately after what she perceived to be an unsatisfactory answer. One of the resident consultants also chided the man for his indecisive attitude to naked weddings. Explicit references to issues regarding wider socio-economic questions are a frequent occurrence on FCWR and the women often take the man's views into account when deciding whether or not to accept him.

A further aspect to consider regarding selection criteria is the man's question asked when there are two remaining women competing for his attention. In this regard, men on TMO are mostly concerned with dating per se rather than long-term relationship prospects, as illustrated in (6)–(8) below:

(6) Stuart: OK, girls, I love to try all new and different types of stuff in my life. When we go on a date, what would you like to try and why?

(7) Fabian: Right, ladies, in the past, I have been described as a party animal. This has caused problems with ex-girlfriends. So what would you do to convince me to stay in with you one evening?

(8) Darren: Right then, girls, I like natural beauty. So if I hid your make-up bag over the weekend, how would you react to that?

As we can see, the Western men on TMO are primarily concerned with the place and content of the dating event – issues relating to personal appearance (8), dating attractions (7), dating adventures (6) and so on. Questions asked by the male contestants on FCWR, on the other hand, are very different (see Example 9).

(9) Zhang: *xiang wen nimen yihou nengbuneng choukong dao chengdu zhebian lai*
I'd like to ask you whether you would come to Chengdu in the future
huozhe shi zai qita difang women yiqi chuangye
or go somewhere else with me to start an enterprise.

Mr Zhang was a vegetable retailer who appeared on the 28 May 2011 edition of FCWR. There were two women keeping lights on for him at the end. He was allowed to ask them a question and to select one of the women on the basis of the answers they provided. The question he was most concerned with, like so many male and female contestants on FCWR, was not the dating event itself, but much further beyond, involving considerations such as career and family planning (some men would ask how many children the women would like to have, with the increasingly flexible official modifications to the existing one-child policy). Alam, Yeow & Loo (2011) note that 'there is a stronger emphasis among women than among men in terms of the partner's income' in online dating (p. 156). However, in the case of FCWR, both female and male candidates seem to emphasize income when choosing a prospective mate.

It seems clear then that women and men on TMO are simply looking for likely partners in a dating event, focusing on compatibility in appearance, habits, interests, and so on. Both female and male participants on FCWR, by contrast, normally come to the show with a view to getting married and with predetermined expectations about the other party and for the partnership. Candidates of the opposite sex not only have to meet these predefined requirements but also have to speak and behave in a satisfactory fashion while being examined within the many Q and A and discussion events happening in the show. No wonder there is a huge difference in successful match rates between TMO (normally 3 or 4 out of 4, or 75–100%) and FCWR (normally 1 or 2 out of 5, or 20–40%). The stricter the criteria, the harder to find a match.

Politics, media and dating shows

I have shown how the Chinese dating show, FCWR, differs from its Western predecessor TMO in terms of programme structure, verbal and non-verbal behaviour of participants, and pragmatic aspects such as criteria for choosing a mate. Referring to programmes on American TV, Gray (2009) says that 'dating shows have long relied on the pleasures of mocking those on screen, not celebrating them' (p. 269). For Chinese dating shows, those on screen are generally respected or at least sympathised with, not mocked, because they are conducting a business of national importance – according to Wright (2011, p. 226), sex ratio imbalance (excess male population) is one of the challenges China faces in the future. In 2010, 19 million people visited various Chinese online dating websites, and the number is expected to rise to 60 million in 2015 (Orlik 2011). Matchmaking is an important function for the service industry in China. With 95.8% people watching television 'often or almost every day' (Miao 2011, p. 111) and an average person watching TV for about three hours a day (Cooper-Chen & Scotton 2010, p. 90), it is small wonder FCWR attracts so much attention and has gained so much popularity. FCWR maintains a viewing rate of between 2.5% and 3.2% of the population, the highest among all TV variety shows in China (Baidu n.d.; Wu 2012).

The entertainment style of FCWR and the pragmatic function it performs might not have achieved its current status had there been powerful rivals from other TV sectors. Xue (2009), for one, notices the lack of current affairs analysis programmes in China and the news programmes are dominated by endless reports of official meetings. Miao (2011) also points out that, 'because propaganda departments exert strict control over Chinese television, official news has been unable to win the public's interest and trust' (p. 111). Current affairs analysis or political talk shows are not encouraged or permitted (except perhaps those supported by the government) in China. It is therefore no surprise that genres that thrive on providing entertainment, with a 'touch of reality', are popular. According to He (2008, p. 21), China uses three means to control the media:

- a series of laws and regulations,
- Party propaganda departments and other agencies, and
- ideological control.

For this author, '[a]s long as the political system built on the dictatorship of the Communist Party of China remains, press freedom will not be realized in China' (p. xx). Furthermore, the government of the People's Republic of China is 'a socialist state under the leadership of the Chinese Communist Party (CCP)' (LaFleur *et al.* 2003, p. 120).

Figure 3.1   Models of power structure amongst government, people and media

Wright (2011, p. 240), for his part, states that 'Chinese people have little direct say in how they are governed', 'there are no meaningful elections in the country' and 'ever since Tiananmen, the Chinese Communists seem to have ruled out any possibility of allowing the emergence of a multiparty democratic system in China' (p. 241). Therefore, we might represent the relationships between the government (i.e. the Chinese Communist Party) and the media and the people in China in a hier-archical structure shown on the left side of Figure 3.1, where the Party rules over both the media and people. This is in contrast to a democratic country like the UK, where the government is elected by the people and the media can criticize the government. Although the government is given the power to govern, it is also open to criticism and can be replaced at the ballot box.

Bearing the power structures suggested in Figure 3.1 in mind, we can move on to consider the different impact that RTV may have on the two different kinds of environments in question, focusing on the way FCWR reflects the cultural-political situation of China and its implications.

Perspectives of 'reality'

On many occasions, male contestants on FCWR mentioned their parents, grandparents and other relatives regularly watching the show and being extremely fond of it. This is not surprising. According to Xue (2009), although there are dozens of TV channels in China, most are dominated by beauty contests, talent competitions, historical costume drama, and so on. We might add RTV to this repertoire after the success story of FCWR – numerous matchmaking programmes and similar shows, such as job-seeking reality shows, 'emotional DIY' shows for couples, 'moving true story' shows and so on, have been spawned by it. For many people in the world, TV news and newspapers are still among the primary sources of information today. Another important source of information is of course the internet, but in China, this is also under rigorous scrutiny via 'tens of thousands of hyper-vigilant cyber-cops' (Wright 2011, p. 238). In addition, major newspapers in China are half-filled with official political articles and half with advertisements (Xue 2009). What is more, if He (2008) is right, then 'all those who work in the media... have become unapologetic spouters of lies' as a result of the Party's 'ideological education' (p. 38). For Cooper-Chen and Scotton (2010, p. 93), 'the curse of Chinese TV, apart from its being state-controlled and defacto censored, is the proliferation of stupid low-budget "reality shows"'. While I do not agree with the criticism that FCWR is a 'stupid low-budget' reality show, I do sympathize with the situation of Chinese TV having to compromise between censorship and audience preference. One possible solution is offering a programme like FCWR, which depicts real people and addresses real needs of a society yet avoids political discussions which might implicate the central government or the Party (except when offering praise or admiration).

The make-up of the audience of FCWR is likely to be different from its UK counterpart, TMO. The British dating show is only one of the wide range of RTV choices including watchdog shows, crime reports, political talks and news reports criticizing the latest government blunder, many of which are more attractive options to mature members of society than the comic fun of TMO. In the case of FCWR, the host Meng Fei once told a story at the beginning of the show involving an older couple on the verge of divorce. The parents saw their son watching FCWR one Saturday and became interested. They ended up watching the show every week together as a family and the divorce issue was dropped. Two generations of family members huddled together in front of the television watching *Take Me Out* seems an inconceivable picture in the UK setting, but it appears to be a common scene in China.

Why the programme is interesting to older and young people alike is perhaps due to its authenticity underlying the entertainment value. Under the tightly controlled media environment of China, it is not possible to criticize the government, but it is possible to attack some business people's inhumane treatment of animals (e.g. extracting bile from live bears or cultivating animal furs), certain ordinary people's poor manners (e.g. speaking loudly in public, eating unfairly large portions in a buffet), damaging acts to cultural heritage or general lack of preservation action (e.g. demolishing older dwellings to create modern compounds, lack of interest in and knowledge of Chinese historical garments). All these topics have popped up at one time or another on FCWR shows. Moreover, the show also brings the viewing public together to reinforce and approve good social practice, moral courage, and conventional values. Gray (2009) notes that (for American TV) '[d]ating shows have always relied heavily on the pleasures of seeing a life more messed up than our own' (p. 261) and 'on the pleasures of mocking those on screen, not celebrating them' (p. 269). While this may be true for Western dating shows like TMO or *Blind Date*, it is certainly not the case for FCWR. The female and male contestants on FCWR often represent the elite groups of society (i.e. company CEOs, managers, entrepreneurs, government officials, shop owners, lecturers, artists, writers...) who go on the show to select potentially life-long partners. This contrast in perspectives of reality may be represented by Figure 3.2.

Because of lack of other engaging RTV genres (e.g. current affairs talk shows), many viewers in China devote their energy and support to available RTV programmes like FCWR, apparently believing or wanting to believe this to be real and helping to make it real. The dotted line in Figure 3.2, however, represents a certain number of sceptics, who no doubt exist, although the number may be negligible and the criticism may be mild. In contrast, reality TV for the UK may be perceived differently by similar categories of people, as the other end of Figure 3.2 shows. According to Turner (2010), there are two opposing views towards reality TV (in the West): although there are 'those who regard reality TV as a positively empowering development' there are also 'those who see reality TV as a tasteless and cynical exploitation of ordinary people's interest in becoming famous' (p. 34). In other words, we can surmise there might be a good proportion of the population in a country like the UK who would question the 'reality' of RTV. Indeed, in the West, 'so much of reality television is devoted to the exposure, humiliation and shaming of its contestants' (p. 37), that it simply cannot represent what ordinary people do in their ordinary life. In the case of China,

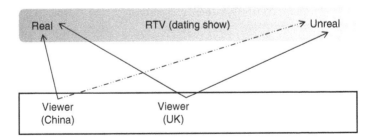

Figure 3.2 Perspectives of reality for dating programmes

however, RTV shows like FCWR are viewed with both pleasure and a kind of seriousness which are not present in their Western counterparts.

Conclusion

FCWR seems to have absorbed the nation's attention in a real sense (having been at the top of the viewing league table since its birth in 2011). In a tightly controlled media environment like that of China, this is not necessarily a bad thing – people get entertained and the government has fewer problems to deal with. To understand the significance of FCWR, even RTV as a whole, in contemporary China, however, we need to look at the wider context. According to Bergsten *et al.* (2008), '[t]hrough its participation in the global order, China has brought hundreds of millions of Chinese out of poverty and firmly tied its economic fate to that of the rest of the world' (p. 235). This is no mean achievement. We might even say China is at one of its strongest periods in its entire history, as it 'surpassed Japan to become the world's second largest economy' recently (Wright 2011, p. 215), next only to the US. Although China still faces many challenges in the future in areas like the natural environment (pollution of air, water, soil) and socio-political stability (corruption, human rights, free flow of information...), it is certainly not on a bad course.

According to Miao (2011), a programme called *Focus* run by the state-owned CCTV and broadcast between 1994 and 1998, investigated and exposed many social problems like homeless children, baby abandonment, business fraud, and even some government officials' wrongdoing and corruption – although understandably 'this program only reported on small potatoes' and 'few cases involving corruption at high levels were being investigated and disclosed' (p. 111). This is in line with Kuhn's (2010) comment that 'China's leaders would prefer the media to focus on failings of local governments rather than question policies of the central government' (p. 315). Kuhn quotes Liu Binjie, Director and Minister of China's General Press and Publication, to say that

> I believe that, in 25 years, Chinese media will be able to meet the people's spiritual and cultural requirements. While safeguarding social and public interests, Chinese media will be more recognized and understood by the West. (Kuhn 2010, p. 320).

Liu's words affirm the Chinese Communist Party's perception of what it is that people need (namely, spiritual and cultural, never political substance). 'Safeguarding' means media control will continue to be tight – or in Kuhn's words, 'censorship is always at the ready' (2010, p. 315). Moreover, the need for Chinese media to be 'recognized and understood by the West' means they will continue to be 'different' from the Western media. As for Chinese people's reaction, Wright's depiction is perhaps the most accurate:

> If the Party can provide the social stability and infrastructural development necessary for continued economic growth, then fine, the public will support the Party and not challenge its rule over China (Wright 2011, p. 214).

In other words, current political analysts believe that Chinese people will not care that much whether they are ruled by a communist party or a democratic government as long as people get fed properly, so to speak, and there is hope of a reasonably good life for everybody. This is what a reality show like FCWR stands for in contemporary Chinese society. The programme appears to be 'real' for most viewers as this might be the only reality they can get from TV and, more interestingly, the only reality they may want for the time being.

References

Alam, S.S., P. H. P. Yeow & H. S. Loo (2011) An empirical study on online social networks sites usage: Online dating sites perspective. *International Journal of Business and Management*, 6: 155–61.

Baidu. (n.d.) China variety show viewing rate league table. *Baidu Zhidao*. Retrieved July 4, 2012, from http://zhidao.baidu.com/question/201431713.

Bergsten, C.F., C. Freeman, N. R. Lardy & D. J. Mitchell (2008) *China's Rise: Challenges and Opportunities* (Washington, DC: Peter G. Peterson Institute for International Economics and the Center for Strategic and International Studies).

Bloor, M. & T. Bloor (2007) *The Practice of Critical Discourse Analysis: An Introduction* (London: Hodder).

Cooper-Chen, A. & J. F. Scotton (2010) Television: Entertainment. In James Scotton & William Hachten (eds.), *New Media for New China* (Chichester, UK: Wiley-Blackwell), pp. 83–97.

Ekström, M. (2000) Information, story-telling and attractions: TV-journalism in three modes of communication. *Media, Culture and Society*, 22: 343–70.

Fairclough, N. (2001) *Language and Power*, 2nd edn. (Essex: Longman).

Ferris, A. L., S. W. Smith, B. S. Greenberg & S. L. Smith (2007) The content of reality dating shows and viewer perceptions of dating. *Journal of Communication*, 57: 490–1.

Gray, J. (2009) Cinderella burps: Gender, performativity, and the dating show. In Susan Murray & Laurie Ouellette (eds.), *Reality TV: Remaking Television Culture* (New York and London: New York University Press), pp. 260–77.

Guadagno, R. E., B. M. Okdie & S. A. Kruse (2012) Dating deception: Gender, online dating, and exaggerated self-presentation. *Computers in Human Behavior,* 28: 642–7.

He, Q. (2008) *The Fog of Censorship: Media Control in China* (New York: Human Rights in China).

Kuhn, R.L. (2010) *How China's Leaders Think: The Inside Story of China's Reform and What This Means for the Future* (Singapore: John Wiley & Sons (Asia) Pte Ltd).

LaFleur, R.A., W. B. Palmer, J. A. Rapp, S. Y. Robson & T. Hamlish (2003) *China: A Global Studies Handbook* (Santa Barbara: ABC Clio).

Laughey, D. (2007) *Key Themes in Media Theory* (Maidenhead and New York: Open University Press/McGraw-Hill).

Lorenzo-Dus, N. (2003) Emotional DIY and proper parenting in *Kilroy.* In J. Aitchison & D. Lewis (eds.), *New Media Language* (London: Routledge), pp. 136–45.

Miao, D. (2011) Between propaganda and commercials: Chinese television today. In Susan Shirk (ed.), *Changing Media, Changing China* (Oxford: Oxford University Press), pp. 91–114.

Orlik, T. (2011) Turning love into money in China's online-dating. *The Wall Street Journal July5.* http://online.wsj.com/article/SB10001424052702303763404576 420001947330580.html).

Palmer, G. (2002) Neighbours from Hell: Producing incivilities. In James Friedman (ed.), *Reality Squared: Televisual Discourse on the Real* (New Brunswick, NJ and London: Rutgers University Press), pp. 221–35.

Turner, G. (2010) *Ordinary People and the Media: The Demotic Turn* (London: Sage Publications).

Ward, L. M. & R. Rivadenrya (1999) Contributions of entertainment television to adolescents' sexual attitudes and expectations: The role of viewing amount versus viewer involvement. *Journal of Sex Research,* 36: 237–49.

Wilkinson, S & C. Kitzinger (2011) Conversation Analysis. In Ken Hyland & Brian Paltridge (eds.), *Continuum Companion to Discourse Analysis* (London and New York: Continuum International Publishing Group), pp. 22–37.

Wodak, R. (2011) Critical Discourse Analysis. In Ken Hyland & Brian Paltridge (eds.), *Continuum Companion to Discourse Analysis* (London and New York: Continuum International Publishing Group), pp. 38–53.

Wright, D.C. (2011) *The History of China* (Santa Barbara, CA: Greenwood).

Wu, F. (2012) Analysis of variety show viewing rate 2011 (in Chinese). *CSM Media Research.* Retrieved July 4, 2012, from http://www.csm.com.cn/index.php/ knowledge/showArticle/ktid/1/kaid/757.

Xue, X. (2009) *China Witness: Voices From a Silent Generation* (Russellville, AR: Vintage Books).

4

The (inter)play of nationality, religiosity and gender: textual mechanisms for the rich representation of Israeli identity on a reality race gamedoc

Michal Hamo

Introduction[1]

Reality television is a significant cultural forum for the exploration of personal, social and national identities. While its characteristic representation of ethnic and sociocultural diversity may promote democratization and pluralism, previous research indicates that this positive potential is significantly limited by reliance on conservative schemes and stereotypes. The present study aims at examining the full potential of reality television to promote pluralism, as well as its immanent constraints and limitations. To this end, it focuses on an extreme case study – an Israeli show intentionally and explicitly dedicated to promoting tolerance and secular–religious dialogue within Jewish-Israeli society. This case study also allows for documenting the unique resources and affordances of a reality television format that has so far received relatively limited scholarly attention – the race gamedoc (e.g., *The Amazing Race*).

Interpretative analysis grounded in media studies and discourse analysis reveals several textual mechanisms for the rich representation of identities. Close examination of these mechanisms allows for exploring tensions and balances between simplicity and complexity, the reaffirmation and challenge of stereotypes, and entertainment and social responsibility. It demonstrates the significance of self-reflection, humour, expectation reversal and playful performance in identity construction and its representation in popular culture texts.

Theoretical background: identities on reality television

Reality television's popularity and salience in the last decade have often been discussed as evidence of its deep rootedness in its cultural backdrop. Particularly, the core tenets, ideological positions and inter-personal relationships of the discourse system of reality television (see Chapter 2) resonate with contemporary values and perceptions regarding personal identity. In keeping with the late modern view of the self as a reflexive project, i.e., the dynamic product of ongoing management (Cameron 2000), reality shows are often framed as offering their participants unique opportunities for self-revelation and personal growth (Holmes 2004). By foregrounding confessional, emotionally charged first-person testimonials (Dovey 2000; Tolson 2006), reality television underscores the value of self-exposure and sincerity, echoing contemporary Western cultures' emphasis on 'good communication' and on therapeutically oriented talk as necessary for (inter)personal growth (Cameron 2000; Illouz 2008). Reality television also highlights consumer and lifestyle choices as resources for self-construction, reflecting their salience in late capitalism (Hawkins 2001; Palmer 2004).

Reality television's preoccupation with personal identity blurs public and private, personal and social identities (see Chapter 2), and is somewhat contradictory. For instance, reality television participants are often progressively transformed from 'ordinary' people to celebrities. Paradoxically, while this transformation entails moving away from one's original identity and blurring the distinction between 'real' and fictional personas, it also emphasizes authenticity, sincerity and staying true to oneself as key values and criteria for evaluating participants. Furthermore, on many formats the search for authentic identity takes place in an artificial and isolated 'pocket world'. This detachment from real-life settings is framed as a social experiment aimed at exposing 'true selves' independent of contextual influences (Brenton & Cohen 2003). These inner tensions position reality television as a central cultural arena for exploring issues of authenticity and personal identity (Holmes 2004; Tolson 2006).

Reality television also reflects the changing character of the contemporary public sphere and the rising dominance of a politics of identity. The growing legitimacy of attention to the personal, the emotional and the ethics of everyday life in public discourse, the increased awareness of multiculturalism and sociocultural differences, and the resulting concern with the possibility of dialogue with the 'other', are all paralleled by the discourse system's thematic foci (Dovey 2000; Hawkins 2001).

Growing attention to multiculturalism is also reflected by reality television's typical representation of ethnic, gender and sociocultural diversity (e.g., Neiger 2012; Piper 2004; Pullen 2004; Taylor 2002).

The increased media visibility offered by reality television, across a wide range of genres and formats, to social minorities and cultural 'others', has sparked discussion of its potential to promote empowerment, democratization and pluralism. Research on reality television within media and cultural studies has increasingly focused on examining its representations of sociocultural identities (Orbe 2008), and has found its pluralistic potential to be considerably constrained.

First, the representation of a wide array of sociocultural identities in a diverse cast of participants is a form of 'institutionalized pluralism' (Neiger 2012) – it is a highly predictable practice, fully controlled by the production staff and aimed at addressing diverse audiences, as well as at providing the basis for dramatic and engaging conflicts among participants (Pullen 2004). Secondly, reality shows draw heavily on stereotypes (Cavender 2004; Pullen 2004; Taylor 2002), and often promote homogenized and essentialist perceptions of ethnic minorities (Harvey 2006; Wang 2010). By frequently employing a form of 'cultural shorthand', i.e., reducing sociocultural identities to lifestyle and consumer choices, they may further foster a superficial view of identity and otherness (Bottinelli 2005; Palmer 2004; Piper 2004).

Furthermore, diversity among participants is often mitigated or negatively framed. Minority participants are often positioned as aspiring to assimilate and adopt mainstream culture, and as having to 'overcome the obstacle' of their otherness in this process of personal growth and achievement (Elias, Jamal & Soker 2009; Neiger 2012; Palmer 2004; Wang 2010). Otherness may also be presented as a challenge to the existence of community and social harmony (Cavender 2004).

Minority participants become complicit in the authentication of these stereotypes and schemes (Wang 2010). Attempts to challenge mainstream perceptions and values or engage in explicit discussions of power and discrimination are downplayed and discouraged (Elias *et al.* 2009; Kraszewski 2004). In reality television formats featuring authoritative experts or judges, who embody hegemonic values and perceptions, such attempts may be strictly penalized, sometimes by elimination from the show (Elias *et al.* 2009; Wang 2010).

Finally, while casting practices highlight the importance of sociocultural group identities, the televisual text itself focuses on personal identities, is often framed in highly individualistic terms, and downplays the impact of sociocultural diversity (Bottinelli 2005; Brenton & Cohen

2003). This conflict between the individual-oriented concept of the self as a reflexive project and the more community-oriented politics of identity is also echoed in the tensions between individual and communal interests and between competition and cooperation, which often shape events, relationships, interactions, self-presentation and discursive patterns on reality television (Cavender 2004; Thornborrow & Morris 2004; Tolson 2006).

As the above findings were documented across a wide range of genres, formats and cultural contexts, they may be discussed as characterizing the discourse system of reality television as a whole. However, attention should also be paid to generic specificity. The present study focuses on race gamedocs, a reality television genre which has received little scholarly attention in comparison to other genres and formats, and aims at addressing this lacuna by focusing on its unique resources and affordances for identity representation. Race gamedocs (the most successful and prototypical of which is the US-originated format *The Amazing Race*) draw on the practices and conventions of both game shows and documentaries to depict a race. In the race, teams of two compete against each other and against the clock in a series of tasks and challenges in order to avoid elimination and ultimately win a large prize. Unlike the majority of reality television formats, in race gamedocs participants are not confined to an artificial 'pocket world' (Brenton & Cohen 2003), but rather interact with 'real life' settings, selected, but not fully controlled, by the production staff. This unique feature allows for a wider array of thematic and narrative resources: in addition to the participants' identities and relationships, the rules of the game and its challenges, race gamedocs draw on the physical and human landscapes of their various locations in the construction of meanings and identities (Aslama & Pantti 2007; Harvey 2006). This may yield unique textual patterns and relatively rich representations of identities, which merit close analytic attention.

The present study

Case study

The present study explores the representation of identities on the Israeli race gamedoc *Sof ha-Derech* ('The End of the Road', Israeli slang for 'excellent, wonderful'). The show aired for two seasons on primetime on Israel's most dominant broadcast channel, the commercial Channel Two. Its second season, which aired May–August 2005, was popular, receiving an average rating of 18.25 per cent and ranking on average fifth on weekly lists of highest rated shows.[2] Based on the general format of race gamedocs, *Sof ha-Derech* featured 12 teams of two, who competed in a series of extreme sport challenges (e.g. bungee jumping), social skills challenges, in which contestants had to enlist the help of passers-by (e.g., recruiting participants for a large-scale folk dance in a public square), 'search tasks' of deciphering clues to reveal the next destination, and 'dare' challenges (e.g., eating vermin).

The competition was conducted in three rounds, each featuring four teams and lasting three days. Each day, the last team to arrive at the finish line was eliminated, and on the third day, one team was named the round's winner. These rounds were then followed by a 'lifeline' round, which gave one team a second chance to return to the race, and a final round, in which the show's winners were named. Each episode of approximately 90 minutes duration depicted a single day of the competition, beginning in the morning at the starting line and ending at night with a victory and an elimination at the finish line. Events of the day were depicted using the heavily edited mix of footage of tasks and interactions, voiceover narration and testimonials typical of reality television.

Sof ha-Derech's unique 'twist' was its cast of participants. While on most race gamedocs, teammates audition for the show together based on previous acquaintance, *Sof ha-Derech* featured teams of two people with no prior acquaintance, who were paired by the production staff so that each team was comprised of one 'secular' contestant and one 'religious' contestant.[3] This casting principle positions *Sof ha-Derech* as markedly dedicated to secular–religious dialogue, and as a clear example of the common practice of adapting a global reality television format to its local production context by incorporating culturally specific and significant themes, issues and symbols (Aslama & Pantti 2007; Waisbord 2004). In the Israeli context, this practice has often resulted in reality shows preoccupied with national identity and social cleavages. These shows function as cultural forums for the negotiation of dilemmas and struggles concerning power, identity and ideology (Newcomb & Hirsch 2000/1983), including those resulting from Israeli society's gradual move from traditional collectivism and the 'melting pot' ethos to growing individualism and recognition of inner diversity (Kimmerling 2001).[4]

In support of its explicit focus on Israeli identity, *Sof ha-Derech* has purposefully employed the unique thematic resources of race gamedocs. The race spanned the country and visited historically significant sites, both from ancient times and from the early days of the Zionist movement (see Aslama & Pantti 2007 for similar patterns). Along the way, contestants interacted with a wide range of passers-by representing the diversity of Israeli society, from Arab fishermen at Jaffa harbour to members of a radical right-wing youth movement protesting the government plan to evacuate the Gaza strip.

Sof ha-Derech's specific focus on the religious cleavage in Jewish-Israeli society can be explained as resulting from the combination of two factors. First, the show was partly financed by, and co-produced with, the organization *Tzav Pius* ('conciliation order'), a branch of the *Avi Chai* Foundation dedicated to the promotion of contemporary Jewish identity and of religious–secular dialogue in Israel. Thus, *Sof ha-Derech* offers an opportunity to examine civil society organizations' use of popular culture as a tool for advancing social causes (see Dardashti 2007 for a discussion of other examples, their political economy and cultural implications).

Second, both seasons of *Sof ha-Derech* aired during a distinct period in the history of Israeli commercial television. Since its commercial debut in 1993, Channel Two was operated through government franchises to three broadcasting companies. In September 2004, a tender was published for new franchises scheduled to begin in November 2005. The tender presented several stipulations and guidelines, key to which was a preference for socially responsible television, that deals with publicly and culturally significant themes and better represents the cultural diversity of Israeli society and its minorities (Avraham & First 2010). In the year leading up to the decision on the tender, Channel Two broadcasters made concentrated efforts to demonstrate their commitment to social responsibility. *Sof ha-Derech* is a prime example of these efforts, as it combines an entertainment format with socially significant content, and focuses on a minority group and on a highly politically charged cleavage.

These factors mark *Sof ha-Derech* as an extreme case study of identity representation on reality television. As the show was intentionally designed to promote pluralism, tolerance and discussions of Jewish-Israeli identity, it is likely that it utilized the affordances of its format for rich and multifaceted identity representation to the fullest degree. Accordingly, examining identity representation on *Sof ha-Derech* may shed light on the full potential of reality television to promote non-stereotypical visibility, democratization and pluralism, as well as on its immanent constraints and limitations, which manifest themselves even under optimal conditions.

To this end, the present study examined the representation of Jewish-Israeli identity in general, and religious Jewish-Israeli identity in particular, in *Sof ha-Derech*'s second season. All episodes of the series were examined as the basis for selecting key scenes for detailed analysis. Particular attention was given to the final round of the competition, which served as the narrative, emotional and thematic culmination of the entire series, and to scenes from earlier episodes featuring teams who made it to the final round, and were accordingly depicted over time and across a large number of episodes, allowing for relatively developed representations.

Analytic framework

The present study was based on interpretative textual analysis informed by the integration of two distinct disciplines, each providing unique theoretical and methodological insights: media studies and discourse analysis.

Two long-established traditions within media studies were employed in the analysis: (1) assessment of the quality of media minority representations, by examining the traits, roles, contexts and relationships with other social groups attributed to specific minorities on screen (Avraham & First 2010); and (2) exploration of the cultural meanings and functions of popular television texts using narrative analysis frameworks, such as uncovering typical plot structures or underlying thematic binary oppositions (Fiske 1987; Piper 2004). These traditions have generated valuable insights about popular television and its sociocultural significance (see above for a review of some of their contributions to the understanding of reality television). However, their analytic approach tends to be holistic, interpretative and content-focused, and less attentive to textual micro-details.

This limitation was addressed in the present study by relying on discourse analysis, with its commitment to close attention to the linguistic and discursive details and particularities of texts. Specifically, the analysis was grounded in the view of identity as an emergent, contextualized and interactional process of ongoing discursive construction, and focused on examining the role of three specific discursive processes in the construction and representation of identities (de Fina, Schiffrin & Bamberg 2006): (1) the constant intersection and constellation of different levels and types of identities, which construct identity as non-monolithic and multidimensional; (2) the use of specific interactional and stylistic choices as resources in indexing, constructing, creating and performing identities (Bell 2001; Rampton 1995; in broadcast talk, Coupland 2001); and (3) the use of explicit references to identity categorizations and labels and of meta-discursive talk as part of the self-reflexive process of identity construction, which may be particularly salient in reality television (Tolson 2006).

While identities are always discursively constructed and performed, on reality television they are *doubly* constructed – first by the interactional and discursive behaviour of participants, and then by the televisual apparatus of editing and narration. The present analysis focused on the finished product of this double construction – a heavily mediated and carefully structured televisual text, which carefully controls our restricted access to contextualized sequences of talk-in-interaction, and does not allow for distinguishing the self-construction of participants' identities from their reconstruction by the televisual apparatus.

Therefore, the integration of media studies and discourse analysis in the present study is manifested in a hybrid analytic approach – an interpretative textual analysis which is informed by discourse analysis, and accordingly is more fine-grained and more language-oriented than usual – rather than in a fully fledged micro-detailed and systematic discourse analysis of televisual data (for further discussions of possible integrations of media studies and discourse analysis, see Blum-Kulka & Hamo 2011; Tolson 2006).

Findings

The analysis revealed three major textual mechanisms that contribute to rich identity representation: representing diversity in the cast of participants, using a recurrent narrative structure of growing complexity, and highlighting the multidimensionality of identity.

Diversity among religious participants

Sof ha-Derech employs reality television's typical feature of a diverse cast of participants in a unique manner. While other reality shows strive to represent the diversity of the general population, *Sof ha-Derech* focuses on the inner diversity of a single minority – religious Jews. Religious participants on the show form a wide spectrum, ranging from the ultra-orthodox to the modern liberal orthodox and from a radical right-wing religious settler to a new-age born-again Jew. This serves to challenge the widespread homogenous perception of religiosity in favour of a more complex and accurate understanding of the diverse positions and possibilities for self-definition it may offer (Goodman & Yonah 2004). Thus, the common conceptualization of a clear dichotomy between religiosity and secularism, which serves as the structuring principle of the show, is somewhat moderated.

Religious participants exhibit diversity not only in the nature and degree of their religiosity, but also in its conspicuousness. While some participants embody visual icons of religious Jewry (e.g., facial hair for men, long-sleeved shirts and skirts for women), others do not exhibit such easily identifiable cues. For example, Tsipi, a married religious woman, appears on the show in trousers and with uncovered hair, in contrast to common religious customs. She may be recognized as religious based solely on her self-definition and on the fact that she is cast as the religious teammate of a secular participant. Consequently, the validity of 'cultural shorthand' (Piper 2004) which allows for coding and decoding identities based on superficial evidence is reaffirmed by some participants but challenged by others. This echoes a more general trend in contemporary television, of challenging the validity of eyewitness and encouraging the viewer to go below the surface of things (Ellis 2008).

Recurrent narrative structure of growing complexity

Many of the tasks on *Sof ha-Derech* are textually structured as gradually unfolding from a seemingly simple clear-cut starting point to more complex and multifaceted situations and meanings, as the following example illustrates. The teams start their day at the ancient Roman hippodrome of Caesarea. They are given a picture of an unfamiliar coin, which they have to obtain in order to discover their next destination. In accordance with the archeological setting, all teams first assume that the coin is ancient, and turn to tour guides, the site's gift shop and the neighbouring antiquity museum in order to identify it. Once these attempts fail, the teams realize that the coin is in fact contemporary and foreign, and accordingly seek help from tourists visiting Caesarea and from travel agencies in the area. Finally, following some effort and frustration, all teams identify the coin as Ethiopian, and recognize that in order to obtain it, they need to turn to the immigrant community of Israeli Ethiopian Jews.

This second shift in the task's frame of reference also alters the significance of its location. Caesarea is no longer framed as an archeological site or a tourist destination, but rather as an affluent all-White town, which the teams have to leave in favour of neighbouring towns with working-class populations, including Ethiopian immigrants. These socio-economic undertones are particularly salient in one incident: the team of Oved (a male right-wing religious settler) and Jenia (a secular female Russian immigrant) goes to the Caesarea golf club in search of tourists. Once they realize that they are looking for an Ethiopian coin, they turn their attention from the club's patrons to its employees, and address a young groundskeeper of Ethiopian descent. In reply to their query, the groundskeeper confirms that the coin is in fact Ethiopian, but explains that he does not have such coins in his possession. At this point, an interaction worthy of closer attention unfolds:

Oved:	*Me-efo ata?*
	Where are you from?
Groundskeeper:	*Me-Hadera.*
	From Hadera.
Oved:	*Yachol lihiyot she-im ani nose'a le-Hadera, ani motse et ze sham?*
	Is it possible that if I go to Hadera, I find it there?
Groundskeeper:	*Sh'al ba-r'chov anashim mevugarim.*
	Ask in the street older people.
Oved:	*Toda raba lecha, kol tuv.* [To Jenia] *Yalla, bo'i nisa le-Hadera. Yesh male Etyopim be-Hadera.*
	Thank you very much, all the best. [To Jenia] Come on, let's go to Hadera. There's tons of Ethiopians in Hadera.

Here, Oved assumes a simplistic and homogeneous view of Israeli-Ethiopian identity, by which the groundskeeper is a 'typical' Ethiopian, who lives in a town with a 'ton of Ethiopians', and is by definition a possible source for the coin. The groundskeeper, by contrast, differentiates himself, who may well have been born in Israel and has no access to the coin, from the older generation who maintain strong ties to their native land. Thus, he implicitly points to the inner diversity of Israeli-Ethiopians – an implication that seems to be entirely missed by Oved, who maintains his initial view. Accordingly, this brief encounter illustrates the potential of interactions with the 'other' for renegotiating identity categorizations and deconstructing stereotypes, as well as the difficulty of realizing this potential. The strained dialogue between the White majority and the Ethiopian minority receives further evidence as none of the (all White) contestants have any Ethiopian friends or acquaintances, and as one team eventually obtains the coin through the assistance of a White Israeli building contractor, who brokers between them and his Ethiopian employees.

The tenuous relationship of *Sof ha-Derech*'s participants with the Ethiopian minority is mirrored by the representation of Ethiopian identity on the show, which is highly ambivalent. On the one hand, the producers of *Sof ha-Derech* created a rare opportunity for positively framed Ethiopian and immigrant media visibility (cf. Avraham & First 2010). Israeli-Ethiopians are positioned as possessing a coveted artifact, and as communicating with them is necessary for the completion of the task, the value of recognition and dialogue with the 'other' is underscored. On the other hand, the representation of Ethiopian identity draws heavily on 'cultural shorthand' and homogenization. For instance, the final shots depicting the successful conclusion of the task feature masses of undifferentiated, nameless Ethiopians and are accompanied by Ethiopian-inspired popular Israeli music.

The Ethiopian coin task is structured as an ongoing learning process: early expectations are challenged and refuted, and participants and viewers alike are required to question seemingly taken-for-granted assumptions in a detective-like quest for the true solution of a puzzle (see Ellis 2008 for a discussion of similar processes in other television genres). This is an uneasy process, as assumptions regarding nationality and identity seem to be highly resistant to change. For *Sof ha-Derech*'s participants, Israel is an ancient historical homeland that may also be understood as part of the modern global world of travel and tourism, but its character as an ethnically and culturally diverse immigrant society is only belatedly acknowledged. The participants' unawareness of the multiculturalism of Israeli society is highly manifest for one team, who seem to be so extremely blind to the existence of Israeli Ethiopians, that their first attempt to confirm the coin's identity is a phone call to the Ethiopian ambassador to Israel.

Accordingly, the Ethiopian coin task may be interpreted as providing its viewers with the opportunity to reflect on the sociocultural changes and challenges faced by their society (Newcomb & Hirsch 2000/1983): it is a miniature illustration of the general move from the traditional ideal of the 'melting pot', and the singular Israeli identity it supposedly produces, to gradual recognition of the country's multiple cultures, and of the difficulty to fully embrace the social and ideological implications of this recognition (Kimmerling 2001).

The Ethiopian coin task demonstrates a recurring narrative structure of scenes and storylines on *Sof ha-Derech* – a gradual move from a simple starting point to growing complexity.[5] It also illustrates the contribution of the unique thematic resources of race gamedocs to the construction of meanings and identities. Finally, it exhibits another textual mechanism for the rich representation of identity, as it points to the intersections of different identity dimensions, including ethnicity, age, class and place of residence.

Highlighting the multidimensionality of identity

The nature of identity as inherently multidimensional and involving the intersection of different levels and types of identities (de Fina *et al.* 2006) is highlighted in the textual construction of events and tasks on *Sof ha-Derech*, as demonstrated by the following example. Participants are assigned the task of enlisting volunteers for the preparation of gift baskets for IDF (Israel Defense Forces, the Israeli army) soldiers. The task's alignment with a highly conservative and hegemonic view of Israeli identity is underscored by the use of military marching music and by the presence of two representatives of the *Association for the Wellbeing of Israel's Soldiers* – a young female soldier in uniform and an elderly male volunteer. This alignment is highly polysemic, and may be read as either celebrating national militarist themes or as ironically depicting them as archaic.

Following this introduction, the textual representation of the task makes ample use of the unique thematic resources of race gamedocs to yield a meaning-laden narrative portraying some of the complexities of contemporary Israeli identity. The narrative focuses on two teams' efforts to enlist volunteers: the all-female team of Emily and Ruthie, who decide, following a passer-by's advice, to target a complex of high-rise buildings, and Oved and Jenia, who follow the directions of another passer-by to a mostly religious neighbourhood of old small single-home houses. The editing juxtaposes scenes of both teams, emphasizing the striking differences between the two locations and the respective results they yield. Emily and Ruthie fail miserably and recruit only a handful of volunteers before abandoning the high-rises in favour of a different location. Their initial choice of the high-rises is labelled as a 'fatal mistake' (*ta'ut fatalit*) by Ruthie and as a 'waste of precious time' (*bizbuz zman yakar*) in the narration. By contrast, Oved and Jenia enlist the help of a group of energetic teenagers, open a gift basket preparation centre at the local synagogue, and quickly accomplish their task. This sharp contrast is deepened even further when Oved and Jenia attempt to expand their efforts and visit a few high-rise buildings, only to disappointedly leave them after a brief stay. As they make their way back to the old neighbourhood, Jenia sums up the experience by saying: 'we're going back to the neighbourhood and that's it… believe me, there it's much nicer' (*anachnu hozrim la-sh'chuna ve-zehu…ta'amin li, sham ze harbe yoter nechmad*).

In this sequence, the show highlights the binary opposition between the two living environments while implying their interrelations with various identities and values: high-rises correlate with a modern

lifestyle, secularism and social detachment, while the old neighbourhood correlates with a traditional lifestyle, religiosity and solidarity.
This allows the gift baskets narrative to serve as a site for exploring
key themes and dilemmas in contemporary Israeli culture, such as the
implications of growing socio-economic gaps or the erosion of the solidarity ethos (Hamo 2010).

As the example illustrates, highlighting the multidimensionality of
identity is a paradoxical mechanism. On the one hand, it constructs
identity as a complex and multifaceted phenomenon, which cannot be
simply reduced to a single attribute. On the other hand, it may serve
to establish clear correlations between different identity components,
resulting in a single, strong and highly value-laden dichotomy (for further discussion of this paradox, see below).

The multidimensionality of identity is particularly highlighted in
the representation of participants' personas and relationships. This is
especially notable when compared to Wang's (2010, fn.9) finding that
the televisual construction of the identity of a reality show contestant
avoided complications by focusing on a single dimension of identity
and disregarding others.

Sof ha-Derech depicts the developing relationships between secular
and religious teammates while often referring to their differences and
similarities on additional identity dimensions. For example, when the
contestant Tsipi (a modern liberal orthodox woman) discusses her hot
temper with her teammate Meidan (a working-class secular man), she
says 'I may be Ashkenazi, but...' (*omnam ani ashkenazia, aval...*), echoing
the common binary perception of Mizrahi Jews (of Asian and African
descent) as hot-blooded and of Ashkenazi Jews (of European descent)
as more reserved and collected. Meidan replies by indicating that he
too is Ashkenazi, a fact that Tsipi finds surprising, most likely because
Meidan's looks and demeanour contrast with the general association of
working-class and Mizrahi cultures (Kimmerling 2001). Here, Tsipi and
Meidan both acknowledge their ethnicity as a significant and relevant
identity category, which carries implications for and correlations with a
range of sociocultural and personal traits. Again, the multidimensionality of identity is paradoxical: Tsipi and Meidan go beyond a simplistic
view of each other as merely 'religious' and 'secular' and enrich their
acquaintance by drawing on other identity dimensions, but they do so
while relying on extremely stereotypical perceptions of ethnicity.

The same paradoxical mechanism is highly evident with regard
to gender. Other than religiosity, gender is the most salient identity
dimension on *Sof ha-Derech*, and it is presented as a key variable with

crucial implications for participants' relationships. For same gender teams, gender is sometimes portrayed as the basis for solidarity and affinity. For example, when the all-male team of Ohad and Yesh'el competes with all-female teams, they encourage each other by emphasizing male pride and the expected physical inferiority of women; and the all-female team of Re'ut and Yehudit often engage in sociable small talk of 'feminine' topics such as cosmetics.

For mixed gender teams, gender differences in interactional styles and values are presented as a major and crucial source of misunderstanding, disparity and conflict. Significantly, their influence is constructed as much more salient and important than that of differences in religiosity, and the depiction of teammates' relationships draws heavily on widespread traditional narrative schemes of male–female relationships, as the following two cases demonstrate.

The relationship of Ariel (a modern orthodox mid-20s single man) and Limor (a secular mid-30s married mother) is presented as a gradual and strenuous process of overcoming clashes of discursive styles and values – a narrative which echoes the popular view of male–female communication as intercultural communication (Tannen 1991), and is accordingly embedded in a conservative, essentialist view of gender. At the beginning of the race, Ariel and Limor constantly argue, to an extent that hinders their performance and questions their ability to continue the race as a team. In keeping with reality television's focus on linguistic aggressiveness (see Chapter 2), such arguments are prominently displayed in the televisual text. The troubled relationship is explicitly explained as stemming from the prototypical differences between the talkative, loud and emotional woman, Limor, and the strong, silent and detached man, Ariel, in statements like Ariel's 'it takes nerves of steel to be with a woman like you a whole day in the car' (*Tsarich azabim shel barzel kedey lihiyot im isha kamoch yom shalem ba-oto*) or 'I understand what your husband has to deal with' (*ani mevin im ma ba'alech tsarich le-hitmoded*). Importantly, while it is evident and at times acknowledged that Limor and Ariel differ significantly on many other dimensions, including age, familial status, ethnicity, place of residence and interests, none of these differences are presented as having such a crucial impact on their relationship.

Following a severe interpersonal crisis, Limor and Ariel attempt, in the words of the narration, 'to cooperate and move their relationship to a constructive path' (*le-shatef pe'ula ve-le-ha'alot et ha-yehasim beneyhen al maslul bone*). To that end, they both make an effort to communicate better and to be more attentive and supportive, echoing contemporary popular perceptions of the importance of 'good communication' in general, and among couples in particular (Cameron 2000). These perceptions are explicitly oriented to by Limor, who tells Ariel 'when you listen to me, everything works' (*kshe-ata makshiv li, ha-kol oved*). Limor and Ariel explicitly address the dangerous potential of their conflictual relationship in the following joint testimonial:

Limor: [To the camera] *Im hu yiten li yad, anachnu oshim et ze kmo gdolim.* [Turning to Ariel, smiling, in an amused tone of voice] *Ve-im lo, az lo.*
[To the camera] If he gives me a hand, we're doing it big time. [Turning to Ariel, smiling, in an amused tone of voice] And if not, then no.

Ariel: [Mimicking Limor] *Az tagid biglalech hifsadnu.*
[Mimicking Limor] Then you'll [masc.] say because of you [fem.] we lost.

Limor: [Smiling] *Biglalech hifsadnu.*
[Smiling] because of you [fem.] we lost.

Here, the teammates exhibit self- and other-awareness of personal and discursive styles and differences, and draw on humour, playful performance and other-orientation to mitigate the tensions such differences create (for further discussion of the humorous performance of identities and relationships, see below).

A different popular narrative scheme of male-female relationships – the romantic scheme of unrequited love – serves as the infrastructure for the depiction of the race's winning team, of Oved (a male right-wing religious settler) and Jenia (a secular female Russian immigrant). This general scheme is adapted to the specific context of *Sof ha-Derech* by focusing on the intersection of gender and religiosity. Many observant Jews refrain from physical contact with members of the opposite sex, a custom labelled *Shmirat negi'a*, ('preserving touch') or *isur negi'a* ('forbidding of touch'). This custom is far more salient on *Sof ha-Derech* than any other religious custom, including much more substantial religious laws. The impossibility of physical contact between a secular woman and a religious man receives focused attention on the show as a major implication of the intersection of gender and religiosity, and serves to concretize, illustrate and deepen the cultural gap between mixed-gender teammates. For example, when Oved and Jenia are (temporarily) eliminated from the race after a long arduous day, Jenia bursts into tears. Oved stands at a safe distance, his arms held together, and asks 'get some girl here to hug her' (*tavi'u le-po eize bat she-tehabek ota*). Here, the intersection of religiosity and gender is evoked as preventing the full realization of Oved's empathy, and contributes to the framing of his relationship with Jenia as unfeasible.

This framing is highly evident on *Sof ha-Derech*'s final episode. In an extreme sport challenge, one teammate is required to walk a tight rope linking two towers in the centre of Tel Aviv. Oved walks the rope, while Jenia, who is waiting on the rooftop of one of the towers, watches in awe, shrieks in fear and calls out in admiration 'what a man' (*eize gever*). The scene evokes the traditional popular image of a damsel in distress waiting for her prince charming, who overcomes physical obstacles in order to rescue her. As it is edited by inter-cutting one-shots of Oved and of Jenia, who are never shot together, the scene also underscores the unbridgeable physical gap between the teammates.

Once the challenge ends, Oved and Jenia are shown sitting in their car. While Oved, sweating and panting, starts reading the instructions for the next task, Jenia wipes the sweat off his face. To a large extent, this first momentary violation of the ban on physical contact is enabled and legitimized by the performance of prototypical gender roles of a male hero and his female caretaker. This offers further evidence of the crucial impact of gender schemes in constructing relationships.

Oved and Jenia make physical contact once more, when they hug after winning the race. A fleeting realization of their relationship, the hug is the emotional culmination of the entire series. As a representation of a secular-religious encounter, the hug is polysemic: on the one hand, it may be read as evidence of Oved's willingness to overcome differences in favour of a truly deep connection with his teammate, and by extension – of the feasibility of secular–religious dialogue based on flexibility and compromise. On the other hand, by hugging Jenia, Oved seems to succumb to mainstream secular values by which physical contact is welcome, and abandon his own religious beliefs and identity. Accordingly, the text's focus on the hug may reflect the general tendency of reality television to co-opt the 'other' and subjugate it to mainstream values and perceptions (Bottinelli 2005).

The above analysis demonstrates the hyper-realism of reality television, as several textual devices, including editing, are used in order to intensify and dramatize relationships, sexual tension and romantic feelings (Tincknell & Raghuram 2002). But this hyper-realistic romantic narrative is not exclusively fabricated by the televisual apparatus. Demonstrating the competence of reality television's participants in the spectacular performance of ordinary identities and emotions (Bonner

2003), Oved himself playfully orients to the romantic undertones of his relationship with Jenia (see below for further discussion). For instance, when he ends a phone call by saying 'I love [masc.] you [fem.]' (*ani ohev otach*), he immediately turns to the group of volunteers surrounding him and says 'that's my mom, that's OK' (*ze ima sheli, ze beseder*). After this dismissal of any possible romance is received with laughter, Oved immediately goes on to say he misses Jenia, implicitly and humorously reinstating the romantic framework he had just dismissed.

Sof ha-Derech's focus on the intersection of religiosity and gender as a significant factor in teammates' relationships reveals the cultural dominance and availability of traditional gender schemes. It also demonstrates the paradox of highlighting the multidimensionality of identity: orienting to gender enables the show to go beyond a simplistic and thin portrayal of religious identity, but this is accomplished while replicating stereotypical and conservative conceptualizations of gender. This paradox is evident in the televisual narratives of Ariel and Limor and of Oved and Jenia, as the development and deepening of their relationships do not challenge traditional gender roles and schemes, but rather authenticate and support them (see Wang 2010).

Conclusions

Three textual mechanisms for the rich representation of identity were observed on *Sof ha-Derech*: demonstrating the inner diversity of religious identity in the cast of participants, using a recurrent narrative structure of gradually growing complexity, and highlighting the multidimensionality of identity. These mechanisms operate on different levels of the televisual text and its production, from casting and locations and tasks selection in pre-production to editing and narration in post-production. While all three mechanisms may be used in a wide range of reality television genres, the realization of the latter two on *Sof ha-Derech* significantly benefits from the unique thematic resources of race gamedocs.

Close textual analysis of these mechanisms uncovers their paradoxical character: while they somewhat contribute to a rich, multifaceted representation of Jewish-Israeli identity, and particularly Jewish-Israeli religious identity, they often evoke stereotypical and conservative perceptions of other identities. Two complementing explanations may account for this ambivalence. First, attending to the specific circumstances of *Sof ha-Derech*'s production, it may be argued that the show was explicitly designed to support the visibility and interests of a particular group – religious Jewish Israelis. Accordingly, *Sof ha-Derech* may have focused on promoting a positive and non-stereotypical representation of Jewish religiosity, while using simplistic and stereotypical representations of other identity dimensions, such as ethnicity and gender, to supplement and enrich it. In a similar manner, the show's explicit focus on promoting intragroup dialogue and tolerance among Israeli Jews results in a restricted, biased representation of Israeli identity as exclusively Jewish, which disregards the ethnonational diversity of Israel, and its Palestinian 'other'. As a result, the rich representation of a single group does not promote pluralism more generally, in keeping with previous findings of the limited realization of reality television's democratic potential.

A second, broader explanation is that as popular television texts, reality shows by definition draw on the given cultural 'toolkits' accessible to their audiences (Newcomb & Hirsch 2000/1983). Identity stereotypes are significant components of these toolkits and readily available and efficient textual resources. Accordingly, the meanings and implications of televisual representations should not be evaluated based on the mere presence of stereotypical conceptualizations, but rather based on the specific ways in which these are employed and interpreted (Gilman 1985). The salience of polysemic messages on *Sof ha-Derech* supports such an approach, and highlights the need to examine reality television's reception. Particularly, assessment of the social significance of such polysemic representations of the complexity of identity requires further empirical research on how they are interpreted by different audiences, and if and how they promote public discussions of identity, nationality and multiculturalism (e.g., Klein & Wardle 2008).

Sof ha-Derech's pluralistic potential is most apparent in those key moments when stereotypes are evoked only to be challenged, reversed or played with. This is accomplished by constructing narratives as learning processes which gradually erode the stereotypical expectations of participants (and ostensibly viewers), and by underscoring participants' ability to reflexively and humorously perform and orient to different identities. The salience of self-reflection and playful performance on *Sof ha-Derech* echoes their importance not only in media discourse but also in everyday life. Sociolinguistic and ethnographic studies increasingly emphasize 'ordinary' people's intentional and sophisticated use of linguistic awareness, self-reflection, humour and creativity in their identity construction, in phenomena such as crossing or stylization (Bell 2001; Coupland 2001; Rampton 1995). In such processes, prototypically recognizable sociolinguistic variation and discursive styles serve as resources for individual performances of flexible, multiple and complex identities. Such phenomena, and their televisual representation on reality shows such as *Sof ha-Derech*, may be interpreted as the integration of the two dominant cultural tropes regarding identity discussed above: the politics of identity, with its emphasis on the importance of sociocultural variation, and the self as an ongoing individual reflexive project.

The present study examined an extreme case study of identity representation on reality television: a co-production of a civil society organization which aired during a highly unique period, and consequently placed intentional emphasis on educational and socially responsible goals, rather than only on entertainment and commercial values. Accordingly, the premise has been that the case study would realize reality television's pluralistic potential more fully than other, more routine cases. When examined against this premise, the findings carry several general implications for our understanding of the discourse system of reality television. First, the fact that the impact of stereotypes was significant even in this extreme case is evidence of their cultural endurance and strength. Second, the findings support the claim that reality television formats are not culturally neutral (Waisbord 2004): although they can be employed for the promotion of various themes and social goals, their basic features and inherent tensions place constraints on such uses.

On the other hand, *Sof ha-Derech*'s popularity demonstrates that reality television's pluralistic potential and its entertainment and commercial values do not necessarily contradict. The textual mechanisms described above contribute to the rich and complex representation of identities, while simultaneously yielding amusing, interesting and engaging televisual moments, and may be used, though less extensively, on other, more routine, reality shows. Accordingly, the present study supports the call for going beyond value-laden dichotomies, such as entertainment/education, in favour of a more careful consideration of reality television's sociocultural significance (Orbe 2008). As the present study indicates, close textual analysis of the role of surprise, expectation reversal and humour in the televisual construction of identities and meanings may contribute to such understanding.

Notes

1. An earlier Hebrew version of this article appeared in 2009 in *Media Frames: Israeli Journal of Communication*.
2. The data used here were provided courtesy of The Israel Audience Research Board (IARB) and produced by The Tele-gal Company. The original figures can be found on the IARB website at www.midrug-tv.org.il.

3. All participants were Israeli Jews. The show's own labels of 'religious' and 'secular' (*dati* and *hiloni*) are adopted here. These labels are grounded in a conservative and simplistic view of Jewish identity as a choice between two distinct categories (Goodman & Yonah 2004). The show itself sometimes works to problematize and complicate this view, as will be discussed below. Note also that the show's exclusive focus on intra-Jewish diversity reflects the widespread biased equation of Israeliness with Jewishness, and is in line with the general symbolic annihilation of non Jewish minorities, and particularly Arab-Israelis, on Israeli commercial television (Avraham & First 2010). For a few exceptions on reality television, see Elias *et al.* (2009), Neiger (2011, 2012).

4. In the case of *Sof ha-Derech* and its contemporaries, this was often done deliberately and explicitly (see below for discussion, and Elias *et al.* 2009; Neiger, 2011 for case studies). More recently, the Israeli commercial primetime has been dominated by highly popular reality shows, such as Israeli *Survivor* and *Big Brother*. While these shows are not predefined as concerned with Israeli identity and nationality, in practice they often involve and yield heated debates of such themes (e.g., Neiger 2012).

5. The same narrative structure is used for the introduction of participants: by carefully designing the revelation of biographical details, *Sof ha-Derech* gradually complicates and deepens viewers' and co-participants' acquaintance with participants' personal and sociocultural identities (see Piper 2004 for similar patterns on *Wife Swap*). In this process, the show often reverses expectations and creates surprise.

References

Aslama, Minna & Mervi Pantti (2007) Flagging Finnishness: Reproducing national identity in reality television. *Television & New Media*, 8: 49–67.

Avraham, Eli & Anat First (2010) Can a regulator change representation of minority groups and fair reflection of cultural diversity in national media programs?: Lessons from Israel. *Journal of Broadcasting & Electronic Media*, 54: 136–48.

Bell, Allan (2001) Back in style: Reworking audience design. In Penelope Eckert & John R. Rickford (eds.), *Style and Sociolinguistic Variation* (Cambridge: Cambridge University Press), pp.139–69.

Blum-Kulka, Shoshana & Michal Hamo (2011) Discourse pragmatics. In Teun van-Dijk (ed.), *Discourse Studies: A Multidisciplinary Introduction*, 2nd edn. (London: Sage), pp. 143–64.

Bonner, Frances (2003) *Ordinary Television: Analyzing Popular TV* (London: Sage).

Bottinelli, Jennifer J. (2005) 'This is reality. Right now, right here. So be real': Reality television and the Amish 'other'. *Western Folklore*, 64: 305–22.

Brenton, Sam & Reuben Cohen (2003) *Shooting People: Adventures in Reality TV* (London: Verso).

Cameron, Deborah (2000) *Good to Talk?: Living and Working in a Communication Culture* (London: Sage).

Cavender, Gray (2004) In search of community on reality TV: *America's Most Wanted* and *Survivor*. In Su Holmes & Deborah Jermyn (eds.), *Understanding Reality Television* (London: Routledge), pp. 154–72.

Coupland, Nikolas (2001) Dialect stylization in radio talk. *Language in Society*, 30: 345–75.

Dardashti, Galeet (2007) The piyut craze: Popularization of Mizrahi religious songs in the Israeli public sphere. *Journal of Synagogue Music*, 32: 142–63.

de Fina, Anna, Deborah Schiffrin & Michael Bamberg (2006) Introduction. In Anna de Fina, Deborah Schiffrin & Michael Bamberg (eds.), *Discourse and Identity* (Cambridge: Cambridge University Press), pp.1–23.

Dovey, Jon (2000) *Freakshow: First Person Media and Factual Television* (London: Pluto Press).

Elias, Nelly, Amal Jamal & Orly Soker (2009) Illusive pluralism and hegemonic identity in popular reality shows in Israel. *Television & New Media*, 10: 375–91.

Ellis, John (2008) Mundane witness. In Paul Frosh & Amit Pinchevski (eds.), *Media Witnessing: Testimony in the Age of Mass Communication* (Basingstoke and New York: Palgrave Macmillan), pp. 73–88.

Fiske, John (1987) *Television Culture* (London: Methuen).

Gilman, Sander L. (1985) *Difference and Pathology: Stereotypes of Sexuality, Race, and Madness* (Ithaca, NY: Cornell University Press).

Goodman, Yehuda & Yossi Yonah (2004) Introduction: Religion and secularity in Israel – alternative views. In Yossi Yonah & Yehuda Goodman (eds.), *Maelstrom of Identities: A Critical Look at Religion and Secularity in Israel* (Tel-Aviv: The Van Leer Institute and Hakibbutz Hameuchad), pp. 9–45. [In Hebrew]

Hamo, Michal (2010) 'The Nation's living room': Negotiating solidarity on an Israeli talk show in the 1990s. *Journal of Israeli History*, 29(2): 175–90.

Harvey, Jordan (2006) *The Amazing 'Race'*: Discovering a true American. In David S. Escoffery (ed.), *How Real is Reality TV?: Essays on Representation and Truth* (Jefferson, NC: McFarland & Co.), pp. 212–27.

Hawkins, Gay (2001) The ethics of television. *International Journal of Cultural Studies*, 4: 412–26.

Holmes, Su (2004) 'All you've got to worry about is the task, having a cup of tea, and doing a bit of sunbathing': Approaching celebrity in *Big Brother*. In Su Holmes & Deborah Jermyn (eds.), *Understanding Reality Television* (London: Routledge), pp. 111–35.

Illouz, Eva (2008) *Saving the Modern Soul: Therapy, Emotions, and the Culture of Self-help* (Berkeley, CA: University of California Press).

Kimmerling, Baruch (2001) *The Invention and Decline of Israeliness: State, Society, and the Military* (Berkeley, CA: University of California Press).

Klein, Bethany & Claire Wardle (2008) 'Theses two are speaking Welsh on Channel 4!': Welsh representations and cultural tensions on *Big Brother 7*. *Television & New Media*, 9: 514–30.

Kraszewski, Jon (2004) Country hicks and urban cliques: Mediating race, reality, and liberalism on MTV's *The Real World*. In Susan Murray & Lauri Ouellette (eds.), *Reality Television: Remaking Television Culture* (New-York: New York University Press), pp. 179–96.

Neiger, Motti (2011) 'Real love has no boundaries'?: Dating reality TV shows between global format and local-cultural conflicts. In Amir Hetsroni (ed.), *Reality Television: Merging the Global and the Local* (Hauppauge, NY: Nova Science Publishers), pp. 123–36.

Neiger, Motti (2012) Cultural oxymora: The Israeli *Idol* negotiates meanings and readings. *Television & New Media*, 13: 535–50.

Newcomb, Horace & Paul M. Hirsch (2000) Television as a cultural forum. In Horace Newcomb (ed.), *Television: The Critical View*, 6th edn. (Oxford: Oxford University Press), pp. 561–73. [Originally published in 1983]

Orbe, Mark P. (2008) Representations of race in reality TV: Watch and discuss. *Critical Studies in Media Communication*, 25: 345–52.

Palmer, Gareth (2004) 'The New You': Class and transformation in lifestyle television. In Su Holmes & Deborah Jermyn (eds.), *Understanding Reality Television* (London: Routledge), pp. 173–90.

Piper, Helen (2004) Reality TV, *Wife Swap* and the drama of banality. *Screen*, 45(4): 273–86.

Pullen, Christopher (2004) The household, the basement and *The Real World*: Gay identity in the constructed reality environment. In Su Holmes & Deborah Jermyn (eds.), *Understanding Reality Television* (London: Routledge), pp. 211–32.

Rampton, Ben (1995) *Crossing: Language and Ethnicity among Adolescents* (London: Longman).

Tannen, Deborah (1991) *You Just Don't Understand: Women and Men in Conversation* (New York: Ballantine Books).

Taylor, Lisa (2002) From ways of life to lifestyle: The 'ordinari-ization' of British gardening lifestyle television. *European Journal of Communication*, 17: 479–93.

Thornborrow, Joanna & Deborah Morris (2004) Gossip as strategy: The management of talk about others on reality TV show *Big Brother*. *Journal of Sociolinguistics*, 8: 246–61.

Tincknell, Estella & Parvati Raghuram (2002) *Big Brother*: Reconfiguring the 'active' audience of cultural studies? *European Journal of Cultural Studies*, 5: 199–215.

Tolson, Andrew (2006) *Media Talk: Spoken Discourse on TV and Radio* (Edinburgh: Edinburgh University Press).

Waisbord, Silvio (2004) McTV: Understanding the global popularity of television formats. *Television & New Media*, 5: 359–83.

Wang, Grace (2010) A shot at half-exposure: Asian Americans in reality TV shows. *Television & New Media*, 11: 404–27.

5
'There's no harm, is there, in letting your emotions out': a multimodal perspective on language, emotion and identity in *MasterChef Australia*

Monika Bednarek

Introduction

This chapter explores the Australian version of the 'reality-competition' cooking show *MasterChef*,[1] focusing on how it celebrates positive, rather than negative emotionality. In so doing, this chapter is intended as a novel contribution to linguistic research on reality television, the majority of which has tended to focus on reality TV programmes and genres that centre around conflict rather than less conflict-rich shows such as *MasterChef Australia* (henceforth also 'MCA').

I will first discuss reality television (RTV) and emotionality in general, before introducing the analytical framework used in this study, which includes linguistic and multimodal analysis. I then offer an in-depth discussion of two extracts, one from *Junior MasterChef Australia* (with child contestants), and one from the 'classic' adult version of *MasterChef Australia*. The discussion will focus on strategies used in the Australian *MasterChef* franchise for projecting an image of MCA as being 'uplifting' and 'supportive'. Finally, this chapter will also discuss the two extracts in terms of identity, introducing the notion of 'emotional identity' as a salient aspect of identity in RTV.

Emotionality and reality television

Most research on RTV recognizes the significance of emotionality: Aslama & Pantti (2006) note that RTV's main attraction is the revelation of 'true' emotions and conclude that RTV 'is one-dimensional in its focus on the emotional' (p. 177). Bonsu, Darmody & Parmentier (2010) emphasize that emotions in RTV are 'mobilized, packaged and sold back to the consumer' (p. 91) with the ultimate aim of profitability. Other researchers (e.g. Lorenzo-Dus 2008; Bonsu *et al.* 2010; DeVolld 2011) have noted that television professionals try to elicit emotional responses from participants, offering these to viewers, and even perform their own emotions – all with the aim of establishing affective relationships with audiences. Such studies have also observed that reality TV interviews are geared towards evoking emotional responses, and strategic scripting and editing also works to these purposes. As noted in the introduction to this volume, RTV 'assigns primacy to emotions in general', because of its emphasis on the personal and private.

There are various ways in which emotions can come into play in RTV programmes, for instance through self-disclosure/confession (e.g., Aslama & Pantti 2006), and there is a vast range of 'emotions considered suitable for broadcast consumption [...]: joy, elation, guilt, embarrassment, sadness, anxiety and so forth' (Lorenzo-Dus 2008, p. 84). However, linguistic analysis of emotions in RTV has mainly centred on *negative* emotions, since researchers have predominantly explored conflict-rich programmes (compare also the introduction to this volume and the five chapters on RTV and aggression). For example, negative emotions such as embarrassment or distress have been seen as 'symptoms of face-loss' (Culpeper 2005, p. 67). Lorenzo-Dus (2008) examines emotionally performed conflict talk in US courtroom shows and argues that these 'offer one of the clearest examples of the ritualized celebration of "negative" emotions in contemporary broadcasting' (p. 85). She also shows how visual and musical elements maximize the entertainment value of emotions and how a systematic analysis of these can show how emotionalism is 'choreographed' and 'packaged' for public consumption (p. 102). While drawing on these studies, this chapter differs from them in exploring a different kind of reality TV genre, the 'reality-competition' cooking show *MasterChef Australia*, and in focusing on positive emotions.

Introducing *MasterChef Australia*

MasterChef Australia (MCA) is a reality television show about a contest to find the 'best' amateur cook in Australia (produced first by Freemantle Media Australia, then by Shine Australia, for Network Ten, Australia). In MCA, contestants compete in a variety of rounds for the title of Australia's 'MasterChef' and associated prizes. The show is not identical to the original British version: As Lewis (2011) explains:

> the Australian version significantly reworked the *MasterChef* format. In Australia, the show aired on primetime commercial television six nights a week and was a glossy, more theatrical and faster-paced take on the BBC concept. [...] Along with a revamped narrative structure, the show has also been strongly indigenised at the level of cultural content and rebranded along strongly nationalistic lines. (Lewis 2011, p. 105)

The official website described the show as '[giving] budding chefs the ulti-mate once-in-a-lifetime opportunity to develop their cooking skills, to be mentored by the best, and ultimately make a change in their lives' (http://www.masterchef.com.au/about-the-show.htm, last accessed 21 July 2010).

MCA has been highly successful in Australia, especially in its second season (2010) when 5.91 million viewers watched the season finale, the official website had 48 million page views and its Facebook page had over 250,000 fans as well as more than 9500 Twitter followers (Ten Network Holdings Limited *Annual Review* 2010, p. 9). Even Australia's then governor-general (Ms Quentin Bryce) featured in the programme. In 2010, the show won an Australian TV industry ('Logie') award in the *Most Popular Reality Program* category. Spin-off series were also created, includ-ing *Celebrity MasterChef Australia* (with celebrity contestants) and *Junior MasterChef Australia* (with child contestants). The Australian version was also the basis for a U.S. version (see MasterChef [U.S. TV series] 2012).

Like other reality TV, MCA is not 'natural' but storyboarded, scripted and edited. While each reality TV programme is unique, common industry techniques for shaping stories that reality TV professional DeVolld (2011) mentions include:

- writing story/episode outlines with plot (divided into acts) and char-acter arcs, writing interview content, narration, and host copy, feed-ing conversation topics to participants;
- editing content in postproduction: compressing time, arranging frag-ments of source material, deleting hesitation phenomena, stringing together fragments, repurposing scenes, introducing fabrications such as deadlines and false subtexts.

Writers, producers and editors thus create the illusion of reality and viewers are usually kept in the dark about exactly how a specific show is produced (DeVolld 2011). Viewers of MCA hence do not know whether the contestants said or did anything else (which was cut); whether or not scenes were shot more than once; whether the dialogue was edited; whether scenes were inserted at the editing stage; and so on:

> Scenes and elements (interviews, dialogue, interactions between characters) don't always occur in the order you see in the final product. For all you know as a viewer, material that looks like a single day in someone's life [...] could be culled from a month or more of shooting and edited to create wall-to-wall drama. Scenes and fragments A, B, and C could have taken place anytime, anywhere, and as for what you're hearing people say, well that's a whole different can of worms. Statements can be handily sliced, diced, and reordered to say almost anything in a process we call 'frankenbyting' (DeVolld 2011, p. 8)

Thus, RTV can be described as choreographed, or manufactured, reality – even if less so than the new 'dramality' programmes like *Geordie Shore* in the UK and *The Shire* in Australia. As DeVolld also notes, each reality television show has some elements that occur naturally and 'at a bare minimum, the *reactions* are real' (DeVolld 2011, p. xvii, italics in original). However, because of the way in which RTV is produced, I will treat the performances analysed in my data as strategically manufactured.[2] In sum, MCA, like other RTV, produces a constructed, simulated reality (see the Introduction to this volume for further discussion).

Interestingly, the success of MCA has been linked to its apparently non-conflictual, comforting and supportive nature (Kalina 2009, in Lewis 2011), with contestants being seen as treated with respect rather than being insulted or bullied by 'nasty judges', and MCA as marking a shift 'from the ritual humiliation of contestants to something more uplifting' (Byrnes 2009). However, as is the case in many other reality TV shows, huge emphasis is nevertheless placed on contestants' emotions, which are regularly elicited. These emotions may be both positive and negative. In this chapter, I will discuss two key issues around emotionality. First, how does MCA project its image of being 'supportive' and 'uplifting'? Second, how does emotionality relate to the construction of contestants' identity? These two issues will be addressed via close analysis of two extracts, one from *Junior MasterChef Australia*, one from *MasterChef Australia*. I will introduce the extracts in more detail below, but will first discuss the analytical framework.

Analytical framework

The two extracts from the *MCA* franchise were analysed qualitatively, incorporating analysis of shot types, dialogue features, salient non-verbal behaviour and audience reactions. Such a multimodal analysis is crucial, since the finished product that audiences interact with is clearly multimodal both in terms of multimodality in the product (shot types) and in terms of multimodality in the performance (facial expression, gesture, posture etc) – see Bednarek (2010) for this distinction. For instance, the shot type determines what we can see, who we can see and how much of them we can see.

In this chapter, I will therefore analyse shots of human participants from the perspective of three of Kress and van Leeuwen's (2006) 'interactive' systems: Social Distance, Involvement and Power. According to Kress and van Leeuwen (2006, pp. 148–9), Social Distance concerns the size of the frame, with close shots realizing an intimate/personal relationship, medium shots realizing a social relationship and long shots realizing an impersonal relationship. Involvement concerns the horizontal angle, distinguishing between Involvement (frontal angle) and Detachment (oblique angle). Power concerns the vertical angle, i.e. whether or not a high angle (Viewer power), a low angle (Represented participant power) or an eye-level angle (Equality) is used. These systems were chosen for analysis because my interest lies in emotionality, which is generally considered as tied to interactive or interpersonal meaning. Additional interactive systems (Contact, Action/Knowledge orientation, Modality) are either not very revealing (as typical of conventional television drama, there is never *direct* eye contact between participants and audience in MCA), not applicable (Action/Knowledge orientation only applies to objective images) or relate to other interpersonal aspects such as issues of truth/reality (Modality). Shots without human participants (for example, a shot showing only a contestant's dish) were not analysed for interactive meanings, although they are included in the transcript.

With respect to other aspects of the analysed interactions (dialogue, salient non-verbal behaviour, etc), the analysis will focus on those resources that have been tied to emotionality in relevant research. Drawing on the long history of linguistic research into the expression of emotion, Bednarek (2008) suggests that emotion can be portrayed by labelling the emotional response directly, including via conventionalized metaphors (*I was afraid; my heart sank*); through psycho-physiological expressions and other behaviour caused by emotion (e.g. crying); by mentioning causes impacting on the speaker emotionally (*my cat died*); or through the use of emotional talk (e.g. interjections, expletives, evaluative language). Paralinguistic and non-verbal features such as facial expressions, vocal cues (e.g. lengthening, loudness, high pitch), gestures, body posture, body movement, and physiological cues have also been linked to emotion (see for example, Selting 1994; Planalp 1999, pp. 44ff). Goodwin and Goodwin (2000) and Enfield and Wierzbicka (2002) are amongst many that have pointed to the importance of considering the body when analysing emotion, talking of the '**embodied performance** of affect, through intonation, gesture, body posture and timing' (Goodwin & Goodwin 2000, p. 26, bold face in original). Thus, the analysis of emotionality will include salient linguistic, paralinguistic and bodily behaviour (see transcription conventions in the appendix to this chapter).

MCA as 'supportive' and 'uplifting'

I will now discuss two strategies that appear to be used to project an image of *MCA* as being 'uplifting' and 'supportive': first, an emphasis on positive emotionality and second, a construction of the judges as 'caring' when negative emotionality is elicited.

Emphasizing positive emotionality

One important strategy for MCA to be seen as 'supportive' and 'uplifting' seems to be an emphasis on positive, rather than negative emotionality. To demonstrate this I will draw on the multimodal analysis of an extract from season 1 (2010), episode 2 of *Junior MasterChef Australia* (Table 5.1). At the time of writing, the video could still be watched online at: http://www.masterchef.com.au/video.htm?movideo_p=41185&movideo_m=131482 (last accessed 4 November 2012). The extract comes from an episode in which 30 children compete in three heats (of ten participants each) for a spot in the top 20. The extract features the announcement of the winners of the first heat (a Seafood challenge). The announcement is explicitly introduced as such by guest judge Matt Preston: *If I call your name that means you're through to the qualifying round and please step forward.* Each child's name is then called out, followed respectively by applause and shots of the child stepping forward, his/her dish and its name, his/her parent(s)' emotional reactions and a reaction shot of the child where s/he talks about his/her response to being selected.

This extract demonstrates the exact opposite of what Lorenzo-Dus (2008, p. 85) calls the 'ritualized celebration' of negative emotionality which is so prevalent in other RTV programmes and genres. In its stead, this extract achieves a ritualized celebration of *positive* emotionality,

Table 5.1 Extract one: from season 1, episode 2 of *Junior MasterChef Australia*

	Shot	Speaker & dialogue	Salient non-verbal behaviour	Audience reaction
1	MCK, medium shot of the four judges; frontal, eye-level angle	Matt Preston [MCK]: If I call your		
2	MCK, long shot of all child contestants; frontal, eye-level angle	name? (.)		
3	MCK, close shot of girl 1; frontal, eye-level angle	that means you're through (.)		
4	MCK, close shot of boy 1; frontal, eye-level angle	to the qualifying round? (.)		
5	MCK, long shot of all child contestants; frontal, eye-level angle	and please step forward (.)		
6	MCK, medium shot of the four judges; frontal, eye-level angle	The first person through?		
7	MCK, long shot showing judges, audience, child contestants, with zoom-in; frontal, high angle	(.) to the qualifying round?		
8	MCK, close shot of girl 2, Ainsleigh; frontal, eye-level angle	(...)		
9	MCK, close shot of boy 2, flanked by two other children who are only partially visible; frontal eye-level angle	(...)		
10	MCK, close shot of girl 2;	(.)		

	Preston; frontal, eye-level angle			
12	MCK, long shot of all child contestants; frontal, eye-level angle		Alex stepping forward	Audience applause
13	MCK, close shot of Alex; frontal, eye-level angle		Alex stepping forward, smiling	Audience applause
14	U, shot of Alex's dish with caption			Audience applause
15	MCK, close shot of audience member, presumably Alex's mother; frontal, eye-level angle		Alex's mother smiling, clapping	Audience applause
16	MCK, close shot of Alex; frontal, eye-level angle	Alex [in SJ]: Wow I think that this is probably	Alex [in MCK]: smiling	Audience applause fading
17	S, close shot of Alex; frontal, eye-level angle	one of the biggest things I've ever done in my life	Alex [in SJ]: smiling	
18	MCK, long shot of judges, audience, children; frontal high angle	Matt Preston [MCK]: Sophie Jane		
19	MCK, medium shot of 5 children, including SJ; frontal eye-level angle	Girl 1 [excited voice] [MCK]: yay (.)	SJ [MCK], smiling, stepping forward Girl 1 [MCK] leaning towards SJ	Audience applause
20	MCK, close shot of SJ; frontal, eye-level angle	go Sophie	SJ [MCK] smiling	Audience applause
21	U, shot of SJ's dish with caption			Audience applause

(continued)

Table 5.1 Continued

	Shot	Speaker & dialogue	Salient non-verbal behaviour	Audience reaction
22	MCK, close shot of SJ; frontal eye-level angle	Sophie J [MCK]: Thank you	SJ [MCK] smiling	Audience applause
23	MCK, close shot of audience member, presumably SJ's mother; frontal, eye-level angle		SJ's mother [MCK] smiling, clapping	Audience applause
24	S, close shot of SJ; frontal, eye-level angle	Sophie J [in S]: I am over the moon I was like wow	SJ [in S] hand gesturing (wow)	
25	MCK, medium shot of Alex and SJ, with other children in background shown in full, zooming-in; frontal, high-angle of children, SJ turned to the side	this is actually happening this is great [laughs]	SJ [MCK] smiling	Audience applause
26	S, close shot of SJ; frontal, eye-level angle	He liked my dish that's really good	SJ [in S] smiling	
27	MCK, long shot showing judges, audience, child contestants, with zoom-in; frontal, high angle	Matt Preston [MCK]: Sophie M		Audience Applause
28	MCK, close shot of SM; frontal, eye-level angle		SM [MCK] breaking into a smile	Audience Applause
29	U, shot of SM's dish with caption			
30	MCK, close shot of SM; children are level angle	Sophie M [MCK]: ⁰⁰Thank you.⁰⁰		Audience applause

#	Visual	Speech	Behaviour	Sound
	audience members, presumably SM's parents; frontal, eye-level angle		[MCK] smiling, clapping	applause
32	S, close shot of SM; frontal, eye-level angle	Sophie M [in S]: When he called out my name I was really exc-		
33	MCK, close shot of SM's clasped hands, camera panning up to settle on SM's face/shoulders; frontal, eye-level angle	ited? it was just (.) really fun cause I knew that	SM [MCK] clasping hands, licking lips	
34	S, close shot of SM; frontal, eye-level angle	everyone was clapping for me?	SM [in S] smiling	
35	MCK, long shot of all child contestants, audience in background; frontal, eye-level angle	Matt Preston [MCK]: Only one place left (.)		
36	MCK, close shot of girl 2, Ainsleigh; frontal, eye-level angle	what I have to do is I have to look at the		
37	MCK, close shot of girl 1; frontal, eye-level angle	dish that shows the most (.)		
38	MCK, close shot of boy 1; frontal, eye-level angle	technical skill		
39	MCK, close shot of Matt Preston; frontal, eye-level angle	as well as (.) those fantastic flavours		
40	MCK, close shot of boy 3; frontal, eye-level angle	and for me that means there's only	Boy 3 [MCK] biting lips	
41	MCK, close shot of girl 3; frontal, eye-level angle	one person who can make up the		

(continued)

Table 5.1 Continued

	Shot	Speaker & dialogue	Salient non-verbal behaviour	Audience reaction
42	MCK, long shot of all child contestants; frontal eye-level angle	fourth place and that's Ainsleigh	Ainsleigh [MCK] stepping forward	Audience applause
43	MCK, close shot of audience members, presumably A's mother and brother; frontal, eye-level angle		A's mother/brother [MCK] throwing hands in the air, then brother clapping	Audience applause
44	MCK, close shot of Ainsleigh, with children/audience in background; frontal, eye-level angle		Ainsleigh [MCK] stepping forward, blushing, slight smile	Audience applause
45	U, shot of A's dish with caption			Audience applause
46	MCK, close shot of Ainsleigh; frontal, eye-level angle	Ainsleigh [S]: I am just amazed I (.)	Ainsleigh [MCK] blushing	Audience applause audible at beginning, then fades
47	S, close shot of Ainsleigh; frontal, eye-level angle	and close to tears and [exhales] ooh it's such a relief	Ainsleigh [S], closing eyes (during ooh)	
48	MCK, close shot of audience members, presumably A's mother and brother; frontal, eye-level angle		Ainsleigh's mother and brother [MCK] clapping	Audience applause

which is strategically manufactured through different conventions and modes.

First, the extract makes use of the reality TV convention of reaction shots, where participants express their emotional response to events (here: being selected to proceed to the next round). These reaction shots appear to be the result of very short interviews, most probably shot 'on the fly' (in the studio) to elicit authentic reactions – see DeVolld (2011, p. 64). Like longer confessionals and self-disclosures (see Aslama & Pantti 2006; Lorenzo-Dus 2009), they are monologic 'one-to-one moments with the camera [...] and offer the viewer a "private audience" with the emotionally expressive participant' (Bonsu *et al.* 2010, p. 101). Across the board, the contestants' dialogue from these interviews realizes highly intensified (e.g. *biggest, ever, really, everyone, such*) positive emotionality (e.g. *over the moon, great, good, fun, relief*) – see shots 16–17, 24–26, 32–33, 46–47 – with marked stress on some of the relevant linguistic features (*wow, great, really excited, ooh, such*).

Both in the reaction shots from the studio (17, 24, 26, 32, 34, 47) and in the shots focusing on the children's more immediate reaction in the MasterChef Kitchen itself (13, 16, 20, 22, 28, 44) the children's visible non-verbal behaviour reinforces this positive emotionality (smiles and laughter). The shots showing immediate reactions from selected audience members (shots 15, 23, 31, 43, 48) – presumably the parents and relatives of the respective child contestant – offer further reinforcement, with all parents shown smiling and clapping, one of them even throwing her hands in the air. Further reinforcement happens in shots 19 and 20, which show another contestant (Girl 1) leaning towards the selected participant (SJ) with clearly audible verbal dialogue, offering a positive emotional reaction from a *non-selected* participant (in an excited voice: *yay (.) go sophie*). In addition, audience applause features highly in most shots from the MasterChef Kitchen (shots 12–13, 15–16, 19–20, 22, 23, 25, 27, 28, 30–31, 42–44, 46, 48), and can even be heard in most of the shots showing the children's dishes (shots 14, 21, 45). Another aspect of the soundtrack that reinforces the positive emotionality is the accompanying music (not transcribed in Table 5.1): Shots 15–34 and shots 34–48 are all accompanied by very upbeat music (while more theatrical or dramatic suspense music can be heard in other shots).[3]

This positive emotionality is skilfully manufactured through the shot types that are used to represent participants. First, some general figures on the represented participants: most of the shots focus on the children, with 15 shots of the winners (SM: 5, SJ: 4, Ainsleigh: 3, Alex: 3), and five further shots of the winners' relatives. Ten shots show child contestants not announced as winners (including shots of Ainsleigh before her selection), and seven shots show several or all child contestants (some including winners). Judges feature in only seven shots in total, with only two shots of the judges alone, two shots of Matt Preston by himself, and three shots of the judges, audience and contestants together. Thus, the focus is clearly on the child contestants, and in particular on the winners and their relatives, contributing to the emphasis on positive emotionality.

Next, we can briefly summarize the shot types (Table 5.2). Concerning Social Distance, most shots are close shots construing an intimate/personal distance (32/44), followed by 8/44 long shots construing an impersonal distance, and 4/44 medium shots construing a social distance. Crucially, the constructed intimate/personal distance of the close shot allows the audience to partake in the participants' emotional reactions, as facial expressions/gestures are clearly visible. With respect to Involvement, the vast majority of angles are frontal (43/44), thus inviting viewers to become more involved with the participants. Significantly, such angles again let viewers partake in the participants' emotional reactions. In contrast to an oblique angle which would show participants sideways, with only parts of their face/body visible, a frontal angle allows the viewer to see how participants react emotionally by showing all or most of their face/body. Finally, looking at Power, most angles are at eye-level (40/44), with only four high angles. This means that equal relationships are constructed with viewers. Again, the audience can partake in the emotional reactions of the participants, because a shot taken from a horizontal, rather than low or high angle, also means that all or most of the participant's face/body is visible, allowing viewers to engage with his/her embodiment of emotions.

Caple (2013) notes that certain configurations of interactive meanings 'tend to cluster together, to the extent that in combination they create stronger or weaker bonds with the audience' (p. 204). Figure 5.1 shows how interactive meanings cluster together in shots from extract one. Arguably, the most frequent combination (a close shot with frontal and eye-level angle) maximizes the potential for emotionality: the frontal and eye-level angles mean that enough of the face is visible, whereas the close shot means that the audience is close enough to read

Table 5.2   Shot types in *Junior MasterChef*

Close	Medium	Long	Frontal	Oblique	Eye-level	High
32/44	4/44	8/44	43/44	1/44	40/44	4/44

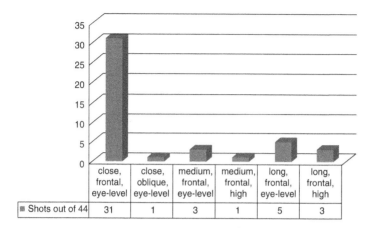

	close, frontal, eye-level	close, oblique, eye-level	medium, frontal, eye-level	medium, frontal, high	long, frontal, eye-level	long, frontal, high
▪ Shots out of 44	31	1	3	1	5	3

Figure 5.1   Clusterings of interactive meanings (*Junior MasterChef*)

the participant's facial expression. Nineteen of these 31 close/frontal/ eye-level shots, i.e. 61 per cent of all such shots, show the winners or their relatives (ten show other contestants and two show Matt Preston).

Junior MasterChef thus achieves a ritualized and strategically manufactured celebration of positive emotionality. The extract I have analysed is (by far) not the only example of such in *Junior MasterChef,* or even in this episode. For instance, during the tasting Matt Preston pronounces positive judgments for the dishes of *all* ten contestants; he also evaluates everyone positively before announcing the heat winners, and after all of the three heats the children who did not make it through are called forward, explicitly congratulated, thanked and applauded as well as presented with gifts and a plaque. Another example of the focus on positive emotionality in *Junior MasterChef* is mentioned in Byrnes (2010), who reports that 'crying scenes' were cut from an episode, with a 'heavily-censored version of events' broadcast instead. The manufacturing of positive emotionality recurs across both *Junior MasterChef Australia* and *MasterChef Australia* and is, presumably, a main reason why the show is perceived as 'uplifting'.

The caring judge

So far we have seen how MCA projects an image of being 'uplifting' through emphasizing positive emotionality. MCA also projects an image of being 'supportive' through constructing its judges as caring, rather than nasty, when negative emotions are elicited. To demonstrate this strategy I will draw on the multimodal analysis of an interaction between one of the judges (Gary Mehigan) and one of the contestants (Claire Winton Burn) in season 2, episode 80 (2010) of MCA (Table 5.3). At the time of writing, the video could still be watched online at: http://www. masterchef.com.au/video.htm?movideo_p=41088&movideo_m=37980 (last accessed 4 November 2012). The interaction comes from an episode in which the five remaining contestants compete in the 'Mystery Box Challenge', where contestants have to create dishes using certain ingredients. The selected interaction takes place immediately after Claire is invited by Gary to come forward (*The final dishes that we'd like to taste ?(.) belong to Claire*) and has presented and introduced her dishes to the judges (*The savoury dish is (.) a mousse and a Muscat sauce and the other dish is a (.) layered lemon curd semifredo with crumble*), and just before they taste them (introduced by Gary's *Shall we taste?* to which Claire replies *Yeah (.) let's do it (.) [laughing] let's get it over with*). For ease of reading, and as only two speaking participants are involved, dialogue and salient non-verbal behaviour are included in the same column in Table 5.3.

In comparison with extract one, it is negative rather than positive emotionality that appears to be emphasized here. Throughout the interaction, Claire negatively evaluates herself (e.g. her behaviour/emotional intelligence: *letting myself down; I don't have the emotional vocabulary to explain; I always fall back on it, I let my food do the talking*), her performance/her dish (e.g. *worse; a dish like that one*), the situation she finds herself in (*I can't do that today; worse; having to stand here*), and labels her emotional state of mind as negative (*how much it hurts*). This negative emotionality is strengthened through intensification/quantification (*so much, worse, everyone, how much* – note also the marked stress on *always*) and through Claire's explicit evaluations of the importance of the event for her (*it matters; this matters so much*). This intensified and negative emotionality in the dialogue is reinforced through other features such as voice quality (voice breaking, almost crying), and non-verbal behaviour (biting her lips, looking down, sniffling, wiping nose, being fidgety, shaking head). An interaction such as this, where emotionality is foregrounded in its visceral form, has been labelled as 'the money shot' (Grindstaff 2002 in Lorenzo-Dus 2008, p. 84). Such emotional intensity develops an affective connection to viewers, making them engage emotionally (Bonsu *et al.* 2010).

It is no surprise, then, that this is strategically *elicited* by the judge, Gary, as he asks a question that both presupposes and elicits negative emotionality: *What's the biggest disappointment for you today?* In fact, Gary's eliciting question is a clear example of how *dominant* participants in reality TV programmes (such as hosts, courtroom judges etc) contribute to the dramatization of *contestants'* performances (Lorenzo-Dus 2008,

Table 5.3 Extract two: from season 2, episode 8 of *MasterChef Australia*

	Shot	Speaker, dialogue and salient non-verbal behaviour
1	long shot of Gary and Claire; oblique, high angle	Gary [*gesturing*]: What's the biggest disappointment
2	close shot of Claire; frontal, eye-level angle	for you (.) <u>today</u> Claire: It's (...) it's partly about the food? (.) it's partly about letting myself down
3	long shot of Claire and Gary; oblique, high angle	[*gesturing with hand while speaking:*] but it's (.) partly also just that sense that
4	close shot of Claire; frontal eye-level angle, C turns head to left so is seen from the side for parts of shot	[*voice starting to break slightly*] you guys don't really get why I'm <u>here</u> or that it matters [*nodding*]
5	close shot of Gary; frontal, eye-level angle	Gary: And why does it matter?
6	close shot of Claire; frontal eye-level angle	Claire [*biting her lips, nodding, looking down, sniffling*]
7	long shot of Claire and Gary; oblique, high angle, R-L pan	[*fidgety with her feet, putting her hand to her nose, sniffling*]
8	close shot of Gary; frontal, eye-level angle	[*almost crying*] I clearly don't have the emotional vocabulary [*sniffle*] [Gary: *slight nodding, possibly encouraging*]
9	close shot of Claire; frontal, eye-level angle	[*hand wiping nose*] to explain to you why this matters so much and I <u>always</u> fall back on it (.) I let my food do the talking (.) I can't do that today [*simultaneous raised eyebrows and shoulders, slight head shake*]
10	close shot of Gary; frontal, eye-level angle	Gary: We've told you before you're so <u>hard</u> on yourself (.)
11	medium to long shot of four contestants; frontal, eye-level angle	look behind you there's just four guys left?
12	close shot of Gary; frontal, eye-level angle	that's a pretty <u>special</u> experience
13	close shot of Claire; frontal, eye-level angle	Claire: [*voice breaking*] It's just that the only thing worse than (.) having to stand here
14	long shot of the three judges, from over the shoulder of Claire, with Claire closer to the camera, shown from head to back; frontal, high angle	with a dish like (.) [*pointing*] that one is
15	close shot of Claire; frontal, eye-level angle	like letting everyone see how much it hurts [*raised eyebrows*]
16	close shot of Gary; frontal, eye-level angle	Gary [*gesturing*]: There's no harm is there of letting your
17	close shot of Claire; frontal, eye-level angle	emotions out [Claire: *looking down; possibly mouthing a silent 'yeah'*]
18	close shot of Gary; frontal, eye-level angle	Gary: Shall we taste? [*turning*]

p. 100). We can see how even a reality television show that is perceived as 'uplifting' strategically elicits the release of *negative* emotions. However, the emotional release is not accompanied by explicit and unmitigated face-attack or humiliation by the judge as is the case in many other reality TV genres (Lorenzo-Dus 2008, 2009; Lorenzo-Dus *et al.* this volume; Garcés-Conejos Blitvich, Lorenzo-Dus & Bou-Franch 2013).

In fact, if we consider Gary's contribution to this interaction, he shows 'active listening' (nodding) and interest (*why does it matter?*), tells Claire she is too self-critical (*We've told you before you're so hard on yourself* – note the *we* which extends this to the other judges), and contests her negative evaluations with positive ones (*just four guys left, a pretty special experience* – note the stress on *special*), thus offering support and encouragement. He also counters Claire's statement that *the only thing worse than having to stand here with a dish like that one is like, letting everyone see how much it hurts*. We can interpret Claire's statement here as referring to a certain *meta-emotion philosophy* (attitudes towards, and thoughts and feelings about, emotions; see Gottman, Fainsilber Katz & Hooven 1996, pp. 243–5) – one where showing emotions in public is disapproved of and where the 'mastering' of emotions is valued (Aslama & Pantti 2006). This is certainly the way Gary interprets her statement, replying with a contrasting meta-emotion philosophy: *There's no harm, is there, of letting your emotions out*. Gary positions himself here in a therapy role, drawing on commonly held attitudes about the positive effect of 'letting emotions out' rather than repressing them.[4] Overall, then, Gary projects a 'caring' and 'supportive' identity in this extract – in stark contrast to the 'nasty' judges of other reality TV programmes.[5] While the judge's contribution clearly elicits the negative emotionality, through his 'caring' and pseudo-therapy role and reference to popular psychology, *MasterChef* escapes the common criticism aimed at RTV of being exploitative, nasty and bullying or humiliating its contestants.

Again, a shot analysis shows more specifically how this reality is manufactured. As before, we will start by looking at some general figures on the represented participants: seven out of 18 shots feature Claire and six feature Gary, with three shots showing them together. There is one shot of the judges (an over-the-shoulder shot showing Claire from the back in the foreground) and one of the other contestants (coinciding with and illustrating Gary's *look behind you there's just four guys left*). Thus, the focus is clearly on the *interaction* between Claire and Gary, albeit with more emphasis on Claire than Gary, since there are more shots of her and the shots showing her are of longer duration.

Table 5.4 Shot types in *MasterChef Australia*

Close	Medium to long	Long	Frontal	Oblique	Eye-level	High
13	1	4	15	3	14	4

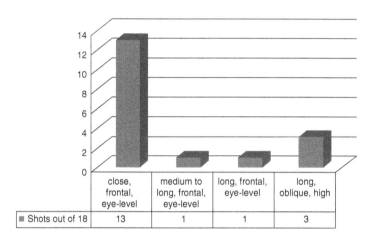

Figure 5.2 Clusterings of interactive meanings (*MasterChef Australia*)

Table 5.4 summarizes the shot types, showing that, as in extract one, a majority of shots are close (rather than medium or long) shots, use frontal, rather than oblique angles, and eye-level rather than high angles. This means that most shots construct a relationship with viewers that is intimate/personal, involved and equal.

Looking at the clustering of interactive meanings (Figure 5.2), the vast majority of shots are examples of close shots with frontal and eye-level angle (showing Gary or Claire individually), followed by long shots with oblique and high angle (showing Gary and Claire together). There is also one medium to long shot with frontal eye-level angle (showing the four other contestants behind their kitchen benches), and one long shot with frontal eye-level angle (the over-the-shoulder shot). Seven of the 13 close/frontal/eye-level shots show Claire and six show Gary, and the shots of Claire are closer than those of Gary. While the close/frontal/eye-level clustering in shots of Claire maximizes the audience's experience of her embodied performance of affect, the shots of Gary allow the audience to experience him as 'caring', for example by making his 'encouraging' nod visible to them.

This in-depth analysis of one interaction from MCA has shown how this reality TV programme strategically manufactures the construction of its judges as 'caring' rather than 'nasty'. Again, this extract is by far not the only example of such in *MasterChef* or even in this episode. For example, the judgments that are pronounced during and after the tasting (in Claire's case and in general) tend to mitigate the negative and/or focus on the positive aspects of dishes.

Commodifying the emotional self

So far I have discussed two strategies for projecting an image of the Australian *MasterChef* franchise as 'uplifting' and 'supportive': an emphasis on positive emotionality reinforced through multiple modes (*Junior MasterChef* extract) and a multimodal construction of its judges as caring pseudo-therapists, rather than nasty bullies, when negative emotions are elicited (MCA extract). The analyses have also shown how *MasterChef* makes use of similar techniques as other reality television genres to 'semiotically boost' behaviour and maximize and dramatize emotional performances (Lorenzo-Dus 2008, 2009). This is achieved through the strategic combination of different modes (e.g. language, visuals, music). Thus, positive emotions, just like negative emotions, are strategically 'mobilized' and 'packaged' for public consumption.

However, emotions do not just exist in a vacuum – they are part and parcel of a person's identity. Through strategic packaging of a range of co-occurring features that create a particular emotional style, RTV constructs particular emotional personae or identities with and for contestants. As pointed out in the introduction, identities are constructed through discursive resources. For example, in extract two above, Claire's emotional identity is quite complex – through a variety of resources she negatively evaluates the self, emphasizes the importance of the competition, and displays intensified negative emotionality. This results in the temporary construal of an upset/emotional identity attributed to a negative self and the importance of the competition. At the same time, we have seen that she is constructed as someone who is in general unwilling to 'let out' her emotions,[6] i.e., a somewhat repressed or controlled 'emotional identity'.[7]

Looking at emotional identity in extract one, the *Junior MasterChef* contestants differ considerably in how they express emotions. To just compare two of the children briefly, Alex only indicates his emotionality through use of an emotive interjection (*wow*) and evaluation of the importance of the event (*one of the biggest...*), without actually labelling his emotional response, leaving viewers to infer it. In contrast, Ainsleigh describes both her emotion (*I am just amazed; it's such a relief*) and her psycho-physiological response (*close to tears*), and also shows her emotions more viscerally (exhaling *ooh*, closing her eyes). The emotional identities of these two participants thus differ quite considerably, and arguably, audiences would also react to them differently. It would seem that the kinds of emotional identities that RTV manufactures with and for individual participants is an important way of allowing audiences to engage with reality TV participants. In fact, for RTV contestants, a successful performance of emotions can be crucial: Those contestants that are particularly good at performing emotions and thereby engaging audiences may become audience favourites and go on to success in other reality TV shows (Bonsu *et al.* 2010, p. 101).[8]

What is being packaged then, is more than just the expression of emotion, it is emotional personae or identities that are being choreographed, or manufactured, commodified and broadcast publicly. RTV is, after all, about the individuals whose journey we follow. In MCA the contestants

> are presented to the audience as 'personalities' [...] – from the glossy opening titles where contestants are individually introduced to the audience (via 'glamour' shots set to American poster Katy Perry's top 40 hit 'Hot N Cold'), to the recurrent use of pop-up text identifying them (and often their age and current occupation/work status), to the names embroidered on their uniforms (along with the *MasterChef* logo) and the focus on their particular 'food styles'. (Lewis 2011, pp. 110–11)

While it is not one of those more generally acknowledged aspects of identity such as age, profession, gender, or ethnicity evoked in Lewis's quote, emotionality appears to be an aspect of identity that is salient in the context of RTV. We need to 'invest emotionally' in reality television characters in order to care about them (DeVolld 2011, p. 10) and arguably their performed emotional identities are crucial for this purpose. RTV thus strategically creates a 'spectacle of the emotional self' (Roscoe 2011).

Concluding remarks

In this chapter I have offered an explorative investigation of emotionality in a reality television programme that has been perceived as 'feel-good' and non-confrontational, discussing two strategies that are used to project a public image of being 'uplifting' and 'caring'. My hypothesis is that *MasterChef* is so successful because it strategically focuses not just on negative but also on positive emotionality, and includes elements that differentiate it from the 'nasty judges' shows that dominate other reality-competition shows. It maximizes television's potential to let viewers experience emotions vicariously (Reiss & Wilz 2004, pp. 367–8), because it does not limit itself to negative emotionality and conflict. Perhaps this kind of programming indicates an awareness on the part of producers that positive emotions appear to correlate with viewer enjoyment (Nabi *et al.* 2006). I have further suggested that it is not simply emotions per se that are sold to audiences, but particular emotional identities, personae or selves.

I call this an *explorative* investigation because clearly much more research needs to be done. Firstly, we need a quantitative (e.g. Lorenzo-Dus 2008, 2009b; Blas-Arroyo in this volume; Lorenzo-Dus *et al.* in this volume) and comparative perspective to complement the qualitative analyses offered here. I would not want to make claims that go beyond the data analysed in this chapter. Challenges that need to be addressed in this context are the time-consuming transcription and analysis of multimodal data. A comparative investigation of differences between, for example, the UK, Australian and US versions of *MasterChef* would also be helpful to tie findings to particular national contexts. For instance, Lewis argues that:

> Australian television producers are often reluctant to overly emphasise aspirationalism or competitiveness on local versions of lifestyle and reality television (Lewis 2009: 303–3). On the surface at least, *MCA* embraces and performs a kind of non-hierarchical, democratic version of Australian 'ordinariness' through shoring up 'a cultural mythos of "mateship" and social egalitarianism (ibid.: 303)'. (Lewis 2011, p. 107)

Thus, it would be interesting to explore to what extent the celebration of positive emotionality in RTV is an Australian phenomenon or a more global phenomenon, indicative of a general shift or trend in RTV. The existence of reality TV programmes such as *Undercover Boss*, which (in the US version at least) often seems to foreground positive emotionality over negative emotionality would suggest that this is not just a localized phenomenon. However, I would expect there to be significant cultural differences with respect to *how* emotional identities are performed across different national reality TV contexts.

Secondly, we need to complement the analyses of the product with analysis both of production processes and reception. While I briefly mentioned common production techniques, these deserve more attention to allow an in-depth investigation of the strategies used in packaging emotional identities. And while some reference was made to how Claire's construal was taken up by parts of the Australian media, how emotional identities are perceived by audience members and what motivates viewers to watch a show like MCA need to be explored with the help of audience research. It must not be forgotten that, as in other broadcast settings, reality television talk involves a 'double articulation', that is an interaction between the on-screen participants on the one hand and an interaction between participants and the audience on the other (e.g. Lorenzo-Dus 2009, p. 161, citing Scannell 1991). It is therefore important to take into account the audience's perspective. One important new way in which this can now be approached by linguists is through analysis of discourses around RTV that are expressed by audience members on new media outlets, such as blogs, websites, Facebook and Twitter.

Thirdly, emotional identity in itself needs further exploration, if it is indeed a salient type of identity in RTV. We could start by charting the different ways in which linguistic, paralinguistic and non-linguistic resources can cluster as particular emotional styles and create particular emotional personae or identities (Bednarek 2011). In the context of RTV, it is obvious that resources such as frame size and camera angles also need to be incorporated into such an investigation. We also need to explore the interaction of emotionality with other identity aspects such as gender, ethnicity and education. Overall, the majority of existing research into these and related aspects in the context of RTV is still located in disciplines outside linguistics. It is now the task of linguists, in particular discourse analysts, to explore systematically the part that language plays in RTV and other products of popular culture. Only then will we gain a fuller understanding of the choreographed reality that is broadcast nightly to our global screens.

Appendix: Transcription conventions

word	marked stress
(.)	short but noticeable pause
(...)	longer pause
°°word°°	quiet speech
?	rising intonation
MCK	in MasterChef kitchen

(continued)

Continued

S	in studio (including audio only or audio/video from studio interviews)
close shot	a shot showing the subject's head, head and shoulders, head and uppermost part of the body [anything less than to the waist]
medium shot	a shot showing the subject from head to waist or knees [anything less than the full subject]
long shot	a shot showing the subject in full [and possibly more of the background]
frontal angle	the subject is facing the camera or is only slightly turned side-ways, with both of the subject's eyes typically visible, with vanishing points within the vertical boundary (see Kress & van Leeuwen 2006, p. 135)
oblique angle	the subject is shown side-on to the camera
high angle	the camera is showing the subject from above
low angle	the camera is showing the subject from below
eye-level angle	the camera is at equal level to the subject

Note that the distinction between the different angles (e.g. frontal vs. oblique) is gradient, rather than clear-cut, and that there are differences *within* shot/angle types (for example, a frontal angle can mean the camera is positioned directly in front of the subject or slightly to one side, a close-up can be 'extreme', i.e. very close to the face or further away), etc.

Acknowledgements

The research in this article was supported by a research grant from the School of Letters, Art and Media at the University of Sydney, for which I am very grateful. I would also like to thank Helen Caple, Nuria Lorenzo-Dus, Pilar Blitvich, and two anonymous reviewers for comments on an earlier version of this chapter, and Sumin Zhao for assistance with parts of the transcription.

Notes

1. See DeVolld (2011) for discussion of the genre of 'reality-competition', from the industry perspective.
2. I was unable to gain insights from the producers into how exactly the performances in the two analysed extracts were produced. DeVolld (2011) notes that there is an 'intentional obscurity of the genre's process from the public', and that 'most of us in Reality TV still try our best to keep the answer to the "Is-it-or-isn't-it-real?" question close to the vest' (p. xvii). In the case of *MasterChef*, the contestants themselves or the parents of child contestants sign confidentiality agreements (Devic 2011). Byrnes (2010) mentions a controversial deletion of scenes from a *Junior MasterChef* episode, with the Australian network for the show stating that: 'only those moments that enhance the storyline or affect the outcome of a challenge, are able to be included in the final edit.' Devic (2011) reports further examples of staging. We can thus safely assume that MCA does choreograph or manufacture reality in the sense in which I have discussed this above for RTV in general.

3. This extract has an emotional arc of suspense (created for example via pauses, dramatic suspense music, etc) and positive emotionality. Less positive emotions such as embarrassment (blushing) and nervousness (clasped hands, lip biting) are also present, but not to the same extent.

4. Gary's statement may also be an attempt to mitigate Claire's implied criticism of MCA as a reality TV programme where contestants' emotions are publicly broadcast to millions of strangers. Gary's attempt to phrase this in terms of popular psychology, then, is an equally implicit defence of the show which ignores the difference between 'letting your emotions out' in private versus doing so in the context of a reality TV show. This interaction is also a good example of the celebration of therapeutic language (Aslama & Pantti 2006, p. 167).

5. It is important to mention that not all judges in other reality TV programmes are necessarily nasty; often there may be a contrast between judges within a programme. For instance, in shows like *American Idol* or *America's Got Talent*, some judges, such as Paula Abdul or Sharon Osbourne, come across as caring. My thanks go to one of the editors for pointing this out.

6. Some in the media have used another contestant's statements about Claire in order to construe her as being too controlled, thereby taking up Gary's evaluation of Claire as someone unwilling to 'let out' her emotions:

> MasterChef's Claire likes control: Courtney
> 12:30 AEST Wed Jul 21 2010
>
> By Jay Savage, ninemsn
>
> She may have survived last night's challenge, but *MasterChef* hopeful Claire Winton Burn will never be the best as long as she takes herself so seriously, the woman she eliminated says.
>   Courtney Roulston was last night booted from the show in a mystery box showdown after a tearful Winton Burn pleaded for the judges to keep her in the competition.
>   'Claire just has that thing where she wants to be perfect all the time,' Roulston said.
>   'She takes things very seriously. The best people will be prepared to make mistakes.'
> (http://news.ninemsn.com.au/entertainment/7932754/masterchefs-claire-likes-control-courtney, last accessed 26 July 2010).

7. In line with the 'emotionale Wende' (Schwarz-Friesel 2007, p. 15) – the affective turn – in the social and cognitive sciences, researchers recently seem to have focused on subjective or expressive aspects of identity. Without going into detail, subjective/expressive features have been linked to the analysis of persona, identity and style in a number of different approaches within linguistics (e.g. Hyland 1999, 2009; Tracy 2002; Englebretson 2007; Martin 2008; Jaffe 2009). While these and other researchers in this area vary with respect to how they define and conceptualize emotion, affect and identity, their ideas do seem to support the view that emotionality is an aspect of identity and that there is such a thing as 'emotional identity'.

8. Hearn (2006) argues that the management of public persona that occurs on the part of reality TV participants is an example of both self-commodification

and self-spectacularization, and that what is produced is 'a branded "self"' (Hearn 2006, p. 133). This means that the particular public selves that are constructed can accrue commercial or market value. Along the same lines, a particular *emotional* self, persona or identity can also accrue market value.

References

Aslama, Minna & Mervi Pantti (2006) Talking alone: Reality TV, emotions and authenticity. *European Journal of Cultural Studies*, 9(2): 167–84.

Bednarek, Monika (2008) *Emotion Talk across Corpora* (Basingstoke and New York: Palgrave Macmillan).

Bednarek, Monika (2010) *The Language of Fictional Television: Drama and Identity* (London/New York: Continuum).

Bednarek, Monika (2011) Expressivity and televisual characterisation. *Language and Literature*, 20(1): 3–21.

Blas-Arroyo, José Luis (2010) La descortesía en contextos de telerrealidad mediática. Análisis de un corpus español. In Francesca Oreletti & Laura Mariottini (eds.), *(Des)cortesía en español. Espacios teóricos y metodológicos para su estudio* (Roma-Estocolmo: Università degli Studi Roma Tre-EDICE), pp. 183–207.

Bonsu, Samuel K., Aron Darmody & Marie-Agnes Parmentier (2010) Arrested emotions in reality television. *Consumption Markets & Culture*, 13(1): 91–107.

Byrnes, Holly (2009) Channel Ten show MasterChef secret recipe. *The Daily Telegraph* online, 11 July 2009 (12.00 am). Downloaded from: http://www.dailytelegraph.com.au/news/channel-ten-show-masterchef-secret-recipe/story-e6freuy9-1225748411764 (accessed 27 July 2011).

Byrnes, Holly (2010) Crying scenes cut from Junior MasterChef. *The Daily Telegraph*, 2 November 2010 (09:00 pm). Downloaded from: http:www.perthnow.com.au/entertainment/crying-scenes-cut-from-junior-masterchef/story-e6frg30c-1225947059375 (accessed 23 October 2012).

Caple, Helen (2013) *Photojournalism. A Social Semiotic Approach* (Basingstoke and New York: Palgrave Macmillan).

Culpeper, Jonathan (2005) Impoliteness and entertainment in the television quiz show: *The Weakest Link*. *Journal of Politeness Research*, 1: 35–72.

Devic, Aleks (2011) Father claims Junior MasterChef contestants are groomed before cooking. *Herald Sun* online, 19 October 2011 (12:00 am). Downloaded from: http://www.heraldsun.com.au/entertainment/tv-radio/junior-chefs-losing-flavour-over-professional-cooking-acting-lessons/story-e6frf9ho-1226170105799 (accessed 23 October 2012).

DeVolld, Troy (2011) *Reality TV: An Insider's Guide to TV's Hottest Market* (Studio City, CA: Michael Wiese Productions).

Enfield, Nick J. & Anna Wierzbicka (eds.) (2002) Special issue of *Pragmatics and Cognition* 10 (1/2) on *The Body in Description of Emotion*.

Englebretson, Robert (ed.) (2007) *Stancetaking in Discourse* (Amsterdam/Philadelphia: John Benjamins).

Garcés-Conejos Blitvich, Pilar, Nuria Lorenzo-Dus & Patricia Bou-Franch (2013) Identity and impoliteness: The expert in the talent show *Idol*. *Journal of Politeness Research*, 9(1): 97–120.

Goodwin, Marjorie H. & Charles Goodwin (2000) Emotion within situated activity. Available to download at <http://www.sscnet.ucla.edu/clic/cgoodwin/00emot_act.pdf>, last accessed 19/5/09. (Originally published as pp. 33–54 in *Communication: An Arena for Development*, edited by Nancy Budwig, Ina C. Uzgris & James V. Wertsch (Stamford, CT: Ablex).

Gottman, John M., Lynn Fainsilber Katz & Carole Hooven (1996) Parental meta-emotion philosophy and the emotional life of families: Theoretical models and preliminary data. *Journal of Family Psychology*, 10(3): 243–68.

Hearn, Alison (2006) 'John, a 20-year-old Boston native with a great sense of humour': On the spectacularization of the 'self' and the incorporation of identity in the age of reality television. *International Journal of Media and Cultural Politics*, 2(2): 131–47.

Hyland, Ken (1999) Disciplinary discourses: Writer stance in research articles. In Chris Candlin & Ken Hyland (eds.), *Writing: Texts, Processes, and Practices*. (London: Longman), pp. 99–121.

Hyland, Ken (2009) Constraint vs creativity: Identity and disciplinarity in academic writing. In Mario Gotti (ed.), *Commonality and Individuality in Academic Discourse* (Bern: Peter Lang), pp. 25–51.

Jaffe, Alexandra M. (ed.) (2009) *Stance: Sociolingustic Perspectives* (Oxford: Oxford University Press).

Kress, Gunther & Theo van Leeuwen (2006) *Reading Images: The Grammar of Visual Design* (London/New York: Routledge).

Lewis, Tania (2011) 'You've put yourselves on a plate': The labours of selfhood on *MasterChef Australia*. In Helen Wood & Beverly Skeggs (eds.), *Reality Television and Class* (London: BFI/Palgrave Macmillan), pp. 104–16.

Lorenzo-Dus, Nuria (2008) Real disorder in the court: An investigation of conflict talk in US television courtroom shows. *Media, Culture & Society*, 30: 81–108.

Lorenzo-Dus, Nuria (2009) 'You're barking mad, I'm out': Impoliteness and broadcast talk. *Journal of Politeness Research*, 5: 159–87.

Martin, James R. (2008) Innocence: Realization, instantiation and individuation in a Botswanan town. In Ahmar Mahboob & Naomi Knight (eds.), *Questioning Linguistics* (Newcastle: Cambridge Scholars Publishing), pp. 32–76.

MasterChef (U.S. TV series). *Wikipedia*, 2012. Downloaded from: http://en.wikipedia.org/wiki/MasterChef_%28U.S._TV_series%29 (accessed 4 November 2012).

Nabi, Robin, Carmen R. Stitt, Jeff Halford & Keli L. Finnerty (2006) Emotional and cognitive predictors of the enjoyment of reality-based and fictional television programming: An elaboration of the uses and gratifications perspective. *Media Psychology*, 8: 421–47.

Planalp, Sally (1999) *Communicating Emotion: Social, Moral and Cultural Processes* (Cambridge: Cambridge University Press).

Reiss, Steven & James Wiltz (2004) Why people watch reality TV. *Media Psychology*, 6: 363–78.

Roscoe, Jane (2011) Reality TV: Manufacturing emotions, or evoking authenticity. Paper presented at the *Manufacturing Emotions* collaboratory, University of Sydney (9 September).

Scannell, Paddy (ed.) (1991) *Broadcast Talk* (London: Sage).

Schwarz-Friesel, Monika (2007) *Sprache und Emotion* (Tuebingen/Basel: A. Francke Verlag).

Selting, Margaret (1994) Emphatic speech style – with special focus on the prosodic signalling of heightened emotive involvement in conversation. *Journal of Pragmatics*, 22: 375–408).

Ten Network holdings Limited (2010) *Annual Review.* Available from http://tencorporate.com.au/annualreport/2010/pdf/TNHL_Annual_Review_2010.pdf (last accessed 30 November 2011).

Tracy, Karen (2002) *Everyday Talk: Building and Reflecting Identities* (New York/London: The Guilford Press).

6
The aesthetics of poverty and crime in Argentinean reality television

María Laura Pardo

Introduction[1]

This chapter seeks to contribute fresh insights into the discursive representation of the extremely poor in reality TV by offering a case study of the Argentinean docudrama *Policías en acción* (*Police in action* – PIA). Extreme poverty is defined in this work by reference to a basic food basket (BFB), the cost of which is determined by the market prices of its items and used to establish the income level that marks the extreme poverty line (Ministerio de Economía de la Provincia de Buenos Aires 2002, pp. 12). The focus on the extremely poor is warranted, both by the postmodern 'spectacularization' of poverty in the media (Debord 1994), and by the importance of extreme poverty as a social problem in the Argentine context (Idnovo Carlier 2001; Ortiz & Pardo 2006, 2008; Pardo 2008). PIA regularly includes a number of destitute individuals, some with mental conditions, and portrays them as criminals or drug-users who often engage in violent behaviour towards their family and neighbours. The interest of the show is twofold. On the one hand, it is currently one of the most watched TV programmes in Argentina.[2] On the other, it displays certain features of postmodernity, such as a particular conception of heroicity (Forster 2002), the fragmentation of image and discourse, and the use of life stories and 'the morbid' as unifying narrative elements (Glusberg 1997).

Discourse fragmentation manifests itself in the written presentation on the television screen of the speech of PIA's characters, which marks the transition from orality to literacy and is limited by the number of characters that can be shown on the screen. As PIA has been broadcast in other Latin American countries (Brazil and Colombia) and similar programmes are shown in Europe and the United States, the chapter might be of interest to both Spanish and English speakers. Discourse fragmentation is indeed a worldwide phenomenon within postmodernity, a philosophy that characterizes the currently dominant neoliberal paradigm. We have adopted Critical Discourse Analysis (Wodak & Meyer 2003; Pardo Abril 2008; García da Silva & Pardo Abril 2010; Resende de Melo 2009) as a theoretical framework, drawing also on Information Hierarchy Theory (IHT) (Pardo 1992, 1996, 2011) and Synchronic–Diachronic Text Analysis (SDTA) (Pardo 2010, 2011).

The chapter starts with a brief review of relevant features of postmodernity and television in the Argentine context. It then provides a detailed explanation of the data, focusing on the docudrama under analysis, and the theoretical framework of this study. A fragment of the programme illustrating the main features of the corpus is then examined. The chapter concludes with some data-driven reflections on PIA's construction of the identity of the extremely poor.

Postmodernity and television – the Argentine context

Debord influentially defines 'spectacle' as not only the outcome but also the goal of the dominant mode of production in postmodernity, considering it the 'very heart of society's real unreality', rather than something that has been 'added to the real world – not a decorative element, so to speak' (Debord 1994 [1967]: 13).[3] For him,

> In all its specific manifestations – news or propaganda, advertising or the actual consumption of entertainment – the spectacle epitomizes the prevailing model of social life. It is the omnipresent celebration of a choice already made in the sphere of production, and the consummate result of that choice. In form as in content the spectacle serves as total justification for the conditions and aims of the existing system. It further ensures the permanent presence of that justification, for it governs almost all the time spent outside the production process itself. (Debord 1994[1967], p. 13).

The 'spectacularization' of private and everyday life in the arts and the mass media has flourished with the rise of what is widely referred to as postmodernity. As Glusberg (1997) has pointed out, postmodernism has been philosophically inspired by Nietzche and Heidegger.[4] It may be conceived of as a current of thought that reacts against modernity and its defining characteristics, and that coincides historically with the late capitalism stage, which Argentina has been going through since

1945 (Ortiz & Pardo 2006). Whereas modernity was marked by a reduction of the self to novelty, postmodernity is characterized, though not exclusively, by the commodification of the self, a feature that reflects the very essence of capitalism (Chiapello & Fairclough 2002, pp. 187–8).

In Argentina, the 1990s marked a period of postmodern splendour, known as the 'pizza and champagne' years (Borón 2000; Klachko 2000; Cristobo 2009). During that decade, the worldwide dominance of financial capital resulted in so-called neoliberal policies being 'applied in depth'. Under the cover of 'globalization', these policies imposed on Latin American citizens a 'single way of thinking' that stresses the inevitability of supposedly efficiency-driven, free market-based economic transformations, whose effects, though at first benefiting only part of the community, would soon trickle down to the rest (Klachko 2000, p. 1).

Postmodernity has promoted the aestheticization of a range of issues, redefining in the process the concepts of the public sphere and of art (Pachenkov & Voronkova 2010).[5] Key amongst these issues in Argentina are torture, the Holocaust, murders committed by the military dictatorship and, importantly for this study, poverty (García Fajardo 2000). This aestheticization of tragic, violent or horrific events provides a clear example of the 'commercialization of human rights' (Ford 2006). Under the heading 'tragedy as commodity', Ford writes about the transformation of 'human suffering indicators' (rape, homicide, accidents, the gap between rich and poor, unemployment and youth crime) into raw material for the culture and advertising industry. The emergence of suffering and the tragic as hard facts, beyond pity, charity, sensationalism or talk of unsatisfied basic needs, is characteristic of our time (Ford 2006).

In a similar vein, the aestheticization of poverty goes beyond the exhibition of pictures or videos showing children and adults starving. It crucially involves the creation of a system of beliefs which often generates discriminatory stereotypes about the extremely poor (Pardo 2008). The aestheticization of poverty in postmodernity is thus not concerned with honesty, moral values or the idea of progress, as may have been the case in modern times. Instead, it is concerned with showing the dark, tragic side of the poor, who are often portrayed as dangerous creatures, the other, or the enemy, thus reinforcing the gap between them and the viewers, whose fear of the strange and different is allayed by the reassuring assertion of this separation (Bauman 2000).

Multiple works have explored the media and their transition from modernity to postmodernity (e.g. McLuhan & McLuhan 1988; Van Dijk 1988a, 1988b, 1991; Barrett 1992; McLuhan 1994; Sreberny-Mohammadi *et al.* 1997) – so much so that today's media can hardly be approached without examining their 'postmodern characteristics'.[6] Much has been written, too, about television, especially newscasts, in postmodern times (e.g. Santander Molina 2002, 2003; Mendo & Mena Rodriguez 2000). Emerging television genres have also been discussed in the context of postmodernity, though not always focusing on philosophical and ideological aspects (Castro 2002; Carlón 2005; Sinclair 2000; Hoynes 1994; Ulanovsky, Itkin & Sirvin 1999; González Requena 1987; Santander Molina 2003; Lorenzo-Dus 2009; Garcés-Conejos Blitvich 2009, 2010). Scholarship on poverty and the media, however, is comparatively scarce (Fuenzalida 1991; Pardo 2008, Pardo Abril 2011; Vasilachis 2003). Little has been published in Latin America about TV programmes that, combining reality and fiction, re-present the plight of certain poor and marginal groups in ways that clearly link them to crime, and hence construct their identities as 'criminals'.

As a mass medium, television is nowadays 'glocalized'. Although adhering to a homogeneous neocapitalist Western ideology, in order to position itself in different countries, cities or places, television has to adapt to their peculiarities and respect certain idiosyncratic cultural values. The resulting tension, common to all homogenizing movements, tends to awaken resistance systems both at the regional and national levels. In Argentina, this process manifests itself in the glocalization of American sitcoms such as *Married with Children* (*Casados con Hijos*) and *Bewitched* (*Hechizada*), and reality shows, such as *The Biggest Loser* (*Cuestión de Peso*), *Dancing with The Stars* (*Bailando por un Sueño*) and *Police in Action* (*Policías en Acción*). The last named, analysed in this chapter, has been also produced in Brazil and Colombia, and constitutes a textbook case of glocalization of the most emblematic postmodern of media discourses: the reality show (Cocimano 2003). Whereas, as a docudrama, it contains discursive representations of the police, the outskirts of Buenos Aires, the poor, crime and families in that city, it is produced, edited and presented by a transnational company according to its own standards and procedures. As a number of other reality television genres, the docudrama – including PIA – is typically postmodern in its hybridity, which packages reality and fiction in ways that are sometimes hard to distinguish.[7]

Methodology

Data and procedure

The reference corpus for this study comprises 17 video-recordings of 2006–2007 PIA episodes provided by the *Endemol* media group. From this corpus, and due to space constraints, a five-minute fragment has been selected for SDTA in this chapter, which comes from the only 2007 PIA episode available (and downloadable) online.[8]

Production team members took part in lively discussions of the reference corpus with my Media Language Analysis students at the University of Buenos Aires, Philosophy and Arts School. The interaction enabled us to achieve a deeper and more detailed understanding of the discursive practice within which the show takes place, an ethnographically revealing experience that shed light on various points of the communicative situations depicted in the videos.

As noted earlier, PIA can be defined as a docudrama – a reality TV genre (although it can also be produced as film and radio) that applies dramatic techniques to real facts proper to the documentary genre. It may be, as in this case, partially fictionalized, i.e., highly edited or featuring actors, and tragic in nature, depicting murders, rapes, accidents, paranormal phenomena, etc. (Idnovo Carlier 2001). PIA thus presents a fictionalized documentary reality (Lorenzo-Dus 2009). It lays emphasis on the social situation of poor families who are seemingly involved with crime, drugs, alcohol or domestic violence. Individuals allegedly involved in crimes can ask for their face not to be shown on camera, but they frequently choose not to. The programme has no on-screen host. Camera in hand, a reporter drives in Buenos Aires police patrol cars about the Greater Buenos Aires districts in search of criminal activity. The audience is thus exposed to police/ham radio jargon: 'Natalia, Natalia' (individual of unknown identity),[9] 'affirmative' (i.e. yes), QTC (message for third parties), QTH (position or location), QSL (understood), QAP (listening, keep up your position), and so forth. PIA portrays a police force that lacks technological or scientific equipment, but generally behaves in a controlled and sympathetic way towards citizens. Also, PIA stories have to be cleared for broadcasting by the Buenos Aires Ministry of Security and the Police Department. This all strongly suggests that police operations are carefully selected by the producers in order to boost the public image of the institution.[10] Narrative sequences are bound together through a careful editing process that shares some of the features of superhero comics, particularly the pop-art presentation.

Despite relying on dramatic stories and plotlines in which citizens living in poverty and believed to transgress the law clash with police forces, the main communicative purpose of PIA is to entertain its audience. To cater to an assumed preference for the morbid, it often selects the life stories of underprivileged alcoholics, transvestites and prostitutes, as well as topics such as the way in which the poor spend their holidays. Unlike 'infotainment' reality TV (Ford 1999), it does not combine entertainment with information, but rather with recreation or representation (Arzeno & Contursi 2006). In this respect, the producer's editorial line is evident in a series of strategies aimed at depicting those 'morbid' individuals whose life stories are narrated as not only poor but also criminal. These strategies include the use of section headings that explicitly characterize them as criminals,[11] as well as of torches in chase scenes for increased dramatic realism.

Speech transcription also serves this purpose. In closed captions, movie and documentary subtitles, speech is transcribed in black or white depending on the screen background and regardless of the speaker. TV subtitles are usually in white on Argentinean television. In PIA, strikingly enough, white is used for social actors except the extremely poor, whose speech is transcribed in yellow captions. A non-marked choice of colour (white) is thus used for those who are on the 'right side' of the law, and a marked colour choice (yellow) is used for the extremely poor. This clearly begs the question about the criteria for such a distinction between groups of people.[12]

Framework

Within a broad CDA framework, our analysis applies Synchronic–Diachronic Text Analysis (SDTA) (Pardo 2011), a specifically linguistic method that accounts for both the language categories required by any basic linguistic theory (Glaser & Strauss 1967) and the linguistic properties through which such categories materialize in a given text (textual practice). Without ruling out the grammatical component of language, SDTA takes, on the whole, a semantic approach, distinguishing between mainly grammatical and mainly semantic categories. Grammatical categories, unlike their semantic counterparts, do not vary from text to text, making it possible to provide a succinct description:

- Speaker/Protagonist (S/P): Any pronominal person or nominal referent that supports the speaker's arguments, regardless of its position as grammatical or logical subject of the utterance.
- Verb 1 (V1): Speaker/protagonist's actions or states.
- Actor/s: Any pronominal person or nominal referent opposing the speaker/protagonist's arguments.
- Verb 2 (V2): Actors' actions or states.
- Time and place (TP): The temporal and spatial orientation necessarily present in every text.
- Pragmatic operator (PO): A category that performs different functions, such as pointing to the correct interpretation of certain parts

of the utterance or to the way in which different utterances should be linked together, or appealing to the listeners/readers and seeking their complicity.

* Negation (N): A non-mandatory 'floating category' that may affect the verb or other words or sectors of the utterance.

Semantic categories, although presupposing grammatical structure, are closely related to the lexicon and, therefore, may vary within the text or even within a given utterance. They are text-specific and allow inductive (text-based) inquiry into speaker-constructed representations of social categories (Pardo 2011). The categories indentified and discussed later in this chapter, therefore, have not been deduced or determined *a priori*, but induced from the text analysed (Pardo 2011). The criterion used to identify semantic categories is drawn from the lexical domain: series of repetitions provide the text with cohesion and therefore entail grammatical repetition as well. Examples of semantic categories in PIA are 'street', 'prison', 'family of origin' and 'street family'.

Both grammatical and semantic/discursive categories serve to construct discursive representations and must be jointly considered. SDTA owes its name to the fact that it enables the analysis of specific linguistic resources within utterances (synchronic analysis) and of individual grammatical and semantic/discursive categories across utterances (diachronic analysis). In addition to semantic categories, SDTA is informed by Information Hierarchy Theory, as I next describe.

Information Hierarchy Theory is a linguistic approach (Pardo 1992, 1996, 2011) inspired by the Functional Sentence Perspective (Weil 1844; Mathesius 1939; Firbas 1992; Pardo 1996, 2011). Information hierarchy is a language principle[13] according to which the information that language users provide follows an order of importance that depends both on the word order of the language spoken and on the speaker's intention to highlight certain features. It is also linked to cognitive processes in which old information is replaced by new information through the repetition of forms and meanings. In Romance languages like Spanish, as Functional Sentence Perspective scholars (Weil 1844; Mathesius 1939; Firbas 1964) have shown, the most significant information is placed at the end of the utterance.[14] Within this part of the utterance, called rheme, a focus can be identified, usually preceded by some suprasegmental element, such as a pause. The focus constitutes the point of orientation of the utterance – its most dynamic communicative space (Firbas 1964, 1992). In Romance languages, speakers use mandatory long pauses intentionally to mark final, focal parts. It goes without saying that, in order to preserve the meaning of the utterance, speech transcriptions should maintain these utterance parts. In the utterance in Example 1 (a) (taken from PIA), for instance, the theme is 'Those who live in this shanty town', and the rheme (i.e., the remaining part of the utterance), contains the focus: 'the government to help them':

Example 1 (a)

rheme

Those who live in this shanty town are tired of waiting for <u>the government to help them</u>./

FOCUS

rheme

Los que viven en la villa están cansados de esperar que <u>el gobierno los ayude</u>/.

FOCUS

In Example 1 (a), the focus is the same in the spoken and written (i.e. transcribed) version. Visually, however, this transcription is shown on three consecutive screen frames in PIA, as can be seen in Example 1 (b).

Example 1 (b)

Frame 1:   Those who live **in this shanty town**/
           *Los que viven **en la villa**/*
Frame 2:   are tired of **waiting**/
           *están cansados de **esperar**/*
Frame 3:   for the government **to help them**/
           *que el gobierno **los ayude** /*

The pauses (/) introduced in the passage create three different foci (in bold in 1b), instead of the single focus that is usually found in a rheme. These visual pauses and the resulting three new spaces (visual frames) give rise to three different meaning units, rather than just one, to which the viewers' attention is drawn. Through this visual/textual fragmentation, therefore, a new orality is generated within this fictional docudrama. Thus, visual/design needs determine the way in which utterances are presented, which ultimately adds intended meaning, stressing certain negative traits that, as the analysis will show, are regularly attributed to the poor.

The fragmentation of discourse in PIA – linking poverty and crime

The fragment transcribed in Example 2 (a and b) includes an introductory segment that provides statistical information about the crimes perpetrated in the Greater Buenos Aires area. This is followed by another segment, 'The flight', which tells the story of a poor man who runs away after having, according to the police and reporter, stolen a motorcycle. He is pursued, taken to the police station and finally released, as it is found out that the motorbike was actually his and he had, therefore, committed no crime. The underlying dual logic thus combines: (a) the expectation that the man is a criminal, created by the way in which the narrative plot is constructed, starting with his escape from jail; (b) the eventual innocence of the man, which might be construed as a trick intended to show viewers that, in linking poverty and crime, they might be prejudiced too. Another possible interpretation, which the analysis of the reference corpus renders more likely (Pardo 2008, 2012; Pardo & Buscaglia 2011) is that we all (even the innocent) may appear suspects and should be treated as such.

Example 2 (a)[15]

[Introductory segment]
Caption:
U1 Greater Buenos Aires area of Buenos Aires province[16] (bottom right)
[Blue box. Each line within this box contains an utterance and takes up a frame.]
U2 A crime is reported every two minutes//
U3 Ninety armed robberies a day are committed//
U4 sixty-four per cent of the crimes perpetrated in Argentina <u>are committed in the Greater Buenos Aires area</u>//
U5 A hundred and six people are arrested every day//
U6 Thirty-eight per cent of armed robberies end up in murder//
U7 Three out of every 10 people released [from prison or police custody] commit a new crime within the next two years//
U8 Eighty per cent of thefts and homicides are committed by minors between 12 and 16 years old//
U9 Only 45% of the violent crimes and 63% of the murders are solved.

This introductory segment of the show, which provides the framework for the text that follows, contains detailed statistics of the number of crimes committed in the Buenos Aires conurbation. This can only make sense as an attempt to prepare viewers to expect a similar situation on their screens, thus inspiring fear. Any information from this point in the episode is thus framed by this editorial line of 'fear'.

After this presentation the narrative begins (Example 2b): an alleged minor crime (a motorcycle theft) is linked to a major flight, and the police deploy all their supposed skills to find out the perpetrator. Eventually, the suspect is released on the grounds of insufficient evidence. But the harm has already been done: the image of the alleged criminal has been watched by everybody. The flight footage succeeds in creating an atmosphere of suspense, similar to that of a chase scene in a film. The biker lives in a disadvantaged neighbourhood and is the object of police and viewer prejudice. The relation between poverty and crime is thus established by discursive representation.

Example 2 (b)

[Story title: The flight]
Police Station No. 3 of Tigre[17]
Reporter (*white captions*) U10 Do you know why you've been detained?//
Man *(yellow captions)* U11 I don't know why, sir, I had the bike, sir/ I had the bike/ and was riding the bike/ and I got afraid and got in the house, but I don't know, I've got nothing, guv, I swear//.
Policeman (*white captions*) U12 We were patrolling the area/ we saw three bikes approaching/ one, on seeing the police/ turned back/ when we tried to intercept him/ he escaped/ through the roofs of the adjoining houses//
Action
Policeman U13 Stay there, mate!//
Policeman U14 He's leapt, he's leapt!//
Policeman U15 He's leapt over!//
Policeman U16 Someone's leapt over from here, madam//
Neighbour U17 No//
Reporter U18 They've never come//
Neighbour U19 No//
Policeman U20 Yes, I'm here searching for him in a house// U21 He's left a bike lying about, I've got him here, inside a house.
Bystander U22 Next door ... He jumped over the wall/ and landed there, next door//
Policeman U23 Go round the back/ mind the window!//
Drunk U24 Don't you scatter my things about!//
Policeman U25 There he is!///

Policeman U26 Next door, next door, next door!/ Go!/ Go!/ S of a b!/

Policeman U27 So, darkie, got him there, darkie?

Policeman U28 A petty thief that has already escaped from us once/ jumps over the walls/ I tell him to stop/ he draws a gun and points it at me/ and I appeal [sic] repeal the attack/ back-up patrol cars come to the scene/ and the criminal is apprehended round the corner.

Caption: Police Station No 3 of Tigre

Reporter (*white captions*) U29 Do you know why you've been detained?//

Man (*yellow captions*) U30 I don't know why, sir, I had the bike, sir/ I had the bike/ and was riding the bike/ and I got afraid and got in the house, but I don't know, I've got nothing, guv, I swear//.

Reporter U31 That was your house?//

Man U32 It's my aunt's house//

Reporter U33 That house?//

Man U34 Yes//

Reporter U35 Did you have a gun?//

Man U36 No, nothing, old man, I never ...//

Reporter U37 And why ...?

Man U38 Because they always beat me, put me somewhere else, I don't know/ I'm afraid, guv.

Reporter U39 Been detained before?//

Man U40 Yes//

Reporter U41 And what have they told you now? What's going on?//

Man U42 Nothing, [what can they say] if I've got nothing.//

Reporter U43 The bike is yours, legally?//

Man U44 Yes, legally/ yes, I've got the paperwork, old man, yes// U45 I've been insulted lots of times/ lots of times I've been beaten, I've been ... do you understand?/ I've been asked to do things that I never ... and impossible things/ on the other side/ I was afraid//

Reporter U46 You ran away because you were afraid?//

Man U47 Because I was afraid, yes, I swear on my children's lives//

Blue box: U48 The man was released a few hours later because he was able to prove that the bike was his//

Application of SDTA to the segment reproduced above (Examples 2a and 2b) yielded the following results as regards grammatical and semantic categories. These are marked in bold and bold italics, respectively, in Table 6.1.

Table 6.2, in turn, shows in non-numerical form the three most frequent oral (*place, crime* and *verb 2*) and the two most frequent visual/written categories (*crime* and *speaker/protagonist*) in focal position in Example 2.

Table 6.1   Grammatical and semantic categories in Example 2 [V3: verb 3]

	Place	S/P	V1	Crime	Time	PO	Actor (Man)	V2	Fear	Woman, neighbours	V3
Oral	13	2	2	7	4	1	6	10	1	1	1
Written/ visual	3	5	3	11	2	1	3	3	0	0	0
Total (oral + written/ visual)	16	7	5	18	6	2	9	13	1	1	1

Overall, the figures show that the fragmentation of discourse through screen frames in this example results in the creation of new foci. The written/visual foci reinforce parts of the utterance (categories) that do not constitute foci in the oral text. In the spoken version, the semantic category *place* has the highest number of foci (n=13), followed by the grammaticalized category *verb 2* (n=10) and the semantic category *crime* (n=7). In the transcription, however, the semantic category *crime* is most often in focal position (n=11), whereas the remaining semantic categories, especially *place*, are less frequently stressed in comparison.

These differences become more significant when we take the oral and written texts together, which is precisely how the fragment is perceived by the audience. This combination results in some categories acquiring considerable importance, most notably the semantic category *crime* and the grammaticalized category *speaker/protagonist*. As shown in Table 6.1, *crime* has only seven foci in the oral version but gains 11 as a result of screen-frame discourse fragmentation. Similarly, *speaker/protagonist* has two foci in the oral text and five in the visual presentation. By highlighting both categories, the editors create a multimodal (oral-visual) link between crime and the chief actor in the story, overlooking the fact that he has been mistakenly arrested. Other categories, by contrast, lose salience by this process: *place* and *verb 2* only gain three foci each, with a total of 16 and 13 foci respectively.

Therefore, the categories in focal position in the oral version may be further reinforced by being visually stressed or, on the contrary, lose that position and therefore their significance. The speaker's hierarchical presentation of the information may thus be modified by the written text or the visual elements, depending on the number of foci a certain category gains in relation to the others. An orally unstressed category may, on the other hand, become visually emphasized, thus distorting the speaker's initial focus.

Table 6.2 Frequent focal categories in Example 2[18]

Focal categories with the highest frequency of occurrence (oral version)			Focal categories with the highest frequency of occurrence (visual presentation)	
Place (N=13)	*Crime* (N=7)	V2 (N=10)	S/P (N=5)	*Crime* (N=11)
U1[Greater Buenos Aires area of Buenos Aires province]	in murder]	are arrested]	Sir	the bike/
in Argentina]	commit a new crime]	swear]	police /	three bikes/
through the roofs of the adjoining houses]	minors between 12 and 16 years old]	u14['s leapt;... 's leapt!]	back-up patrol cars	escaped
from here]	45% of the violent crimes and 63% of the murders]	u15['s leapt over!]	Sir	has already escaped
in a house]	gun?]	u17[No]	on the other side /	to stop
here, inside a house	legally?]	is apprehended]		the attack /
Next door ... there, next door]	Yes[19]	detained]		the criminal/
round the back/ mind the window!		swear]		riding the bike /
my things[20]		never]		u44[Yes, legally/
round the corner]		u40[Yes]		things that I never ...and impossible things/
That was your house?]				
U33[That house?]				
U34 [Yes][21]				

Table 6.3   Hierarchical information in Example 1[22]

Participants	Place	Speaker/ Protagonist	V1	Crime	PO	Actor/ Man	V2	Fear	Neighbour	V3
Reporter							U10 [Do			
						you	know			
				why		you	've been detained?]			
Man						U11 [I	don't know			
				why						
		Sir				I [23]	had			
				the bike						
		sir/				I [24]/	had			
				the bike	and		was riding			
				the bike/	and I		got	afraid		
					and I		got			
	in the house				But I		don't			
							know			
						I	've got			
				Nothing						
		Guv				I	swear]			

We will now examine the hierarchical presentation of information (Table 6.3). Owing to space constraints, this is restricted to utterances 10 and 11 (Example 1).

Oral and visual foci have been underlined to aid visualization, followed by closing brackets and slashes respectively. The term *participants* refers to the speakers and does not indicate a grammatical/ semantic category. Co-occurring categories can be seen from left to right (synchronic approach). *Crime* and *fear* are linked to each other. The *actor/man*'s attitude towards the former is not defiant or threatening: in spite of his innocence, he is afraid. Each column displays instances of the category in question throughout the text (diachronic approach). In the *actor/man* column, for example, the pronoun *I* is placed after the verb in two cases,[25] in which he also mentions the 'bike', the supposedly stolen item included in the *crime* category. The man's agency is thus stressed. *Why* appears twice in the *crime* column, and *bike* three times, the latter emphasized by the man's denial of the theft. These repetitions point to the high degree of isomorphism of the text.

Two oral foci belong to the *verb 2* category, while three visual foci fall under *speaker/protagonist*, *crime* and *actor/man*. Through visual fragmentation, the editorial line of the programme draws attention to the crime, the suspect, and his interlocutor, the reporter. The oral version, on the other hand, highlights the arrest and the detainee's earnest protestation of his own innocence. Thus, his imagery contrasts with that of the show, which deals with crime and its perpetrators.

Conclusion

In this chapter, evidence has been presented of the way in which editorial processes of visual/textual fragmentation of oral discourse create new rhemes and foci. In the case of the docudrama PIA, they are used to stress the link been poverty and crime, which might lead to inspiring fear and prejudice in the audience. This kind of discursive representation, based on false beliefs about those who live in poverty, is not restricted to the illustrative example analysed in detailed in this chapter. It is, on the contrary, representative of the reference corpus. Given the popularity of the genre in which it occurs, it is not difficult to see how, through large-scale mass media reproduction, this kind of discursive representation may become socially shared. Discourse and image fragmentation are, as we noted at the start of this chapter, among the typically postmodern features that characterize the docudrama genre.

One should be also mindful, however, that postmodern support for cultural diversity entails enabling non-mainstream voices to be heard. Like other reality shows, such as *Bailando por un Sueño*[26] (Dancing for a Dream), *Calles Salvajes* (Wild Streets), and *Cámaras de Seguridad* (Security Cameras), PIA purports to give voice to those who have not traditionally had it, drawing attention to their life stories. The presence of the poor, the mentally ill and other disadvantaged groups on screen and particularly on reality TV is no longer unusual. In PIA, 'the voiceless' appear as the actual authors of their stories. Thus, storyline development, previously in the hands of the learned, wealthy and powerful elite, has now been partly replaced by the newly found voice of the so-called minorities.[27] As we have seen in this chapter, though, their narrative is heavily editorialized and often used against them.

Postmodernity has also introduced important changes to the notion of heroicity. The hero is no longer someone who, believing in science or in their own willpower, is capable of performing daring feats or undertaking collective projects. Contemporary heroes are ordinary men and women (see Pardo & Lorenzo-Dus 2010), whose claim to fame often lies in their being able to endure daily life and the utter hopelessness of this world. Accordingly, PIA shows everyday scenes of incredible suffering by ordinary people. Although postmodern heroes do not possess superpowers in real life, their fictional counterparts often do. The postmodern pop-art boom can be seen in comic-inspired American TV series, such as *Heroes and Smallville*. The opening of PIA and the shifts between news items seem to have been similarly influenced.

Tragedy, death, horror and the cult of memory without an official story have been not only aestheticized (i.e. painted, drawn, carved, filmed, reported by the press or shown on TV) in postmodern times but also spectacularized (i.e. paraded and massively marketed). Such aestheticization and spectacularization have also resulted in the boom of the bizarre and freakish (Debord 1994; González Requena 1987; Hoynes 1994), with the extremely poor as a favourite subject. In reality TV programmes such as PIA they are also presented as a 'minority' routinely engaged in criminal activities, arousing a feeling of fear and insecurity in the audience. The show thus reflects and further constructs within the Argentine context a morbid kind of voyeurism, typical of postmodernity, in which watching poor people depicted as criminal and 'bizarre' (prostitutes, transvestites, the insane, etc.) has become an aesthetic experience (Pardo and Buscaglia 2011).

Appendix

Example 2 (Spanish text):

Introduction

Caption **u1**[*Conurbano bonaerense* (bottom right)//]
[Blue box. Each line within this box contains an utterance and takes up a frame.]
u2. [*Se denuncia un delito cada dos minutos//.*]
u3. [*Se cometen 91 robos con armas por día//.*]
u4. [*En el conurbano se registran el 64% de los delitos de toda la Argentina//.*]
u5. [*106 personas por día son detenidas//.*]
u6. [*El 38% de los robos terminan en homicidios//.*]
u7. [*3 de cada 10 personas que recuperan la libertad vuelve a delinquir a los dos años//.*]
u8. [*El 80% de los robos y homicidios los cometen menores de entre 12 y 16 años//.*]
u9. [*Solo se esclarecen el 45% de los crímenes violentos y el 63% de los asesinatos//.*]
Story title: *La fuga*
Comisaría tercera de Tigre
Reporter (*white caption*) **u10** [*¿sabes por qué te detienen?//*]

Man (*yellow captions*) **u11** *[No sé por qué, Don, tenía la moto, yo, Don/ tenía la moto yo/ y venía en la moto/ y me dio miedo y me metí en la casa pero no sé, no tengo nada, jefe, se lo juro//]*

Reporter(*white captions*) **u12** *[Veníamos recorriendo la zona/ vemos que vienen tres motos/ la cual una al ver la presencia policial/ se vuelve/ cuando nosotros tratamos de interceptarlo/ se da a la fuga/ entra a saltar por los techos de las casas linderas//]*

Action

Policeman **u13**. *[Parate ahí, flaco//.]*

Policeman **u14**. *[Saltó, saltó//.]*

Policeman **u15**. *[Saltó por el otro lado//.]*

Policeman **u16**. *[Saltó alguien Sra. por acá//.]*

Neighbour **u17**. *[No//]*

Reporter **u18** *[No vinieron en ningún momento//]*

Neighbour **u19** *[No//]*

Policeman **u20**. *[Si estoy acá buscándolo en un domicilio//]* **u21** *[Dejó una moto tirada acá, lo tengo acá dentro de una casa//]*

Bystander **u22**. *[En la casa de al lado por el muro saltó/ y ahí cayó de ahí de la casa de al lado//]*

Policeman **u23** *[Andá por atrás/ cuidado la ventana//]*

Drunk **u24**. *[No me vayas a tirar las cosas//.]*

Policeman **u25** *[Allá está//]*

Policeman **u26**. *[Al lado, al lado, al lado/ Dale/Dale/H de P//]*

Policeman **u27**. *[¿Y, pardo, lo tenés ahí, pardo?//]*

Policeman **u28**. *[Un caco que ya/ se nos había dado una vez a la fuga/salta los paredones/ le doy la voz de alto/saca un arma de fuego me apunta/ y yo (apelo SIC) repelo la agresión/ vienen móviles de apoyo/ y es aprehendiendo el delincuente/ a la vuelta a la manzana//]*

Caption: Comisaría tercera Tigre

Reporter (*white captions*) **u29** *[¿sabes por qué te detienen?//]*

Man **u30** (*yellow captions*). *[No sé por qué Don tenía la moto, yo/ tenía la moto yo, Don/ y venía en la moto/ y me dio miedo y me metí en la casa pero no sé, no tengo nada, jefe, se lo juro//]*

Reporter **u31**. *[¿Y era tu casa esa?//]*

Man **u32** *[Es la casa de mi tía//]*

Reporter **u33**. *[¿Esa casa?//]*

Man **u34**. *[Sí//]*

Reporter **u35**. *[¿Tenías arma?//]*

Man **u36**. *[No, nada, papá yo nunca//]*

Reporter **u37**. *[¿Y por qué?//]*

Man **u38**. *[Por que siempre me pegan, me ponen en otro lado, qué se yo/ yo tengo miedo, jefe//]*

Reporter **u39** *[¿"Tuviste" detenido antes?//]*

Man **u40**. *[Sí//]*

Reporter **u41** *[¿Y ahora qué te dijeron? ¿Qué pasa?//]*

Man **u42**. *[Nada, si no tengo nada yo//]*

Reporter **u43**. *[La moto es tuya, ¿es legal?//]*

Man **u44**. *[Sí, legal/sí tengo los papeles padre, sí//]* **u45***[A mi me verduguearon muchas veces/muchas veces me han pegado, me han… ¿me entiende?/me han pedido cosas que jamás y cosas imposibles/del otro lado/me dio miedo a mí//]*

Reporter **u46**. *[¿Huías por el miedo?//]*
Man **u47**. *[Por el miedo, sí, se lo juro por mis hijos//]*
Blue box: **u48**. [El hombre fue liberado a las pocas horas porque pudo probar que
la moto era suya//.]

Table 6.A1 Translation

Focal categories with the highest frequency of occurrence (oral version)			Focal categories with the highest frequency of occurrence (visual presentation)	
Place	*Crime*	V2	Speaker/ Protagonist	*Crime*
13	7	10	5	11
u1[Conurbanobonaerense]	*en homicidio]*	*detienen]*	*Don/*	*en la moto/*
de toda la Argentina]	*a delinquir]*	*juro]*	*la presencia policial/*	*tres motos/*
por los techos de la casas linderas]	*menores de entre 12 y 16 años]*	*u14[saltó, saltó]*	*móviles de apoyo/*	*a la fuga/*
por acá?]	*el 45% de los crímenes violentos y el 63% de los asesinatos]*	*u15[Saltó por el otro lado]*	*Don/*	*a la fuga/*
en un domicilio]	*arma?]*	*u17[No]*	*del otrolado/*	*la voz de alto/*
acá dentro de una casa]	*legal?]*	*está]*		*la agresión/*
de ahí, de la casa de al lado]	*sí/]*	*detienen]*		*el delincuente/*
por atrás, cuidado la ventana]		*juro]*		*en la moto/*
las cosas]		*nunca]*		*u44[Sí, legal/ sí*
a la vuelta a la manzana]		*u40[Sí]*		*sí/]*
tu casa esa/?]				*cosas que jamás, y cosas imposibles/*
u33[esa casa?]				
u34 [Sí]				

Table 6.A2 Translation

Participants	Place	Speaker/ Protagonist	V1 *Crime*	PO	Actor/ *Man*	V2	*Fear*	*Neighbour*	V3
Reporter						u8[Sabes			
			por qué						
					te	detienen]			
Man			por qué			u9 [No sé			
		Don	la moto			tenía			
		Don/			yo				
			la moto		yo/	tenía			
				y		venía			
			en la moto/	y	me	dio	miedo		
				y	me	metí			
	en la casa			pero		no sé			
			nada			no tengo			
		jefe se	lo			juro]			

Notes

1. An earlier version of this chapter was presented at a specialist panel of the 2011 International Pragmatics Association Conference: The Discourse of Reality Television. Multidisciplinary and Cross-Cultural Approaches (Convenors: Nuria Lorenzo-Dus, Swansea University, UK; and Pilar Garcés-Conejos Blitvich, University of North Carolina at Charlotte). The research has been partly conducted within the UBACYT 200100100120 project, led by me and funded by the University of Buenos Aires, Philosophy and Arts School. It has also benefited from discussions with my Media Discourse Analysis (under)graduate students and my work with the Argentine National Council for Scientific and Technological Research (Consejo Nacional de Investigaciones Científicas y Técnicas - CONICET). I am grateful to Adriana Podesta and especially to Mónica Descalzi for translating this chapter into English. I am also grateful to the anonymous reviewers and the editors for their helpful suggestions.
2. http://losanalisisdelatv.blogspot.com.ar/2010/01/policias-en-accion-lo-mas-visto-del.html or http://www.primiciasya.com/rating/Policias-en-acci243n-lo-m225s-visto-del-viernes---20091107-31121.html
3. Original edition available online at http://library.nothingness.org/articles/SI/fr/pub_contents/7
4. Nietzsche was also a precursor for postmodernism in his genealogical analyses of fundamental concepts, especially what he takes to be the core concept of Western metaphysics (Aylesworth 2012). He was, too, an interest shared

by postmodern philosophers and Martin Heidegger, whose meditations on art, technology, and the withdrawal of being they regularly cite and comment upon. "...Those looking for personal condemnations of Heidegger for his actions and his 'refusal to accept responsibility' (for the Holocaust) will not find them in postmodernist commentaries. They will, however, find many departures from Heidegger on Nietzsche's philosophical significance and many instances where Nietzsche's ideas are critically activated against Heidegger and his self-presentation' (Aylesworth 2012).

5. About the links between aestheticization and the public sphere, see Hannah Arendt (1958) and Jurgen Habermas (1989), the two most influential social philosophers, who formulated the idea of public sphere. As Pachenkov and Voronkova (2009, p.1) point out, 'When we look at these most famous definitions, we realize that all of them understand the public space as a place for gathering – not for "moving through".' Arendt was concerned about Agora and Forum, which by definition were spaces for citizen gathering – for meeting and speaking, for spending leisure time, for encounters with others. To Habermas the typical public spaces were the coffee and tea houses where the bourgeois gathered, read newspapers, talked, and discussed their common interests. Those ideas, however, are quintessentially modern and, as such, opposed to fundamental features of postmodernity and its concept of public sphere. 'If nothing is eternal and stable, if everything changes and moves, why should these city quarters stay the same forever? Why should artists stay in the same city areas for long?' (Pachenkov and Voronkova 2009, p. 5). Thus, the notion of aestheticization redefines the concepts of both public sphere and art.

6. However, it is important to avoid over-interpreting the frequent presence of life histories on TV shows, the fragmentation of discourse and image, and the emphasis on architecture as new social or linguistic phenomena that characterize contemporary media. We would rather see them as features of postmodernity that should be taken into account by ethnography and social practice.

7. Neapolitan (1993) has demonstrated how the formal features of reality shows lead to their being confused with fictional shows. The mixture of reality and entertainment seems to have encouraged production trends that combine formal characteristics of both shows. The production incorporates a narrative of the story together with takes of real scenes, interviews with real people involved in the events and dramatization by professional actors following a fiction-like script. The expressions 'true' and 'actually happened' are often used (Neapolitan 1993). In this rhetorical mix, the content considered and called 'real' is delivered as drama; the reconstruction of crimes, accidents and lovers' reunions shares the rhetorical markers of fiction: music, off-screen narrators and voices, on-set shooting, special effects ... In many cases the reconstruction or construction is combined with real or documentary scenes. (Ministerio de Educación y Ciencia de España, Proyecto Pigmalión, available online at http://ares.cnice.mec.es/informes/03/documentos/part02_cap05_87.htm)

8. www.eltrecetv.com.ar. The selected fragment lasts from minute 41.30 to 46.38 and contains 48 utterances.

9. Literally 'Natalie'. (Translator's note)

10. This has been under a cloud because of its members' role in the crimes against humanity perpetrated during the last military dictatorship, and, more recently,

their perceived corruption and links to both organized and petty crime. Several publicity campaigns have aimed at improving the institutional reputation of the Buenos Aires police by different means, including the production of PIA, a goal that has never been explicitly acknowledged on the show.

11. For example: 'The flight: go hard on them' (*'La fuga: duro con ellos'* in Spanish), in the episode analysed.
12. Editorial comments are by and large in black, placed within a coloured box. They mostly provide information about the places where the allegedly criminal action occurs, which tend to coincide with the Greater Buenos Aires districts explicitly characterized in the boxes as poverty-stricken/crime-ridden areas.
13. We call it a 'principle' because it is common to all languages.
14. The term 'utterance' is used here to refer to a unit with a communicative goal, a rheme and a theme.
15. For the Spanish version of this fragment see the Appendix to this chapter. Transcription conventions are as follows: U1, u2, etc.: utterances; /: (visual) frame separation; // full stop. Comments in italics describe visual aspects of the segment.
16. Significantly, the theme has been elided from this utterance, leaving only the rheme.
17. Tigre is a Greater Buenos Aires district.
18. For the Spanish version see Table 6.A1 in the Appendix to this chapter.
19. This 'yes' answers the question whether the motorcycle has been legally purchased or not, and therefore falls under the category of *crime*.
20. This is the focus of utterance 24, where the drunk asks the policemen not to scatter his possessions, which are lying about on a patio. This is his way of telling them that this is his patio, where his things are untidily spread because such is the nature of the place, and therefore 'things' belongs to this category.
21. This 'yes' answers the question whether that is his aunt's house, and thus stresses that it is the *place* they have been looking for.
22. See Table 6.A2 in the Appendix to this chapter for the Spanish version.
23. The pronoun is placed after the verb in the original.
24. The pronoun is again placed after the verb in the original.
25. The use of personal pronouns before or after finite verbs is not mandatory in Spanish. Pronouns are sometimes colloquially placed after the verb, even in affirmative sentences. (Translator's note)
26. Poor people and NGOs take part in this contest in order to raise funds for different causes. Poor members of such organizations make an appearance in order to arouse empathy in the viewers and do not turn up again until the end of the season. Their voice serves the interests of the producers, boosting ratings and providing a justification for the competition.
27. Paradoxically, these include large groups of people – the poor, for instance, make up more than half the world's population.

References

Arendt, H. (1958) *The Human Condition*. (Chicago: University of Chicago Press).
Arzeno, F. & M. E. Contursi (2006) Policías en acción: ficcionalización, representación de la policía bonaerense y caos de las clases subalternas. In *X Jornadas*

nacionales de investigadores en comunicación (Buenos Aires: Universidad de Ciencias Sociales-UBA). Available online at: http://www.redcomunicacion.org/memorias/pdf/2006ararzeno-contursi.pdf.

Aylesworth, Gary (2012) Postmodernism. In Edward N. Zalta (ed.), *The Stanford Encyclopedia of Philosophy*. Available online at: http://plato.stanford.edu/archives/fall2012/entries/postmodernism/

Barrett, E. (ed.) (1992) *Sociomedia,Multimedia, Hypermedia, and the Social Construction of Knowledge* (Cambridge MA: The MIT Press).

Bauman, Z. (2000) *Trabajo, consumismo y nuevos pobres* (Barcelona: Gedisa).

Borón, A. (2000) América Latina: crisis sin fin o fin de la crisis. In Segrera López & D. Filmus (eds.), *América Latina 2020. Escenarios, alternativas, estrategias*, (Buenos Aires: Unesco-Flacso-Temas Grupo Editorial).

Brumme, J. & H. Resinger (eds.) (2008) *La oralidad fingida: obras literarias. Descripción y traducción* (Madrid: Iberoamericana).

Carlón, M. (2005) Metatelevisión: un giro metadiscursivo de la televisión argentina. *deSignis*, 7/8. Available online at http://www.designisfels.net/designis78.htm

Castro, C. (2002) La hibridación en el formato y pautas para el análisis de Gran Hermano. *ZER Revista de estudios de comunicación (komunikazioikasketenaldizkaria)*,13. Available online at http://www.ehu.es/zer/zer13/hibridacion13.htm (accessed 10 September 2010).

Cocimano, G. (2003) *El Fin del Secreto. Ensayos sobre la privacidad contemporánea* (Editorial Dunken: Buenos Aires).

Cristobo, M. (2009) El neoliberalismo en Argentina y la profundización de la exclusión y la pobreza. *Margen*, 55. Available online at http://www.margen.org/suscri/margen55/cristobo.pdf

Chiapello, E. & N. Fairclough (2002) Understanding the new management ideology: A transdisciplinary contribution from critical discourse analysis and new sociology of capitalism. In N. Fairclough (Guest editor), *Language in New Capitalism* (Special Issue of *Discourse and Society*, 13 (2).

Debord, G. (1994) *The Society of Spectacle* (New York: Zone Books).

Firbas, J. (1964) On defining the theme in Functional Sentence Analysis. *Travaux Linguistiques de Prague*, 1: 267–80.

Firbas, J. (1992) *Functional Sentence Perspective in Written and Spoken Communication* (Cambridge: Cambridge University Press).

Ford, A. (1999) *La marca de la bestia* (Buenos Aires: Norma).

Ford, A. (2006) La construcción discursiva de los problemas globales. El multiculturalismo, residuos, commodities y pseudofusiones. Multi(Inter)culturalidad: perspectivas y convergencias. *Signo y pensamiento*, 24: 46.

Forster, R. (2002) La muerte del héroe. In *Crítica y sospecha* (Buenos Aires: Paidós).

Fuenzalida, V. (1991) *Televisión, pobreza y desarrollo* (Santiago de Chile: CPU).

García Fajardo, C. (2000) Estetización de la cultura: ¿pérdida del sentimiento sublime? *Espéculo. Revista de estudios literarios*. Available online at http://www.ucm.es/info/especulo/numero16/estetiz.html (accessed 15 March 2011).

García Fajardo, C. (2002) El gusto estético en la sociedad postindustrial. *Espéculo. Revista de estudios literarios*. Available online at http://www.ucm.es/info/especulo/numero21/gusto_es.html (accessed 2 March 2011).

Garcia Da Silva, D. & N.G. Pardo Abril (2010) Miradas cruzadas hacia la pobreza desde una perspectiva crítica transdisciplinaria. *Cadernos de Linguagem e Sociedade*, 11(1): 66–90.

Glaser, B. & A. Strauss (1967) *The Discovery of Grounded Theory: Strategies for Qualitative Research* (New York: Aldine Publishing Company).

Glusberg, J. (1997) *Moderno Post Moderno* (Buenos Aires: Emece).

González Requena, J. (1987) *El discurso televisivo: espectáculo de la posmodernidad* (Madrid: Cátedra).

Habermas, J. (1989) [1962] *The Structural Transformation of the Public Sphere: An Inquiry into a Category of Bourgeois Society* (Cambridge, MA: The MIT Press).

Haßler, G. (2008) Temas, remas, focos y tópicos en la oralidad fingida y en su traducción. In J. Brumme, & H. Resinger (eds.), *La oralidad fingida: obras literarias. Descripción y traducción* (Madrid: Iberoamericana).

Hoynes, W. (1994) *Public Television for Sale. Media, the Market, and the Public Sphere* (San Francisco: Westview Press).

Idnovo Carlier, S. (2001) El secreto está en el relato: fortalezas y retos del docudrama en la era posmoderna. *Comunicación y Sociedad*, 14(2): 37–70.

Klachko, P. O. (2000) *La conflictividad social en la Argentina de los '90: el caso de las localidades petroleras de Cutral Có y Plaza Huincul (1996–1997).* (Buenos Aires: CLACSO Libros). Available online at http://biblioteca.clacso.edu.ar/ar/libros/levy/klachko.pdf

Koch, P. & W. Oesterreicher (1985) Sprache der Nähe – Sprache der Distanz. Mündlichkeit und Schriftlichkeitim Spannungsfeld von Sprachtheorie und Sprachgeschichte. *Romanistisches Jahrbuch*, 36: 15–43.

Mathesius, V. (1939) On the so called functional sentence perspective. *Slovo a slovesnost*, 5: 171–84.

McLuhan, M. (1994) *Understanding Media. The Extensions of Man* (Cambridge, MA: The MIT Press).

McLuhan, M. & E. McLuhan (1988) *Laws of Media. The New Science* (Toronto: University of Toronto Press).

Mendo, A.H. & E. Mena Rodríguez (2000) Análisis de las diferencias comunicativas en los telediarios de las cadenas de televisión. *Psicothema*, 12(2): 389–92.

Neapolitan, D.M. (1993) An analysis of the formal features of 'reality-based' television programs. ERIC. Available online at http://eric.ed.gov/ERICWebPortal/search/detailmini.jsp?_nfpb=true&_&ERICExtSearch_SearchValue_0=ED360063&ERICExtSearch_SearchType_0=no&accno=ED360063

Lorenzo-Dus, N. (2009) *Television Discourse. Analysing Language in the Media* (Basingstoke and New York: Palgrave Macmillan).

Ministerio de Economía de la Provincia de Buenos Aires (2002) *Pobreza: definición, determinantes y programas para su erradicación.* Special Issue of *Cuadernos de Economía*, 65.

Ortiz, T. & M.L. Pardo (2006) *Estado posmoderno y globalización: transformación del estado- nación argentino* (Buenos Aires: Departamento de Publicaciones, Facultad de Derecho, UBA).

Ortiz, T. & M. L. Pardo (eds.) 2006. *Estado posmoderno y globalización. Transformación del estado-nación argentino.* Buenos Aires: Departamento de Publicaciones de la Facultad de Derecho de la Universidad de Buenos Aires y Editorial MPS.

Ortiz, T. & M.L. Pardo (eds.) (2008) *Desigualdades sociales y Estado. Un estudio multidisciplinar desde la posmodernidad.* Buenos Aires: Departamento de Publicaciones. Facultad de Derecho. Universidad de Buenos Aires y A3 Plus.

Pardo Abril, N. (2008) *¿Qué nos dicen? ¿Qué vemos? ¿Qué es pobreza? Análisis crítico de los medios* (Bogotá: Antiquus Editores).

Pardo, M.L. (1992) *Derecho y Lingüística. ¿Cómo se juzga con palabras?* (Buenos Aires: Centro Editor de América Latina).

Pardo, M.L. (1996) *Derecho y Lingüística. ¿Cómo se juzga con palabras?* 2nd edn, revised and enlarged. Prólogos de Teun van Dijk & Carles Duarte y Monserrat (Buenos Aires: Nueva visión).

Pardo, M.L. (1998) La estetización y espectacularización de la pobreza: análisis crítico del discurso posmdoerno televisivo en la Argentina. In T. Ortiz & M.L. Pardo, *Desigualdades sociales y Estado. Un estudio multidisciplinar desde la posmodernidad* (Buenos Aires: Departamento de Publicaciones, Facultad de Derecho, Universidad de Buenos Aires).

Pardo, M. L. (ed.) (2008) *El Discurso sobre la pobreza en América Latina*. Editorial Frasis. Colección Poder, Discurso y Sociedad Santiago de Chile: Chile Prólogo de Robert De Beaugrande.

Pardo, M.L. (2010) Discourse as a tool for the diagnosis of psychosis: A linguistic and psychiatric study of communication decline. In N. Lorenzo-Dus (ed.), *Spanish at Work. Institutional Discourse in the Spanish-Speaking World* (Basingstoke and New York: Palgrave Macmillan), pp. 227–51.

Pardo, M.L. (2011) *Teoría y metodología de la investigación lingüística. Método sincrónico- diacrónico de análisis lingüístico de textos* (Buenos Aires: Tersites).

Pardo, M.L. (2012) Asociación discursiva entre pobreza y delito en un programa televisivo reproducido en *YouTube*. In N. Pardo Abril (ed.), *Discurso en la web: pobreza en YouTube* (Bogotá: Universidad Nacional de Colombia – GRAFIWEB, impresores publicistas), pp. 270–93.

Pardo, M.L. & N. Lorenzo-Dus (2010) The Falklands/Malvinas 25 years on: A comparative analysis of constructions of heroism on Argentinean and British television. In M. L. Pardo (Guest editor) *Critical and Cultural Discourse Analysis from a Latin American Perspective*. Special Issue of *Journal of Multicultural Discourses*, 5(3), pp. 253–70.

Pardo, M. L. & V. Buscaglia (2011) Delirio, pobreza y televisión: análisis del discurso y psicoanálisis. In M.J. Coraccini (ed.), *Identidades silenciadas e (In)visíveis: entre a inclusão e a exclusão (identidade, midia, pobreza, situação de rua, mudança social, formação de profesores)* (Campinas: Editorial Pontes).

Pachenkov, O. & L. Voronkova (2009) Urban public space in the context of mobility and aestheticization: Setting the problem. In *Urban Public Space in the Context of Mobility and Aestheticization: Facing Contemporary Challenges* (Berlin: Institute for European Ethnology, Humboldt University). Available online at http://www.cisr.ru/files/news/INTRO_short.pdf

Patrone, L. (2009) *Policías en Acción: Desgracia Ajena, Éxito Propio*. Available online at http://www.monografias.com/trabajos37/policias-en-accion/policias-en-accion.shtml (accessed 3 October 2009).

Resende de Melo, V. (2009) *Análise de Discurso Crítica e Realismo Crítico. Implicaçacões Interdisciplinares* (Campinas, SP: Pontes Editores).

Robertson, R. (1992) *Globalization: Social Theory and Global Culture* (London: Sage).

Santander Molina, P. (2002) Acceso y poder discursivo en las noticias de la televisión chilena. *Signos*, 35: 51–2, 243–69.

Santander Molina, P. (2003) El acceso invisible en las noticias de televisión. *Estudios Filológicos*, 38: 139–56.

Sinclair, J. (2000) *Televisión: comunicación global y regionalización* (Barcelona: Gedisa).

Sreberny-Mohammadi, A., D. Winseck, J. McKenna & O. Boyd-Barrett (eds.) (1997) *Media in Global Context. A Reader* (New York: Arnold).

Ulanovsky, C., S. Itkin & P. Sirven (1999) *Estamos en el aire. Una historia de la televisión argentina* (Buenos Aires: Planeta).

Van Dijk, T. (1998a) *News as Discourse* (Hillsdale, NJ: Lawrence Erlbaum Associates).

Van Dijk, T. (1998b) *News Analysis: Case Studies of International and National News in the Press* (Hillsdale, NJ: Lawrence Erlbaum Associates).

Van Dijk, T. (1991) *Racism and the Press* (London and New York: Routledge).

Vasilachis, I. (2003) *Pobres, pobreza, identidad y representaciones sociales* (Barcelona: Gedisa).

Verón, E. (1986) *Perón o muerte. Los fundamentos discursivos del fenómeno peronista* (Buenos Aires: Hyspamérica).

Weil, H. (1844) *De l'odre des mots dans les langues anciennes comparées aux langues modernes, Questiones de grammaire générale* (Paris: Joubert).

Wodak, R. & M. Meyer (2003) *Métodos de análisis crítico del discurso* (Barcelona: Gedisa).

7
Heroic endeavours: flying high in New Zealand reality television

Philippa Smith

Introduction

Tune into New Zealand television in any given week and the menu of reality programmes in a multi-channel environment is certain to keep the hungriest of viewers satisfied. A weekly diet of 'reality' emanating mainly from Australia, the United States and the United Kingdom, as well as from New Zealand, is proof of the global popularity of reality television (RTV). The 1990s saw the emergence of the first RTV programmes to screen in New Zealand, such as *Fear Factor, The Amazing Race, Who Dares Wins, Extreme Makeover* and *Popstars*. Criticism was initially raised both locally and internationally that RTV was cheap, superficial, and tabloid (Hill 2005; Lealand & Martin 2001). But the fact that two decades later RTV rates regularly in the top ten most-watched programmes on New Zealand's free-to-air terrestrial channels each week (New Zealand Film and TV 2011) is testimony that it has become a commonly accepted part of the nation's media landscape.

Defining RTV as unscripted programmes that involve ordinary people, rather than actors, provides a wide scope when it comes to examining locally made programmes from New Zealand. Both terrestrial and pay-TV channels within a commercialized broadcast environment have embraced a wide range of formats from game shows, cooking contests, and makeovers of people, their homes and their gardens, to competitions to be the country's next top model, farmer of the year or latest pop idol. Some programmes have been adapted from formats originating in other countries (*Survivor, Treasure Island, The Apprentice, Dancing with the Stars*) while others represent the home-grown ideas of local producers (*Popstars, The Chair*).

Although viewing the global phenomenon of RTV from a 'national' perspective is not new, it has received minimal academic attention, as

140

pointed out by Aslama and Pantti (2007), whose own study of Finnish RTV is an exception in this area. This chapter therefore contributes to the wider body of literature about RTV by not only examining its nation-building role in a New Zealand context, but also demonstrating how discourse analysis enables a better understanding of how this occurs.

I focus on the discourse of RTV through a case study of the emergency services genre, specifically *Rescue 1* – a popular New Zealand programme that has screened since 2009. *Rescue 1* follows the missions of an emergency helicopter team based in Auckland – New Zealand's largest city with a population of 1.4 million. The portrayal of ordinary people as being extraordinary in saving the lives of others as part of their day-to-day job reflects the qualities that New Zealanders like to believe are characteristic of the national psyche, as discussed later. In the analysis of this programme, I concentrate on the positive projection of the helicopter rescue team as 'local heroes' which, in turn, contributes to constructing an optimistic view of New Zealanders in the twenty-first century.

Underlying my approach to RTV's role in nation-building is Anderson's (1983) theory that the media are instrumental in enabling people to imagine their communities in certain ways through the dissemination of discourses about national identity. I also incorporate Billig's (1995) view that nationhood is constantly, and often banally, flagged in popular culture through symbols and language. Both these theorists serve to align my work with the stance of the *Real Talk* editors who, in acknowledging the role of culturally recognizable acts and stances in identity construction, call for a discursive analytical approach when considering RTV (see Chapter 1).

To investigate discourses about national identity in RTV – where discourse is 'language in use' and 'a way of representing the world' (Fairclough 2003, p. 124) – requires a broad approach that goes beyond the text itself. Accepting that 'texts are not produced and interpreted in isolation but in real-world contexts with all their complexities' leads me to follow an approach that goes beyond the microanalysis of language in order to explain 'why a text might be as it is and what it is (really) aiming to do' (Paltridge, 2000, pp. 157–9). As explained in Chapter 2, Critical Discourse Analysis (CDA) is an approach that can be used to indicate social and cultural change by considering the context in which a text exists, and my application of one of Fairclough's CDA analytical frameworks will be discussed later. First, however, it is necessary to consider the emergence of national identity as a key feature within New Zealand broadcasting.

Setting the scene of RTV in New Zealand

The New Zealand Government has long recognized the potential for media to play a substantive role in nation-building, which is essential to the cultural, social and economic stability of the nation. As far back as the 1930s, documentary films, mostly produced by the state's National Film Unit, were based upon a Griersonian tradition that promoted the idea that fostering a sense of national identity through film was important, particularly during the years of the Second World War (Goldson 2004). Even post-war documentary movies presented an idealized representation of a harmonious New Zealand with positive depictions of its politicians and the policies and services that reinforced its image as a wonderful place in which to live (Goldson 2004). From these early beginnings, and with the arrival of the first television sets in New Zealand in 1960, a small broadcast environment emerged of one state-owned television channel under the New Zealand Broadcasting Service. By 1975 there were two state-owned channels under the name of Television New Zealand – TV1 and TV2. These stations included some local content, but the airwaves were dominated by cheaper overseas programming from the United States and Britain.

It was the deregulation of the broadcasting industry in the late 1980s that led to a more proactive stance in cultivating local content. The introduction of private and pay-TV channels in the 1990s put pressure on TV1 and TV2 to return dividends to the Government through advertising revenue while retaining at least some aspects of a public-service style of television. Local-content quotas for New Zealand had been talked about but were never introduced. Rather, encouragement came from the establishment of a government broadcast funding agency under the Broadcasting Commission in 1989, later renamed New Zealand On Air (NZOA). The 1989/90 annual report of NZOA stated that one of its goals was to 'ensure that mainstream audiences have access to a variety of quality programmes made for New Zealanders, by New Zealanders and about New Zealanders' (NZOA 1990, p. 3). A public-service Charter, introduced later by the Labour-led Government in 2001, directed TVNZ to 'provide shared experiences that contribute to a sense of citizenship and national identity' (TVNZ Charter n.d.). Eight years later, the Charter legislation was repealed with a change in government, though NZOA still remained with its objectives intact.

Economically, however, deregulation of the broadcasting industry, which occurred in New Zealand as in other countries in an era of neo-liberalism, meant that television became fiercely competitive as more channels vied for the advertising dollar. Deregulation saw a move to the production of both 'fast turnaround' documentary series (Goldson 2004) and of RTV; these were less-expensive options when compared with the traditional quality documentary and drama programmes.

Although the first imported RTV programmes received a mixed reception, with some viewers critical of their superficiality and cheapness (Horrocks 2004; Lealand & Martin 2001), they still rated highly amongst the viewing population. Local producers realized the potential for New Zealand's own versions or adaptations of RTV programmes to garner support from broadcasters and, in some circumstances, from NZOA. RTV also went some way to meeting the growing desire of New Zealanders to see locally made programmes that showcased the country's uniqueness, that evoked 'emotions of pride and nostalgia' and that 'represented New Zealand's culture and identity to ourselves and the rest of the world' (Varcoe & Curran 2009, p. 1). It was the 'blue light' (crime) observational, factual programmes that were the first type of RTV to appear in New Zealand in the 1990s and this signalled a move away from traditional documentary, as other countries had already experienced.

American crime shows, such as *Unsolved Mysteries* (1987), *America's Most Wanted* (1988) and *Cops* (1989), first set the wheels in motion for RTV. Hill (2005) believes that Rupert Murdoch's launch of the Fox Television Network in the United States in the late 1980s in the newly deregulated and fiercely competitive broadcast environment of television saw the introduction of RTV that was not only cheap to produce, but also attracted attention through dramatic raw footage using newly developed technology such as satellite cameras and mini-cams. On-the-spot footage of the police and also of emergency service teams in the late 1980s practically guaranteed fast-moving, action-packed sequences keeping viewers riveted to their television screens (Kilborn 1994). Other countries were quick to copy or adapt these emergency-focused shows for their local viewers and New Zealand was no exception, with a flow of these programmes such as *Emergency Heroes* (1998), *Police* (1998), *Kids' Hospital* (2002), *Firefighters* (2004), *111 Emergency* (2004), *Coastwatch* (2004), *Piha Rescue* (2005), *Rapid Response* (2010), *Danger Beach* (2011) and *High Country Rescue* (2012) stretching into the new millennium.

The scholarly literature about emergency RTV programmes has focused mainly on police shows, which suggests the dominance of this particular type of programming in a variety of countries (see Chapter 6 on the Argentinean context). Fishman and Cavender's (1998) edited book *Entertaining Crime* presents a range of topics about television reality crime programmes including televised violence, the reconstruction of law and order, the ratings of crime RTV and the social context of changes in US crime policy in the 1970s that led to a flourishing of programmes in the genre. Bonner (2003) devotes a section of her book *Ordinary Television* to law and order, concluding that programmes that treat crime in a solemn and serious manner, such as *Crimewatch UK*, are a specific genre where the viewers are addressed as citizens who can help catch criminals. For her part, Hill (2000) surveyed viewers about *999* and the emergency programme *Children's Hospital*, concluding that while the audience was well aware of the 'unrealistic and "edited" version of real-life rescue and medical operations' (p. 210), this was something expected even from a public-service channel to attract a wide audience. The research participants claimed that they enjoyed these programmes for their entertainment and educational value.

Emergency RTV programmes in New Zealand have not been a main concern of academics. Rather, researchers have chosen to examine local adaptations of challenge programmes such as *Survivor, Temptation Island* and *100 Hours* (Kavka & West 2004), as well as *Flatmates* – New Zealand's version of *Big Brother* that was broadcast via the internet (Kavka & Turner 2004). A tendency to consider nation-building within RTV has however received some attention. West (2006) investigated the 'presentness' of New Zealand RTV in both a temporal and physical sense as a way to engage with the 'domain of the real' (p. 16). Part of her examination of a range of programmes, such as *Neighbourhood Watch, Caught on Tape, Treasure Island, Survivor* and *Pioneer House*, included the ongoing production of culture and identity through aesthetic and discursive practices. Kavka (2004), in particular, focused on the concept of home as a noticeable feature of New Zealand RTV, evident in programmes that dealt with home renovation such as *DIY Rescue* (2001), real-estate *Location, Location, Location* (1999) and *Hot Property* (2000), and lifestyle *Home Front* (1999) and *My House, My Castle* (1999). These programmes, Kavka (2004) argued, showed ordinary people in – or doing things to – their homes, which she said symbolized the 'cultural rootedness' (p. 232) that was so important for New Zealanders living in a British settler society.

My analysis of *Rescue 1* moves from Kavka's (2004) concept of the home as providing a 'feeling of situatedness' (p. 234), to a similar feeling experienced in New Zealand's scenic outdoors – the playground where leisure activities are looked upon as a distinctive part of the nation's lifestyle and culture. But this is also a place where accidents can occur. It is this metaphorical playground, in fact, where the drama of *Rescue 1* is situated and in which the heroic Auckland helicopter rescue team operates. The following section outlines the analytical framework and the data I use in my study.

Methodology

Acknowledging the power of the Government and the broadcast media in nation-building processes requires a methodological approach in this piece of research that goes beyond the sole analysis of discourse to a description, an interpretation, and an explanation of the representation of the social world through human action. An analytical framework developed by Fairclough (2010) since the late 1980s serves this purpose because it reinforces his view of Critical Discourse Analysis (CDA) as the 'analysis of dialectical *relations between* discourse and other objects, elements or moments, as well as analysis of the "internal relations" of discourse' (p. 4). The dimensions of the framework are detailed next, followed by a description of the data.

Framework

Fairclough's CDA framework involves analysis of three dimensions – text, discourse practice, and sociocultural practice – with the purpose 'to make visible through analysis, and to criticise, connections between properties of texts and social processes and relations', which are not necessarily obvious to either the producers or interpreters of these texts (2010, p. 132). Fairclough, in fact, used this framework in his 1995 analysis of two of Britain's early RTV crime programmes – *Crimewatch UK* and *999* – to argue that they assisted in re-establishing a positive relationship between the people and the state following a decline in support for the police between the 1970s and the 1990s. An elaboration of these three interconnected dimensions and the application of them in my analysis of *Rescue 1* are as follows:

(i) The text – the main object of discourse analysis (Le & Le 2009) – is examined closely to understand how written or spoken language in combination with visuals and sound is part of a discursive event. In my analysis of *Rescue 1*, I look at how the text negotiates and produces a discourse about national identity through the construction of the members of the emergency team as both ordinary New Zealanders and as local heroes. Analysis of the text involves examination of the verbal styles used by the narrator and the social actors (the rescue team and the public) to convey stereotypical or evaluative traits of New Zealand national identity.

(ii) An examination of discourse practice looks at the processes of text production, distribution and consumption. It asks why a text might be constructed in a certain way when alternative choices might have been made. In the case study of *Rescue 1*, I firstly discuss its standard format and narrative structure within the conventions and constraints of television, looking at the editing process of camera footage, along with the music and dialogue that are used. This demonstrates how discourse practices within RTV create excitement and drama surrounding real-life emergency heroes in New Zealand. Secondly, I examine how the heroic rescue team attains positive values of 'ordinariness, informality, authenticity and sincerity' (Fairclough 2010 p. 158) through three forms of talk:

> *Narration* – the voice-over by the unseen narrator who mediates between the audience and the social actors;
>
> *Conversationalization* – whereby private world discourse of ordinary people (such as the narrator's interpretation of events, or the words or actions of a social actor) is infused into the public domain (medical discourse) contributing to the informalization of discourse of contemporary society (Fairclough, 2010);
>
> *Testimony* – where social actors speak for themselves as witnesses to an event.

Given that the permeation of other genres and discourses in the programme (interdiscursivity) are also examples of discourse practice (Fairclough, 2010), I highlight aspects of the drama, comedy, adventure movie, and travel log genres found in *Rescue 1*, as well as the promotional discourse used to appeal to the charitable nature of New Zealanders to support the good work of Auckland's helicopter service.

(iii) Sociocultural practice as a dimension of the framework looks at the wider conditions in which the text and discourse practice are embedded. It offers an interpretation of the 'construction of social identities and representations of the social world' through the text (Fairclough 2010, p. 172) by considering aspects such as 'the context of the situation, the institutional context and the wider societal context or "context of culture"' (Fairclough 2010, p. 95). Looking at *Rescue 1*, I explain the discourse about national identity that has historically dominated in New Zealand society and its impact on the production of locally-made programmes.

Although Fairclough describes his three-dimensional framework in the above sequence, this is not to say that the presentation of data necessarily follows suit as this is dependent on a study's research question and the different types of texts analysed. In fact, Fairclough (2010) often explains his own analyses either by firstly referring to discourse practice or by integrating analysis of all three dimensions. My analysis of *Rescue 1* introduces features of discourse practice first because of their role in shaping the programme. Text analysis is referred to as it becomes relevant. The third dimension of sociocultural practice is in turn considered in a concluding section to explain the relationship between discursive processes and social processes.

Data

Rescue 1, which provides the data for my analysis, is produced by the New Zealand company Great Southern Television and broadcast on TV2 in prime time. It won the award for best factual television series in the New Zealand television awards following its first screening in 2009 and has rated highly since then. *Rescue 1* takes viewers on real-life helicopter emergency rescue missions covering Auckland and its surrounding environs. The city is located on an isthmus on the country's North Island: to the east is the Waitemata Harbour with its numerous recreational islands and, to the west are the more treacherous surf beaches and the Manukau Harbour. The potential for accidents to occur is high, particularly when considering New Zealanders' passion for an active, outdoor recreational lifestyle which can be accessed right at their doorstep. The helicopter is often the fastest and most efficient way to transport accident victims to hospital. Its distinctive red and yellow colouring means it is easily identifiable by the public, who are aware of its lifesaving ventures as it flies high in the sky. I have selected one episode of *Rescue 1* (the third in series one) for detailed analysis. This episode, typical of the emergency rescue genre, is used to demonstrate the discursive nature of the programme's nation-building function.

Analysis

Format and narrative structure

The discursive practices of format and narrative structure are standard in each *Rescue 1* programme and can therefore be considered representative of the series. They are important elements in the programme as they provide the framework for the construction of the discourse of national identity. They transform the day-to-day activities of the helicopter rescue team – those unsung heroes attempting 'dangerous and thrilling rescues' (TVNZ n.d.) – into a dramatic story that seeks to excite and transfix the audience. The rollercoaster of emotion the programme seeks from the audience is reliant on the conflict-resolution structure of the narrative, which is instrumental in reinforcing a worthy and honourable image of New Zealanders.

The standard format of each *Rescue 1* programme involves the presentation of several 'missions' that, although occurring at different times, are brought together for dramatic effect and to show the variation in the types of accidents the rescue team attends. In the episode under analysis, the call-out emergency stories are:

1. A stick has pierced the jugular vein of four-year-old Jack,[1] who has fallen from a tree during a sunny day out at the beach with his family. He has internal bleeding – a life-threatening situation – and must be ventilated before being airlifted to hospital.
2. A BMX rider and the driver of a quad bike have collided while racing in the sand dunes of a military bombing range. Both patients are concussed and one has broken bones.
3. A 47-year-old intoxicated hiker has fallen and gashed his head in a large lava cave on the island of Rangitoto – a dormant volcano in Auckland's Waitemata Harbour. The helicopter is unable to land on the uneven terrain and the rescue team must winch the patient up and fly him to hospital.

This is how the 23-minute-long episode, broken into three parts of six, seven and then nine minutes long, was structured to cater for TVNZ's requirement for advertisement breaks:

Prologue (standard introduction for all episodes including music, voice-over, visuals and title)
    Mission One (introduction)
    Mission Two (introduction and climax)
Ad Break
    Mission Two (resolution – reaching hospital)
    Mission Three (introduction and climax)
    Mission One (intensification of situation and climax)
Ad Break
    Mission Three (resolution)
    Mission One (further intensification of drama maintaining climax, then resolution)

Epilogue (summary of outcomes of all three patients, concluding with a personal tribute to the *Rescue 1* team by a family member or friend of the patient).

This format plays an essential part in structuring the drama in which the missions are related and the *Rescue 1* team members are positioned as heroes. The narrative works within the constraints of the broadcaster's requirements to include advertisement breaks by building the tension to the end of each section to retain audience attention. Attempts to create anxiety in the audience are assisted by a consistent theme of the race against time to save people's lives: not only in locating accident victims in the New Zealand landscape, but also in administering medical treatment in the face of adverse conditions – climate, terrain, or victim's injuries for example – and airlifting them to hospital as quickly as possible. This sense of urgency dominates the programme, enhanced by linguistic, audio and visual features such as the narrative, background music, camera work and film editing which often involves speeded-up footage of the helicopter flying over spectacular terrain. This has the hallmarks of an adventure movie, indicating the discursive practice of introducing other genres and discourses into RTV, which is discussed later.

Although working within a minimal narrative structure (Todorov 1971) in each individual mission that moves from a state of equilibrium (team at the helicopter base), to one of disequilibrium (accident scene), and finally back to equilibrium (resolution of the drama), the storytelling is more complex in its need to create, and increase, the tension that makes the audience appreciative of the *Rescue 1* team members. Rather than relating each mission in a linear fashion, the story weaves back and forth between the emergencies to maintain the heightened interest of the audience. As a result, the audience must consume a great deal of information to follow the three stories of ordinary New Zealanders – people just like them – in dangerous and often life-threatening situations. Anxiety and a sense of jeopardy about what will happen next surrounds each mission as the story climaxes in each section but is then temporarily suspended to allow for commercial breaks. Apart from exposing the audience to advertisements, this suspense-building narrative device of a 'cliffhanger' – a standard technique commonly found in serial programming such as soap-operas (Lorenzo-Dus 2009) – keeps viewers riveted to the channel during this break by increasing their desire to find out what will happen next. The more serious the mission, the more time is allocated to the individual story.

While mission one in this episode involves the most serious case of the young patient Jack, the weaving of the two other missions into the narrative delays the resolution of the first and thus intensifies the drama. The concept of time is handled purposively as the anxiety has increased for the audience in the first instance through fast music and accelerated camera action and, in the second instance, through the narrative structure with the emphasis on the 'race' to the location. Yet, once the team arrives on site the pace of the programme slows as the members assess the situation and make the necessary plans for patient recovery. In each mission, the audience is positioned as voyeurs in that they become privy to the conversations between team members and accident victims or witnesses to assess what has happened, or between the medics and rescuers as they decide what action needs to be taken. As a result the audience hears various forms of talk which are commonly found in RTV, as I next discuss.

Forms of talk

The different forms of talk expressed by the narrator and social actors, in conjunction with the sound and camera work, reinforce the discourse of RTV as 'authentic' and 'real'. Three forms of talk are discussed in this section – narration, conversationalization and testimony – demonstrating the discursive practice of the mixing of discourses and other programme genres in RTV.

(i) *Narration*

The viewers are reliant on the voice-over of the unseen narrator – given a degree of familiarity through his New Zealand accent – to guide them through each episode. The narrator's responsibility lies not only in introducing each episode, but also in providing important information about each rescue mission to help the audience keep track of the stories in the fast-paced, action-packed narrative. The narrator, therefore, mediates between the audience and the *Rescue 1* team describing the accident that has occurred, explaining the concerns about the injuries and the actions of the *Rescue 1* team, and repeatedly updating each scenario as the narrative jumps between missions. But, as Fairclough (1995) points out, such narrative is external to the actual events and the narrator should not be seen as just one person employed to voice the part and to personalize the programme. The narrator is in fact a collective of the production team, such as the cameraman, director, editor, and writer, who all play their parts in the construction of the programme and how meaning is conveyed.

To illustrate this point, specifically the interplay of the standard narrative, camera work and sound to construct New Zealand national identity, I focus here on the prologue of *Rescue 1* (reproduced in Table 7.1). The words in this prologue have remained the same throughout each series, but some of the images, although similar in the action they convey, have been changed in later series, presumably as a way of updating the programme and giving it a fresh look. The opening shot sequences in this prologue launch the viewer straight into the drama, which is a key discursive feature of the programme. This entails voice-over narrative using a variation of tone and pauses for dramatic effect, along with rapidly changing camera shots that match the rhythm of the accompanying upbeat music, and the background sound of the rotating helicopter blades – all working to gain audience attention from the first second.

The voice-over narrative informs the audience of the who, what, where and how of the emergency helicopter team, matched with the selected images. It immediately sets up the *Rescue 1* team members as heroic lifesavers within a New Zealand context. The pronoun 'they' in the first sentence –'they call them *Rescue 1'*– assumes viewer familiarity with the *Rescue 1* service. The viewers are also told what to expect of the team through adjectives such as 'elite' and 'highly trained', denoting their professionalism and the high esteem in which they are held. Establishing the team's experience in relating the 500 'mercy missions' carried out each year implies that these are rescues for which New Zealanders should be grateful. The skill involved in *Rescue 1's* job covering the Auckland metropolis is immersed in a sense of the urgency associated with emergency situations, emphasized through the camera work and the fast-paced music. Later, the narrator introduces the team members of each mission by name, with individual photographic shots, and clarifies their roles as either pilot, advanced paramedic or crewman. This is somewhat reminiscent in style of the selection of the expert teams in fictional television dramas such as *Mission Impossible*. This personalizing of the *Rescue 1* team is designed to enable the audience to establish a connection with these people, who look like ordinary New Zealanders yet demonstrate 'extra-ordinary' (specialized) knowledge, skills and courage in their job.

Location is also an important feature of the programme in constructing New Zealand identity. The nation is flagged in the scenery which acts as the backdrop for *Rescue 1* missions and at times the sweeping aerial camera shots of dramatic land-, sea- and city-scapes seem reminiscent simultaneously of a travel log, tourism promotion video and an

Table 7.1 Rescue 1 prologue – opening scenes

Time (in seconds)	Voice-over narrative	Images
1		Speeded-up aerial shots from viewers' perspective inside the helicopter as
2		it flies along the coastline. Cut-away shots zooming in to close-up of turning helicopter blades, then to
3	*They call them Rescue 1.*	view of the helicopter parked at its base headquarters. Zoom-in shots to pilot inside helicopter. Cut to team member rushing on board.
5		Helicopter door slides shut. Team member runs from landed helicopter with medical bag in hand.
6	*An elite team of highly trained*	Inside shot of pilot at helicopter controls high above rural landscape.
	patrolmen and	Montage of exterior and interior shots
9	*paramedics*	from various angles showing rescue team loading a patient on a stretcher into the helicopter.
10	*who fly over*	Montage of six exterior aerial action
	500 mercy missions a year	shots of helicopter viewed from above
13	*and*	with water and landscape below.
14	*patrol*	Speeded-up motion shots approaching Auckland city with its multi-storey buildings lit up against the night sky.
15	*a 150km zone around*	Satellite map of New Zealand, zooms in on Auckland to show location.
	the bustling	Aerial shots show helicopter flying
17	*Auckland metropolis.*	above the city of Auckland in daylight.
18	*Working to save lives*	Shots inside helicopter with close-up of stretchered patient's head rolling from side to side. Team member puts oxygen mask on patient.
	in a relentless race against	Aerial view from above looking at helicopter hovering above the city. Cut to three different views of helicopter flying in the city.
21	*time* (pause)	Zoomed-in, full-screen close-up of the helicopter with its main sponsor trademark on its side, and the bold
	In (pause)	words RESCUE painted across it.

(*continued*)

Table 7.1 Continued

Time (in seconds)	Voice-over narrative	Images
23 24–29 30	*Rescue 1* (narrator slows dialogue for emphasis)	Fast-paced montage of scenes of various rescue missions, patients, team members being winched up into a helicopter holding patient, interior shot of pilot looking out of helicopter window to city below, team attending to patient, rugged coastal scenery, close-up of helicopter blades, helicopter landing on roof of hospital. Includes flashes of maps, and captions such as 'serious car crash', 'emergency storm warning', 'Auckland hospital' over these shots. Full screen graphic of *Rescue 1* programme title.

adventure movie. The narration in the prologue establishes the size and the area of the '150 kilometre zone' for which the helicopter is responsible and uses the adjective 'bustling' to imply how 'busy' and 'in a hurry' people are, and the noun 'metropolis' (in conjunction with cityscape visuals) to indicate Auckland's importance as a city. Auckland's location is highlighted in the prologue with the camera zooming in on it in the graphics of a satellite aerial map – much like the Google map process. The expanse and contrasting terrain of Auckland's city, beach and rural landscapes are reinforced as the area is magnified, creating a sense of how spread out it is, but also of the varied recreational lifestyle it offers. Much of this sense of the nation would be lost if viewed only from ground level.

In the prologue, however, the audience barely has time to concentrate on one aspect as the scenes transition rapidly from helicopter, to scenery, to rescue team members, to patients, to the aerial shots of Auckland city and to flying to the hospital. This dramatic visual sequencing ties in with the narrator's description of 'the relentless race against time' implying the urgency of the situation and the necessity of speed to save lives, as well as reinforcing a sense that the crises never stop and that the *Rescue 1* team never gives up. There are more than 40 camera-shot or scene changes within the 30 second prologue for the audience to consume and 'get a taste' of what the programme will offer. This presentation of the prologue, and in fact the whole programme, enables the audience to experience the action of the *Rescue 1* team recognizable as New Zealanders with fortitude and skill. However, as the programme progresses, it is the different forms of talk and the variation of verbal styles of the narrator, the emergency team members and other social actors which continue to construct a particular version of New Zealand national identity.

As noted earlier, the three interweaving missions in the narrative of each episode keep the audience in suspense and waiting for the outcome of each scenario. In what follows, I concentrate on the first rescue mission, involving young Jack. Jack's accident, in fact, is the most heart-wrenching given that he is only 4 years old. His story dominates this episode – it is the first to be related and the last to be resolved. I focus specifically on the combination of different voices and shifting verbal styles to demonstrate that it is through the words of New Zealanders – whether the narrator, the rescue team members themselves, or Jack's mother who gives testimony about what happened – that the identity of local heroes is negotiated.

(ii) *Conversationalization*

Conversationalization in *Rescue 1* involves the breaking down of the barriers of official medical/emergency services discourse into a more informal and 'lay' discourse for the viewers. This seeks to bring a closer relationship between the rescuers, the social actors and the audience, which is indicative of what Fairclough (2010) refers to as a trend towards the increasing informalization of modern society. The following extract demonstrates conversationalization at work through the interaction between different verbal styles – the dramatic narrative of the unseen narrator, the medical talk of an on-the-ground ready response paramedic (RRP), and a *Rescue 1* paramedic's shift to a 'lifeworld discourse' (that is, the talk of ordinary people) when communicating with Jack's mother:

The camera focuses on young Jack whose jugular vein has been pierced by a stick. In this sequence of shots he is lying limp under the trees at the beach with the *Rescue 1* emergency team working alongside the ground rapid response paramedic (RRP) who has arrived at the scene:

Narrator voice-over:

They need to paralyse Jack's throat so a tube can be passed between the vocal cords and he can be artificially ventilated...

The procedure is extremely dangerous but it is the only way to keep Jack alive...

RRP [out of camera shot]:

[sub titles on screen accompanied by sound of voice]

He's still got a GCS of what people?... one... two... one...five. I'm going to give him one milligram of Midaz... Just to knock him out.

[Jack's mother can be heard as she leans over him trying to encourage a response: 'Where's Mummy's hand? Where's Mummy's hand?']

RRP: *Can somebody please explain to Mum what we are going to do?*

Close-up shot of *Rescue 1* paramedic speaking in the direction of Jack's mother: *We are just going to give him a relaxant you see... just to relax him a little bit... We are just going to stick a tube into his throat there...*

In the first instance the narrator acts as a medical interpreter in explaining the technical term 'artificial ventilation' as passing a tube between Jack's vocal cords. This narration heightens tension in foreshadowing the potential danger of this delicate procedure. The combination of the adverb 'extremely' and the adjective 'dangerous' are effective in suggesting that the procedure requires great skill. The gravity of the situation is further intensified when the narrator uses the words 'only way' to indicate that there is no other option to keep Jack alive. The audience is well aware that the rescue team offers the only hope for Jack's survival.

In the next part of the extract, the audience takes a 'fly on the wall' or observational position as it listens in on conversations involving medical discourse. This entry into the domain of emergency workers' medical discourse gives insight into the skills and level of knowledge crucial in their work. The RRP's subtitled medical talk to her colleagues provides evidence of the shared knowledge and expertise of the medics as they communicate with each other and work collectively to save Jack. Even though some of the terminology is unlikely to make sense to the audience, subtitles are sometimes used purposively to convey the technical language. As the RRP consults with the team about the level of medication she is about to administer, this contrasts with the words of Jack's mother as she hovers over him desperately seeking a response. Hearing the anxious words of 'where's Mummy's hand?' the RRP seeks assistance from the *Rescue 1* paramedic to reassure Jack's mother, which he does by shifting from medical discourse to a lifeworld discourse.

The paramedic informalizes his discourse by telling Jack's mother that their intention is simply to 'stick a tube into his throat'. He chooses his words carefully and his repetition of the hedge 'just' in 'just going' and 'just to relax' seeks to minimize the danger of the procedure. His explanation that the medical team is going to 'relax him a little bit' is in contrast to the narrator's earlier alarmist description informing the audience that it would be necessary to 'paralyse his throat'.

This scene demonstrates the paramedic's use of different frames of talk where he shifts his 'footing' within an interaction to keep 'different circles in play' (Goffman 1974, p. 156; see also Chapter 2 and Chapter 11 in this volume). On the one hand, he positions himself as a professional paramedic using and responding to medical discourse to communicate with the rest of the rescue team involved in an extremely dangerous emergency procedure. At the same time, he must interact with a different audience – Jack's mother. To respond to her anxiety he must alter his footing by re-aligning his verbal and non-verbal behaviour. This shift from using medical discourse to a lifeworld discourse involves addressing Jack's mother directly, adopting a calm voice, and using clear and reassuring language based on his own 'knowledge schema', that is, his expectations of her as a mother and how he thinks she might respond to 'people, objects, events and settings in the world' (Tannen and Wallat 1999, p. 334).

An appropriation of a lifeworld discourse is also evident in the *Rescue 1* team members' direct address to the audience, which occurs frequently in the series. This creates a sense of familiarity with the viewers as information about an accident is explained to them in simple terms. As the discourse is informalized and shifts to take on the characteristics of chat or a casual conversation with the audience, the likable personalities of the emergency team emerge, showing their human side. In one instance, for example, the camera focuses on the pilot who, on returning from a mission, has been abandoned by the others to clean the inside of the helicopter. He jokes to the camera:

Oh yeah the crewmen always just bugger off and leave the pilot to clean up – the lazy pricks!

This injection of comedic discourse into the narrative presents a moment of light relief from the intensity of drama by illustrating the playful camaraderie amongst the rescue team. It also creates a sense of the rescuers as ordinary people – even heroes have to clean. Although the rescue team's on-camera activities have portrayed them as heroes, the pilot's comment and actions minimize the concept of them as being extra-ordinary. This demonstration of humbleness is a characteristic that has been linked to the New Zealand psyche (ASB 2013).[2] The pilot's self-construction of the rescuers as ordinary people just carrying out their everyday job is reinforced by combining colloquial language, banter and swear words in a humorous context. In fact the word 'bugger' was the subject of much public discussion in early 1999 when it was used as almost the sole text in a Toyota car advertisement. The popularity of a New Zealand farmer (portrayed by an actor) repeatedly exclaiming 'bugger' in a humorous way resulted in its legitimization and subsequent referencing frequently in conversation and in the media (Bell 2001).

The informalization of society through conversationalization, as illustrated in this section, contributes to enabling the audience to identify the rescue team in the programme as 'real', 'ordinary' New Zealanders. Conversationalization is in fact the 'general rejection in contemporary societies of elite, professional, bureaucratic practices' resulting in a 'valorisation of ordinariness, naturalness, being oneself and so forth in discourse and more generally' (Fairclough 2010, p. 542).

At the same time, the verbal styles of the narrator and the rescue team position *Rescue 1* members as heroes with the characteristics of intelligence, compassion and knowledge. But there are other social actors who also reinforce this, which I illustrate next via another form of talk, the testimony, of one of the social actors – Jack's mother (referred to from here on as JM).

(iii) *Testimony*

Testimony is a form of talk where people can speak for themselves (Fairclough 1995) and is a regular feature of RTV discourse, often conveyed through a social actor's direct address to the audience. The programme has been structured to include the testimony of an accident victim and/or one of their friends or family members at the conclusion of each *Rescue 1* episode to validate the importance of the emergency team. A social actor recalling what happened on the day provides a much more personal account of the mission than might be conveyed by the narrator and presents an opportunity to further construct heroic New Zealanders. In the story about Jack, his mother – now personalized through her first name appearing on screen – recalls the day of her son's accident. In particular, her testimony fills the gaps in the story of

Jack's air transportation to hospital by helicopter which the audience was unable to witness. The following extract relates her emotions as she tearfully describes her experience:

> *Jack's Mother (JM): I was just kind of willing that it would be okay...*
>
> *I had my head turned around just in between the seats of the helicopter watching that little chest go* [indicates up and down movement with her hand]...
>
> *My heart was just...I just thought – my God – I am losing my little boy and – no way – I just had to keep fighting in my mind....no way...*

JM's heart-wrenching testimony relating her fear of losing her son is intensified through the recollection of her actions and thoughts. Verbs such as 'willing', 'thinking', and 'fighting in my mind' indicate the intensity of her emotion as she flew with Jack to hospital for emergency surgery. JM's repetition of 'just' in association with these verbs that involve the mind rather than any physical action emphasizes how she draws on all of her inner resources to will Jack's survival, including a formulaic expression containing a biblical reference – 'my God'. Her use of first person singular pronouns demonstrates self-reflexiveness on her actions and the situation to form a biography or a narrative of the self (Giddens 1991), while her self-positioning in the role of the despairing mother is reinforced by her repetition of the adjective 'little' ('that little chest') and in conjunction with the possessive deteminant 'my' ('my little boy').

In constructing her own vulnerability, JM validates the service of the *Rescue 1* team in saving Jack. Her slow and deliberate on-camera monologue contrasts with the fast pace of the helicopter rescues that featured earlier in the programme. As she gives a blow-by-blow account of her fears and concerns, JM's testimony is interspersed with cutaway aerial scenes of the helicopter and flashbacks of the medics working to save Jack as he lay 'lifeless' on the ground beneath the trees. She recounts the anxious wait at the hospital as surgeons cut open Jack's chest and worked relentlessly to locate and repair the hole in his jugular vein. But as the emotion intensifies with JM's drawn out narrative, the close-up camera shot that has concentrated on her face during the testimony gradually pulls back and widens to reveal Jack sitting on her lap, smiling and playing with a toy helicopter – a symbolic representation of the rescue service that saved his life. This story has reached its happy conclusion and Jack's mother ends with a personal tribute. Her testimony becomes a testimonial for Jack's rescuers:

> *JM: If they hadn't come and he would have had to have gone by ambulance or taken him in the car we wouldn't have Jack. They got there just in time!*

JM's use of pronouns in these final two sentences brings together three types of identity: 'they' for the *Rescue 1* team which, as has already been stated, represents them as heroes that at least by now everyone should know; 'he' for Jack – the link between the team and his mother; and 'we' – indicating that, if Jack had died, it would have affected others and not just her. In evaluating what might have happened using past-tense conditional clauses and posing the alternate forms of action (*if they hadn't... he would have... we wouldn't have*) JM paints the scenario of what was a very near tragedy.

The audience are made to become co-members of JM's lifeworld as they are drawn sympathetically to her story and are encouraged to feel grateful for the helicopter service, which one day might also help them. However, JM's testimony indicates a multifunctional role of the *Rescue 1* programme in its discursive practice of introducing yet another discourse into the RTV realm. Besides entertaining and informing the audience using elements drawn from the genres of drama, comedy, adventure movie, and travel log, *Rescue 1* also has a strong promotional discourse. Regardless of the advertising of *Rescue 1's* sponsor – a bank – through its logo prominently displayed on the sides of the helicopter, the programme is in fact a public relations exercise for the helicopter emergency service (operated by The Auckland Helicopter Trust).

Commentary from one of the *Rescue 1* producers published on the charitable trust's website relates his personal experience of being saved by an emergency helicopter service. This, he says, motivated him to approach the Trust's marketing and public relations manager about making the programme ('TV producer sees the light' 2012). The programme's promotional objective is further evidenced in more recent series of *Rescue 1*, where a mobile telephone number for texting donations features in the end credits. Such promotion further enhances the nation-building role of *Rescue 1* as it calls on New Zealanders to show a caring attitude and a sense of gratitude by supporting the local heroes.

The various forms of talk identified in this section as part of the analysis of both text and discursive practice demonstrate the shifting of verbal styles and the conversationalization that impacts on the heroic construction of the *Rescue 1* emergency team. It is those enviable New

Zealand characteristics of being skilful, capable, strong and knowledge-able, yet down-to-earth and genuine, which can be found in other contexts about national identity, that I now discuss as part of the socio-cultural dimension of this programme.

Sociocultural practice

So far, this analysis has considered the dimensions of text and discourse practice of Fairclough's CDA framework and how these have contrib-uted to the construction of the *Rescue 1* team as heroes. The third dimension of sociocultural practice is used to interpret and explain the findings in a wider context by considering the impact of discourses about national identity found in New Zealand history and particularly in political rhetoric.

At the beginning of this chapter, I noted Billig's (1995) theory suggest-ing that we are reminded of our homeland on a daily basis through less obvious forms of nationalism – symbols and habits of language. This includes banal words, such as 'I', 'you', 'we', 'here' and 'now', or signs such as flags, the weather, the beach or, in the case of this research, the rescue helicopter. Such daily reminders of 'us' are often unobtrusive because they are so familiar, but Billig also notes that drawing attention to them through research creates a greater awareness about the depths of our identity and, in particular, how we construct ourselves as differ-ent from 'them' – that is, other nations and peoples. This has particular relevance to New Zealand which, as a small country, has historically sought to display its uniqueness and to position itself as remarkable in a global setting.

National identity, in signifying collective belonging, is a desirable concept, given that the guaranteed existence of the nation through signs and symbols 'preserves its distinct identity, and provides a ter-ritory where the national culture and ethos are dominant' (Byrnes 2007, p. 2). The signing of the Treaty of Waitangi in 1840 between the indigenous Maori and the British Crown established New Zealand as a bicultural nation, though the early settlers still regarded them-selves as British, working hard to recreate a superior England (Binney, Bassett & Olssen 1990) or a 'better Britain' (Belich 2001) in the South Seas. A more distinct New Zealand identity reinforcing a pioneering, hardworking and innovative spirit set within the scenic beauty of the nation developed slowly over time as the country's loyalties and trade ties to Britain lessened particularly in the latter part of the twentieth century. Simultaneously, a rise in Maori nationalism and increased diversity through immigration caused feelings of insecurity amongst some New Zealand Europeans, who felt their status as the dominant ethnic group was threatened (Belich 2001). Although progressive governments addressed these feelings through the promotion of tolerance and understanding of others, certain myths and symbols about New Zealanders remained from those early years and were reassuring that the older identity had not been forsaken.

Historian Michael King (2003) noted that New Zealand characteristics that exist in contemporary culture, such as the country being 'special' with its lakes and beaches, the informal social attitudes, the do-it-yourself approach to home maintenance and the resourcefulness of people, reiterate long-held attitudes and values of New Zealanders. Given that these characteristics form the basis for positive imaginings about the nation, it is not surprising that they resurface in political rhetoric under the guise of 'traditional Kiwi values' (Brash 2004) or mainstream, core values (Murphy 2007). Those characteristics of honesty, tolerance, friendliness, humour, informality and helpfulness that denote New Zealand national identity are foregrounded in other discourses, such as advertising (Bell 2001; Bulmer & Buchanan-Oliver 2010) and local surveys about New Zealanders (Larson 2008). They also feature in the recollection of national role models or heroes such as Mt. Everest conqueror Sir Edmund Hillary, yachtsman Sir Peter Blake and aviator Jean Batten (King 2003).

Although challenges of increased globalization and the state's desire for New Zealand to become a competitive player in the world economy prompted the Labour-led government in the early 2000s to rebrand the nation with a 'shared national purpose' and an economic vision for the future (Skilling 2010, pp. 178–9), the same positive characteristics of national identity remained embedded in this discourse. Evidence for this can be found in texts such as a government budget media release in 2006, which focused on areas for investment that concentrated on abstract characteristics such as independence, strength, pride, responsibility, creativity, competitiveness and commitment to success, with the objective of positioning New Zealand positively on the world stage. As the release stated, 'It is about who we are, what we do, where we live, and how we are seen by the world' (New Zealand Government 2006).

King's (2003) observation that the 'dominant realities of New Zealand life... are still those of a mainstream Pakeha [New Zealand European] culture in which almost every citizen has to participate' (p. 513) still rings true and is well engrained within many different texts whether books, advertisements, policy documents or television programmes. So almost ten years following King's comment, when we analyse

RTV programmes such as *Rescue 1* in a wider sociocultural context we become aware of the interdiscursive presence of a dominant discourse about national identity that has been constructed and reified by government, institutions and media over many years.

Rescue 1 in review

In applying Fairclough's three-dimensional framework of CDA to *Rescue 1*, I have argued that New Zealand's economic, social and cultural background has been instrumental in the way the discursive practices of this RTV programme have impacted on the social construction of national identity in New Zealand. My examination of the text and of discourse practice in *Rescue 1* has shown how the producers have created a fast-paced and exciting programme based on the real-life missions of Auckland's helicopter rescue team. Their use of format, content, narrative structure, and features drawn from a range of genres and discourses assures that *Rescue 1* meets the broadcaster's objective for high ratings on prime time television[3] in a competitive media environment. At the same time it fulfils broadcast policy's call for more local content that relates stories about New Zealanders.

Analysis of three forms of talk in *Rescue 1* – narration, conversationalization and testimony – has shown how different verbal styles and some of the linguistic features used by the narrator and the social actors serve to create a greater sense of commonality amongst New Zealanders. Informal discourse contributes to constructing a national identity that unites New Zealanders by confirming faith in what might be seen as the unique and distinctive characteristics of the nation. On another level, *Rescue 1* operates in a promotional capacity in not only show-casing the desirable scenery and lifestyle of New Zealand and in featuring advertising of its main sponsor's logo (see Table 7.1, at 21 seconds), but also in its reconstitution of the audience from citizens to consumers in validating the need for public donations to support the helicopter rescue service.

Importantly, through CDA I have shown how the discourse of RTV contributes, perhaps unknowingly and in a banal way, to a complex nation-building process. It draws on a dominant discourse about national identity, taking many historically based characteristics and perceptions surrounding the New Zealand psyche and recontextualizing them in the promotion of the *Rescue 1* team members as local heroes – constructed to epitomise what it means to be New Zealanders in the twenty-first century. In essence, this highlights a consistent theme within CDA – that discourse is not only socially shaped, but also socially shaping (Fairclough 1995, 2010).

Notes

1. Social actors' names have been changed for confidentiality purposes.
2. The downplaying of heroism has also been evident in other factual television contexts as shown in Pardo and Lorenzo-Dus's (2010) study of documentaries and news reports containing narratives from British soldiers from the Falklands War. These narratives expressing extraordinary actions as being part of a soldier's everyday duty were sometimes used to mitigate the ugly side of war.
3. Mid-year ratings in 2010 showed that *Rescue 1* was the second-highest rating programme on TV2 with 509,400 viewers (Lewis 2010).

References

Anderson, Benedict (2013) *Imagined Communities: Reflections on the Origins and Spread of Nationalism* (London: Verso).

ASB/ASB Bank (2013) ASB survey reveals Kiwis overindulging on 'humble pie'. ASB press release, 18 February 2013. Scoop News website. Retrieved 3 March 2013 from http://www.scoop.co.nz/stories/BU1302/S00567/asb-survey-reveals-kiwis-overindulging-on-humble-pie.htm.

Aslama, Minna & Mervi Pantti (2007) Flagging Finnishness: Reproducing national identity in reality television. *Television & New Media*, 8: 49–67.

Belich, James (2001) *Paradise Reforged: A History of the New Zealanders from the 1880s to the year 2000* (Auckland: Allen Lane, Penguin Press).

Bell, Allan (2001) 'Bugger!' Media language, identity and postmodernity in Aotearoa/New Zealand. *New Zealand Sociology*,16(1): 128–50.

Billig, Michael (1995) *Banal Nationalism* (London: Sage Publications).

Binney, Judith, Judith Bassett & Erik Olssen (1990) *The People and the Land: Te Tangata Me Te Whenua: An Illustrated History of New Zealand, 1820–1920.* (Wellington: Allen and Unwin).

Bonner, Frances (2003) *Ordinary Television* (London: Sage Publications).

Brash, Don (2004) *Nationhood.* Address to the Orewa Rotary Club of New Zealand, 27 January 2004. Retrieved 5 August 2010, from http://www.national.org.nz/article.aspx?articleid=1614.

Bulmer, Sandy & Margo Buchanan-Oliver (2010) Experiences of brands and national identity. *Australasian Marketing Journal*, 18: 199–205.

Byrnes, Giselle (2007) Rethinking national identity in New Zealand's history. Conference paper at the Dominion Status Symposium. Retrieved 28 March 2010, from http://www.nzhistory.net.nz/files/documents/giselle-byrnes-national-identity.pdf.

Fairclough, Norman (1995) *Media Discourse* (London: Edward Arnold).

Fairclough, Norman (2003) *Analysing Discourse: Textual Analysis for Social Research* (London: Routledge).

Fairclough, Norman (2010) *Critical Discourse Analysis: The Critical Study of Language* (Harlow: Pearson Education Ltd).

Fishman, Mark & Gray Cavender (eds.) (1998) *Entertaining Crime: Television Reality Programs* (New York: Aldine de Gruyter).

Giddens, Anthony (1991) *Modernity and Self-identity: Self and Society in the Late Modern Age* (Cambridge: Polity Press).

Goffman, Erving (1974) *Frame Analysis* (New York: Harper & Row).

Goldson, Annie (2004) A look in: Documentary on New Zealand television. In Roger Horrocks & Nick Perry (eds.), *Television in New Zealand: Programming the Nation* (Oxford: Oxford University Press), pp. 240–54.

Hill, Annette (2000) Fearful and safe: Audience response to British reality programming. *Television & New Media,*1(2): 193–213.

Hill, Annette (2005) *Reality TV: Audiences and Popular Factual Television* (London: Routledge).

Horrocks, Roger (2004) Construction site: Local content on television. In Roger Horrocks & Nick Perry (eds.), *Television in New Zealand: Programming the Nation* (Oxford: Oxford University Press), pp. 272–85.

Kavka, Misha (2004) Reality estate: Locating New Zealand reality television. In Roger Horrocks & Nick Perry (eds.), *Television in New Zealand: Programming the Nation* (Oxford:Oxford University Press), pp. 222–39.

Kavka, Misha & Stephen Turner (2004) Kiwiflatmates.com: When reality tv goes wrong. In Claudia Bell & Steve Matthewman (eds.), *Cultural Studies in Aotearoa New Zealand* (Melbourne: Oxford University Press), pp. 251–67.

Kavka, Misha & Amy West (2004) Temporalities of the real: Conceptualising time in reality TV. In Su Holmes & Deborah Jermyn (eds.), *Understanding Reality Television* (London: Routledge), pp. 136–53.

Kilborn, Richard (1994) How real can you get? Recent developments in 'reality' television. *European Journal of Communication*, 9: 421–39.

King, Michael (2003) *The Penguin History of New Zealand* (Auckland: Penguin Group).

Larson, Virginia (2008) The North and South survey: She'll be right (fingers crossed). *North and South,* July; 40–5.

Le, Thao & Quynh Le (2009) Critical discourse analysis: An overview. In Thao Le, Quynh Le & Megan Short (eds.), *Critical Discourse Analysis: An Interdisciplinary Perspective* (Hauppage, NY: Nova Science Publishers), pp. 3–16.

Lealand, Geoff & Helen Martin (2001) *It's All Done with Mirrors: About Television* (Palmerston North: Dunmore Press).

Lewis, Rebecca (2010) Reality TV a big turn on. *The New Zealand Herald,* 4 July 2010. Retrieved 2 June 2012 from http://www.nzherald.co.nz/entertainment/news/article.cfm?c_id=1501119&objectid=10656363

Lorenzo-Dus, Nuria (2009) *Television Discourse: Analysing Language in the Media* (Basingstoke and New York: Palgrave Macmillan).

Murphy, Nigel (2007) A failure of multiculturalism? New Zealand's reaction to the French and Australian riots of October–December 2005. *British Review of NZ Studies*, 16: 93–127.

New Zealand Film and TV (2011) *Reality TV.* Retrieved 1 June 2012 from http://newzealandfilmtv.co.nz/reality-tv/.

New Zealand Government (2006) *Budget 2006 Theme 3 – National Identity.* Media release (18 May). Retrieved 9 September 2012, from http://www.scoop.co.nz/stories/PA0605/S00409.htm (2006).

NZOA (1990) *Broadcasting Commission Annual Report 1989/90.* Retrieved 3 June 2012 from http://www.nzonair.govt.nz/media/32331/ar%2089-90.pdf.

Paltridge, Brian (2000) *Making Sense of Discourse Analysis* (Gold Coast, Queensland: Antipodean Educational Enterprises).

Pardo, Laura & Nuria Lorenzo-Dus (2010) The Falklands/Malvinas 25 years on: A comparative analysis of constructions of heroism on Argentinean and British television. *Journal of Mulitcultural Discourses*, 5(3): 253–70.

Skilling, Peter (2010) The construction and use of national identity in contemporary New Zealand political discourse. *Australian Journal of Political Science*, 45(2): 175–89.

Tannen, Deborah & Cynthia Wallat (1999) Interactive frames and knowledge schemas in interaction: Examples from a medical examination and interview. In Adam Jaworski & Nikolas Coupland (eds.), *The Discourse Reader* (New York: Routledge), pp. 332–48.

Todorov, Tzevetan (1977) *The Poetics of Prose*, translated by Jonathan Culler. (New York: Cornell University Press).

TV producer sees the light. (5 July 2012) *TV Guide*. Retrieved 9 September 2012 from http://www.rescuehelicopter.org.nz/index.php/news/news-headlines/218-tv-producer-sees-the-light.html

TVNZ (n.d.) Rescue 1. Television New Zealand website. Retrieved 14 January 2013 from http://tvnz2013.co.nz/detail.php?id=99 (n.d.).

TVNZ Charter (n.d.) Television New Zealand website. Retrieved 30 May 2012 from http://tvnz.co.nz/view/tvnz_story_skin/111535?format=html

Varcoe, Jude & Karin Curran (2009) NZ On Air, public perceptions research, 2008/2009. Retrieved 1 June 2012 from http://nzonair.govt.nz/media/40394/public%20perception%20executive%20summary%202008-2009.pdf

West, Amy (2006) *Here and now: intimacy, immediacy and authenticity in New Zealand's reality television*. Unpublished doctoral thesis, The University of Auckland.

Part III
Reality Television and Aggression

8
(Im)politeness and exploitative TV in Britain and North America: *The X Factor* and *American Idol*

Jonathan Culpeper and Oliver Holmes

Introduction

Biressi and Nunn (2005, p. 2) note that 'the highly visible presence of ordinary people in "unscripted" situations is both the watermark of reality TV (RTV) and arguably an explanation of its success with audiences'. RTV creates entertainment through its likeness to what audiences recognize as *real*. That sense of the 'real' can be enhanced by the use of language that is unscripted (not predictable), unstandardized (not conforming to prestige dialects or styles) and personal (not selected for a public audience). Such language is entertaining: the unpredictable, non-conforming and personal make for exciting TV. Impoliteness is not dependent on such language, but it is typically associated with it. It is thus not surprising that the rise of RTV has seen a rise in impoliteness on TV, as many lay commentators have bewailed (see Lorenzo Dus *et al.* in this volume, for academic evidence). Indeed, one might note that over the last two decades traditional chat, quiz and talent shows have developed popular exploitative genres (see Chapter 1). The key feature that separates the exploitative from standard non-exploitative genres is that the former are characterized by impoliteness, something which has been a focus of recent research (e.g., Culpeper 2005; Bousfield 2008; Lorenzo-Dus 2009; Garcés-Conejos Blitvich, Lorenzo-Dus & Bou-Franch 2010; Garcés-Conejos Blitvich, Bou-Franch & Lorenzo-Dus 2013).

This chapter focuses on the highly successful UK exploitative talent show *The X Factor* and its equivalent in the USA, *American Idol*. We investigate the nature of the interactions that constitute these shows, and, specifically, whether there are interactional differences between the two – differences which might shed light on more subtle ways in which the show is constituted differently in different cultural contexts.

We stress that we are not aiming at pan-generalizations about any culture, as characterizes much traditional work in cross-cultural pragmatics (for instance, Blum-Kulka, House & Kasper 1989). People belong to many different cultures, and those cultures are not closed, coherent and neatly bounded (see, e.g., Mills 2009). This is not to say that labels such as 'North American' or 'British' culture have no meaning; they are labels that people use to make sense of behaviours. What we pursue are cultural 'rich points', a notion proposed by Agar (for instance, 2006). Rich points are 'moments of incomprehension and unmet expectations' (Agar 2006, p. 4). Agar (2006, p. 5) suggests that if one observes '*patterns* across certain kinds of persons and/or certain kinds of situations', we get a clue that something is 'neither universal nor unique nor random', but part of a 'culture of those persons in that situation' which is '*not* understandable to an outsider'. We will focus on the singing auditions of our shows, specifically the interactions that occur after a contestant's performance and where impoliteness is often perceived to be. What triggers our hunch that these are cultural rich points is the unexpected – from our British perspective – quantity of supportive politeness in the USA show, even if the contestant's performance had been terrible by any estimation.

(Im)politeness

Broadly speaking, politeness involves the maintenance or enhancement of social harmony through the expression of positive evaluations of the target and/or through doing what is accepted, expected or wanted (for instance, displaying consideration for the target by mitigating imposing or unwelcome acts). We take an eclectic approach to politeness in our analyses. Like many researchers, including the classic Brown and Levinson (1987 [1978]), we will deploy the notion of 'face'. The English idiom 'losing face' refers to the damage one's public image suffers, often resulting in humiliation or embarrassment. Although currently differing views are emerging (see, for example, the special issue on face, identity and (im)politeness in the *Journal of Politeness Research*, 2013, volume 9, issue 1), much modern writing draws upon the work of Goffman (1967, p. 5), who defines face thus:

> the positive social value a person effectively claims for himself by the line others assume he has taken during a particular contact. Face is an image of self delineated in terms of approved social attributes.

Note that it is not just the positive values that you yourself want, but what you can claim about yourself from what *others* assume about you. All this, of course, is pertinent to the talent show: the contestants' face is publicly exposed, the judges articulate positive or negative evaluations of contestants, and contestants demonstrably experience humiliation and embarrassment. Whilst the concept of face is particularly useful, we will occasionally complement it by referring to Spencer-Oatey's (2008, p. 13) concept of 'sociality rights', involving perceived rights and obligations in interaction. With regard to how politeness might be realized, traditional politeness models have proposed strategies for achieving politeness constituted by words and grammar. For example, using an interrogative structure (as opposed to an imperative one), hedges, or a friendly or deferential vocative could all potentially increase the politeness of a request. We take a broader view that politeness can be achieved by any kind of behavioural signal, including non-verbal signals.

Although the study of impoliteness has a fairly long history (specifically, in the guise of the study of swearing; see, for example, Montagu, 1973), only relatively recently is momentum truly gathering, as evidenced by, to name but a few fairly recent items, Bousfield (2008), Bousfield and Locher (2008), Garcés-Conejos Blitvich (2010) and Culpeper (2011). Here, we are concerned with the opposite of politeness, namely the disruption of social harmony through the expression of negative evaluations of the target and/or through doing what is not accepted, expected or wanted. Culpeper (1996) proposed various strategies for achieving impoliteness, including 'Ignore, snub the other', 'Condescend, scorn or ridicule', 'Call the other names', 'Invade the other's space', 'Seek disagreement' and 'Put the other's indebtedness on record'. Although not without their problems, these have proved an effective means of analysing various types of data (see, e.g., Cashman 2006; Bousfield 2008; Lorenzo-Dus, Garcés-Conejos Blitvich & Bou-Franch 2011; and Chapter 9 in this volume). Of course, just as with politeness, impoliteness can be achieved by any kind of behavioural signal.

Two important points about both politeness and impoliteness need to be borne in mind. (Im)politeness is not something simply created by a speaker or actor. Targets of (im)politeness are not passive but active co-constructors of (im)politeness (see Hutchby 2008). Both politeness and impoliteness are often reciprocated (see Culpeper 2011, pp. 203–7). Hence, in British culture, 'how are you' might receive the response 'how are you'; 'hello' might receive the response 'hello'; 'thank you' might receive the response 'thank you' or a polite acknowledgement such as 'it's a pleasure'. Politeness puts pressure on the target to reciprocate in kind (for instance, not only comply with a request, but produce subsequent similarly polite behaviours). As for impoliteness, Culpeper, Bousfield & Wichmann (2003, p. 1562) noted that reciprocal impoliteness may be the best way of restoring face (for instance, 'fuck you' might receive a response 'fuck you'). Alternatively, direct contradiction is common (for instance, 'you're an idiot' might receive a response 'no I'm not'). And there are also various ways of deflecting or accepting the impoliteness (see Culpeper *et al.* 2003, pp. 1564–8 and Bousfield 2008, pp. 195–200). Of course, how one might respond to politeness or impoliteness will be more or less constrained by the context. Theoretically, one might think, game show contestants do not have the right to respond in kind to impolite judges.

Context is in fact crucial for all politeness and impoliteness. It is at the conjunction of behaviour and context that politeness or impoliteness is generated and understood. An utterance such as 'eat your food' would hardly count as impolite if said by a parent to a child, but would more than likely be so if said by the child to the parent. Power, as illustrated by this example, is particularly important. Furthermore, 'mezzo' level notions of context are particularly important for (im)politeness. Terkourafi (for instance, 2005) deploys the notion of frame; Garcés-Conejos Blitvich (2010) the notion of genre; and Culpeper (2005) the notion of activity type. Culpeper (2005, p. 66) suggests 'the (im)politeness value of an utterance is partly determined by the activity of which it is a part'. The notion of 'activity type' is central to our chapter (Levinson 1992[1979]). In a nutshell, an activity type (such as a seminar, a family dinner event, or a birthday party) is a collection of particular speech acts (such as requests, questions and offers) that stand in particular pragmatic relationships to each other and have become a relatively conventionalized whole. Game shows are one such activity type. In exploitative game shows, a certain degree of impoliteness is sanctioned; it is both accepted and expected. This is not to say that the effects of impoliteness are necessarily neutralized for all participants. As elaborated in Culpeper (2005), people are not good at factoring the context to the extent that it can overrule the salience of impolite behaviours.

Activity types

The notion of activity type, according to Levinson (1992, p. 69), refers to:

> [...] any culturally recognized activity, whether or not that activity is coextensive with a period of speech or indeed whether any talk takes

place in it at all [...] In particular, I take the notion of an activity type to refer to a fuzzy category whose focal members are goal-defined, socially constituted, bounded events with *constraints* on participants, setting, and so on, but above all on the kinds of allowable contributions. Paradigm examples would be teaching, a job interview, a jural interrogation, a football game, a task in a workshop, a dinner party, and so on.

What do these constraints consist of? Levinson gives some clues, referring to, for example, 'participants, setting' and, most importantly of all, 'allowable contributions' (1992, p. 96). He is less explicit about what constitutes a 'contribution', but it seems from his analyses that they are conceived of largely in terms of particular speech acts. Subsequent researchers have sought to clarify and detail the ways in which activity types are interactionally constituted. Thomas (1995, pp. 190–2), for example, provides a list of elements, including:

- the goals of the participants
- allowable contributions
- the degree to which Gricean maxims are adhered to or are suspended
- the degree to which interpersonal maxims (cf. Leech's Politeness Principle, 1983) are adhered to or are suspended
- turn-taking and topic control
- the manipulation of pragmatic parameters (for instance, power, social distance)

These elements are the analytical framework for our qualitative analyses, though, rather than 'interpersonal maxims', we will focus specifically on (im)politeness.

It is important to note, however, that activity types have a cognitive side as well as an interactional side. Levinson writes:

Because of the strict constraints on contributions to any particular activity, there are corresponding strong expectations about the functions that any utterances at a certain point in the proceedings can be fulfilling. (1992, p. 79)

[Activity types] help to determine how what one says will be 'taken' – that is, what kinds of inferences will be made from what is said. (1992, p. 97)

Activity types involve both what interactants do in constituting the activity and the corresponding knowledge they have of that activity.

Their cognitive dimension helps account for interpretative variability across cultures. Those 'strong expectations' are normative expectations. But normality, as Sarangi (2000, p. 7) reminds us, is not an all or nothing affair: activity types have fuzzy edges (less prototypical elements) and focal points (more prototypical elements). Furthermore, knowledge about activity types is acquired through culturally mediated experience. Bednarek (2005, p. 690), discussing the related notion of frames, remarks:

> [...] knowledge structures are not innate but acquired through socialization, 'constructed' out of experience (out of our own experience or accounts of experiences by others and so on), and are hence both *diachronically* and *culturally dependent*.

Differences in the experiences of different cultural groups or even different individuals will lead to them having activity type knowledge with different focal points. Hence, participants with different experiences (for instance, different cultural backgrounds) will have different conceptions of what might appear to be the same activity type (see Culpeper, Crawshaw & Harrison 2008, for an illustration). Here lies a connection with cultural rich points, those '*patterns* across certain kinds of persons and/or certain kinds of situations', which are part of a 'culture of those persons in that situation' and '*not* understandable to an outsider' (Agar, 2006, p. 5). These patterns can be conceived of in terms of activity types. People who interact but do not share the cultural experiences that led to an activity type being formed may well experience 'moments of incomprehension and unmet expectations' (Agar 2006, p. 4).

Exploitative and reality television

Of course, not all genres of RTV are exploitative. As Hill (2007, p. 197) points out:

> Not all reality TV is about humiliating people. In Britain, and to a lesser extent Sweden, there are a variety of categories that make up popular factual television, from health-based reality programmes about people overcoming accidents and illness, to inspiring examples of people experiencing new things, to tips and advice on gardening or buying a home, all of which can present a positive message to viewers.

Furthermore, exploitation is not simply one way, that is, the programme makers exploiting their subjects, as Holmes (2004, p. 111) remarks:

> [...] Reality TV's relationship with the 'ordinary' person is used to invoke different positions in debates over the form. For example, according to its critics the relationship between Reality TV and its participants is fundamentally 'exploitative': either the programme-makers exploit their subjects through 'manipulation' and editorial control, or the participants exploit the programme in an entrepreneurial bid for media exposure.

However, it must be acknowledged that exploitation is a major component. Hill (2007, p. 197) continues:

> [...] some of the most dominant types of reality TV have been the reality game show (*Big Brother, Survivor*) and reality talent show (*Pop Idol, X Factor*). These formats, and their celebrity cousins, have concentrated on putting people in difficult, often emotionally challenging, situations. Audiences have come to categorise this specific type of reality TV as 'humiliation TV'. [...] *Pop Idol* includes the regular humiliation of contestants in their auditions to be on the show.

This observation is echoed by Turner (2010, p. 2): 'the media's interest in their reality and gameshow contestants is at least as exploitative as it is enabling'.

Culpeper (2005) uses the term 'exploitative TV' specifically to refer to exploitative chat, quiz or talent show genres that are structured to maximize potential for impoliteness. Face is sensitive to public exposure, and talent show contestants have face invested in their performances. Those performances take place in public, in front of the immediate audience (judges, television crew, and others) and the distant TV audience, thereby creating the potential for dramatic face loss. Moreover, the situation is not conducive to a good performance: typically, auditions take place in a fairly large room without backing music or microphone, and in front of the glaring judges. Crucially, performances and performers are not scored or ranked, but given a verbal assessment, where there are opportunities for impoliteness. Impoliteness is the linguistic tool by which the face of contestants is exploited, thereby achieving humiliation. Of course, it is a game and the judges may well just be playing the role of being impolite. However, as noted above, this contextual mitigating factor may not be adequately brought into play.

One of the key functions of impoliteness is entertainment: somebody (in talent shows, usually the contestants) is the target of impoliteness from somebody else (in talent shows, usually the host(s)) for the purpose of entertaining a third party (in talent shows, the studio and TV audience) (Culpeper 2011, pp. 233–5 and 249–52). However, there is no guarantee that the mere presence of impoliteness within a TV show will result in entertainment. Impoliteness is triggered in many different ways. It is often the more creative, less conventional types that appear with unusual frequency in exploitative TV shows, as Culpeper (2005) demonstrates. Moreover, just as with humour, entertainment is highly culture-sensitive. One symptom of this is the fact that particular exploitative shows have not been equally successful in all cultures, sometimes leading to them being adapted or withdrawn. *The Weakest Link*, for example, has been a huge global success, its format having been franchised to 42 countries across the world. But its acerbic and disrespectful style did not lead to straightforward success in all cultures. According to the website www.realitytvworld.com, the version aired in India lasted barely a year, because of falling ratings, whilst the version aired in Hong Kong required 'softening' of the presenter's style in order to bring it more into line with cultural norms, because of complaints.

The shows *The X Factor* and *American Idol* are singing talent shows. Both originate from *Pop Idol*, a British television series which first appeared on ITV in 2001. A second series followed in 2003, and the format has been franchised around the world as the 'Idol' series (cf. *American Idol*). For reasons of copyright and ownership, in the UK it was relabelled *The X Factor*. Simon Cowell, a judge on all of these programmes, has developed a reputation for his impolite remarks on contestants' performances. His autobiography is called *I Don't Mean To Be Rude, But: The Truth about Fame, Fortune and my Life in Music* (Cowell 2004). The reputation of these shows for impoliteness coupled with their enactment in many different countries makes them good candidates for cross-cultural impoliteness exploration.

Data and method

Our core dataset is sourced from three DVDs: *The X-Factor Revealed: The Greatest Auditions Ever* (2004), *The X-Factor: The Greatest Auditions Ever* (2005), and *The Best and Worst of American Idol: Series 1–4* (2005). Of course, these particular auditions are likely to have been selected for their entertainment value, and thus quite possibly contain more confrontation than 'normal' auditions. However, what is important for us is that the datasets are comparable, as our purpose is to identify differences. Regarding participants, in the British version, the judges include Simon Cowell and two other judges, one British (Sharon Osbourne) and one Irish (Louis Walsh), interacting with British contestants. In the American, the judges include Simon Cowell and two American judges (Randy Jackson and Paula Abdul) interacting with American contestants.[1]

Forty auditions were fully transcribed, 20 from *The X Factor* and 20 from *American Idol*. We only transcribed full auditions (not, for example, cases where the auditionee voluntarily gave up and walked off). Moreover, we collected each set of 20 so that it comprised ten that could be classified as 'successful' (that is, the auditionee progressed), and ten that could be classified as 'unsuccessful' (that is, the auditionee failed to progress). Two successful auditions and two unsuccessful auditions from each set of 20 were randomly selected using an online random number generator. This gave a total of eight auditions that we will analyse qualitatively in the following section.

In the process of transcribing the 40 auditions and qualitatively analysing them, we developed four hypotheses about general differences between the two shows.

(1) *The X Factor* judges are more likely to make critical comments on the auditionees' performances and the auditionees are more likely to accept them than their *American Idol* counterparts.
(2) The *American Idol* judges mitigate their initial face threat more often than *The X Factor* judges in the unsuccessful auditions.
(3) The *American Idol* judges give more advice to the unsuccessful auditionees than *The X Factor* judges.
(4) The *American Idol* judges applaud successful auditionees more often when they leave the room than do their *The X Factor* counterparts.

The point of these hypotheses is that they pinpoint possible differences in the focal points of the culturally embedded activity type, differences that could constitute cultural rich points with their associated moments of incomprehension and puzzlement. In the penultimate section of this chapter, we address these hypotheses with quantitative analyses. In order to boost frequencies, we have included a supplementary dataset of 20 interactions. We created this dataset from YouTube clips of the shows, following the same selection criteria as the DVD data (except, for reasons of availability, the period, which was 2006 to 2008).[2] The supplementary data did not change the nature of emerging patterns but made them more pronounced. Even so, each individual piece of statistical evidence may not carry much weight. However, each piece is pointing in similar directions.

The X Factor and *American Idol*: Qualitative analyses of (im)politeness in the post-performance interactions

Four successful auditions

The X-Factor: Rowetta's audition[3]

R: I'm begging (1.0) you can't not put me through ((shrugging arms)) (0.5) my mum will go mad ((breaks out into song again, this time a different song)) (5 seconds) don't say you are not through because you are mad (.) that's wrong .hhh the x-factor is *mad* ((breaks out into song again in which she points at each judge separately as she steps closer to them))
((scene fades out with clock ticking and then returns))

R: (xx) ((walks closer to the judges)) (1.0) put me through

L: no:::

R: why

L: you are dreadful

R: you know I am not dreadful

L: you are (0.5) you are quite mad as well

R: thank you ((nods and then walks backwards looking sad with head down))

SH: I don't think she's dreadful

R: please Sha[ron]

L: [she is]

R: thank [you]

SH: [I don't] think you are dreadful (.) I think you have [got a real old] belters voice

L: [she is [mad as] well]

R: [please] (1.0) I'm thirty eight .hhh please .hhh I (.) this is it for me ((arms behind back))

S: Sharon yes or no

SH: yes

R: thank you ((smiles with arms behind back)) (0.5) will Louis say no

L: ((leans over desk pointing to his chest)) I would hate to have you in my category=

S: =Rowetta occasionally you have to make a decision [which you are going to]

R   [I'll never speak I swear]
S: regret
SH: Rowetta shut up
S: you do (1.5) which is why I am going to say::: (4.0)
R   please
S: yes (1.5) you are through to the next round (2.0) off you go (.)
        leave ((points to door))

Prior to this interaction, Rowetta has taken three turns, self-selecting each time. Her unusual, for this activity type, hogging of the conversational floor does not go unnoticed. Sharon comments 'do you stop for air Mrs', implying, via Grice's (1975) maxim of quantity, that there is evidence she does not. Rowetta invades space (an impoliteness strategy noted in Culpeper 1996, p. 358), not only conversational space, but also physical by walking closer to the judges despite not being invited to do so. She violates perceived equity rights (Spencer-Oatey 2008), specifically, rights to space. This potential impoliteness is combined with direct commands, 'don't say you are not through' and 'put me through', which could be seen as challenging the power hierarchy in this context. Louis intensifies his rejection of Rowetta's commands by saying 'no:::' with an elongated vowel. Rowetta defends by asking for justification from Louis, who replies with a conventional face threatening insult 'you are dreadful'. Note the ambiguity here: 'dreadful' could refer to the performance and/or her nature (this kind of ambiguity is a feature of many insults in our data). Rowetta defends through direct contradiction, 'you know I am not dreadful' (this could also be seen as a challenge to the power hierarchy, as she presumes to assert what the judges know). Louis continues with a further conventional insult, 'you are quite mad', which is clearly geared towards her nature. Surprisingly, Rowetta responds by saying 'thank you', with prosody apparently reinforcing sincerity. Non-verbally, she displays sad acceptance. Certainly, polite thanks makes further criticism and insult from Louis more difficult (because of the reciprocal nature of (im)politeness it is more difficult to be impolite to somebody who is being polite than the opposite).

Sharon does not follow Louis. Perhaps sensing an injustice, she intervenes by directly contradicting Louis's insults, 'I don't think you are dreadful'. She builds on this point with a face-giving compliment: 'I think you have got a real old belters voice'. Although Sharon agrees to Rowetta progressing, Louis implies 'no': 'I would hate to have you in my group'. Not being liked, not being allowed to be a member of a group, or presumably thought fit for a group violates perceived association rights (Spencer-Oatey, 2008, p. 16). Simon, despite being interrupted, follows Sharon in agreeing to Rowetta progressing, though it is not fulsome agreement, as he hints that he thinks he may come to regret it. Finally, one might note the direct and perfunctory way with which Simon commands Rowetta to leave ('off you go (.) leave'), exercising his power, although we should remember that Rowetta has proven herself somewhat resistant to direction.

The X-Factor: Peter and Emma

PE: ((sing for 47.0 seconds))
S: thank you very much (0.5) Louis
L: I like Peter's voice (1.5) ((looks down, then back at the duo)) I think he has got a really good soulful voice
P: thank you
L: I didn't like your voice ((shakes head looking at Emma)) (2.0) Emma I didn't like you very much but I think *Pete* has got a great voice ((nods head))
E: thank you ((twitches and strokes her hair, her bottom lip moves and she nods her head slowly and looks towards the sides))
S: Sharon
SH: yeah I love your voice Peter (0.5) you've got an amazing voice but I (.) I love the chemistry between the two of you=
S: =well you are not equal singers and that's what it is isn't it

Simon's 'thank you very much' is mere conventional politeness, and a discourse signal marking the transition from the performance to the evaluation. Louis gives face to Peter, 'I like Peter's voice', reinforcing his act with a third-party compliment: 'I think he has got a really good soulful voice'. Peter acknowledges the face enhancement ('thank you'). The fact that Louis did not include Emma in his comments already allows an impolite implicature, via Grice's maxim of quantity, that he liked Emma less. He then attacks Emma's face in a somewhat mitigated fashion by shaking his head and saying 'Emma I didn't like you very much'. 'Very much' allows the possibility of a scalar implicature, via the maxim of quantity, that she is still liked but not very much. Despite this, and despite it being a context in which contestants know that impoliteness is likely, Emma gets visibly upset. This is consistent with the argument made in Culpeper (2005) that the salience of impolite behaviour engulfs contextual factors that theoretically mitigate impoliteness (for instance, it's all a game). Nevertheless, she says 'thank you'. This usage is not as odd as Rowetta's, given the possible implicature that she is still liked. Still, it appears to accept rather than rebuff the implied face attack, possibly because it is a way of taking the focus off the face attack and warding off further attack. Sharon, like Louis, gives face to Peter: 'love your voice Peter (0.5) you've got an amazing voice'. But she explicitly diverges from Louis (cf. 'but') by praising the two as a group: 'I love the chemistry between the two of you'. In contrast, Simon is critical of the group: 'you are not equal singers' implies, via the maxim relation, that Emma is the worse singer. Sharon and, in fact, Louis vote for them to progress, but Simon does not.

American Idol: Fantasia

F: ((sings for 70 seconds))
P: thank you Fantasia
R: this girl can sing ((points and makes eye contact with Fantasia))
P: you got to watch your pitch though
F: yeah= ((nods))
P: = you got to watch your pitch a little bit but you are definitely a *strong wonderful* singer
F: thank you
P: you're welcome (1.0) Simon
S: well you see the girl has got a great voice it's just I always um er try and imagine people at this stage *where you go:::* ((folds arms and looks at Paula)) throughout the competition
P: ((nods head facing Simon))
R: hmmm (.) hmmm=
S: =because you have such a *distinct* voice (1.0) erm and what at one moment is deemed as an advantage will then *possibly* become a disadvantage because you are what you are
P: [right]
R: [well] Simon do you guys want to hear another song or what do you think
S: yeah I would be interested yeah
R: yeah
P: with different colours shoot away
F: erm I could do Tina Turner rolling
S: ok
F: ((sings for 25 seconds))
P: there you go (3.0) excellent ((while Fantasia sings))
R: ((holds his hand up))

P: ((puts both hands out with thumbs up)) thank you now that's what I was talking about that's what I was talking about
R: yeah she's great
P: yes or no
R: I definitely say this competition would be far less interesting without her
P: I totally agree absolutely
S: I actually think you're one of the best we have ever had
F: woo ((claps hands together smiling))
S: that's what I think
P: guess what
S: I really do
P: guess what that means ((signalling to Fantasia))
S: you are through=
F: =I'm going to Hollywood
R: yeah ((begins to clap and cheer))
P: you are going to Hollywood ((claps and cheers))
F: ((smiles and claps back))
P: congratulations

Randy gives face with a compliment: 'this girl can sing'. The fact that Fantasia is referred to in the third-person, 'this girl', may suggest that Randy is seeking confirmation from his fellow judges, but it could also be a device to intensify the compliment. Third person compliments in the hearing of the target, just as third-person insults (cf. Culpeper 2011, p. 135), notionally have a stronger claim to reflect the speaker's true views, as they are more remote from the kind of strategic modification an addressee as sole target might require. Paula offers qualified agreement: 'you got to watch your pitch though'. But her overall positive assessment is clear: 'you are definitely a strong wonderful singer' not only deploys the emphatic 'definitely', but also carries stress on 'strong' and 'wonderful'. Fantasia acknowledges the compliment with 'thank you'. Simon is also complimentary and adopts the third-person strategy: 'the girl has got a great voice'. The three judges are like-minded, and support each other in their positive evaluations (Paula nods; Randy voices agreement, 'hmmm'). However, Simon does strike a (somewhat convoluted) note of pessimism: 'what at one moment is deemed as an advantage will then possibly become a disadvantage because you are what you are'. This leads to Fantasia being offered a chance to sing another song, which results in fulsome compliments from the judges, including 'now that's what I was talking about' (twice), 'she's great',

'I definitely say this competition would be far less interesting without', and 'I actually think you're one of the best we have ever had'. There are also conventional non-verbal positive signals: Paula puts out both hands with thumbs up, and the judges clap. Clapping is a conventional non-verbal way of signalling approval of a performance, somewhat like saying 'congratulations', as indeed Paula does in the final turn. All this contributes to 'exaggerating approval' (Brown & Levinson 1987[1978], p. 106).

American Idol: Justin

P: I think you did just a wonderful joyful audition I love everything about you you have got great confidence
J: thank you ((nods head smiling))
P: and presence and I'll say you're a star in the making
J: thank you so much
S: and this is the point where I am going to admit that the American talent is probably better than the English talent

Paula opens with effusive approval: 'I think you did just a wonderful joyful audition'; 'I'll say you're a star in the making'. Likewise, Simon delivers face enhancement. His statement 'this is the point where I am going to admit that the American talent is probably better than the English talent' implies, via the maxim of relation, that Justin is better than the singers he has judged in England. Given this compliment involves violating his own face, assuming he has face invested in 'English talent', it is praise indeed. Paula puts a hand to Simon's forehead, as if to check whether he has a fever. All three judges vote for Justin to progress and clap as he leaves the room.

Four unsuccessful auditions

The X Factor: Two anonymous females

A1: ((sings for 20 seconds))
S: ((holds hand up signalling stop)) no::: (1.0) girls (.) individually you sound horrendous together you sound even worse I don't think anyone would ever pay to want to hear you sing
A1: oh they do [they do and they]
A2: [they have done]
A1: have done for a few years and at the end of the day you want something different *we've got* whatever *you want* we can give *you* ((motions hand from herself to the judges)) (2.0) we've got it

L: you are certainly different
A1:   yeah
L: but in the *wrong* way
S: yeah it's just the worse image I have ever seen=
SH: =it's very very dated *honestly* girls the look is= ((shakes head and tilts head))
S: =horribly so
SH: really
A1:   what are you actually looking for then ((points to judges))
S: the absolute opposite of you (0.5) it's awful
SH: you are not unique you are not stars you are not special=
S: =and never will be (1.0) girls it's a no

Simon interrupts, both verbally and non-verbally, the auditionees' singing, a possible violation of equity rights, specifically, the right to space in which to perform their song. Simon continues with conventional insulting negative assertions, 'individually you sound horrendous together you sound even worse' and 'I don't think anybody would ever pay to want to hear you sing', the former intensified by parallelism ('X you sound Y') and the latter by the adverb 'ever'. The auditionees directly contradict Simon. Louis picks up on their claim to be 'different', a feature which they clearly meant to be positive, but the ambiguity allows Louis to exploit 'garden path' impoliteness effects. After allowing supportive engagement from an auditionee ('yeah'), he cancels the implicit positive meaning: 'but in the *wrong* way'. Simon picks up this negative note ('yeah'), and produces a negative evaluation, 'it's just the worst image I have ever seen', something which flouts the maxim of quality (it is improbable that he has really compared the auditionees with all the bad images he has ever seen) and implicates that they look extremely bad. Sharon negatively evaluates their appearance: 'it's very very dated'. Apart from intensification through the repetition of 'very', a flout of the maxim of manner, interestingly, this clause is fronted, a further flouting of the maxim of manner, and further intensification of the assertion (compare with 'honestly girls the look is very very dated'). Sharon's adverbials 'honestly' (which is stressed) and 'really' serve to strengthen the epistemic claim that their look is indeed dated. Simon supports and intensifies Sharon's negative evaluation ('horribly so'). In defence, the auditionees ask the judges 'what are you actually looking for?' Simon responds with implicational impoliteness saying 'the opposite of you', implicating, via the maxim of relation, that they have none of the positive values associated with *The X Factor* stars, and adds an explicit conventional negative assertion: 'it's awful'. Sharon, picking up the idea of opposites, uses a series of parallel structures ('you are not X') to reinforce their lack of positive qualities. Simon continues this, adding an intensifying 'and never will be'. Normally, there is a voting procedure, but Simon declares on behalf of everybody: 'it's a no'. The auditionees enact the defensive strategy of 'opting out on record' (Culpeper *et al.* 2003, p. 1566) by walking out.

In fact, the auditionees re-enter in order to attempt to negotiate the verdict. Similar strategies ensue. Interestingly, an auditionee's defensive strategy is to attempt to reverse the power positions, 'just feel sorry for them', something which implies that the judges are an object of pity. Somewhat like previous extracts, later the other auditionee says 'thank you very much', with prosody suggesting sincerity. Perhaps at this point there is acceptance that they are not going to go any further.

The X Factor: Female duo

<pre>
       ((sings for 19 seconds))
A1:   oh see we cocked that right up didn't we oh never mind
S: Fiona why I found this difficult is because you look like the girl on
       what's the programme with Matt Lucas
L: Little Britain
A1:   VICKY POLLARD ((turns to face the girl who is being called this))
S: do you know who I mean
SH: Vicky Pollard
S: Vicky Pollard ((laughs and holds hands in the air))
A2:   do I look like her
A1:   yeah but no but yeah
S: yes
A2:   oh thanks ((laughs))
S: you do ((laughs))
A2:   so I look like a man
SH: NO
S: no no no no no you don't look like a man you look like a man
       dressed as a woman
A2:   so I look like a drag
A1:   ((turns away laughing))
S: you do a bit (1.0) girls if I am being honest with you the act isn't
       great and the image is is is horrendous
A1:   huhh
L: you looked like the odd couple from the minute you walked in
S: you look like a stretched version of her ((points to the taller one))
</pre>

Simon's comment, 'you look like the girl on what's the programme with Matt Lucas', is neutral with respect to politeness (if one cannot guess who he is talking about). Once it is established that it is Vicky Pollard, negative implications can be drawn through the maxim of relation (Vicky Pollard is a caricature of an ugly 'chav' played by a man). Auditionee 2's response is 'oh thanks', but said with exaggerated prosody signalling insincerity (she also laughs). 'Insincere agreement' is a regular defensive strategy (Culpeper *et al.* 2003, p. 1566). But Simon reaffirms his belief, 'you do'. The auditionee challenges Simon to make explicit the point of comparison: 'I look like a man' (with rising intonation). Sharon denies this, and in so doing contradicts Simon's presumed implied insult. However, Simon also vigorously denies this, but then highlights the specific unflattering nature of the comparison: 'you look like a man dressed as a woman'. When asked to confirm whether she looks like 'a drag', Simon confirms using, a minimizer, 'a bit'. 'A bit' is a conventionalized politeness formula, regularly used to soften the impact of something for the target. Here, however, even being drag-like to a small degree could well be construed as offensive. In fact, a feature of Simon's (im)politeness style is to mix elements of politeness and impoliteness in such a way that the politeness does not counterbalance the impoliteness but instead strikes a note of sneering sarcasm (see Culpeper 2011, pp. 174–8, Garcés-Conejos Blitvich, Bou-Franch & Lorenzo-Dus 2013). He then asserts that the act as a whole 'isn't great' and that their image is 'horrendous', reinforcing the truth of the claim with 'if I am honest with you'. Louis takes over from Simon, saying 'you looked like the odd couple from the minute you walked in', which is amplified through a parallel structure by Simon 'you look like a stretched version of her'. All three judges vote 'no'.

American Idol: Tamika

R: erm I know you are not a super singer girl er do you sing in your church choir
T: ((moves head to one side)) yes I do
R: I think that=
S: =I was going to ask that
R: that that will be a better thing for you I don't think you are a solo singer at all I think
T: ((frowns)) I'm sorry
R: I don't feel that you are a solo singer I don't feel that you have a solo singer's voice
T: ((laughs)) that that I really don't believe I been singing solo ever since I could sing so for you to tell me that I should be singing in a

choir when I have been leading every song in my choir since I was
five years old for you to tell me that (.) ha I laugh at you
R: it is definitely only my opinion but=
T: =yes it is
R: but my expert music industry opinion
T: but like you said it is only your opinion ((points at Randy))

This interaction comprises 95 turns, making it one of the longest auditions we have encountered. Generally, unsuccessful auditions consume
more discourse space than successful, for the obvious reason that a
negative verdict is (a) more difficult to deliver (in Conversation Analysis
terms, one might see it as a dispreferred second, and as such is structur-
ally more complicated, involving pauses, prefaces, accounts, and so on),
and (b) often challenged by the auditionee. For reasons of space, we will
focus on representative discourse patterns.

Randy begins with the utterance 'I know you are not a super singer
girl [...] do you sing in your church choir?' We have met this kind of
strategy before. Although he asserts that she is not 'super', one can still
draw scalar implicatures such that she is nevertheless 'good' or 'okay'.
But, of course, if one has face invested in being 'super', this utterance
is still a potentially face-attacking insult. Simon acts collaboratively:
'I was going to ask that'. It emerges that the question about the church
choir is motivated by Randy's opinion that she should not be a solo
singer. This produces signals of disbelief from the auditionee, Tamika.
Not only does she frown, but the expression 'I'm sorry' feigns that she
has not heard properly: she implicates by flouting the maxim of quality that what Randy has said cannot possibly be true. She also offers an
account of why it cannot be true, and she laughs, explicitly directing
the laughter at Randy: 'I laugh at you'. This has obvious impoliteness
implications, as laughter is often directed at what is not serious or is
ridiculous. With humbleness, Randy responds 'it is definitely only my
opinion but'. Clearly, he is going to qualify his assertion ('but'), but is
impolitely interrupted by Tamika who exploits his humbleness: 'yes it
is'. Randy continues: 'but my expert music industry opinion'. He claims
expert power (see French & Raven 1959). This, however, is rebuffed by
Tamika, reminding him that he had said it was only his opinion. This
power struggle is played out over a further 31 turns. Simon steps in to
get a 'second opinion' from Paula, who says:

P: I'm kind of blown away by erm (1.0) just your (1.0) your erm self
righteousness and erm and your lack of respect for quite possibly
the network that chose us to be judges erm::: we are all we are all

in a field that it is just our opinion (.) however it is our opinion and we are able to give feedback to you that may just possibly may be constructive to you so that if this is really what you want to do it takes a little bit of constructive criticism and take it on to the next audition

Paula comments on the auditionee's impoliteness, notably the 'self-righteousness' and 'lack of respect'. What the auditionee is doing constitutes a challenge to the power hierarchy.

Simon gives his negative opinion: 'you are not good enough to go through to the next round'. This is rebuffed by Tamika: 'I have my own [opinion] you have yours'. What follows is somewhat surprising, at least from our perspective, coloured as it is by British cultural experiences; it is a cultural rich point:

P: carry your confidence and keep going forward
R: keep it
P: keep it and try
R: keep it
P: keep trying for the next audition (.) one thing about I know what it is like to be up there auditioning (.) I've been rejected bazillions of times but it never stopped me from going on to the next audition because eventually who knows you will get something

Despite the auditionee's impoliteness, Paula, supported by Randy, identifies a positive feature in Tamika, namely, her confidence. They urge her to 'keep' this, and continue 'trying' at auditions. Paula even expresses a kind of deference by putting herself down: 'I've been rejected bazillions of times'. It is conceivable that there may be a racial component at play here, given that Tamika is a black female and both judges are black and one is female. However, there is no evidence that this factor influences the judges in their interactions with other auditionees. Moreover, constructive advice, incorporating the 'keep trying' message to a degree, for auditionees whose singing is abysmal is a relatively frequent feature of the American judges (see the next auditionee's interaction and also the following quantitative section).

The following 20 turns revolve around Randy's advice that Tamika should take singing lessons, advice that is rejected:

T: ha oh I am hurt I am hurt and I am angry and I am really starting to get angry because for you to sit there ((arms stretch out pointing at Randy)) you are not standing where I am standing you are not coming where I am coming from (.) you are stood here being judges by people about how you sing (.) you are not singing are you and for you to tell me that I need lessons

S: Tamika Tamika

R: Tamika

T: it's Tami::ka Tami::ka

S: Tamika ((holds hand up))

T: Tami::ka

S: Tamika

T: it's Tami::ka

S: Tami::ka ((smirks)) please go to an audition where they lie to you (.) thank you very much indeed

T: oh no I am not about to go to an audition where they lie to me but

R: we are telling you the truth and you don't want to hear it

S: go there (.) thank you very much

R: thank you

T: ((begins to walk out)) thank you because you all got problems you all got mega issues

Interestingly, Tamika identifies the two emotions that are central to impoliteness, 'hurt' and 'anger' (Culpeper 2011, pp. 62–5). The particular kind of impoliteness Tamika articulates is 'affective impoliteness', specifically, the type which involves blaming a target for the particular negative emotional state one is in (Culpeper 2011, pp. 221–5). The following eight turns involve the particular pronunciation of Tamika's name. Simon mispronounces Tamika's name, saying [ɪ] instead of [iː] three times. The striking issue here is that Tamika does not let an incorrect pronunciation go, but instead repeatedly corrects Simon (and Randy). Again, Tamika is talking out of turn and challenging power relations. Simon signals that the interaction is at an end by saying 'thank you very much indeed'. The fulsome thanks is perhaps to underscore the end of the interaction, but could also contain a note of sarcasm. Simon has to reiterate his thanks, which Randy echoes. Tamika reciprocates with 'thank you'. Not only does this illustrate the power of automatic routines for finishing interactions, but also the powerful nature of reciprocal politeness. As if restoring the balance of her true impoliteness agenda, Tamika immediately follows with two insults 'you all got problems you all got mega issues'.

American Idol: Keith

S: Keith
K: yeah
S: erm last year I described someone as being the worst singer in America (.) I think you are possibly the worst singer in the world (1.0) based on that performance and I am absolutely serious (.) I have never ever heard anything like that in my life (1.0) ever
R: Keith that was horrific man (.) when you said you were interesting and unique you said a mouthful (1.0) oh my God
S: no but Keith you've got to hear yourself to believe it (1.0) there is nobody on this planet that sings like you (2.0) really
K: you got to be kidding me

In this audition, Simon and Randy are the only judges. Simon describes Keith as 'possibly the worst singer in the world'. Ostensibly, the epistemic marker 'possibly' mitigates the assertion that he really is 'the worst singer in the world'. However, the assertion is so extreme that is difficult to think that Simon is mitigating its impact on Keith or making the most accurate statement he can (he has not heard every singer in the world, so it is not possible to say that Keith is the worst singer). As with 'a bit' discussed above, 'possibly' has a sarcastic ring to it; it is not there as a sincere attempt to mitigate the impact of what he is saying. This is consistent with his meta-pragmatic comment 'I am absolutely serious'. Strictly speaking, Simon's comment 'I have never ever heard anything like that in my life' is neutral with respect to whether it is a positive or negative evaluation, but it is easy to infer the relevance of the comment in context (that is, he has never heard anything as bad as that in his life). In his following turn, Simon simply flouts the maxim of quality in making a hyperbolic statement 'there is nobody on this planet that sings like you', implicating, in this context, that Keith sounds worse than anybody else on earth. Randy supports Simon with an explicit face-attacking assertion 'that was horrific'. Interestingly Randy refers to Keith with the familiarizing vocative 'man', and later he uses 'dude'. Both reflect a certain sympathetic warmth towards Keith. Keith's response 'you got to be kidding me' counters the face-attack with the suggestion that it is non-serious.

A few turns later, the judges offer advice despite the criticism they have made:

R: what else do you love to do
K: well I like to dance ((holds heart))
R: just maybe you know get into dancing ((laughs to self))

Here, Randy 'attends to the hearer' (Brown & Levinson 1987, p. 103). Keith does not rebut the advice. He receives a verdict of 'no' from both judges, acknowledging the verdict with 'fine', though the prosody may suggest that he is less than happy with it.

Quantitative comparisons

In this section we report quantitative results for four hypotheses concerning general differences between the shows.

> (1) *The X Factor* judges are more likely to make critical comments on the auditionees' performances and the auditionees are more likely to accept them than their *American Idol* counterparts.

If criticism was given in a post-performance interaction, it was counted as one instance, regardless of how many criticisms were made. Only explicit acceptances of criticism were counted, that is, when it was realized as an (apparently sincere) 'thank you' or an explicit agreement with the stated criticism immediately after it was performed or in the closing interaction.

The results in Table 8.1 show that *The X Factor* judges in fact made criticisms only slightly more frequently than the *American Idol* judges. However, whereas only 40 per cent of the *American Idol* auditionees accepted the criticisms they received, 64 per cent of *The X-Factor* auditionees accepted theirs.

> (2) The *American Idol* judges mitigate their initial face threat more often than *The X Factor* judges in the unsuccessful auditions.

Mitigation is taken to mean any attempt (including clear non-verbal devices) during the post-performance evaluation by the judges to lessen the impact of their first impoliteness targeted at the auditionee. If

Table 8.1 The frequencies with which judges performed criticism and auditionees accepted it

Talent show	Amount of times criticism is given	Amount of times criticism is accepted
The X-Factor	22	14 (64%)
American Idol	20	8 (40%)

mitigation was given, it scored a count of one regardless of how many mitigating devices were used. Table 8.2 displays our results.

Though the numbers are low, the *American Idol* judges mitigate their initial impoliteness in the bad auditions nearly three times as much as *The X Factor* judges.

(3) The *American Idol* judges give more advice to the unsuccessful auditionees than *The X Factor* judges.

By advice, we refer to constructive suggestions about how to become a better singer or what ambitions to follow. Advice for the unsuccessful auditionees tends to be rare: the combined figure for both shows is only 22 per cent of the auditions. However, the *American Idol* judges offer advice more than twice as often as *The X Factor* judges (eight as opposed to three times).

(4) The *American Idol* judges applaud successful auditionees more often when they leave the room than do their *The X Factor* counterparts.

In only five of the 15 successful *The X Factor* auditions did the judges clap the auditionees, compared with 11 of the 15 *American Idol* auditions.[4]

Concluding remarks

Flowing from our qualitative analyses of the post-performance evaluations, we would highlight the following five points: Firstly, power emerges as key. Judges are in a position of power, not only by virtue of their expertise, but also their legitimate role: they are appointed by the TV company to evaluate contestants. However, as Locher points out, 'interactants with low status can decide to exercise power over people

Table 8.2   The frequencies of face threat mitigation in the bad auditions

Talent show	Amount of times impoliteness is given initially	Amount of times initial impoliteness is mitigated
The X Factor	15	3 (20%)
American Idol	18	11 (61.1%)

with relatively greater status' (2004, p. 31, see also pp. 208 and 218). So we see auditionees, especially in unsuccessful auditions, challenging the power of judges to deliver negative verdicts. This is done through impolite linguistic behaviours, such as interruptions, commands and even insults. Importantly, note that these behaviours violate the power hierarchy. This has the consequence that they are more likely to be perceived as impolite. An empirical study in Culpeper (2011, pp. 183–93) provided evidence that being in a position of high relative power licenses certain behaviours to the extent that they are not seen as impolite, whilst being in a position of low relative power results in the converse.

Secondly, both judges and auditionees use a range of (im)politeness devices. Compliments or insults can be couched in relatively conventional ways to enhance or attack face, and they can be performed verbally or non-verbally (for instance, clapping or laughing). However, as was shown, there is a considerable density of implicational impoliteness, and of rhetorical devices (for instance, ambiguities, parallelism). Creativity has a much stronger association with implicational matters. Discussing well-known truths expressed through implicit rather than direct statements, Carter comments 'their indirectness prompts interpretation and a "creative" inference of meaning' (Carter 2004, p. 134). And parallelism, of course, is one of the staples of literary stylistics (for instance, Leech 1985).

Thirdly, we repeatedly drew attention to the way in which the judges, in particular, acted in concert. If a judge diverged, it was highly marked. Yet, with a few notable exceptions (for instance, Graham 2008; Lorenzo-Dus, Garcés-Conejos Blitvich & Bou-Franch 2011), the bulk of (im)politeness research has focused on dyadic interactions. Calculating the face-damaging effects of an utterance in isolation, a move familiar in Brown and Levinson (1987) inspired research, makes no sense. We need to consider – to use a musical metaphor – the overall harmonics created through the concord (or discord) of (im)politeness work across interaction in context.

Fourthly, participants met impolite utterances with an array of responses from counter-impoliteness through to polite acceptance. Perhaps the most interesting strategy to have emerged is the use of 'thank you'. Sometimes it acts to close the interaction, and thus the flow of impoliteness. Sometimes as a response to an insult it may appear to 'accept' the face damage. Of course, this will partly depend on how it is said. Prosody can be manipulated to signal sarcasm. Even if it is said with apparent seriousness, one might suppose that the short-term pain of accepting an insult might be worth bartering for blocking further impoliteness. Because of the reciprocal nature of politeness, it is much more difficult for an interactant to respond with impoliteness.

Finally, (im)politeness studies rarely comment on the (im)politeness characteristics of individuals (see, however, Garcés-Conejos Blitvich *et al.* 2013, also on Simon Cowell). A characteristic of Simon Cowell that emerged in our data was his usage of mixed messages, specifically, the usage of conventionalized linguistic politeness in contexts where it cannot conceivably counterbalance impoliteness effects. For example, describing somebody as 'a bit' of a drag [queen], or referring to somebody as 'possibly' the worst singer in the world. We suspect that this insincere lip service to politeness phenomena may well have the opposite effect of exacerbating the impoliteness.

Our quantitative analyses were designed to capture recurring differences. Although we found that *The X Factor* judges only made critical comments slightly more often than those in *American Idol*, those comments were much more frequently accepted by their auditionees, perhaps because they considered that acceptance to be a more normal part of their activity type than did auditionees in *American Idol*. *The X Factor* judges mitigated their critical comments much less frequently than their *American Idol* counterparts, again perhaps because a higher level of criticism is expected within their conception of the activity type. In contrast, *American Idol* judges were much more likely to give advice for improving singing or fulfilling future ambitions in the case of bad performances, and also were likely to be much more fulsome in their celebration of good performances. As a whole, one can see that the post-performance feedback sessions are constituted somewhat differently in the two shows. Both shows involve a similar activity type, yet those activity types have somewhat different focal points, and those differences are potential cultural rich points. From our own British perspective, our hunch that the US show has a rather odd quantity of supportive politeness, relative to the UK show, is borne out. Moreover, the patterns we have observed seem to reflect different underlying values and attitudes. A stereotype maybe, but it is often said that North Americans place particular value on success and its achievement through personal endeavour (see Ash 1999, pp. 205–6, and Nussbaum 2005, Chapter 1). The notion of the 'American dream' encapsulates these values. It is not surprising then that *American Idol* orientates more to the celebration of achievement (for instance, clapping) and to striving for future achievement (for instance, 'keep trying'). As we saw in the case of Tamika, what looked like deluded confidence in one's own ability from our perspective was positively viewed by the North American judges as confidence in one's own ability to achieve success. With regard to the British English,[5] the social anthropologist, Kate Fox, writes 'can there be any other nation so resolutely unpatriotic, so prone to self-flagellation, so squeamishly reluctant to accept praise?' (2004, p. 174), and the commentator Jeremy Paxman writes 'why [...] do the English seem to enjoy feeling so persecuted?' (1998, p. x). Such values and attitudes may underlie the more muted approach to success on *The X Factor*, and the greater willingness to engage in and accept criticism.

Media scholars, such as Hill (2007), Holmes (2004) and Turner (2010), correctly observe the importance of exploitative TV. But they do not have the apparatus to explain what makes it tick. This chapter has argued that impoliteness is key. It demonstrated a way of describing impoliteness in the context of two talent shows, showing how participants use language and non-verbal behaviours exploitatively, causing humiliation and offence to targets, at least in part for the entertainment of the audience. Impoliteness interacts with context, and so this chapter also introduced the notion of the activity type to account for the context of the talent show. Activity types give shape to and are shaped by cultural practices and experiences, with the consequence that activity types vary across cultures. Even an ostensibly identical activity type may have different focal points. Differences in focal points may become cultural rich points – those moments of difference in cultural patterning that may result in puzzlement.

Appendix: Transcription key

Symbol	Example	Explanation
[ ]	A: I like [them] B: [so] do I.	Portions of utterances that overlap.

=	A: that was awful
	    truly awful=
	B: = give me
	    another chance
		Latching: there is no audible pause between the end of a prior turn and the start of a next piece of talk.

YES	YES	Capital letters: speech that is noticeably louder than surrounding talk.
No	*No*	Italics indicate particular stress.
(0.5)	what (0.5) as a group	Numbers in parentheses mark silences in seconds.

(continued)

Continued

Symbol	Example	Explanation
(.)	Simon (.) why do you do that	Parentheses around a full stop indicate a brief pause of less than half a second.
:::	We::::ll	Colons indicate an elongated vowel.
(( ))	((smirking))	Double parentheses enclose descriptions of non-verbal actions.
( )	(fucking)	Single parentheses enclose uncertain (for instance, difficult to clearly hear) transcriptions.
.hh	Rowetta .hh how are you	A series of letter 'h's preceded by a dot marks an in-breath.
Hhh	Louis hhh don't be so mean	A series of letter 'h's with no dot marks an outbreath.
eh-heh-heh	Okay eh-heh-heh	These letters indicate laughter
(x)	(x) What	Parentheses enclosing one or more of the letter 'x' indicate a disfluency.

Notes

1. Although Simon Cowell is a constant feature, two *American Idol* auditions have only one American judge, and two *The X Factor* auditions have Cheryl Cole instead of Sharon Osbourne.
2. The auditionee gender balance for the entire dataset is: *The X Factor* 13 females / 8 males; *American Idol* 16 females / 14 males. Nine of the *The X Factor* auditionees were comprised of groups (usually duos). Groups are not a feature of *American Idol*.
3. See the Appendix for our transcription conventions.
4. Clapping could be heard, but rarely seen, as the camera tended to focus on the auditionee leaving the room. Thus, we do not know whether all judges clapped on these occasions.
5. As we have mentioned, Louis Walsh is Irish, though the majority of the show's participants (judges, contestants, TV crew, and so on) are English.

References

Agar, Michael (2006) Culture: Can you take it anywhere? *International Journal of Qualitative Methods*, 5: 1–12.
Ash, Sherry (1999) The United States of America – the land of opportunity. In Eddie Ronowicz & Colin Yallop (eds.), *English: One Language, Different Cultures* (London: Continuum), pp. 197–263.
Bargiela-Chiappini, Francesca (2003) Face and politeness: New (insights) for old (concepts). *Journal of Pragmatics*, 35: 1453–69.

Bednarek, Monika A. (2005) Frames revisited – the coherence-inducing function of frames. *Journal of Pragmatics*, 37: 685–705.

Biressi, Anita & Heather Nunn (2005) *Reality TV: Realism and Revelation* (London: Wallflower Press).

Blum-Kulka, Shoshana, Juliane House & Gabriele Kasper (eds.) (1989) *Cross-Cultural Pragmatics: Requests and Apologies*. Vol. XXXI in the Advances in Discourse Processes series (Norwood NJ: Ablex).

Bousfield, Derek (2008) *Impoliteness in Interaction* (Philadelphia and Amsterdam: John Benjamins).

Bousfield, Derek & Miriam Locher (eds.) (2008) *Impoliteness in Language: Studies on its Interplay with Power in Theory and Practice* (Berlin and New York: Mouton de Gruyter).

Brown, Penelope & Stephen Levinson (1987)[1978] *Politeness. Some Universals in Language Usage* (Cambridge: Cambridge University Press).

Carter, Ronald (2004) *Language and Creativity: The Art of Common Talk* (London and New York: Routledge).

Cashman, Holly (2006) Impoliteness in children's interactions in a Spanish/English bilingual community of practice. *Journal of Politeness Research*, 2: 217–46.

Cowell, Simon (2004) *I Don't Mean To Be Rude, But...: The Truth about Fame, Fortune and My Life in Music* (Ebury Press: London).

Culpeper, Jonathan (1996) Towards an anatomy of impoliteness. *Journal of Pragmatics*, 25: 349–67.

Culpeper, Jonathan (2005) Impoliteness and entertainment in the television quiz show: *The Weakest Link*. *Journal of Politeness Research*, 1: 35–72.

Culpeper, Jonathan (2011) *Impoliteness: Using Language to Cause Offence* (Cambridge: Cambridge University Press).

Culpeper, Jonathan, Derek Bousfield & Anne Wichmann (2003) Impoliteness revisted: With special reference to dynamic and prosodic aspects. *Journal of Pragmatics*, 35: 1545–79.

Culpeper, Jonathan, Robert Crawshaw & Julia Harrison (2008) 'Activity types' and 'discourse types': Mediating 'advice' in interactions between foreign language assistants and their supervisors in schools in France and England. *Multilingua*, 27: 297–324.

Fox, Kate (2004) *Watching the English: The Hidden Rules of English Behaviour* (London: Hodder and Stoughton).

French, John R.P. & Bertram Raven (1959) The bases of social power. In Dorwin Cartwright (ed.), *Studies in Social Power* (Ann Arbor: University of Michigan Press), pp. 150–67.

Garcés-Conejos Blitvich, Pilar (2010) A genre approach to the study of im-politeness. *International Review of Pragmatics*, 2: 46–94.

Garcés-Conejos Blitvich, Pilar, Nuria Lorenzo-Dus & Patricia Bou-Franch (2010) A genre approach to impoliteness in a Spanish television talk show: Evidence from corpus-based analysis, questionnaires and focus groups. *Intercultural Pragmatics*, 7: 689–723.

Garcés-Conejos Blitvich, Pilar, Patricia Bou-Franch & Nuria Lorenzo-Dus (2013) Identity and impoliteness: The expert in the talent show *Idol*. *Journal of Politeness Research*, 9: 97–121.

Goffman, Erving (1967) *Interactional Ritual: Essays on Face-to-face Behavior* (Garden City, New York: Anchor Books).

Graham, Sage L. (2008) A manual for (im)politeness? The impact of the FAQ in an electronic community of practice. In Derek Bousfield & Miriam A. Locher (eds.), *Impoliteness in Language: Studies on its Interplay with Power in Theory and Practice* (Berlin: Mouton de Gruyter), pp. 281–304.

Grice, H. Paul (1975) Logic and conversation. In Peter Cole & Jerry Morgan (eds.), *Syntax and Semantics 3: Speech Acts* (London and New York: Academic Press), pp. 41–58.

Hill, Annette (2007) *Restyling Factual TV: Audiences and News, Documentary and Reality Genres* (Abingdon and New York: Routledge).

Holmes, Su (2004) 'All you've got to worry about is the task, having a cup of tea, and doing a bit of sunbathing': Approaching celebrity in *Big Brother*. In Su Holmes & Deborah Jermyn (eds.) *Understanding Reality Television* (London: Routledge), pp. 111–35.

Hutchby, Ian (2008) Particpants' orientations to interruptions, rudeness and other impolite acts in talk-in-interaction. *Journal of Politeness Research*, 4: 221–41.

Leech, Geoffrey N. (1983) *Principles of Pragmatics* (London: Longman).

Leech, Geoffrey N. (1985) Stylistics. In Teun A. van Dijk (ed.), *Discourse and Literature* (Amsterdam and Philadelphia: John Benjamins), pp. 39–57.

Levinson, Stephen C. (1992[1979]) Activity types and language. In Paul Drew & John Heritage (eds.), *Talk at Work* (Cambridge: Cambridge University Press), pp. 66–100.

Locher, Miriam (2004) *Power and Politeness in Action: Disagreements in Oral Communication* (Berlin and New York: Mouton de Gruyter).

Lorenzo-Dus, Nuria (2009) 'You're barking mad – I'm out' – impoliteness and broadcast talk. *Journal of Politeness Research*, 5: 159–87.

Lorenzo-Dus, Nuria, Pilar Garcés-Conejos Blitvich & Patricia Bou-Franch (2011) On-line polylogues and impoliteness: The case of postings sent in response to the Obama Reggaeton YouTube video. *Journal of Pragmatics*, 43: 2578–93.

Mills, Sara (2009) Impoliteness in a cultural context. *Journal of Pragmatics*, 41: 1047–60.

Montagu, Ashley (1973) *The Anatomy of Swearing* (London and New York: Macmillan and Collier).

Nussbaum, Stan (2005) *American Cultural Baggage: How to Recognize and Deal With It* (New York: Orbis Books).

Paxman, Jeremy (1998) *The English: A Portrait of a People* (London: Michael Joseph).

Sarangi, Srikant (2000) ATs, DTs and interactional hybridity: The case of genetic counselling. In Srikant Sarangi & Malcolm Coulthard (eds.), *Discourse and Social Life* (Longman: Harlow), pp. 1–27.

Spencer-Oatey, Helen (2008) Face, (im)politeness and rapport. In Helen Spencer-Oatey (ed.), *Culturally Speaking: Culture, Communication and Politeness Theory*, 2nd edn. (London and New York: Continuum), pp. 11–47.

Terkourafi, Marina (2005) Beyond the micro-level in politeness research. *Journal of Politeness Research*, 1: 237–62.

Thomas, Jenny (1995) *Meaning in Interaction* (London: Longman).

Turner, Graeme (2010) *Ordinary People and the Media: The Demotic Turn* (London: Sage).

9
Impoliteness in US/UK talent shows: a diachronic study of the evolution of a genre

Nuria Lorenzo-Dus, Patricia Bou-Franch and Pilar Garcés-Conejos Blitvich

Introduction

Reality television (RTV) has been under considerable scrutiny within the academic fields of media/cultural studies and, to a lesser extent, linguistics. Here, and within the context of 'exploitative reality shows', research has focused on impoliteness by lay participants (for example, Bousfield 2007, 2008; Culpeper 1996; Culpeper, Bousfield & Wichmann 2003) and 'experts', ranging from forthright property and lifestyle gurus and no-nonsense courtroom judges to draconian entrepreneurs, and offensively witty quiz presenters or judges (Culpeper 2005; Garcés-Conejos Blitvich *et al.* 2013; Lorenzo-Dus, 2006a, 2006b, 2008, 2009a, 2009b). These shows, moreover, are seen as representative of a 'rise of spectacular incivility' in the media, that is, of a rise of incivility as spectacle or as conscious performance for the purposes of entertainment (Lorenzo-Dus 2009a). RTV has arguably experienced increasing levels of, predominantly, verbal conflict and aggression over time (Coyne *et al.* 2010; Crook *et al.* 2004; Culpeper 2005; Holmes 2004; Redden 2008; Turner 2010). Yet, to our knowledge, no empirical analysis has been conducted of levels of impoliteness over time in these shows, despite the proven links between (i) verbal conflict and impoliteness in the media (see, for example, Lorenzo-Dus 2007) and (ii) verbal conflict and the evolution of media genres such as the talk show (Hess-Luttich 2007) and the news interview (Garcés-Conejos Blitvich 2009). The aim of this study, therefore, is to test the hypothesis that impoliteness has *progressively* come to characterize 'exploitative' RTV. To do so, we undertake a diachronic case study – spanning eight years – of the RTV genre known as the talent show, specifically focusing on the UK and US versions of one of its most popular instantiations – the *Idol* franchise.

The diachronic dimension in analyses of (im)politeness has been mostly ignored (see Culpeper & Kádár 2011, p. 11). Even less common are analyses that trace the development of (im)politeness within a specific genre. We thus see our longitudinal study as a contribution to the field of historical (im)politeness research (Culpeper & Kádár 2011; Kádár & Haugh 2013). Further, to be truly meaningful, diachronic analyses need to be circumscribed to genres. As we have argued elsewhere (Garcés-Conejos Blitvich 2010a; Garcés-Conejos Blitvich *et al.* 2010), genres – which we equate with social practice (Pennycook 2010) – provide a better anchor for cross-cultural analyses of im/politeness than, as posited by Mills (2009), communities of practice (see Chapter 8 for the use of 'activity type' to serve a similar purpose). We believe that the evolution of (im)politeness needs to be scrutinized within genres, as both (im)politeness manifestations and genre constraints on (im)politeness evolve over time. A diachronic approach, furthermore, is the best way to tackle the study and definition of genres (Neale 1990). Due to the intrinsic hybridity of genres and their nature as processes – that is, they are dominated by repetition, but also by variation and change – 'historicizing generic definitions and the parameters of both any single generic corpus, and of any specific generic regime' (Neale 1990: 58) is a must.

Reality television and the talent show genre – the role of impoliteness

RTV is not a new creation but one that traces its origins back to U.S. 'actuality programming' in the 1940s (Penzhorn & Pitout 2007). Due to its enormous popularity, RTV has been the focus of much academic debate within media/cultural studies scholarship. However, theorizing RTV has posed significant problems, including how to define it. Most of these problems, as noted in Chapter 1, seem to arise from treating RTV as a genre rather than as a 'discourse system' – in the sense of Scollon and Scollon (2001) or Gee (2005) – into which different chains of genres, exhibiting different degrees of hybridity, coalesce. The label 'reality' has also been problematized (Mittel 2004; Tolson 2001).

Whether regarded as shameless, cynical exploitation of ordinary individuals or as democratizing, empowering television, reality shows have placed ordinary people at the centre of attention (Turner 2010). This is precisely one of the four features that, according to Penzhorn and Pitout (2007), contribute to its essence. Other features include its voyeuristic nature, the encouragement of audience participation and the attempt to simulate real life.

RTV has been described variously as 'trash TV', 'tabloid TV, 'humiliation TV', 'exploitative TV' and 'victim TV'. Such labels indicate criticism of RTV on different grounds; the two most frequently given include superficiality/banality and humiliation of ordinary people. Yet reality television remains incredibly popular. Nabi *et al.* (2006) applied a 'uses and gratifications' approach to ascertain why people continue to watch reality television. This approach posits that viewers make an active choice of what media to consume and this choice is based on certain needs that are fulfilled by the programmes chosen. Satiating feelings of voyeurism was identified as one of those needs. It was also reported that viewing reality shows increased feelings of happiness, parasocial relationships, negative outcomes and feelings of dramatic challenge. Reiss and Wiltz (2004) added vengeance as a very important reason, after status, why people are drawn to RTV. Since RTV shows contain a large amount of competition and interpersonal conflict, audiences can satiate their need for vindication through viewing them. Crook *et al.* (2004) found that not necessarily voyeurism but morbid curiosity was the personality characteristic most strongly associated with watching RTV. They concluded that, since individuals are morbidly curious, it is not surprising that the networks and cable stations come up with more extreme RTV shows each season. Since most violence enacted in RTV is verbal violence (Coyne *et al.* 2010), that would mean an increase in the level of conflict and rudeness found in the shows. Also, it has been shown that (both verbal and non-verbal) aggression and violence heighten arousal, which is closely tied to levels of attention (Mutz & Reeves 2005). Furthermore, our brain cannot distinguish between – that is it does not react differently to – non-mediated and mediated violence (Reeves & Nass 1996). Scholars, therefore, conclude that mediated verbal aggression is a good attention-grabbing device (Mutz & Reeves 2005). It is hence not surprising that linguistics scholars have found RTV to contain impoliteness (see for example, Culpeper 2005; Bousfield 2007, 2008; Lorenzo-Dus 2006a, 2006b, 2007, 2008, 2009a, 2009b; Garcés-Conejos Blitvich *et al.* 2010; Garcés-Conejos Blitvich *et al.* 2013).

Additionally, impoliteness is associated with raw emotions (Garcés-Conejos Blitvich *et al.* 2010; Kienpointner 2008) and could be related to 'authenticity' in the context of RTV shows, which trade in the performance of this kind of emotionality (Lorenzo-Dus 2009a). At the same time, though, impoliteness can be used strategically (see Beebe 1995; Kienpointner 1997; Garcés-Conejos Blitvich 2009). And within the 'emotional public sphere' that RTV fosters (Lunt & Stenner 2005), impoliteness is indeed used strategically, that is, as an 'openly constructed and dramatic' construct that seeks to provide entertainment effects via the spectacular performance of 'negative' emotional expressiveness (Lorenzo-Dus 2009a: 119).

Im/politeness scholars have debated whether this strategic use of impoliteness in RTV can be considered 'really' impolite, rather than part-and-parcel of the genres in which it features systematically (see Culpeper 2005; Garcés-Conejos Blitvich 2009, 2010b; Lorenzo-Dus 2009b; Mills 2005). It is important to note, in this respect, that 'exploitative', confrontational reality shows have evolved from, and against the backdrop of, standard (non-confrontational) ones. In particular, they have evolved 'through the subversion of the politeness norms of the standard shows' (Culpeper 2005, p. 47). Also, and as discussed above, verbal aggression and impoliteness are effective attention-grabbing devices. Furthermore, there is available empirical evidence that shows that sections of the audience of reality television perceive the confrontainment of these shows as truly impolite (Garcés-Conejos Blitvich 2013a; Garcés-Conejos Blitvich *et al.* 2010; Lorenzo-Dus 2009b).

The genre of reality television on which our diachronic study is based is the talent show *Idol*. Describing the talent show as a genre of the reality television discourse system entails identifying the show's communicative purpose, as this shapes its structure and rhetorical choices. Like other reality television shows, the talent show has a double communicative purpose: one is civic in nature and is related to a didactic dimension; the other is economic and achieved through an entertainment dimension (Burger 2006). Specifically, the talent show constitutes a hybrid genre (Redden 2008). Its evolution shows clear influences from the traditional game show, in as much as it is articulated around suspenseful competition, and the lifestyle show, since it contains narratives of personal transformation. These influences combine with the general focus of RTV on ordinary people to produce a successful form of light entertainment.

In talent shows a panel of judges assesses different abilities or skills – talents – by ordinary people in front of them and, often, in front of a live studio audience. In shows like *Britain's Got Talent*, for example, talent can be of any kind, ranging from dog training to dancing or making eyeballs seemingly pop out of their sockets. In other shows, talent is restricted to a specific sphere of activity, for instance dancing, as in the UK's *So You Think You Can Dance*. Singing talent shows, of which *Idol* is a case in point, are particularly popular.

Features of *Idol* that contribute to its popularity include its competition format, the material (a lucrative recording contract) and symbolic (celebrity status) prize it offers and the salient role played by its viewers in, especially, the last stages of the show during which their votes are more decisive than the judges'. This no doubt creates additional conflict potential (see Holmes 2004; Redden 2008; Turner 2010).

Idol's specific move structure, in turn, is designed to maximize the show's coaching and entertainment purposes. The programme revolves around a five-stage selection process (see Methodology section). In the stage on which this study focuses – the live auditions – the turn-taking system is that of a polylogue (or multi-party interaction, see Kerbrat Orecchioni 2004). It includes an exchange of greetings between judges and contestants, a brief interview by the judges of the contestants that serves also to introduce them, the singing performance itself, and the judges' assessment thereof. Another important, genre-specific feature of *Idol* is that contestants have the opportunity to respond to the judges' assessments of their performance – a situation that sometimes leads to (escalating) conflict (Holmes 2004; Redden 2008; Turner 2010).

The formal choices of content and style that make up the *Idol* rhetoric include contestants' articulation 'through crucial elements of a telesual rhetoric such as close proximity to the viewer, [...] ordinariness and direct address (liveness)' (Holmes 2004, p. 153) – as is characteristic of RTV (Cowell 2003; Turner 2010). For their part, the judges' rhetoric, in relation to the entertainment dimension of the genre, fluctuates between the harmonious, non-confrontational strategies typical of some lifestyle shows (Lorenzo-Dus, 2006a, 2006b; Smith 2010) and the verbally aggressive, confrontational strategies that characterize other exploitative shows (Lorenzo-Dus 2008, 2009b). Important for our study is the fact that, although judges relate to the entertainment purpose of the show in different ways (not all necessarily confrontational), journalists and scholars generally agree in placing Simon Cowell within the confrontational side (Cowell 2003; Garcés-Conejos Blitvich *et al.* 2013; Holmes 2004; Redden 2008; Turner 2010; Culpeper and Holmes, Chapter 8 this volume).

In light of the above, our study seeks to answer two research questions:

- *Research Question 1:* given both the general contention that aggression has come to characterize exploitative RTV, to which the talent show genre belongs, and the link between aggression and impoliteness, has the discourse of the judges in *Idol* become progressively more impolite?
- *Research Question 2:* If so, what kind of impoliteness characterizes the judges' performance in *Idol*?

Methodology

Data

Our case study is based on data from the UK and US versions of *Idol*. Since its inception in 1998 by Simon Fuller in the UK (*Pop Idol*) and the US (*American Idol*), *Idol* has enjoyed unprecedented success in the over 30 countries to which the franchise has been sold (Livio 2007).[1] By 2005, for example, it had become the biggest show on U.S. television, a position that it still holds at the time of writing. And in the UK, average viewing figures rose from 7.40 million in 2004 to 14.3 million in 2010, with the finals consistently topping audience shares. Since then, however, viewing ratings have dropped significantly, the most recent figures at the time of writing (*X Factor* 2012) being an average of 8.6 million viewers.

Idol claims to be mainly concerned with identifying singing talent. However, appearance, personality, stage presence and dance routines are also regarded as important aspects of the contestants' performances. Regular comments made by, for instance, the UK judges about contestants having (or not) the 'x factor' in respect of these features demonstrates this.

Idol employs a panel of experts who, in their role of judges, act as gatekeepers in the initial stages of the show and then critique the performances of the finalists. Five stages can be differentiated within *Idol*: Stage 1 consists of the producers' auditions, during which it is decided who will perform in front of the judges. This is the only stage that is not broadcast, for obvious reasons. The judges' auditions comprise Stage 2. Those candidates who are successful proceed to Stage 3, also known as 'bootcamp'. Here the selection process is further refined through a series of performances in front of the judges, who are also at the 'bootcamp', and then at the 'judges' houses' (Stage 4). A reduced number of candidates, divided into several categories ('girls', 'boys', 'over 25s', 'groups'), eventually make it to the live shows (Stage 5) and are assigned one of the judges as their 'mentor'.[2] The auditions (Stage 2) and shows (Stage 5) take place in front of a panel of judges and a live audience.[3] Audience involvement is crucial in the live shows for, in addition to the judges' vote, viewers are encouraged to vote for their favourite contestant to stay in the competition. The least voted contestant after each live show leaves the competition. In both Stages 2 and 5 contestants have the opportunity to respond to the judges' assessments of their performance, either directly or through the show's presenter/s.

Our corpus consists of 160 live audition sequences, each lasting between two and eight minutes, during the period 2002–2009, and totalling 91,650 words. Half of the sequences are from the UK shows (n=80) and the other half from the U.S. shows (n=80). Simon Cowell is the only member of the panel of judges present in all the sequences in the corpus. The other judges vary, and include Dannii Minogue, Louis Walsh and Sharon Osbourne, in the UK shows, and Paula Abdul and Randy Jackson, in the US shows. Sequences in our corpus, therefore, are evenly spread across time, show and show phase.

While sizeable, our corpus does not claim to be representative of the talent show genre, let alone RTV, as a whole. In other words, it does not make a case for 'typicality'. Instead, it makes a case for a key principle of case study research, namely one in which the inference is 'that the theoretical relationship among conceptually defined elements in the sample will also apply in the parent population' (Mitchell 1984, p. 239).

Procedure

The corpus was recorded and transcribed in its entirety following the conventions developed for the multimodal transcription of television texts (see Lorenzo-Dus 2009a and the Appendix to this chapter for a key). It was then coded for impoliteness by a small team of trained researchers under the supervision of one of the authors of this chapter.[4] Inter-coder agreement was reached by discussing and assessing each individual instance where there was initial disagreement.

Classification of discourse stretches within the sequences in the corpus to specific individual impoliteness strategies was interpreted as indicative of *salient* – rather than absolute – orientation towards attacking/preserving either positive or negative face. As we have argued elsewhere (Garcés-Conejos Blitvich 2010a; Lorenzo-Dus *et al.* 2011), we agree with Bousfield (2008) that it is difficult to establish a clear-cut distinction between the two sides of face, positive and negative, along the lines of Brown and Levinson (1987). However, we believe that the distinction is still conceptually and methodologically useful, and we have advocated for maintaining it in, rather than eliminating it (as Bousfield 2008 proposed) from extant frameworks. Viewing the relationship between both aspects of face in terms of a cline and accepting that although both may be simultaneously threatened in interaction, one of them – either positive or negative face wants – is saliently threatened on a given occasion, solves most problems associated with maintaining the original distinction.

Our research questions sought to investigate whether the discourse of talent show judges in *Idol* had become more impolite (Research Question 1). Were that to be the case, we also sought to find out what kind of impoliteness had progressively come to characterize their performance (Research Question 2). In order to answer these related questions, a quantitative analysis of the coded corpus was finally conducted in which we divided the 160 coded sequences as follows:

- Corpus 2002–5: 40 sequences from UK shows, 40 sequences from US shows.
- Corpus 2006–9: 40 sequences from UK shows, 40 sequences from US shows.

Framework

Our study adopted primarily an 'impoliteness2' framework, in so far as results emerged from analysts' categorization of instances of impoliteness according to an existing taxonomy of impoliteness. This taxonomy is based on an adaptation of those put forward by Culpeper (1996), Culpeper *et al.* (2003) and Culpeper (2005). Modifications include analysis of the individual strategy 'explicitly associate the other with a negative aspect' (ANA) as a manifestation of saliently positive rather than negative impoliteness (Lorenzo-Dus *et al.* 2011), and the addition of implicated impoliteness within off-record strategies (Garcés-Conejos Blitvich 2010a).[5]

There are two reasons why we regard use of a taxonomy of impoliteness strategies as beneficial to this study. Firstly, within a large corpus it helps discriminate or unveil *patterns* of impoliteness (on/off record, positive/negative, and different individual impoliteness strategies) for their subsequent qualitative analysis (see also Terkourafi 2005; Lorenzo-Dus *et al.* 2011). Secondly, it allows for a bird's eye view of the evolution of impoliteness across time, which is the main aim of this chapter.

It is important to clarify, however, that analysts' categorizations were guided by examination of the actual ways in which participants (contestants and judges in our case) realized and/or ascribed impoliteness to others in the course of interaction (see Hutchby 2008). Analysts' decisions *and* participants' realization/ascription of impoliteness, moreover, stemmed from (different levels of) knowledge of generic constraints applicable to the corpus. Therefore, an approach to the study of im/politeness based on genre (as understood by Fairclough 2003) seems to us the most comprehensive way to approach these phenomena. We believe that im/politeness assessments are tied to genre constraints. Also, Fairclough's model allows for a combined politeness1/politeness2 approach that takes into consideration polylogal, intergroup communication such as the one under analysis. Furthermore, as stated above, a genre approach to the study of im/politeness (see Garcés-Conejos Blitvich 2010) fits in well with the diachronic angle of our study.[6]

Results

Table 9.1 shows the total number of impoliteness strategies used by the *Idol* judges in the 2002–05 and the 2006–09 periods; as well as the distribution of impoliteness according to the superstrategies of positive impoliteness (P-IMP), negative impoliteness (N-IMP) and off-record impoliteness (OR-IMP). P-IMP and N-IMP constitute types of on-record impoliteness (ON-IMP).

The figures in Table 9.1 reveal an overall increase of impoliteness across time, from 472 in the 2002–05 period to 593 in the 2006–09 one. They also show, though, that this was not evenly distributed *within* impoliteness superstrategies: OR-IMP figures were nearly halved in the 2006–09 period vis-à-vis the 2002–05 period (but note that their numbers are very small in the first instance). Within ON-IMP, N-IMP hardly experienced an increase, whereas P-IMP not only had the largest number of instances in both periods but it also experienced the most dramatic increase, from 280 instances in 2002–05 to 426 instances in 2006–09.

Figure 9.1 shows the frequency of use of individual impoliteness strategies within each impoliteness superstrategy across the two time periods.

The occurrence of individual impoliteness strategies within each of the three impoliteness superstrategies was next calculated. T-tests (paired, two sample for means; Bonferroni correction applied) revealed only one statistically significant difference in the use of individual impoliteness strategies across the two time periods, namely 'explicitly associate the other with a negative aspect' (ANA) [t (159) $=-5.906$, $p<.001$]. ANA was also the most frequently used strategy in both periods, followed by 'condescend, scorn, ridicule' (CSR) and 'be disinterested, unconcerned, unsympathetic' (DUU). Results therefore reveal

Table 9.1   Use of impoliteness superstrategies across two time periods

Impoliteness	Total	ON-IMP		OR-IMP
		P-IMP	N-IMP	
2002–05	472	280	127	65
2006–09	593	426	137	30

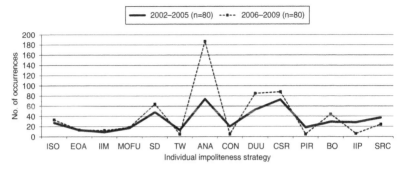

Figure 9.1 Use of individual impoliteness strategies across the two time periods

an overall increase of impoliteness across time, especially in relation to P-IMP and, specifically, to ANA.

Idol: A progressively impolite genre?

The quantitative analysis shows both change and continuity across the two time periods. The most noticeable change concerns the overall increase in the frequency of use of impoliteness strategies in *Idol*. This, as we saw in Figure 9.1, is principally due to the dramatic increase in the frequency of use of one individual impoliteness strategy: ANA. As noted earlier, ANA is located within the superstrategy category of P-IMP. It is also functionally very similar to another P-IMP strategy – 'call the other names' (CON) – which was used very infrequently in the entire corpus (see Figure 9.1). This is probably because of the programme's audience, which includes all age groups and requires the shows to observe certain guidelines as regards use of language. In the UK, *Idol* shows are broadcast before 21:00, that is, before the so-called *watershed* period (also known as *safe harbor* in the US). Name calling through swear words (taboo words), therefore, could not be part of the discourse of either the judges or the contestants. When it occurred, it was either bleeped or edited out prior to the show's being broadcast.

As for continuity, with the exception of ANA, the results show that individual impoliteness strategies display similar frequencies of use across the two time periods. Also, and as the two data lines in Figure 9.1 show, the actual distribution of strategies is remarkably similar across the two time periods. This suggests generic preferences regarding the type of impoliteness to be performed in *Idol*. Specifically, in addition to a marked preference for the use of ANA, the results show CSR, DUU,

SD ('seek disagreement') and BO ('block the other') to be the next most frequently employed individual strategies in both time periods. DUU, SD and BO are all likely to occur within instances of conflict talk, which is what our data largely consist of, specifically in the form of (negative) assessments of contestants' performances by one or more of the judges.

Coding of impoliteness by speaker enabled us to map use of the CSR and ANA mainly onto the discourse of one judge: Simon Cowell. CSR and ANA could in fact be described as his two 'trade-mark' impoliteness strategies, for 79 per cent of all instances of CSR and 61 per cent of all instances of ANA in the corpus were used by him. CSR, moreover, has been shown to be one of the most frequent impoliteness strategies in other quantitative studies of impoliteness in exploitative RTV (Garcés-Conejos Blitvich *et al.* 2013; Lorenzo-Dus 2009b). This seems to indicate that use of condescension, scorn and ridicule is a discourse (the discourse of exploitative RTV) rather than a genre trait.

We noted above that ANA and CRS were mainly used by Cowell, who often realized them through witty, verbal fireworks. Examples (1a–1b), from the 2006–09 corpus, contain typical realizations of these strategies.

(1a) Contestant (C) has just auditioned.

MLS – contestant looking	62	C	it is the sort of thing I
nervous. CU – C	63		would expect someone
(to contestant)	64		to be standing outside a subway doing (.) with a hat (.)
CU – contestant looking very	65		and the hat would be
stern			empty

(1b) – Contestant (C) has just auditioned.

MLS – contestant	45	C	you sound like
CU – C (to C)	46		someone who should
	47		be singing on a cruise ship (.) and then halfway through the
CU – contestant looking	48		song (.) I imagine the
shocked			ship sinking

In these examples Cowell humiliates the contestants by comparing their performances to unsuccessful busking (1a) and 'disastrous' cruise entertainment (1b). In terms of showbiz performance, both busking and cruise entertainment are, of course, poor relations of those within the music industry to which the contestants aspire. Busking and cruise entertainment implicitly work here as 'music career choices' open to those who do *not* have star quality (the x factor), which is what *Idol* claims to be all about. But Cowell's assessments go beyond denying the contestants access to the music industry. Through witty – and wittily delivered – metaphors and hypothetical scenarios, the contestants' inability to pursue even busking and cruise entertainment options is made plain to them, and used to humiliate them publicly. Note, in this respect, Cowell's use of a list-of-three style in (1a) and (1b), the last component of which delivers the 'punch-line' for the assumed entertainment of the audience. These rhetorically delivered one-liners are of course more creative and more entertaining than a literal verbalization of their implicated meaning would be, that is, for example, 'You sound like an inadequate busker' in (1b). They therefore contribute to Cowell's own impression management in ways that mark him as distinctive from other reality show experts (for a discussion of experts' impression management / identity construction in RTV, see, for example, Garcés-Conejos Blitvich *et al.* 2013; Lorenzo-Dus 2008, 2009a).

Cowell's use of CSR in examples (1a) and (1b), and more widely in our corpus, can also be seen as instances of 'snark' (Dorfman 2010). Dorfman (2010) argues that, while it is easy to be annoying and bitchy, being snarky requires a certain level of intelligence and interactional power. And, although snark is not always entertaining (Richardson 2010), this seems to be the purpose behind Cowell's use of it. His scornful put-downs both belittle their direct recipients and aim at amusing the viewing/studio audience. Put-down humour can be simultaneously inclusive *and* exclusive. It can be inclusive in so far as it shows camaraderie and contributes to strengthening bonds between those who laugh. And it can be exclusive in as much as it can distance its author (and those who laugh with him/her) from those parties who are its target (Dynel 2008). Cowell's frequent use of condescension (CSR) and association of contestants with negative aspects (ANA) in, especially, the 2006–09 period, served to raise him at the expense of the contestants, making them the butt of his 'jokes'. The rhetorical structure of these often followed an 'XYZ formula' where X involved the 'offending event' (Bousfield 2007, 2008), Y highlighted the offending event by associating the contestant with a negative aspect, and Z further emphasized this negativity. This is similar to ritualistic African-American banter in classic Labovian work (1972, p. 311): 'Your mother (X) so old (Y) she got spider webs under her arms (Z)'.

In Cowell's three-part formula, the Z component – the final blow in the build-up of impoliteness – was frequently the contestant. Note in this respect that the strategically placed micro-pauses between the X, Y and Z components in (1a) and (1b) emphasize the delivery of the witty hyperbole (Z). The examples illustrate the use of humorous, wittily produced impolite criticism in order to show off his power over the contestants (see Chapter 10 for a contrasting situation) and expert identity (for a detailed analysis of Cowell's identity construction see Garcés-Conejos Blitvich *et al.* 2013) They provide the audience with voyeuristic pleasure and a spirit of *schadenfreude*, both of which are known to grab attention and lead to entertainment in the context of 'exploitative' RTV (Culpeper 2005; Chapter 8 in this volume). Furthermore, these negative associations and scornful remarks highlight Cowell's expert status and the power relations between him and the other judges.

Cowell was the only judge in the corpus who *systematically* used verbal creativity as put-down. Yet he is not unique within 'exploitative' RTV in his delivery of humiliation and impoliteness through verbal wit. A number of reality television experts have become 'celebrity experts' – and in the process stolen the limelight of the shows in which they appear – precisely because of their display of impolite, verbal wit aimed against ordinary folk. Some of these celebrity experts have become known for their catch-phrases, like the UK presenter of *The Weakest Link* ('you are the weakest link – good bye', Culpeper 2005), some courtroom show judges on US television (for example, 'you redefine chutzpah' *Judge Milian*, Lorenzo-Dus 2008), and even some of the 'property gurus' of makeover shows (for example, Ann Maurice, *The House Doctor*, Lorenzo-Dus 2006a, 2006b; and Gillian McKeith, *You Are What You Eat*, Lorenzo-Dus 2009a).

In terms of qualitative changes across time, then, what our results show is a progressive mapping of the discourse of the judges, or rather of one judge (in our case Cowell), into a more general trend in exploitative RTV whereby verbal wit and impoliteness go hand in hand in the strategic performance of celebrity expert personas. Each of them may then develop their own idiosyncratic style, but strategic performance of impoliteness as entertainment – of 'impolitainment' (Lorenzo-Dus 2009a) – seems to emerge as their common denominator.

Conclusion

The aim of our study was to carry out a diachronic analysis of the manifestations of impoliteness in a genre, the talent show, within the broader discourse of RTV. Aggressive verbal behaviour has become a staple of the talent show genre in particular and of the discourse of RTV in general (Turner 2010; Chapter 1 of this volume). In fact, it has been claimed that non-exploitative shows, belonging to different genres, evolved into their exploitative versions as a result of the constant introduction of non/verbal behaviour that could be interpreted as impolite or aggressive (Culpeper 2005; Hess-Luttich 2007; Garcés-Conejos Blitvich 2009, 2010a). The evolution of the exploitative versions of these genres may have involved further interactional coarsening over time. It is precisely this claim, for which no empirical evidence exists, that our study was designed to test in the two periods (2002–05; 2006–09) under scrutiny. More specifically, our research questions sought to answer whether panel judges' verbal behaviour had become more impolite over time and, if so, what types of impoliteness had come to characterize it. The results of our analysis indicated that statistically significant changes had occurred in relation to the use of P-IMP (which went from 280 in the earlier period to 426 in the most recent). More specifically, the results of the analysis revealed that the two most frequently used P-IMP strategies were ANA and CSR, both of which could be considered the discursive trademark of celebrity judge Simon Cowell. Thus, and in response to our research questions, it would seem that interactional coarsening in the form of especially P-IMP has indeed taken place over time.

The increase in impoliteness would make sense in a genre that relies on the audience's voyeuristic needs (Nabi *et al.* 2006), as well as on their needs for status and vengeance, for its success (Reiss & Wiltz 2004). In a market saturated by generic forms of the RTV system – many of them equally reliant on the same commercial formula (aggressive non/verbal behaviour) – more displays of impolite behaviour would seemed geared towards securing the continued attention on the audience's part that producers seek (Mutz & Reeves 2005).

A boost in the use of impoliteness would also make sense from the point of view of the evolution of the genre. Neale (1990), discussing generic, social and cultural verisimilitude, argues that it is often the generically verisimilitudinous elements that are least compatible with the regimes of cultural verisimilitude that constitute a genre's pleasure. This would make sense in the case of politeness and impoliteness. Politeness is socially sanctioned – the default term – in public discourse (Fraser 1990; Sellers 2004). Thus, use of impoliteness, a common occurrence in the discourse of reality television, would be verisimilitudinous within its many genres, even if in sharp contrast with daily societal usages. The pleasure derived by audiences would lie herein. It would make sense that after the 'canonization' and 'automation' of the genre (its first two stages according to Jass, cited in Neale 1990, p. 60), an increase in impoliteness were tied to a third stage – the 'reshuffling'. This would seek to exploit the generically verisimilitudinous feature (impoliteness) that is most sharply in contrast with culturally verisimilitudinous ones (such as politeness). We believe that diachronic analyses of impoliteness need to be circumscribed to genres, which we understand as social practice (Pennycook 2010), for norms underlying expectations of im/politeness go back to generic constraints rather than to communities of practice as a whole (Garcés-Conejos Blitvich 2010a; Garcés-Conejos Blitvich *et al.* 2010). In the same way that we cannot make overarching generalization of im/politeness across cultures (Mills 2009; Culpeper and Holmes, Chapter 8 in this volume), the evolution of impoliteness manifestations and the norms to which these are related need to be studied in connection to specific genres in given periods rather than to historical periods as a whole.

Appendix: Transcription key (simplified from Lorenzo-Dus 2009a)

<u>always</u>	marked stress
a- an	hesitation
(.)	short pause (less than half a second)
MLS/CU	medium long shot/close up

Notes

1. *Pop Idol* was replaced in the UK by *The X Factor* in 2004, as part of the *X Factor* franchise, created by Simon Cowell after legal disputes regarding the *Idol* franchise. Throughout this article, we use *Idol* to refer to both the US version (*American Idol*) and the UK versions (first *Pop Idol*, then *X Factor*) of this talent show.
2. Stages 3 and 4 have been introduced into the format in recent years.
3. Stage 2 is not always conducted in front of a live audience (for example in *Pop Idol* and earlier versions of *American Idol*).
4. We are grateful to the researcher team, and specially to A. Allsebrook, for their discussion of some of the findings.
5. The individual impoliteness strategies, within their respective superstrategy category, are shown in the list below. With the exception of 'implicated impoliteness', which comes from Garcés-Conejos Blitvich (2010b), all the individual impoliteness strategies were first identified in Culpeper (1996).

      ON RECORD IMPOLITENESS

      POSITIVE IMPOLITENESS

'Ignore/snub the other' [ISO]
'Exclude other from the activity' [EOA]
'Dissociate from the other' [DFO]
'Be disinterested, unconcerned, unsympathetic' [DUU]
'Use inappropriate identity markers' [IIM]
'Use obscure secretive language' [OSL]
'Make the other feel uncomfortable' [MOFU]
'Seek disagreement' [SD]
'Use taboo words"'[TW]
'Call the other names' [CON]

NEGATIVE IMPOLITENESS
'Frighten' [FR]
'Condescend, scorn, ridicule' [CSR]
'Invade the other's space' [IOS]
'Explicitly associate the other with a negative aspect' [ANA]
'Put the other's indebtedness on record' [PIR]
'Hinder or block the other, either physically or linguistically' [BO]

OFF RECORD IMPOLITENESS
'Implicated impoliteness' [IP]
'Sarcasm' [SRC]

WITHHOLD POLITENESS

6. For a more detailed description of the genre approach to im/politeness, see Garcés-Conejos Blitvich 2010a, 2013b).

References

Beebe, Leslie M. (1995) Polite fictions: Instrumental rudeness and pragmatic competence. In James E. Alatis, Carolyn. A. Straehele, Maggi Ronkin & Brent Gallenberger (eds.), *Georgetown University Round Table on Languages and Linguistics* (Washington, DC: Georgetown University Press), pp. 154–68.

Bousfield, Derek (2007) Beginnings, middles and ends: A biopsy of the dynamics of impolite exchanges. *Journal of Pragmatics*, 39: 2185–216.

Bousfield, Derek (2008) *Impoliteness in Interaction* (Philadelphia and Amsterdam: John Benjamins).

Brown, Penelope & Steven Levinson (1987) *Politeness: Some Universals of Language Usage* (Cambridge: Cambridge University Press).

Burger, Marcel (2006) The discursive construction of the public and the private spheres in media debates: The case of television talk shows. *Revista Alicantina de Estudios Ingleses*, 19: 45–65.

Cowell, Simon (2003) All together now! Publics and participation in *American Idol. Invisible Culture: An Electronic Journal for Visual Culture*, 6. http://www.rochester.edu/in_visible_culture/Issue_6/cowell/cowell.html

Coyne, Sarah M., Simon L. Robinson & David A. Nelson (2010) Does reality back-bite? Physical, verbal, and relational aggression in reality television programs. *Journal of Broadcasting & Electronic Media*, 54(2): 282–98.

Crook, Sarah F., Tracy Worrell, David Westerman, Jeffrey Davis, Emily Moyer & Scott Clarke (2004) Personality characteristics associated with watching reality programming. Paper presented at the meeting of the International Communication Association, New Orleans, LA.

Culpeper, Jonathan (1996) Towards an anatomy of impoliteness. *Journal of Pragmatics*, 25: 349–67.

Culpeper, Jonathan (2005) Impoliteness and entertainment in the television quiz show: *The Weakest Link*. *Journal of Politeness Research*, 1: 35–72.

Culpeper, Jonathan, Derek Bousfield & Anne Wichmann (2003) Impoliteness revisited: With special reference to dynamic and prosodic aspects. *Journal of Pragmatics*, 35(10–11): 1545–79.

Culpeper, Jonathan & Dániel Z. Kádár (2011) *Historical (Im)politeness* (Berlin: Peter Lang).

Dorfman, Lawrence (2010) *The Snark Handbook: Insult Edition – Comebacks, Taunts and Effronteries* (New York: Skyhorse Publishers).

Dynel, Marta (2008) No aggression, only teasing: The pragmatics of teasing and banter. *Lodz Papers in Pragmatics*, 4(2): 241–61.

Fairclough, Norman (2003) *Analysing Discourse: Textual Analysis for Social Research* (London: Routledge).

Fraser, Bruce (1990) Perspectives on politeness. *Journal of Pragmatics*, 14: 219–36.

Garcés-Conejos Blitvich, Pilar (2009) Impoliteness and identity in the American news media: The 'Culture Wars'. *Journal of Politeness Research*, 5(2): 273–304.

Garcés-Conejos Blitvich, Pilar (2010a) A genre approach to the study of im-politeness. *International Review of Pragmatics*, 2: 46–94.

Garcés-Conejos Blitvich, Pilar (2010b) The *YouTubification* of politics, impolite-ness and polarization. In Rotimi Taiwo (ed.), *Handbook of Research on Discourse Behavior and Digital Communication: Language Structures and Social Interaction* (Hershey, PA: IGI Global), pp. 540–63.

Garcés-Conejos Blitvich, Pilar (2013a) El modelo del género y la des/cortesía cla-sificatoria en las evaluaciones de Sálvame por parte de la audiencia. In Catalina Fuentes (ed.), *(Des)cortesía para el espectáculo; Estudios de pragmática variacionista* (Madrid: Arco Libros) pp. 167–96.

Garcés-Conejos Blitvich, Pilar (2013b) Face, identity, and im/politeness: Looking backwards, moving forward – from Goffman to Practice Theory. *Journal of Politeness Research*, 9: 1–33.

Garcés-Conejos Blitvich, Pilar, Patricia Bou-Franch & Nuria Lorenzo-Dus (2013) Identity and impoliteness. The expert in the talent show *Idol*. *Journal of Politeness Research*, 9: 97–120.

Garcés-Conejos Blitvich, Pilar, Nuria Lorenzo-Dus & Patricia Bou-Franch (2010) A genre approach to impoliteness in a Spanish television talk show: Evidence from corpus-based analysis, questionnaires and focus groups. *Intercultural Pragmatics*, 7: 689–723.

Gee, James P. (2005) *An Introduction to Discourse Analysis Theory and Method*, 2nd edn. (New York: Routledge).

Hess-Luttich, Ernest W. B. (2007) Pseudo-argumentation in TV debates. *Journal of Pragmatics*, 39: 1360–70.

Holmes, Su (2004) 'Reality goes pop!': Reality TV, popular music, and narratives of stardom in *Pop Idol*. *Television & New Media*, 5: 147–72.

Hutchby, Ian (2008) Participants' orientations to interruptions, rudeness and other impolite acts in talk-in-interaction. *Journal of Politeness Research*, 4: 221–41.

Kádár, Dániel Z. & Michael Haugh (2013) *Understandings of Politeness* (Cambridge: Cambridge University Press).

Kerbrat-Orecchioni, Catherine (2004) Introducing polylogue. *Journal of Pragmatics*, 36: 1–24.

Kienpointner, Manfred (1997) Varieties of rudeness: Types and functions of impolite utterances. *Functions of Language*, 4: 251–87.

Kienpointner, Manfred (2008) Impoliteness and emotional arguments. *Journal of Politeness Research*, 4: 243–65.

Labov, William (1972) *Language in the Inner City* (Philadelphia: University of Pennsylvania Press).

Livio, Oren (2007) Performing the nation. A cross-cultural comparison of Idol shows from the UK, US, Canada and Israel. Paper submitted to Popular Communication Division of the International Communication Association's 57th Annual Conference.

Lorenzo-Dus, Nuria (2006a) Buying and selling: Mediating persuasion in British property shows. *Media, Culture & Society*, 28: 739–61.

Lorenzo-Dus, Nuria (2006b) The discourse of lifestyles in the broadcast media. In P. Bou-Franch (ed.), *Ways into Discourse* (Granada: Comares), pp. 135–48.

Lorenzo-Dus, Nuria (2007) (Im)politeness and the Spanish media – The case of audience participation debates. In M.E. Placencia & C. García-Fernández (eds.), *Research on Politeness in the Spanish Speaking World* (Mahwah, NJ: Lawrence Erlbaum Associates), pp. 145–66.

Lorenzo-Dus, Nuria (2008) Real disorder in the court: An investigation of conflict talk in US courtroom shows. *Media, Culture & Society*, 30(1): 81–107.

Lorenzo-Dus, Nuria (2009a) *Television Discourse. Analysing Language in the Media* (Basingstoke and New York: Palgrave Macmillan).

Lorenzo-Dus, Nuria (2009b) 'You're barking mad – I'm out': Impoliteness and broadcast talk. *Journal of Politeness Research*, 5: 159–87.

Lorenzo-Dus, Nuria, Pilar Garcés-Conejos Blitvich & Patricia Bou-Franch (2011) On-line polylogues and impoliteness: The case of postings sent in response to the Obama Reggaeton YouTube video. *Journal of Pragmatics*, 43: 2578–93.

Lunt, Peter & Paul Stenner (2005) *The Jerry Springer Show* as an emotional public sphere. *Media, Culture and Society*, 27: 59–81.

Mills, Sara (2005) Gender and impoliteness. *Journal of Politeness Research*, 1: 263–80.

Mills, Sara (2009) Impoliteness in a cultural context. *Journal of Pragmatics*, 4: 1047–60.

Mitchell, C. (1984) Typicality and the case study. In R. F. Ellen (ed.), *Ethnographic Research: A Guide to General Conduct* (London: Academic Press), pp. 228–41.

Mittel, Jason (2004) *Genre and Television: From Cop Shows to Cartoons in American Culture* (London: Routledge).

Mutz, Diana & Byron Reeves (2005) The new videomalaise: Effects of televised incivility on political trust. *American Political Science Review*, 99: 1–15.

Nabi, Robin L., Carmen S. Stitt, Jeff Halford & Keli L. Finnerty (2006) Emotional and cognitive predictors of the enjoyment of reality based and fictional television programming: An elaboration of the uses and gratifications perspective. *Media Psychology*, 8: 421–47.

Neale, Stephen (1990) Questions of genre. In Oliver Boyd-Barrett & Chris Newbold (eds.) *Approaches to Media: A Reader* (London: Arnold), pp. 460–7.

Pennycook, Alastair (2010) *Language as Local Practice* (London: Routledge).

Penzhorn, Heidi & Magriet Pitout (2007) A critical-historical discourse analysis of reality television. *Communication*, 33: 62–76.

Redden, Guy (2008) Making over the talent show. In Gareth Palmer (ed.), *Exposing Lifestyle Television: The Big Reveal* (Aldershot: Ashgate), pp. 129–44.

Reeves, Byron & Clifford Nass (1996) *The Media Equation* (Cambridge: Cambridge University Press).

Richardson, Kay (2010) *Television Dramatic Dialogue. A Sociolinguistic Study* (Oxford: Oxford University Press).

Reiss, Steven & James Wiltz (2004) Why people watch reality TV. *Media Psychology*, 6: 363–78.

Scollon, Ron & Suzanne W. Scollon (2001) *Intercultural Communication*, 2nd edn. (Oxford: Blackwell).

Sellers, Mortimer (2004) Ideals of public discourse. In Christine Sistare (ed.), *Civility and its Discontents* (Lawrence, KS: University Press of Kansas), pp. 15–24.

Smith, Angela (2010) Lifestyle television programmes and the construction of the expert host. *European Journal of Cultural Studies*, 13: 191–205.

Terkourafi, Marina (2005) Beyond the micro-level in politeness research. *Journal of Politeness Research*, 1: 237–62.

Tolson, Andrew (ed.) (2001) *Television Talk Shows: Discourse, Performance, Spectacle* (London and Mahwah, NJ: Lawrence Erlbaum Associates).

Turner, Graeme (2010) *Ordinary and the Media: The Demotic Turn* (London: Sage).

10

'No eres inteligente ni para tener amigos... Pues anda que tú' ['You are not even clever enough to have any friends... Look who's talking!']: a quantitative analysis of the production and reception of impoliteness in present-day Spanish reality television

José Luis Blas Arroyo

Introduction[1]

One of the conclusions reached in many of the studies conducted on impoliteness is that the nature and degree of impolite behaviour are closely linked to the contexts in which it takes place, whether private or institutional. With regard to the latter, for example, attention has been paid to certain kinds of discourse in which verbal aggressiveness and impoliteness are part of the interactional behaviour that is expected of participants, as occurs in political debates that take place in parliament and at election time (Martín Rojo 2000; Fernández 2000; Harris 2001; Pérez de Ayala 2001; Bolívar 2005; Blas Arroyo 2011) or in television programmes about military training (Culpeper 1996; Bousfield 2008), to mention but a few. In recent years there has been a growing interest in analysing impoliteness in different media genres, especially from television. Of course, in other (not-so-distant) times it was difficult to find many such programmes. Along with pseudo-debates and talk shows of different kinds (Grindstaff 2002; Patrona 2006; Brenes 2007; Lorenzo-Dus 2007, 2009a; Hutchby 2008; Garcés-Conejos Blitvich 2009, 2013; Garcés-Conejos Blitvich *et al.* 2010; Fuentes 2013), researchers have recently found reality shows to be an important source of material for studying impoliteness (see, e.g., Culpeper, Bousfield & Wichmann 2003; Culpeper 2005; Lorenzo-Dus 2008, 2009b; Blas Arroyo 2010a, 2010b).

One of the most debated topics concerns the very essence of impoliteness in these programmes, which are mainly concerned with entertaining and the commercial interests of television company executives. Hence, it comes as no surprise that some scholars have raised serious doubts about the 'reality' of this impoliteness. Are the sequences of stark conflict in many of these programmes really impolite? Do instances of such conduct coincide with those that can be observed in daily life, away from the television spotlights? Further still, do their protagonists interpret the verbal (and non-verbal) aggression directed towards them as a threat to their face? And what about the viewers? Do they see things the same way as journalists, television critics, and other 'experts' do? Moreover, can we expect to see significant behavioural differences between individuals and different social groups?

Until recently, and coinciding with an important change in the role granted to the hearer in the interpretation of impoliteness (Eelen 2001; Locher & Watts 2008; Lorenzo-Dus 2009b; Garcés-Conejos Blitvich *et al.* 2010; Lorenzo-Dus, Garcés-Conejos Blitvich & Bou-Franch 2011), few empirical studies have adopted a perspective that goes beyond the analyst's own appreciations, however suggestive these may be. Both the paucity of quantitative approaches, which would allow the researcher's impressions to be supported or rejected, and the scarcity of works that address the way viewers receive impoliteness are weak points in this line of research.

Also, many of the studies published to date on impoliteness in reality shows have looked at formats in which there are very important differences among the protagonists in terms of the power axis and social distance (Culpeper 1996, 2005; Bousfield 2008; Brenes 2009; Lorenzo-Dus 2009b; Blas Arroyo 2010a; Chapters 8 and 9 in this volume). Specifically, in most of the genres examined impoliteness tends to run in basically one direction (expert to lay contestant), and the possibility of true conflict is practically ruled out because the recipient of the offence has barely any capacity to defend him or herself, let alone attack the offender. What happens, however, in programmes in which such distance appears to be much less, when not altogether neutralized? In this work my aim is to answer this question through an empirical analysis of a reality show genre – the dating game (see also Chapter 3) – on Spanish television. The programme is called *Mujeres y hombres y viceversa* (MHYV) [Women, men and vice-versa] and is broadcast daily by the privately owned channel Tele 5, which has a considerable following in Spain.[2]

Methodology

The work reported in this chapter comprised two studies: an Impoliteness Production (IP) study and an Impoliteness Reception (IR) study. This follows the design pioneered in Lorenzo-Dus's analysis of a British TV reality show (Lorenzo-Dus 2009b) and later adapted in Garcés-Conejos Blitvich *et al.* (2010) and Lorenzo-Dus *et al.* (2011). Methodological adaptations to Lorenzo-Dus's (2009a) work in this chapter include evaluation of different social groups for the production and reception of impoliteness. The IR study also includes samples from a Spanish talent show (*Operación Triunfo* ['Operation Success'] with the aim of evaluating potential differences across reality TV genres as regards the power imbalance axis – something that is made far more explicit in *Operación Triunfo* than in MHYV.

The reference corpus for the IP study consisted of 21 episodes of MHYV, aired in November 2011. In MHYV a number of contestants of both sexes (*pretendientes* [pretenders]) seek to 'conquer the love' of a *tronista* ['thronist']³ (two per sex each season). As part of the process of seduction and conquering, *pretendientes* and *tronistas* go on several dates together in different settings with the aim of getting to know each other better. They are recorded and what goes on during those dates is discussed in great detail in the television studio by a number of characters, such as the hostess (Emma García), a couple of 'experts in love'⁴ and, more sporadically, members of the public or relatives of the contestants. Additionally, there are other characters, known as *ganchos* [literally 'hooks'], usually former contestants who left their mark owing to their peculiar personality and who judge the performance of current contestants. These *ganchos* play a key role as far as this study is concerned, since it is their interventions that start off many of the impolite moves in the show.

Data for the IP study draw on a collection of the most aggressive sequences of MHYV as selected by Tele 5 and posted on its website, where many unsolicited comments were later posted by followers of the show. In this sense, it is important to underline the fact that, although I use some of the analytical tools of seminal second-order impoliteness studies (Brown & Levinson 1987; Culpeper 1996, 2005; Culpeper *et al.* 2003; Bousfield 2008), this analysis starts out from a selection of the most conflicting relationships between the participants in the contest, based on what lay persons have previously conceived as (undoubtedly) first-order impolite scenes, whatever nomenclature might be used to name them (on this issue, see below). In sum, impoliteness in both the IP and, even more so, later in the IR study, is not an aprioristic analytical label, but a real category defined previously by members of the audience.

The resulting sample – or actual analytic corpus for the IP study – comprises 25 video clips, each lasting between three and ten minutes, which have been transcribed and coded by the author in accordance with the following factors: (a) the person who starts the verbal conflict (name, role in the programme and gender); (b) its addressee – the person who will probably continue that impoliteness in successive moves (name, role and gender); (c) the type of moves in which the impolite utterances are produced; (d) the impoliteness strategies employed; and (e) the motivation underlying the impoliteness. In the more complex factors, such as the types of moves or the strategies used by the participants, the coding was also performed by a second coder, who is a university colleague in the area of Spanish linguistics. All the instances that the two coders did not agree on were removed from the analysis. This affected only 8 per cent of the utterances that were originally selected.

As regards the IR study, a sample of 50 first- and second-year university students[5] ('the audience') were asked to assess four video clips – three from MHYV and one from the last season (2009) of the talent show *Operación Triunfo* (OT). This was in order to check for any differences in the way impoliteness was received by the audience in different reality show genres. The differences among the participants in the power axis, as well as in their interactional rights and obligations, in these two reality shows are so important that – I hypothesize – they can be reflected in the way impoliteness is evaluated by the audience.

Once each video had been viewed twice, the members of the audience were asked to answer a series of questions concerning their beliefs about:[6]

(a) whether the protagonists' behaviour could be considered impolite or not ('Do you think the first speaker behaves badly towards his/her interlocutor? And what about the latter when he/she responds to the former?')
(b) its nomenclature ('What term(s) would you use to define that behaviour?')
(c) the level of impoliteness ('If you thought it was impolite, to what extent would you say it was impolite?')
(d) the extent to which the recipients were affected ('Do you think the interlocutor was offended by the speaker's behaviour?')
(e) the extent to which the members of the audience would be affected in a potentially similar situation, that is, in a TV show such as

MHYV ('Try to put yourself in the interlocutor's shoes: do you think you would have reacted in the same way in that situation?')

(f) the reality or fiction of that impoliteness in a programme shown for entertainment ('Although it is an entertainment programme, do you think the interlocutors have a reason to feel upset by the speaker?')

For the purposes of the sociological analysis mentioned above, different social factors regarding the respondents were also considered, namely sex (man/woman), age (under 20/over 25 years old)[7] and habitat (urban/rural).[8]

Although some reservations about analysing quantitatively complex and interactional phenomena like those contemplated in these pages have been reported (Herring 2004, p. 370), quantitvative methods have proven a valid instrument for empirically analysing impoliteness (see Blas Arroyo 2001, 2003; Lorenzo Dus 2009b; Garcés-Conejos Blitvich 2010; Lorenzo-Dus *et al.* 2011), as well as an indispensable toolkit with which to test hypotheses. In this case, the quantitative analysis in both the IP and IR studies was performed using the software application SPSS 18.0.[9] Together with the most common descriptive statistics (absolute and relative frequencies, averages, and so on) and the contingency tables and graphs that derive from them, a chi-square test (X^2) was also used to determine the reliability of some of the differences that were observed (level of significance: $p < 0.05$).

The IP study: the discursive realization of impoliteness in MHYV

Impolite moves

A first glance at the data shows that most of the discourse moves containing impoliteness in MHYV appear in the answers given by participants who have felt offended (N = 158; 60.5%) by the earlier interventions of their interlocutors in the initial offensive turns (N = 93; 35.6%).[10] These quantitative differences, together with almost negligible no-answer figures (N = 10; 3.8%), reflect marked differences vis-à-vis reality shows broadcast in other countries, such as *Dragon's Den* (DD), the one analysed by Lorenzo-Dus (2009b). In DD, where several entrepreneurs pitch their business ideas to five successful venture capitalists from whom they seek investment, the contestants have more room to manoeuvre. This, however, does not prevent 34 per cent of the discourse moves from not having a direct answer – a figure that contrasts sharply with the far lower number of such occurrences found in MHYV (3.8%). These differences become even clearer when we analyse the type of counter moves that the participants carry out in the sequences containing openly impolite behaviours. As can be seen in Figure 10.1, the overwhelming majority of these moves are offensive (65.5% vs. a meagre 9.8% in DD), followed a long way behind by others of a defensive nature (19.9% vs. 37% in DD) and a third group whose initially defensive essence contains the seed of an attack on the interlocutor (9.6%). In contrast, the moves in which the participant accepts or compromises with the offences received are reduced to the minimum expression in MHYV (0.6% vs. 19.5% in DD).

In short, we are dealing with a reality show in which, rather than justifying oneself when criticized, what the participants are really interested in is defending their face with all the verbal weapons at their disposal, including replying offensively, with the most hurtful insults, to the person who has previously offended them.

This overview offers several important qualifications regarding some of the institutional and social factors analysed in this study. One of the most important is the role played by the different interlocutors taking part in the programme. Thus, the quantitative analysis reveals the existence of significant differences among the main protagonists of the reality show (p. 0.003). As can be seen in Table 10.1, *ganchos'* moves are mainly offensive (78.8%) – their defensive moves provide only 8.7 per cent of the total. In contrast, *tronistas* (28.1%) and *pretendientes* (26.5%) invest significantly more time in defending themselves, as is to be expected in a contest in which the ability to react and ride out criticism without being affected by it seems to be an ingredient for success. Now, the fact that both *pretendientes* (56.6%) and *tronistas* (54.4%) use more than half

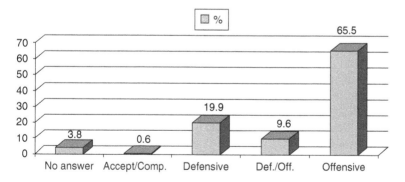

Figure 10.1 Types of counter moves in long sequences (%)

Table 10.1 Types of discourse moves in long sequences by roles (%)

Role	No answer		Accept/ Compromise		Defensive		Defensive/ Offensive		Offensive	
	N	%	N	%	N	%	N	%	N	%
Gancho	3	2.9	2	1.9	9	8.7	8	7.7	82	78.8
Tronista	1	1.8	1	1.8	16	28.1	8	14	31	54.4
Pretendiente	5	6	0	0	22	26.5	9	10.8	47	56.6
Others	0	0	0	0	3	33.4	0	0	6	66.6

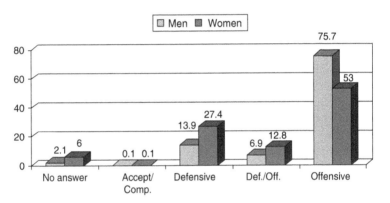

Figure 10.2 Types of discourse moves in long sequences by gender (%)

their moves to attack whoever has previously attacked them tells us something about what is expected of a show like MHYV. In this respect, attention must be drawn again to the quantitative differences between this study and the data reported by Lorenzo-Dus (2009b) in her analysis of *Dragon's Den*. Unlike what is observed in MHYV, in DD by far the greater part of all impolite activity is carried out by the experts (dragons), who devote no fewer than 94 per cent of their discourse moves to being offensive, versus only 9 per cent in the case of the contestants. Apart from cultural differences, this sharp contrast could be mainly related to the distance in the power axis between experts and contestants, which is much greater in DD than in MHYV.

Returning to MHYV, we can also see significant differences related to the gender of the participants in the contest (X^2: 18.694; p. 0.002; see Figure 10.2). Men (75.7%) realize a greater number of offensive moves than women (53.0%). In contrast, the latter realize twice as many defensive moves (27.4%) as the former (13.9%). Yet, the fact that there is a close relationship between this factor and that of the role played by participants makes it difficult to evaluate them independently. Indeed, the participants playing the role of *gancho* are mostly males, which is just the opposite of *tronistas*, who, in the corpus analysed in this study, are three females.

Impoliteness strategies and motives in offensive moves

In order to examine the use of impoliteness strategies in the offensive moves, regardless of whether they occurred in initiating or counter moves, I drew upon impoliteness classifications put forward by Culpeper (1996, 2005), later improved by Bousfield (2007, 2008) and then also tested by Garcés-Conejos Blitvich (2010) and Lorenzo-Dus *et al.* (2011); see also Chapter 8). Two changes were made to provide a more faithful account of the interactional behaviour of the contestants in MHYV. Firstly, the insult strategy was considered in isolation, since it plays a significant role in the relationships among some of the protagonists of the programme. Secondly, the strategies of 'Explicitly associate the other with a negative aspect' (Culpeper) and 'Criticize – dispraise h, some action or inaction by h, or some entity in which h has invested face' (Bousfield) were merged because they refer to similar attitudes and actions on the part of attackers towards their victims.

As can be seen in Table 10.2, the strategy that participants in MHYV prefer to use is scorn ('...no eres ninguna modelo/ más bien eres poco agraciada/ muy poquita cosa' [... you're no model/ in fact you're pretty unattractive really/ there is nothing remarkable about you at all]) (22.9%), including all and any of its variants, whether that means belittling their interlocutor's intellectual or any other capacity ('No eres inteligente ni para tener amigos' [You are not even clever enough to have any friends]), or ridiculing their present or past conduct ('... esos tatuajes me parecen una horterada' [I think those tattoos are a bit tacky]). The rest of the strategies are divided out in fairly equal proportions, although they all stand some way behind this scorn. This finding is similar to that obtained by Lorenzo-Dus (2009b), where the strategy 'Condescend, scorn, ridicule' topped the ranking of impoliteness in DD with even higher figures (31%) than those in MHYV – something to be expected given that in DD, as in other programmes of the same kind (*Operación Triunfo; Idol*), a set of experts with a considerable degree of competence in their field are judging the mistakes and failings of contestants who do not make the grade. What stands out is that in MHYV, where the distance between the main characters in the power axis is

Table 10.2   Impoliteness strategies in MHYV offensive moves

Impoliteness strategies in offensive moves	Number of occurrences	%
Condescend, scorn or ridicule	43	22.9
Criticize – dispraise h, some action or inaction by h, or some entity in which h has invested face	27	14.4
Sarcasm	26	13.8
Challenges	25	13.3
Hinder/block (deny turn, interrupt, shouting...)	24	12.8
Insult	22	11.7
Other	21	11.2
Total	188	

Note: The strategies that offered low figures in our corpus ('Be uninterested, unconcerned', 'Disassociate from the other', 'Use inappropriate identity markers') have been included within a ragbag labelled 'Other', in order to facilitate the statistical analysis. No examples of the strategy 'Use obscure or secretive language' were identified in the corpus.

much more balanced than in DD or OT (because of the absence of any true difference in professional competence of any kind), this strategy of scorning and ridiculing the other has a similar weight. Even more, unlike what happened in those other shows, in MHYV both the aggressor and the victim implement this strategy, with the result of continuous loops of impoliteness. This finding points to the salience of scorn as a form of impoliteness that has become a true goldmine for the media (see also Chapter 9).

Harshly criticizing one's interlocutor and associating him or her with negative aspects is another of the favourite strategies used by the participants in MHYV. One of the most harshly condemned aspects is lack of honesty. This is a recurring accusation, for example, in many of the addresses the *ganchos* aim at *tronistas* and *pretendientes*, who are accused of acting according to spurious interests and principles that have nothing to do with the 'spirit' of the programme (that is, to find love).[11] Excerpt (1) illustrates one of these accusations. David *(gancho)* is harshly criticizing Gina *(pretendiente)* for manipulating and deceiving José Luis *(tronista)* for her own interests.[12]

(1) David: ... es quee→ vamos, lo que dices↑ cómo hablas↑cómo lo
               dices↑cómo lo manipulas↑ me recuerda mucho a ellas!
               [mujeres que David conoció en el pasado]

Gina: pero qué dices!!
David: lo que oyes/ y se pasa muy mal!! QUE TE ESTÁS
       APROVECHANDO DE ÉL PARA MONTAR TU PAPELÓN!!
Gina: perdona?!
David: así de claro y así de sencillo! y como yo lo ve mucha gente...

[David: ... I meeean→ come on, what you say↑ how you speak↑how
        you say it↑how you manipulate things ↑ you really remind
        me of them! [some women that David had known in the
        past]
Gina: what are you on about?
David: You heard me/ and that makes you really suffer, you know!
       YOU'RE JUST TAKING ADVANTAGE OF HIM TO SHOW
       YOURSELF OFF TO EVERYONE!!
Gina: I beg your pardon?!
David: you heard me! And just like me a lot of other people see
       through you too...]

On some occasions (13.8 per cent), impoliteness is also conveyed by
means of sarcasm, a strategy by which the interlocutor indirectly loses
face through the use of implicatures (Culpeper 1996; Kienpointner
1997; Bousfield 2008; Garcés-Conejos Blitvich 2010; Blas Arroyo 2010b).
Although most of the protagonists of MHYV do not reach the levels of
dialectic competence and subtlety that are generally associated with the
technique (Ruiz Gurillo & Padilla Garcia 2009), there are several occasions
when a more prosaic version of this strategy is produced in the most heated
interactions. For instance, in Excerpt (2), Fabián, one of the *pretendientes*,
interrupts Elena, an old *gancho* (and girlfriend), with an ironic comment
in order to contradict Elena's statement about her pretended romanticism:

(1) Elena: ...pues yo soy bastante romántica (risas de Fabián)// y me
           encontré con una persona mayor/ un
           cate [drático
    Fabián: [es el romanticismo en persona (risas del público)
    Elena: te quieres callar ya pesao!! (risas del público)

   [Elena: ...well I'm quite romantic (Fabián laughs)// and I found
           myself with an older person/ a pro
           [fessor
    Fabián: [she's romanticism itself (the audience laughs)

> Elena: can you shut up, you are such a pain...!! (the audience laughs)]

Another impoliteness strategy involves attempts to hamper and, in extreme cases, prevent any chance of the interlocutor's expressing him or herself (12.8%). The tactics that are most commonly used to achieve this consist in continual interruptions, raising one's voice to the point where the other person can no longer be heard, and, in some extreme cases, standing up and addressing the other in an intimidating way.

Moreover, several instances (11.7%) were found in which the offender literally insults his or her interlocutor by using coarse language (*bocazas, paleto, poligonera, analfabeta, macarra*, and so on [big-mouth, peasant, chav, illiterate, lout]) that are clearly recognized as such in the linguistic community they both belong to.

The analysis of the interaction among these strategies and the role played by the different protagonists in the programme shows statistically significant differences (X^2: 37.475; p. 0.005). Indeed, some of the tactics described above are closely linked to certain characters in the contest. Thus, the intention to scorn the interlocutor is used above all by the *ganchos*, whose star role is to criticize (pitilessly) the contestants (both *tronistas* and *pretendientes* alike). Likewise, *ganchos* also top the lists in the use of sarcasm (53.8%),[13] the wish to hinder other participants (54.2%) and even the use of insults (47.6%).

The differences related to the gender of the participants are equally significant (X^2: 14.223; p. 0.027). The men employ more belligerent language than the women in the use of nearly all the strategies. This is true in the case of scorning their opponent, a strategy the males (67.4%) use literally twice as often as the females (32.6%), but also realizing sarcasm (69.2% / 30.8%), insults (68.2% / 31.8%) and many other strategies taken into account in the analysis (Other) (76.2% / 23.8%). It is interesting to note how this genderlect profile is maintained, and even increases, among the *pretendientes*. Indeed among these *pretendientes*, men outdo women in each and every one of the macro-strategies that were analysed, which confirms the idea that, under the same conditions, the men in this programme display considerably more aggressive and impolite behaviour than the women.

At the same time, men also outdo women in some of the motives underlying the impolite moves (X^2: 16.279; p. 0.012). Particularly striking in this regard are the differences that are seen when the interlocutor's intelligence is being criticized, where the figures for the men (82.4%) are four times higher than those of the women (17.6%). Yet, the same can also be said for other human qualities of a moral nature (honesty, sincerity...) (71.7% / 28.3%), or the skills needed to establish romantic relationships (60.9% / 39.1%). The only area in which the females (69.6%) rank higher than the males (30.4%) is in criticizing the discursive behaviour of their interlocutors, whom they accuse of being too aggressive, and in which those involved are (not by chance) nearly always men.

Now, if the men nearly always 'outdo' the women in terms of abundance of that kind of attacks, who are these aimed at? The women (70.6%) are the object of offensive comments regarding their intelligence far more commonly than the men (29.4%) (p. 0.021). This reveals sexist attitudes that are deeply rooted in Spanish society[14] and, it appears, are also taken up by the younger generations (or, at least, by those lower sectors of society that take part in these programmes). In contrast, in the other categories that were mentioned, it is the men who are the main targets of the attacks, although this time the differences are not statistically significant (X^2: 8.597; p. 0.198).

The IR study: the reception of impoliteness in MHYV by the audience

In the IR study, an 'audience' made up of 50 undergraduate students were asked to act as raters and consider four videos that contained sequences previously selected by the Tele 5 staff as being openly impolite. Through a number of questions included in a questionnaire, we sought to evaluate the way in which impoliteness was judged by members of this audience, as well as the degree of their personal involvement regarding the way the participants in a reality show like MHYV behave, that is, how the raters would have reacted if they found themselves in a similar situation. Complementarily, and with the aim of comparing these same judgments with reality shows that offer a different format and rules of behaviour, in this part of the research we also included a recording from the last episode of *Operación Triunfo*, a programme that I have analysed in previous studies (Blas Arroyo 2010a, 2010b).

The videos, each lasting between two and three minutes, contained the following material:

• Video 1: one of the members of the OT judging panel, Risto Mejide, evaluates one of the contestants (Tania) in a very negative manner, criticizing her for her atrocious performance in one of the galas of the programme, and also blaming her for her partner's poor performance. Following a row between Risto and other members of the panel, who endorse Tania's performance and consequently prevent her from being 'nominated' (for eviction and thus having to leave the contest), she reacts by swearing at Risto ('vete a tomar por culo' [fuck off]) and insulting him ('hijo de puta' [you bastard!]).

- Video 2: one of the *ganchos* in MHYV, David Morales, harshly criticizes one of the female *pretendientes* in the programme (Abi), whom he accuses of being an impostor, as well as lacking intelligence for having said that her participation in the contest had nothing whatsoever to do with 'finding love' (the aim, it should be remembered, of the programme) but with making money and becoming famous. After a timid attempt to deny it, Abi bursts into tears and rushes off the set.

- Video 3: another of the *ganchos* usually present on the show, Vicente, accuses another *pretendiente* (María) of entering the contest for spurious, selfish reasons. Yet, in contrast to what happened in the previous video, this time the contestant lashes back with a furious retort against her opponent's attacks; amidst screams and continual interruptions and reproaches, she accuses him of being disrespectful to her, as well as of having other physical and moral defects.

- Video 4: two former participants in the programme, Elena (*tronista*) and Fabián (a *pretendiente* who had seduced Elena some months before), appear on the show in order to make public the reasons why their relationship had failed. Fabián accuses Elena of not being honest and going out with another boy while, supposedly, their relationship had already begun. Elena reacts to these accusations by condemning Fabián for having done hardly anything to help their relationship which was, as a result, bound to fail. These and other tough reproaches (including the dubious sexual abilities of both) alternate throughout the three minutes the video lasts.

In the first part of the analysis, the members of the audience were asked whether the behaviour of the first participants in each video (Risto, David, Vicente and Fabián) could be considered impolite. As can be seen in Figure 10.3, an overwhelming majority (89%) believed this was the case, versus only 7.2 per cent who did not think so. The opinion of a number of media commentators and scholars who think that everything that happens in these programmes is just part of the 'game' or the 'community of practice' in which the participants take part, and therefore cannot be taken seriously (Montgomery 1999; Mills

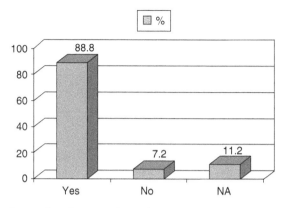

Figure 10.3   Respondents' ratings of impoliteness by first speakers in videos 1 to 4

2002;[15] but see against, Culpeper 2005; Garcés-Conejos Blitvich *et al.* 2010; Lorenzo-Dus *et al.* 2011) was thus not shared by the audience in the IR study.

Among the terms that are used to describe the behaviour of these protagonists, *impolite* is found only in third place (14.8%), behind those that refer to their *lack of respect* (*lack of respect, he has no respect,* and so on) (22.4%) and the term *rude* (21.5%). Behind these we find others such as: *thoughtless* (9%), *excessive* (8.4%), *coarse* (5.5%), *bad-mannered* (2.6%), *uncouth* (2.3%) and *cocky* (1.5%). Lastly, and occurring fewer than five times in the corpus, we find a host of derogatory terms, such as: *arrogant, disgusting, silly bugger, cynical, gossip, fault-finder, rabble, defiant, unpleasant, hard, disrespectful, childish, conceited, arrogant, spiteful, retarded* and *gross,* as well as a few phrases along the same lines: *with no feelings, tactless, lacking in tact* (for issues of nomenclature on impoliteness analysis, see Watts 2008; Garcés-Conejos Blitvich 2013; Garcés-Conejos Blitvich *et al.* 2010).

With regard to the degree of this impoliteness, the answers were sorted into several groups using a 7-point Likert scale (see Lorenzo-Dus 2009b): 1-2 (not at all or not very impolite), 3 (impolite), 4-5 (very/extraordinarily impolite), 6 (Other), 7 (No answer). These results are shown in Table 10.3.

Not only do most of the raters consider the characters' behaviour to be offensive, but they also see it as being 'very or extraordinarily' impolite (46%). Fabián, the protagonist in video 4, is the one who is judged in the most balanced way. Nevertheless, characters 2 and 3, *ganchos* in

Table 10.3 Respondents' ratings of participants in videos 1 to 4

Ratings	Participants									
	Risto (Video 1)		David (Video 2)		Vicente (Video 3)		Fabián (Video 4)		Total	
	N	%	N	%	N	%	N	%	N	%
Not at all/Not very impolite (1–2)	12	20	7	11.6	5	8.3	15	25	39	15.6
Impolite (3)	13	21.6	16	26.6	11	18.3	12	20	52	20.8
Very/ Extraordinarily impolite (4–5)	31	51.6	32	53.3	33	55	19	31.6	115	46
Other	2	3.3	3	5	6	10	0	0	21	8.4
NA	2	3.3	2	3.3	5	8.3	14	23.3	23	9.2

MHYV, are evaluated very strictly by the audience, with frequencies for answers 4 and 5 above 53 per cent, while the opinions of those who interpret their behaviour as not at all or not very impolite barely reach 10 per cent. Lastly, mention should be made of one special case – that of Risto, the panel member in OT. Although the majority consider his behaviour to be very impolite (51%), the proportion of those who see his behaviour as meeting the expectations of TV experts is by no means negligible (20%) and, in any case, is twice that obtained by the *ganchos* in MHYV.

In sum, it seems that at least part of the public establishes differences between the ways the 'experts' behave in the two reality shows under analysis: while it could be considered acceptable and constructive for a competent member of the panel to criticize – even harshly – the performance of a contestant who wishes to be successful in the music world, the same is not the case when less professional goals are involved.

By gender, more women (59.6%) than men (46.7%) selected the most extreme ratings ('very/extraordinarily impolite'). Yet, these differences are not statistically significant (X^2: 3.511; p. 0.172). In contrast, those related to the age of the respondents are significant. While the younger group (<20) gave the more benevolent answers of 1 and 2 (not at all or not very impolite) (23%), the older group (>25) were far stricter (90% consider the protagonists' behaviour to be impolite or very impolite, versus 77% of those in the first group) (X^2: 3.388; p. 0.046).

The raters who live in large towns and cities (63.4%) were stricter in their assessments than those who live in smaller towns and villages (46.8%). These statistically significant differences (X^2: 6.069; p. 0.048) could be related to the existence of an almost hidden – but often real – feeling of superiority from many inhabitants of big cities towards customs and attitudes of people identified these days as *canis* and *chonis* – two pejorative words often associated with participants in these reality shows.

Furthermore, respondents' opinions were almost identical to those that were given to another question in the questionnaire: 'Do you think the interlocutor felt offended by the first speaker's behaviour?' (see Figure 10.4). The bars of almost identical height in Figure 10.4 reflect this fact. Observe how, again, an overwhelming 86.5 per cent think that the contestants felt offended by the behaviour of those that criticize them, versus a very small 6.7 per cent who think the opposite (figures that are again almost identical to the ones given by those who believed that the participants had not been impolite).

When the members of the audience were asked about the reasons that led them to think that way, the answers were distributed relatively uniformly. Those who believed that the interlocutors really felt insulted, repeatedly pointed to certain reactions that the TV camera picked up on from time to time. Thus, nearly all of them highlighted Abi's (video 2) inability to go on speaking and her untimely departure from the television studio in tears. Raters also noticed how Tania (video 1) was unable to control her facial expression, which unmistakably reflected the fact that Risto's merciless criticism has deeply hurt her. In contrast, raters

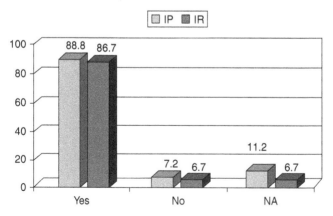

Figure 10.4 Comparison between the respondents' ratings of impoliteness by first speakers and the feeling of offence by the interlocutors (videos 1 to 4)

were not so unanimous about Elena (video 4), whose smiling attitude at nearly all times was, for some, a clear sign of nervousness resulting from the cutting remarks she has received. For others, however, it was the correlate of a cynical attitude that has nothing to do with being the target of real impoliteness, but instead with the rules of TV reality shows, which this contestant was believed to handle with great expertise.

Regarding this last fact, much can be gathered from the answers to the question: 'Although it is just a TV show designed to entertain, do you think the interlocutors have reasons to feel hurt by the speaker's words?' Although, as shown in Figure 10.5, responses were far from the unanimous agreement seen in the foregoing questions, the majority gave an affirmative answer (58.7%), which represents over twice the number of negative answers (24.2%), followed by 7.6 per cent who were undecided and 9 per cent who gave no answer (NA). These differences were significant (Chi-square test; p. 0.025). In any case, in view of the quantitative differences between the data obtained now and those mentioned earlier, it would seem that, initially, some raters evaluated (out of context) the impression they got of those who behaved impolitely and how this impoliteness was received by the targets of such behaviour. Only afterwards did they react upon realizing (now in context) that this behaviour may be a part of the rules of the media game. Note how a far-from-negligible 17 per cent of the sample (the sum of the undecided and the NA) was undecided, whereas for another significant 24 per cent, the diagnosis was then negative. Whatever the case may be, attention must be drawn to the fact that this proportion is significantly lower than the majority of raters, who believed that there were sufficient reasons for taking offence, even in entertainment programmes like OT and MHYV. We might well ask ourselves (and this could be an issue for future research) what would have happened if the questions in the questionnaire had been asked in a different order.

As we have seen so far, the behaviour of the speaker who introduces the first offence in dyadic interactions is overwhelmingly viewed as impolite by the audience (with some qualifications introduced later due to the fact that the shows are considered entertainment programmes). But how does this same audience see the behaviour of the interlocutors, who nearly always react to the offensive moves with a snappy retort? As shown in Figure 10. 6, there are some significant quantitative differences between these characters and the previous ones. Indeed, almost 35 per cent of the raters now deny that the behaviour of these second participants can be labelled as impolite (versus 7.2 per cent, remember, in the case of the first participants). Nevertheless, this figure is surpassed

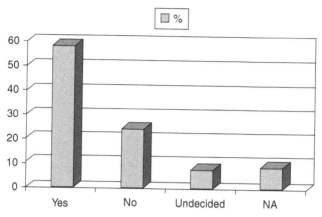

Figure 10.5 Respondents' ratings to the question: 'Although it is just a TV show designed to entertain, do you think the interlocutors have reasons to feel hurt by the speaker's words?'

by those who also see these characters as behaving in a rude and inconsiderate way (57%).

Thus, we can see how, unlike other reality shows,[16] impoliteness is a cornerstone of the interactional behaviour of almost all the characters in a programme like MHYV, including the contestants. And as shown by the example analysed here, it is also reflected sporadically in other talent shows, such as *Operación Triunfo*, in which this sort of behaviour was initially forbidden. The difference between the two is that if a contestant in OT insults or is disrespectful to a member of the panel, s/he may end up having to leave the programme. Nothing of the sort happens in MHYV, where the participants are free to come back with a retort – even violent – in response to those who have attacked them at some earlier time.

Now, on this occasion, there are clear differences in the way each protagonist is assessed (see Table 10.4). At one end of the spectrum, there is a character like Abi, who unsuccessfully attempts to deny David's accusations and, finding herself powerless, rushes out of the TV studio in tears. It is therefore not surprising to find that for the vast majority of the raters (70%) Abi's behaviour is considered not at all or not very impolite. She is followed by María (44%), who (unlike Abi) decides to stand up to the person who criticizes her (Vicente) using a good number of reproaches. Perhaps that is the reason why a considerable proportion of raters also considers her performance to be impolite (15.3%) or very impolite (30.7%). This opinion is mainly based on the fact that she yells and interrupts a lot, which is an attitude that almost from the

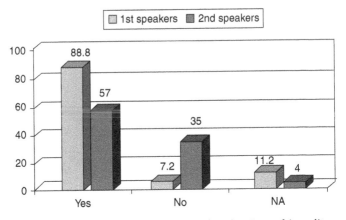

Figure 10.6 Comparison between the respondents' ratings of impoliteness by first and second speakers (videos 1 to 4)

Table 10.4 Respondents' ratings of impoliteness by second speakers in videos 1 to 4

Ratings	Participants									
	Tania (Video 1)		Abi (Video 2)		María (Video 3)		Elena (Video 4)		Total	
	N	%	N	%	N	%	N	%	N	%
Not at all/Not very impolite (1–2)	6	10	42	70	23	44	7	13.7	78	35
Impolite (3)	6	10	5	8.3	8	15.3	13	25.4	32	14.3
Very/ Extraordinarily impolite (4-5)	44	73.3	6	10	16	30.7	28	54.9	94	42.1
Other	1	1.6	2	3.2	1	1.9	0	0	4	1.8
NA	3	5	5	8.3	4	7.6	3	5.8	15	6.7

start clashes with that of the *gancho*, and which leads to a true battle between them.

At the other end of the spectrum, we find Elena (MHYV) but, above all, Tania (OT), whom three-quarters of the sample considered extraordinarily impolite following her foul-mouthed, insulting reply to the member of the panel who had previously condemned her performance. This is the only case in which the negative opinions of the contestant actually exceeded those of the person who previously attacked her. For the audience, it seems that breaching the rules in a contest like OT is considerably worse than if it occurs in a reality show in which the power relationships among the participants are more evenly balanced, such as those underlying MHYV.

Lastly, an analysis of the social factors linked to the audience also reveals a number of interesting differences. Thus, for instance, the women in the sample are significantly more sympathetic towards these contestants than the men. This may be due to the fact that in the four videos that contestant-role was played by members of their same gender, who were the victims (also in all the cases) of cruel dialectic blows from males. The percentage of female raters who saw these characters' behaviour as not at all or not very impolite stands at around half the sample (43.1% versus only 27.6% among the men). And, additionally, female raters produced fewer harsh opinions (answers 4 and 5 on the questionnaire) (41%) than their male counterparts (56.9%) (X^2: 4.852; p. 0.028).

Regarding age, the younger group (<20) was more indulgent to the behaviour of these characters than the older one (>25). Of this latter group, 63.6 per cent interpret these contestants' reactions as impolite or very impolite, versus 47.5 per cent among the younger members (X^2: 3.239; p. 0.085).

The purpose of the final question was to find if the raters would have reacted as the contestants did, had they found themselves in a similar situation. As can be seen in Figure 10.7, the proportion of raters who gave an affirmative answer dropped sharply (33.6%) and the number of those who answered 'no' was considerably higher (48.4%). Furthermore, we must also consider those who said they would react in a different way (9.4%) and, to a lesser extent, those who were undecided (4%) or did not answer – NA – (4.5%).

These data now show a clear distancing on the part of the raters from the participants. On this occasion, over half the sample (which many of those who previously considered that there were sufficient reasons to feel annoyed undoubtedly belong to) claim that they would not have reacted in the same way as the contestants. This distancing probably derives from the feeling of superiority as well as satisfaction due to their not finding themselves in the same circumstances as the ill-treated youngsters in the programme (see Culpeper 2005). This was referred to in some of the raters' comments for whom the contestants' replies were too visceral – a 'mistake' that they would never make, either by keeping quiet ('no insulta quien quiere, sino quien puede' [a Spanish saying meaning something along the lines of 'You are not offended by those who wish to offend you, but by those who can']) or by reacting in a considerably more even-tempered way. Indeed, some raters had no qualms about underlining that they had much better manners than the

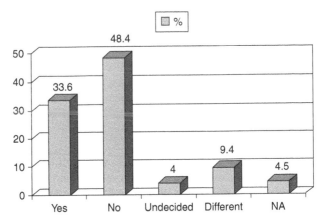

Figure 10.7   Respondents' ratings to the question: 'Try to put yourself in the interlocutor's shoes: do you think you would have reacted in the same way in that situation?'

contestants, while others acknowledged that when one takes part in a reality TV show, one is fully aware of what one is in for. As one member of the audience put it: 'qui no vulga pols, que no vaja a l'era' (something like: 'if you don't want to get burnt, don't play with fire').

Conclusions

By undertaking a quantitative analysis, this research has shown that there are important differences between the realization of impoliteness between a Spanish reality show like MHYV and other television shows in which there is a greater difference between the participants in terms of power. In this regard, we have seen how many of the impolite utterances in MHYV arise in the course of counter moves, that is to say, in the reply turns of those who have previously been offended. This is one considerable difference with respect to other reality shows (OT, *The Weakest Link*, *DD*), in which impoliteness is almost exclusively found in initiating moves.[17] The differences are even more manifest when we evaluate the kind of counter moves that are carried out by the protagonists, which are predominantly of an offensive nature. Yet, this general outlook displays an interesting co-variation with the role of the protagonists of the contest, where the *ganchos* stand out above the rest, as the main champions of the offence moves, while *tronistas* and *pretendientes* spend more time on defending themselves from criticism, although their potential for being offensive is also quite high.

Therefore, it comes as no surprise that *ganchos* are recorded as the highest users of the main impoliteness strategies, most of which have been pointed out in earlier studies (Culpeper 1996, 2005; Bousfield 2008; Lorenzo-Dus 2009b). Some peculiarities have been identified in the present context, for example, that scorning and ridiculing the opponents tops by far the list of these strategies. This is striking given the fact that none of the participants can boast of being more competent or knowledgeable than the other participants (which is something that the panels in other reality shows are able to brandish). If we also take into account the frequent presence in this programme of insults and swear words, which are less usual in other contests, we find ourselves faced with a singular profile of impoliteness.

With regard to the IR study, we have seen how the audience initially interprets the behaviour of those who begin the offensive moves as being very impolite, but also views those who answer them back in the same way. Nevertheless, in this latter group some variability is observed, as some participants were classified as being very impolite while other raters did not see things the same way. At the same time, it seems that the raters are even harsher on the contestants who behave impolitely in reality shows regulated by stricter rules and where the interactional power distance between the interlocutors is greater (the case of OT, as opposed to MHYV).

A more detailed analysis of these attitudes reveals that they are more complex than they may initially appear. On the one hand, the vast majority of respondents answered that the contestants had felt offended and that they also had good reason to feel so. Nevertheless, these figures started to diverge somewhat when the programme was inserted within the context of a TV show. In this context, most of the respondents continued to believe that the participants were justified in feeling bad about the criticism from their co-participants, but the figures for those who disagreed with this belief grew substantially with respect to the previous questions. One gets the impression, then, that the members of the audience (at least part of this audience) follow these reality shows with great interest and involvement, and that it is only when someone reminds them that it is just an entertainment programme that they begin to see things from another angle. Furthermore, this interpretation varies even more when the respondent is put in a hypothetical situation that is similar to the one undergone by the participants in these reality shows. Under these circumstances, most of the audience moved away from the fate of those participants whose behaviour, just a short time before, they had justified due to the offences they had received.

The statistical analysis has also enabled us to uncover some differences in the sample of social groups analysed in this chapter. Thus, we have been able to observe that both the younger members of the audience and those who live in small towns and villages are the most benevolent towards the participants. In contrast, the older ones and those living in large towns and cities display a considerably more critical attitude, perhaps as a result of a greater sense of superiority vis-à-vis those who take part in these reality shows, who are frequently associated with a vulgar taste and behaviour. There are also differences related to gender: women were tougher on those who start the offence move, but at the same time they were more sympathetic towards those who reply to that impoliteness (often also by means of offensive moves, as we have seen). This finding may be related to the fact that the members of this second group were always women, whereas the members of the first (those who begin the impoliteness) were in all cases men. This is also a fact that points towards the particular degree of involvement with which the majority of this (mostly female) audience watches these programmes.

Notes

1. I wish to thank my daughters, Silvia and Paula, for their help in selecting and interpreting the corpus. I am also indebted to Juan González for his help with the statistical processing of the data, as well as two anonymous referees for their invaluable comments on an earlier draft of this chapter. In any case, they are not responsible for the errors that may be found.
2. *Mujeres y hombres y viceversa* is the Spanish version of the original Italian programme *Uomini e Donne*. In its debut in 2008, it obtained an audience share of more than 18 per cent in its time slot, and has since been leader for several seasons.
3. The word *tronista* is a Spanish neologism made up by the show's creators, which literally refers to the person who is sitting on the 'throne of love'.
4. At that time, a former Spanish porn star (Miriam Sánchez) and her husband, the sports journalist Pipi Estrada.
5. All the members of the audience, except three, were familiar with the programme, which they watched on a more or less regular basis, although this familiarity was significantly higher among the females. All of them were undergraduate students taking History and Education degrees, and can therefore be considered lay judges with no background in (im)politeness models.
6. All members of the audience were told beforehand that they were participating on a completely voluntary basis and that it was in no way part of their regular academic curriculum.
7. An intermediate group of raters lying between the two intervals was left without being coded for this factor.

8. The first case includes the raters who live in the provincial capitals of Castellón and Valencia, while the second contains all the others. Our interest in this fact derives from the traditional opposition between the inhabitants of big cities and those of (mainly) rural places in Spain on attitudes and behaviours. Although many of these differences have clearly been attenuated in today's globalized world, they still persist in many ways. This is something that can be applied to many places in Spain, including the Valencian Community, where this study was conducted.

9. For the purpose of quantification in different sections of the study, we follow some analytical procedures used previously in the literature (see Holmes & Schnurr 2005; Lorenzo-Dus 2009b; Garcés-Conejos Blitvich *et al.* 2010).

10. All the categories used in this IP study are taken from previous research (Bousfield, 2008; Lorenzo-Dus 2009b), with the exception of what I have called 'defensive-offensive' moves, that is, those interactional moves within an initially defensive essence that contains the seed of an attack on the opponent.

11. For more details on the question of authenticity in media discourse, see also Lorenzo-Dus (2008, 2009a).

12. In transcribing the examples we followed a simplified and partially modified version of the conventions employed by the Valesco group in their analysis of Spanish colloquial speech (Briz & Valesco 2002).

13. As regards this matter, *ganchos'* performance is very similar to that of the experts in talent shows (Chapter 9) or the judges in courtroom shows (Lorenzo-Dus 2008). The difference seems to lie in the degree of know-how in the performance of sarcasm as a witty resource for conflict and verbal duelling. (I am grateful to one of the reviewers for suggesting this interpretation.)

14. According to a recent opinion poll carried out by the Federación de Mujeres Progresistas (FMP) among young people, younger generations are today at least as sexist as their parents, if not more. Thus, although traditional sexism is now frowned upon, many young couples still consider that 'the girl must please the boy' or that 'women need protection'. More than 40 per cent of the males in the poll believed that females feel fulfilled when they get a boyfriend and 60 per cent think that jealousy is normal in a romantic relationship. Moreover, the majority of respondents identify females with personality traits such as tenderness and supportiveness, and males with aggressiveness and bravery. These attitudes were considered very alarming by the FMP, who saw them as potentially leading to young females '… justifying male mistreatment, considering that it is a natural behaviour of men'.

15. Among the Spanish TV commentators, the following quote from Antonio Rico is illustrative of this way of thinking that emphasizes the deceit of everything that happens in these reality shows: 'The contestants and the audience of *Mujeres y hombres y viceversa* (Telecinco) dance more or less stuck, while a terrible song is playing. Everyone pretends to have fun, everyone pretends to share confidences with others, everyone makes allegedly knowing gestures, everyone smiles nonstop. And, as in *On the road*, the apocalyptic novel by Cormac McCarthy, where raining ash and hunger is the measure of all things, then *Mujeres y hombres y viceversa* seems the first sign of a cold glaucoma fogging the world' (*Levante-El Mercantil Valenciano*, 18 October 2012).

16. This is the case of *Operación Triunfo* and many other recent talent shows, such as *Tú sí que vales* and *La voz*.
17. Although an intriguing matter, it is difficult to reach a conclusion about eventual differences between MHYV and the British shows, due to cultural divergences between the Spanish and the British way of making television. On the one hand, both *The Weakest Link* (Culpeper 2005) and *Dragon's Den* (Lorenzo-Dus 2009b) match the interactional profile of the – also Spanish – *Operación Triunfo* (Blas Arroyo 2010a) better than the one of *Mujeres y hombres y viceversa*, because of the above-mentioned differences among the contestants in institutional roles and power access. But on the other, the kind of rudeness that we have seen in all these programmes seems to be part of a global tendency to make confrontation and impoliteness a key element of today's television.

References

Blas Arroyo, José Luis (2001) 'No diga chorradas..' La descortesía en el debate político cara a cara. Una aproximación pragma-variacionista. *Oralia*, 4: 9–45.

Blas Arroyo, José Luis (2003) 'Perdone que se lo diga, pero vuelve usted a faltar a la verdad, señor González': Form and function of politic verbal behaviour in face-to-face Spanish political debates. *Discourse and Society*, 14(4): 395–423.

Blas Arroyo, José Luis (2010a) La descortesía en contextos de telerrealidad mediática. Análisis de un corpus español. In Francesca Orletti & Laura Mariottini (eds.), *(Des)cortesía en español. Espacios teóricos y metodológicos para su estudio* (Roma-Estocolmo: Università Degli Studi Roma Tre-EDICE), pp. 183–207.

Blas Arroyo, José Luis (2010b) Niveles en la caracterización de las estrategias discursivas. Aplicaciones al estudio de la descortesía en un corpus mediático. *Español Actual*, 94: 47–76.

Blas Arroyo, José Luis (2011) *Políticos en conflicto. Una aproximación pragmático-discursiva al debate electoral cara a cara* (Bern: Peter Lang).

Bolívar, Adriana (2005) La descortesía en la dinámica social y política. In Jorge Murillo (ed.), *Actos de habla y cortesía en distintas variedades de español: Perspectivas teóricas y metodológicas. Actas del II Coloquio Internacional del Programa EDICE* (San José de Costa Rica: Universidad de Costa Rica), pp. 137–64.

Bousfield, Derek (2007) Beginnings, middles and ends: Towards a biopsy of the dynamics of impoliteness. *Journal of Pragmatics*, 39(12): 2185–216.

Bousfield, Derek (2008) *Impoliteness in Interaction* (Amsterdam: John Benjamins).

Brenes, Ester (2007) Estrategias descorteses y agresivas en la figura del tertuliano televisivo: ¿transgresión o norma? *Linred*, 2: 1–19.

Brenes, Ester (2009) *La agresividad verbal y sus mecanismos de expresión en el español actual*. Doctoral thesis, Universidad Sevilla.

Briz, Antonio & Grupo Valesco (2002) *Corpus de conversaciones coloquiales* (Barcelona: Ariel).

Brown, Penelope & Stephen Levinson (1987) *Politeness. Some Universals in Language Use* (Cambridge: Cambridge University Press).

Culpeper, Jonathan (1996) Towards an anatomy of impoliteness. *Journal of Pragmatics*, 25(3): 349–67.

Culpeper, Jonathan (2005) Impoliteness and entertainment in the television quiz-show: *The Weakest Link. Journal of Politeness Research*, 1(1): 35–72.

Culpeper, Jonathan, Derek Bousfield & Anne Wichmann (2003) Impoliteness revisited with special reference to dynamic and prosodic aspects. *Journal of Pragmatics*, 35: 1545–79.

Eelen, Gino (2001) *A Critique of Politeness Theories* (Manchester: St. Jerome Publishing).

Fernández, Francisco (2000) *Estrategas del diálogo. La interacción comunicativa en el discurso político-electoral* (Granada: Método Ediciones).

Fuentes, Catalina (ed.) (2013) *(Des)cortesía para el espectáculo: estudios de pragmática variacionista* (Madrid: Arco Libros).

Garcés-Conejos Blitvich, Pilar (2009) Impoliteness and identity in the American news media: The 'Culture Wars'. *Journal of Politeness Research*, 5(2): 273–304.

Garcés-Conejos Blitvich, Pilar (2010) The YouTubification of politics, impoliteness and polarization. In R. Taiwo (ed.), *Handbook of Research on Discourse Behavior and Digital Communication: Language Structures and Social Interaction* (Hershey, PA: IGI Global), pp. 540–63.

Garcés-Conejos Blitvich, Pilar (2013) El modelo del género y la des/cortesía clasificatoria en las valoraciones de *Sálvame* por parte de la audiencia. In Catalina Fuentes (ed.), *(Des)cortesía para el espectáculo: estudios de pragmática variacionista* (Madrid: Arco Libros).

Grindstaff, Laura (2002) *The Money Shot. Trash, Class, and the Making of TV Talk Shows* (Chicago/London: The University of Chicago Press).

Harris, Sandra (2001) Being politically impolite: Extending politeness theory to adversarial political discourse. *Discourse and Society*, 12(4): 451–72.

Herring, S. C. (2004) Computer-mediated discourse analysis: An approach to researching online behaviour. In S. A. Barab, R. Kling & J. H. Gray (eds.), *Designing for Virtual Communities in the Services of Learning* (New York: Cambridge University Press), pp. 338–76.

Holmes, Janet & Stephanie Schnurr (2005) Politeness, humor and gender in the workplace: Negotiating norms and identifying contestation. *Journal of Politeness Research*, 1(1): 121–49.

Hutchby, Ian (2008) Participants' orientations to interruptions, rudeness and other impolite acts in talk-in-interaction. *Journal of Politeness Research*, 4(2): 221–43.

Kienpointner, Manfred (1997) Varieties of rudeness: Types and functions of impolite utterances. *Functions of Language*, 4(2): 251–87.

Locher, Miriam & Richard J. Watts (2008) Relational work and impoliteness: Negotiating norms of linguistic behaviour. In Derek Bousfield & Miriam A. Locher (eds.), *Impoliteness in Language* (Berlin and New York: Walter de Gruyter), pp. 77–101.

Lorenzo-Dus, Nuria (2007) (Im)politeness and the Spanish media: The case of audience participation debates. In María E. Placencia & Carmen García (eds.), *Research on Politeness in the Spanish-Speaking World* (Mahwah, NJ and London: Lawrence Erlbaum Associates), pp. 145–66.

Lorenzo-Dus, Nuria (2008) Real disorder in the court: An investigation of conflict talk in US courtroom shows. *Media, Culture and Society*, 30(1): 81–107.

Lorenzo-Dus, Nuria (2009a) *Television Discourse: Analysing Language in the Media*. (Basingstoke and New York: Palgrave Macmillan).

Lorenzo-Dus, Nuria (2009) 'You're barking mad, I'm out': Impoliteness and broadcast talk. *Journal of Politeness Research*, 5(2): 159–87.

Lorenzo-Dus, Nuria, Pilar Garcés-Conejos Blitvich & Patricia Bou-Franch (2011) On-line polylogues and impoliteness: The case of postings sent in response to the Obama Reggaeton YouTube video. *Journal of Pragmatics,* 43: 2578–93.

Martín Rojo, Luisa (2000) Enfrentamiento y consenso en los debates parlamentarios sobre la política de inmigración en España. *Oralia,* 3: 113–48.

Mills, Sara (2002) Rethinking politeness, impoliteness and gender identity. In Lia Litosseliti & Jane Sunderland (eds.), *Gender, Identity and Discourse Analysis* (Amsterdam/Philadelphia: John Benjamins), pp. 69–89.

Montgomery, Martin (1999) Talk as entertainment: The case of *The Mrs. Merton Show.* In Louann Haarman (ed.), *Talk about Shows: La Parola e lo Spettacolo* (Bologna: CLUEB), pp. 101–50.

Patrona, Marianna (2006) Conversationalization and media empowerment in Greek television discussion programs. *Discourse and Society,* 17(1): 5–27.

Pérez de Ayala, Soledad (2001) FTAs and Erskine May: Conflicting needs? Politeness in *Question Time. Journal of Pragmatics,* 33(2): 143–70.

Ruiz Gurillo, Leonor & Xosé Padilla García (2009) *Dime cómo ironizas y te diré quién eres: Una aproximación pragmática a la ironía* (Frankfurt: Peter Lang).

Watts, Richard J. (2008) Rudeness, conceptual blending theory and relational work. *Journal of Politeness Research* 4(2): 289–318.

11
'You are killing your kids': framing and impoliteness in a health makeover reality TV show

Cynthia Gordon

Introduction[1]

Honey We're Killing the Kids is a reality television programme that addresses the childhood obesity epidemic in two ways: by providing expert health education to individual families, and by packaging these families' experiences as 'makeovers' for public consumption. *Honey We're Killing the Kids* (hereafter: *Honey*) aired in the United States in 2006 and 2007 on TLC (The Learning Channel) and in Canada on The Food Network; the show was developed and originally aired in the UK; Australia and New Zealand also produced versions. *Honey* has become perhaps best known for a focal scene that occurs in every episode: Parents of children with bad health habits – and the at-home viewing audience – are presented with larger-than-life, morphing computer-generated images that predict how the children will look as they mature to age 40, given a nutrition expert's analysis of their current physical health and everyday habits. In speaking with the parents in this scene, the nutrition expert directly, and very negatively, evaluates the children's health habits and tells parents 'you are killing your kids'. Following an understanding of impoliteness as tied to identity (e.g., Garcés-Conejos Blitvich 2009), the expert's discourse is readily interpretable as 'impolite': It questions and undermines the parents' positions (in this case, as 'good parents'). In fact, the parents use various accounting strategies to save face (see Gordon 2011), supporting the contention that impoliteness has occurred.

(Im)politeness, however, is generally not well understood as a discursive phenomenon in 'intergroup, institutional, mediated' communication between three or more participants (Garcés-Conejos Blitvich, Lorenzo-Dus & Bou-Franch 2010, p. 692). The aforementioned scene from *Honey* is of this type: Interaction occurs between individuals who orient to one another through social categories (nutritionist and parents) in a specialized encounter occurring on reality television (hereafter: RTV), which involves heavy editing and a displaced audience. Ways of approaching such communication include the concept of 'genre' (Garcés-Conejos Blitvich 2010) and a cognitive interpretation of 'frame' (Terkourafi 2002, 2005). In this chapter, I suggest an alternative (yet complementary) approach, following Locher and Watts (2005), who identify Goffman's (1974) social, interactional notion of 'frame' as productive for investigating (im)politeness. Tannen and Wallat (1993, p. 59) refer to this notion as 'interactive frame', or a 'definition of what is going on' at any given conversational moment. I demonstrate how RTV's complex framing shapes impoliteness in this context.

Specifically, I expand Goffman's (1974, 1981) notion of 'laminated' or 'layered' frames, and argue that different laminations lead to multiple interpretations of the nutritionist's discourse, for both the parents and RTV audience: Her discourse is impolite, but also potentially interpretable as appropriate or 'politic' (Watts 1989), depending on how the frame is understood. This view builds on research conceptualizing (im)politeness primarily from participants' and native speakers' evaluations – first-order (im)politeness (e.g., Chapter 1; Locher & Watts 2005), while also explaining the complexity of impoliteness on *Honey* and in other (mediated, multiply-framed) contexts. The analysis contributes to understanding impoliteness in discourse, while also adding the idea of laminated interactive frames to the expanding 'impoliteness' toolbox – which includes (among others) 'genre', a cognitive understanding of 'frame', the notion of 'face', and the idea that (im)politeness strategies are intertwined with identity-work. It also offers an alternative perspective to the recent suggestion that Goffman's 'frame' concept is too static, and ill-suited for contemporary impoliteness scholarship (see Garcés-Conejos Blitvich 2013).

My analysis treats frames not as fixed, but as discursively created to constitute multiple social realities and identities. I show how frames are *blended* (Gordon 2008, 2009): at least two definitions of the situation co-exist, as when a conversation simultaneously accomplishes both parent–child pretend play and the child's naptime preparations; they are also *embedded* (Gordon 2002, 2009), meaning one frame is fully contained within another, as when characters in a novel play a card game (see Goffman 1974). The recurring scene I analyse is framed both as a health consultation and an intervention; I show how this blended frame is created through various discourse strategies, most notably word choice of the nutritionist and narrator, as well as through visual cues. While in a health consultation, the nutritionist's behaviour is 'impolite' – clinicians generally try to minimize face-threat for patients and families (e.g., Lutfey & Maynard 1998) – it can be read as 'appropriate' (and indeed, necessary) in a life-saving intervention frame.

Further, the blended frame is embedded in a 'larger' frame providing the 'rim of the frame' (Goffman 1974, p. 82): 'the RTV makeover'. This rim indicates a text's genre in that it works 'to define the text against those things which it is not' (Frow 2005, p. 106). Impoliteness is sanctioned in the makeover genre; it helps to establish the participants' desperate need for the upcoming 'transformation' (Weber 2009, p. 7) by threatening participants' interactional positions. In addition, this and other genres exist within a larger discourse system (see Chapter 1). The RTV discourse system sanctions (though does not neutralize) impoliteness; its presence is arguably for the audience's benefit (e.g., Culpeper 2005). The dual orientation of televised contexts – to participants and at-home audiences – needs to be considered, too (see Chapter 2). Thus, impoliteness on RTV is nuanced and productive, meriting further exploration.

In what follows, I first introduce the concept of (interactive) frame as a means of approaching (im)politeness. Second, I introduce *Honey* in more detail. Third, analysis reveals how creating laminated frames shapes interpretations and functions of the nutritionist's verbal behaviours, thus highlighting the multifaceted nature of her 'impoliteness' and the layered nature of RTV. I also discuss the parents' (limited) discourse in the encounter. The conclusion outlines this study's contributions to discourse-analytic approaches to (im)politeness and RTV.

Background

Communication always occurs within – and creates – what Bateson (1972) and Goffman (1974) call a *frame*. A frame – or what Tannen and Wallat (1993, pp. 59–60) term an *interactive frame* – is a 'definition of what is going on in interaction, without which no utterance (or movement or gesture) could be interpreted'. For example, in a teasing frame, 'you are killing your kids' means something different than in a serious, medical diagnosis frame. An utterance's meanings and functions, including regarding (im)politeness, arise within the frame of uttering.

Discourse analysts have demonstrated how participants use linguistic and paralinguistic features – what Gumperz (1982) calls *contextualization cues* – to indicate how they mean what they say, or to construct a frame (e.g., Tannen & Wallat 1993; Gordon 2009). For example, analysis of pretend play involving a preschool-age child and her mother (Gordon 2002) demonstrates how the mother uses a high-pitched voice and addresses her daughter as 'Blue Fairy' (among other strategies) to signal a *play frame* (Bateson 1972). However, framing is often more complex than this and multiple situational definitions can exist simultaneously: Goffman (1974, 1981) observes that frames are laminated, or layered, in interaction; he explains that 'Every possible kind of layering [of frames] must be expected' (Goffman 1974, p. 157).

Extending Goffman's theorizing, Gordon (2002, 2008, 2009) demonstrates how frames are *blended* and *embedded* in family conversations. For instance, when the aforementioned mother uses the same high-pitched voice and says to her daughter, 'Blue Fairy, will you help me pick a book' (to read before the child's naptime), the situation is simultaneously play and not-play. The frame is blended; the mother uses play to accomplish a parenting task. In contrast, embedded frames are created, for example, when the mother and child engage in mommy-baby role-reversal pretend play, and the child begins to repeat language from a shared prior experience. This embeds a re-enactment frame in the play frame, the latter of which Goffman (1974, p. 82) would call the 'rim of the frame', indicating 'just what sort of status in the real world the activity has, whatever the complexity of the inner laminations'. Differently stated, whether the mother and child re-enact a specific event or enact generalized pretend roles (such as 'mommy' and 'baby'), the activity's overall status – the rim – is 'play'.

As frames are created moment-by-moment in talk, so too is (im) politeness, (see, for example, Locher & Watts 2005; Culpeper 2005). In fact, Watts (1989, p. 137) suggests that 'the nature of the social activity' must be considered in assessing behaviour as (im)polite or 'politic' (appropriate). This indirectly acknowledges that (im)politeness is fundamentally connected to interactive frame. Yet the notion, along with the idea of laminated frames, has not been systematically applied to explore it.

A related (though distinct) understanding of frame underpins Terkourafi's (2002, 2005) *frame-based approach* to impoliteness. Terkourafi (2005, p. 247) suggests that frames are cognitive, representing 'situations holistically as structures of co-occurring components'. This builds on Schank and Abelson (1977) and corresponds with what Tannen and Wallat (1993, p. 60) call 'knowledge schemas', or 'expectations about people, objects, events and settings in the world'. These two understandings of 'frame' – as 'interactive frame' (the understanding

I adopt) versus 'knowledge schema' (Terkourafi's understanding) – are interconnected. For example, interlocutors' knowledge schemas about medical encounters shape how they produce and interpret discourse moment-by-moment, and specific experiences alter medical encounter knowledge schemas.

For Terkourafi (2005, p. 247), frames capture what is 'normal' and 'expected' in different circumstances. Her quantitative analysis of recorded everyday conversations uncovers patterns of co-occurrence between politeness forms (e.g., verb type) and sociological variables (e.g., interlocutors' age, the setting). She argues that politeness resides 'in the regularity of this co-occurrence': Forms are 'polite' '*because* they are regular' (Terkourafi 2005, p. 248). These forms arise out of identity concerns; they are 'face-constituting' and usefully understood as 'politic' (see Terkourafi 2005, p. 252).

Qualitative research also observes particular politeness forms in different communication activities (roughly, 'frames') and suggests that identity concerns motivate politeness. Especially relevant for this study are analyses of health communication finding that clinicians typically treat encounters with patients and families with what Lutfey and Maynard (1998) call 'interactive caution'; they aim to minimize face-threat for others by using numerous politeness strategies, including mitigation, hedging, and hesitation. Clinicians' 'interactive caution' surfaces in various encounters, including between physicians and oncology patients (e.g., Lutfey & Maynard 1998), nurses and diabetic patients (e.g., Karhila *et al.* 2003), and even veterinarians and pet owners (e.g., Stivers 1998). In particular, politeness strategies cluster around sensitive topics, such as patient's lifestyle (e.g., food and alcohol consumption) and 'life or death' issues (e.g., serious diseases) (Linell & Bredmar 1996). Thus, within 'health consultation' frames, physicians tend to use polite forms, especially in talk about delicate matters.

Garcés-Conejos Blitvich's (2010) genre approach also links patterns of (im)politeness to context. Texts belonging to a genre share communicative purpose and intended audience, higher-level structural elements such as 'moves', and micro-discursive choices (Garcés-Conejos Blitvich *et al.* 2010, p. 692; see Swales 1990). Analysing Fox News' *The O'Reilly Factor*, Garcés-Conejos Blitvich (2010) argues that the host's frequent impoliteness typifies the 'confrontational news' genre of which the show is a key example; while face-threatening to guests, Bill O'Reilly's behaviour builds rapport with the audience. Similarly, Culpeper's (2005) analysis of *The Weakest Link* – an 'exploitative' quiz show 'designed to humiliate contestants' (p. 35) – argues that the impolite comments of the host-persona (Anne Robinson), are primarily intended for audience entertainment (though contestants experience face-attack). Thus, while the impoliteness of O'Reilly and Robinson is arguably an essential generic element, it is still treated as 'impolite' by show participants.

Impoliteness is also typical of RTV as a broader 'discourse system'. As discussed in Chapter 1, a discourse – 'a system of communication shared by certain communities' – is enacted in various genres. A discourse system involves recognizable patterns of language use, language socialization, ideological positions, and interpersonal relationships (Scollon & Scollon, 2001 p. 107). For RTV impoliteness is common (e.g., Culpeper 2005; Gordon 2011); participants' situated identities – or 'subject positions' (Anton & Peterson 2003, as cited in Garcés-Conejos Blitvich 2009; see also Davies & Harré 1990) – are threatened and delegitimized as a matter of course.

In summary, research suggests that impoliteness relates to: (1) regularity of forms by 'context', whether in the sense of a situational frame or more abstract schema; (2) identity implications for participants; and (3) assessments by participants and viewers. My research draws on the concept of layered frames to reveal how RTV's framing affects interpretations and functions of seemingly 'impolite' behaviour.

Methods and data

I use discourse analysis to explore the 'impoliteness' displayed by Dr Lisa Hark, the nutritionist on *Honey We're Killing the Kids,* in a key scene that occurs once per episode. In this scene, Hark shares with parents her (negative) assessment of their children's health practices and her (negative) prediction of how the children will physically mature, given their habits. Using conventions associated with interactional sociolinguistics (e.g., Gordon 2009), this scene was transcribed across all 13 episodes of season one of *Honey.*[2] Each episode features one family, and the scene of interest typically lasts between four and five minutes. My analysis presents representative extracts.

Honey fits into the 'makeover' genre of reality TV (e.g., Weber 2009). As Lewis (2008, p. 452) explains, *Honey* offers families and especially children 'a complete lifestyle makeover' and 'combines social observational elements and melodramatic spectacle with a strongly didactic approach to issues of diet, health, and family relations'. The show has 'a moral/pedagogic agenda' (Skeggs & Wood 2011, p. 5) while also featuring the transformation narrative typical of a makeover show (e.g., Weber 2009). 'Makeover' RTV shows publicly scrutinize people's private lives and behaviours (Lunt 2008); *Honey* is no exception. The following extract from a TLC (The Learning Channel) press release for the programme gives a sense of the show's purpose:

> HONEY WE'RE KILLING THE KIDS! [...] issues a critical wake-up call for parents. [...] nutrition expert Dr. Lisa Hark shows how everyday choices can have long-term impacts on children [...] Using state-of-the-art computer imaging and certified assessments based on measurements and statistics, Dr. Hark first gives Mom and Dad a frightening look at the possible future faces of their children – and a dramatic reality check. Then, introducing her new guidelines and techniques, Dr. Hark works with parents to reverse course and give their kids a healthy diet and active lifestyle. [...]

Each episode begins with the introduction of one family (with at least two approximately school-aged children) in which a narrator (heard but not seen) provides an overview of the family's poor health habits. He also gives previously gathered background information on the children's medical information (including height, weight, and blood pressure measurements; fitness test results; etc.). Clips of family life are spliced into this introduction. Hark, the show's nutrition expert, is also introduced by the narrator and does some self-introduction in speaking directly to the camera. The scene discussed above, wherein Hark gives the 'reality check' to the parents, next appears. This scene, for which the children are not present, comprises the primary data for my analysis and includes the multiple 'impolite' verbal behaviours this study explores. The scene also includes the morphing computer-generated images that show the prediction (formulated by Hark and her 'team of experts') of how the children will look as they mature to age 40. These images promise not only weight gain and poor health, but also 'that chubby kids will turn into burn-out losers with sallow faces, mullets, missing teeth, paunches, and a general air of felonious misery' (Weber 2009, p. 140). At the end of this scene the parents agree to participate in the family health makeover programme.

Of the 13 families participating in season one, 12 are headed by wife-husband pairs and one by a single mother. They seem to be from various places around the United States. Ten families are identified as white, two as African American, and one as Hispanic. The socio-economic status of families is not discussed, though it has been suggested that transformational reality TV shows promote middle-class values (e.g., Ferguson 2010; see also Gordon under review, regarding *Honey* specifically).

After the scene in which Hark presents the images and confronts the parents, she is shown introducing new rules to the families in their homes over the course of three weeks. Each week the families are portrayed as struggling to comply with these rules, such as 'dump the junk' (i.e., avoid eating sweets and other low-nutrition foods) and 'limit screen time' (i.e., cut down on television and video games). Family members ultimately improve and generally succeed. At the end of each episode, Hark shows the parents new visual images predicting how the children will look as they mature into adulthood, provided that they continue to follow her rules. As Kendrick (2008, p. 389) remarks, 'these new, healthier adults are clear-skinned, well-groomed, smiling, and, vitally, thin'.

Analysis

Characterizing the nutritionist's discourse

In the recurring scene I analyse, Hark makes it known to parents that their children have bad habits that will impact their future health in profound ways. One way she does this is through showing the visual images predicting how (terribly) the children will look as they age. This threatens the parents' face, or their parental identities, as I have argued elsewhere (Gordon 2011): When a child has a 'spoiled' identity (Goffman 1963) – such as when he or she looks unkempt (Collett 2005) – parental identities are damaged. Hark also prompts the parents to react to and take blame for what is depicted in these images, producing utterances such as 'Do you feel at all responsible for the way he [the child] looks as an adult'? (Gordon 2011, p. 3560). Parental reactions to these images and Hark's comments, as Gordon (2011) demonstrates, include 'response cries' (Goffman 1981) like *oh my God, wow,* and *terrible*; emotional displays (such as crying); avowals of emotion (such as when one mother says, voice breaking, that she feels *really bad* that her son could look as is predicted); and statements of culpability (as when a father utters, while crying, *it's my fault*). These strategies can be understood as face-saving in that they facilitate parents' *accounting* for the situation and their behaviours (Gordon 2011; see Buttny 1993). Collectively, their presence suggests that what transpired in the scene – both the images that parents were shown and what was said to them – has threatened their parental identities, and that Hark's discourse is worthy of close attention.

The nutritionist threatens the parents not just in what she says but how she says it. Overwhelmingly, she reports negative information about the children's diets in direct ways, using little mitigation and often emphatically stressing highly evaluative words, both of which threaten parents' interactive positions as 'good parents' and are therefore interpretable as impolite, by the parents themselves and by the witnessing audience at home.

For instance, in episode 4, Hark begins her discussion by providing a negative assessment of the food diary (a record kept of food consumed over the course of several days, prior to the family's participation in the programme) of the couple's 9-year-old daughter.

(1) Dr Hark: Now let's start with Autumn.
  Her food diary was APPALLING.

Through the negatively evaluative (and emphatic) adjective *appalling*, Hark threatens not only the face of Autumn (who is not present), but of the parents too, because monitoring and directing children's behaviours, including food intake, are responsibilities that are socio-culturally linked to parents (e.g., DeVault 1991). Similarly, in episode 9, Hark addresses the sugar consumption of an 11-year-old girl, stating: *The amount of sugar-filled sweets and drinks that Skylar consumes, is frankly STAGGERING. Over a GALLON of sweetened tea . every two days!* Again, she uses a highly evaluative word (*staggering*) with emphatic stress to highlight inappropriate consumption.

Additional examples include the nutritionist describing 4-year-old James' current diet as *a real mess* (episode 13) and 8-year-old Mateo's diet as *a liquid time-bomb* (episode 8). She observes that 7-year-old Jessie's *diet and eating behavior* are *simply OUT OF CONTROL* (episode 3) and that 9-year-old Patrick's *food intake is almost OFF the scale* (episode 7). Hark likewise comments on children's lack of physical activity (though less frequently), such as when she notes in episode 2 that 10-year-old Kevin *spends up to SIX HOURS A DAY watching television, and he hardly gets ANY exercise.*

In addition to freely offering negative, value-laden assessments of the children's practices (thereby indirectly threatening parental face), Hark also directly accuses the parents, often using '*you*'. In the following extract (from episode 13) Hark describes not only a child's poor eating behaviour (5-year-old Jessica takes only one bite of food to determine if she likes it) but also the parents' inappropriate response (offering her an unhealthy food if she rejects the first food).

(2) Dr Hark: Unfortunately, when it comes to trying a new food,
  she simply takes one bite,
  and if she doesn't like it,
  you quickly offer her an alternative.
  A TASTY UNHEALTHY snack!

Here Hark makes clear that the parents are failing in their duties and thereby are responsible for the child's poor health outlook. The next extract shows a similar strategy, with Hark addressing the behaviour of 5-year-old Bradley (in episode 12).

(3) Dr Hark: I know he's only five,
               but he is learning VERY FAST
               that if he screams loud enough,
               he's gonna get his way, no matter what!

In this extract, the nutritionist does not use '*you*', but it is clear that it is the parents who are going to give the child *his way, no matter what*. They are not appropriately strict; elsewhere Hark notes that Bradley and his two brothers eat *VAST amounts of junk food*.

Hark is also very direct in predicting that each child will not reach average predicted life expectancy given his or her gender and race. This suggests that the parents, far from being 'good parents', are actually shortening their children's lifespans. A typical example, from episode 1, shows Hark speaking with the parents of two boys:

(4) Dr Hark: The average African-American man lives to be sixty-nine.
               Unless you make a radical change,
               I predict,
               that the actual life expectancy for both of your children,
               will be about FIFTY-EIGHT . years of age.

Again, Hark uses emphatic stress here to draw attention to the children's shortened predicted lifespans. And, she places blame on the parents, using '*you*'. Immediately after giving the life expectancy information, Dr Hark's 'impoliteness' reaches its peak: She says to parents, *you are killing your kids*. In stating this, Hark usually emphasizes the word *killing*, as shown in the examples below, from episodes 7 and 2.

(5) Dr Hark: By feeding them THAT diet,
               and allowing them to lead such an inactive lifestyle,
               you are KILLING your kids.
(6) Dr Hark: If your children continue to eat a high-fat,
               high-sugar, high-calorie diet,
               there is a HIGH likelihood
               that they will develop diabetes,
               heart disease, cancer, and other medical problems.

You've HAD a chance to keep them healthy,
but in reality,
you're KILLING your kids.

In this final (ultimate) attribution of blame, Hark discursively constructs the parents as failing in their role and as contributing to the
children's (predicted) shortened lifespan. It is perhaps not surprising
that this often elicits uncomfortable glances between parents (if not
greater emotional displays like crying or tearing up); their positions
as good parents are threatened. However, they typically are not given
the discursive space to contradict Hark: Across episodes, parents accept
what she says as truth. In only one episode do parents momentar-
ily question the validity of the projections and what Hark says: They
chuckle quietly, and the father utters of the prediction of what his
daughter will look like at age 40, *Good thing it's only a computer projection, not a def- definite.* Hark, however, quickly reasserts her expertise,
emphasizing her years of practice and using medical terms such as
clinically obese.

Following Culpeper's (2005) discussion of how *The Weakest Link* host
repeatedly utters 'you are the weakest link, goodbye', Hark's repetition
of *you are killing your kids* can be viewed as creating her own on-screen
persona for the benefit of at-home viewers. In addition, however, it
affects the co-present parents, who react as if they have experienced
face-threat: On *Honey*, the parents use accounting strategies in response
(see Gordon 2011). And, the face threat seems to 'work': at the end
of the scene, Dr Hark offers the parents a chance for redemption, an
opportunity to participate in her *intensive nutrition and fitness regime,*
which they all accept.

In summary, in the encounter with the parents, Dr Hark uses direct
language in negatively assessing children's health habits. This can be
read (by the participants and the audience) as highly impolite toward
the parents, who arguably are responsible for the children's food intake
and exercise practices. Hark also is direct in stating how long she thinks
the children will live, and in blaming the parents for the situation. And
indeed, parental reactions to what takes place in the scene suggest that
their faces have been threatened; crying, for instance, is a 'symptom of
face-loss' (Culpeper 2005, p. 57). This face-loss is presumably connected
to not only the information Hark presents, but also to how it is presented. In the following sections, I suggest that her behaviour, however,
is difficult to categorize as simply 'impolite' when the layered frames of
the scene are considered.

Impoliteness in a health consultation frame

Hark's verbal behaviours take place within an interaction framed as a health consultation. Narrator commentary and the splicing together of particular scenes accomplish this framing for the viewers. Further, within the scene itself, which is experienced by the show's participants and witnessed by the audience, Hark's use of language helps construct this frame. The health consultation frame is thus created through various strategies, including words used by the narrator, visual cues, and Hark's use of 'medical' and 'scientific' language in speaking with the parents. However, within this frame her discourse contrasts sharply with everyday clinical health communication behaviours, and is thus interpretable as impolite.

Before Hark's encounter with the parents, the show's narrator introduces her to the viewing audience as *nutrition expert Dr Lisa Hark* (though as the show unfolds she is most often referred to as *Lisa* and sometimes as *Dr Lisa*). Her health knowledge and expertise are repeatedly foregrounded: The narrator notes that Hark is in consultation with the *Harvard School of Public Health,* she has *twenty years experience,* and she is *one of America's TOP nutritionists* (note that Hark is a Registered Dietitian and has a PhD in Education; she is not an MD). He remarks that Hark draws on *scientific data* and uses *state-of-the-art* (or *cutting-edge*) *technology* in producing (with input from her *team of experts*) the *computer-projections* that the parents are shown. It is noted that she puts each child's every behaviour *under the microscope.*

Visual elements of the show preceding the scene also frame it as a health consultation for the audience. Hark is shown early in each episode wearing a white lab-coat, speaking with another expert who is also wearing a lab-coat (a medical doctor, who is identified as *Dr Keith Ayoob, Albert Einstein College of Medicine*). Hark is also shown looking at charts and graphs. These details reinforce the impression that scientific data and Hark's medical expertise will be relevant in the upcoming interaction between the parents and Hark; it is thus foreshadowed to be a kind of medical health consultation. (In the scene itself, she wears a pants suit, not a lab-coat, however.)

In addition to the narrator's talk and visual details framing the scene as a health consultation, Hark also uses discourse that constructs this frame as she talks to the parents. In extract 7 (from episode 1), Hark explains the preparation behind the encounter:

(7) Dr Hark: As you know, we've wei:ghed and measured them, ((*the children*))

and we've done a series of tests.
I've also had a chance to review their current diet.
And combining ALL of that information,
with the LATEST computer technology?
We have the ability to project
how your children MIGHT look,
in the years to come.

Hark here indicates that she has undertaken empirical scientific study (she mentions the activities of *weighing, testing, measuring, reviewing,* and *combining information*) and has used *the LATEST computer technology.* Hark's word choice conveys to the parents (and the television audience) how the computer-generated images – the 'scientific' predictions – were created. Simultaneously, her words create a particular frame: It is a kind of health consultation in which she is the medical expert.

This frame is more subtly created through the repeated mentioning of numbers and measures as Hark interacts with the parents. When speaking about children's weight, for example, she consistently refers to comparative measurements, noting for example that a 10-year-old girl (episode 7) *weighs more than most EIGHTEEN YEAR OLDS,* and that a ten-year-old boy (episode 3) *weighs almost TWICE as much as he should;* when speaking about food consumption, she makes remarks that one child (episode 1) is eating *nearly a thousand calories a day MORE than he needs,* and another (episode 8) is eating *THREE TIMES the amount of calories that he needs.* These numerical comparisons, connecting weight to age, and actual versus ideal calorie consumption, have a medical, scientific air about them (although in fact, they are quite general). They thus help construct the situation as a health consultation.

Overall, contextualization cues in the form of word choice and visual elements of the programme are used to frame the encounter as a health or medical consultation between an expert clinician and laypersons. Yet, Hark's behaviour strays in notable ways from the conventionally polite ways of interacting in such encounters. Compare what Hark says to the parents of three children – *The diet that you are feeding them now . is KILLING your kids* (episode 3) – to how it is recommended that veterinarians confront an owner of an obese pet: 'Deliver the information without making it personal. Instead of saying, "You've been feeding the dog far too much and that's why he's having problems," try something like, "Sometimes, when dogs take a little more food than they need, they can develop this type of problem"' (Jackson & Gray 2005, p. 220). Hark's use of *you* and *killing* are especially notable. She approaches the sensitive issues of food consumption and potential future disease and shortened lifespan in ways that clearly contrast with typical clinician discourse in health consultation frames, encouraging an 'impolite' reading of her talk both by the co-present parents who experience face-threat, and the show's viewers.

Impoliteness (?) in an intervention frame

Assessing Hark's 'impoliteness' is made more complex however by the fact that the situation is also framed in another way. The physical surroundings hint that the 'health consultation' between the nutritionist and parents is actually (or also) something else. The parents do not meet Hark in a medical office, for example; instead, the set for the scene looks something like a cross between a medieval dungeon and an abandoned warehouse. (In the BBC version, the parents and expert meet in a cell-like, white room, reminiscent of a futuristic hospital.) The physical setting not only may serve to appear dramatic and to interest the audience, but also may function to 'scare' the parents. In fact, through discourse too, the encounter is constructed as not 'only' being a health consultation: It is simultaneously an 'intervention', creating *blended frames* (Gordon 2008, 2009). While interventions typically take place in people's homes (not dungeons), a fundamental feature is that the target person is 'unsuspecting' (van Over 2009); the unfamiliar scene in *Honey* may contribute to catching the parents off-guard.

Following van Over's (2009) analysis of episodes of the A&E documentary *Intervention*, the practice of intervention unfolds when 'a group of collaborators exert social pressure to bring about change in another interlocutor's perceived identity, usually when that person is deemed to be an "addict," in need of "help," who is likely to resist lesser persuasive attempts'. Addicts participating in *Intervention* are not informed about the intervention in advance, but instead are surprised by it (this brings up ethical considerations for RTV; see Kosovski & Smith 2011). Recurring kinds of statements made by an addict's family members and friends during the confrontation itself include, among others, blunt statements about a negative future (e.g., *if you continue like this you will be dead*) (van Over 2009). These are similar to Hark's *you are killing your kids*. Because *Honey*'s scene between the parents and Hark is framed as an intervention, her bluntness is understandable as appropriate.

Language is used to foreshadow the encounter as an extra-persuasive, intervention event. *Honey*'s press release, for example, refers to giving parents *a frightening look at the possible future faces of their children – and a dramatic reality check*, as well as a *critical wake-up call*. Similar language occurs on the programme, used by both Hark and the show's narrator, and heard by the at-home audience. For instance, across episodes the narrator notes that because changing the family's behaviour *won't be easy*, Hark is *going for shock tactics*. Near each episode's beginning, Hark emphasizes that she will be *tough* or *really tough* because radical changes are needed. And, just before the scene, she utters some version of the following directly to the camera: *What I need to do now is show Mom and Dad how their children will look at the age of forty if they continue on this path. If this doesn't motivate them, I don't know what will*. This suggests an intervention. Thus, the upcoming encounter – including the shocking images and direct discourse – appears to be motivated by these families' desperate need of help; it is a life-saving intervention (though it could be motivated by other factors too, like ratings).

This framing is reinforced in the actual encounter with the parents. As mentioned, the dungeon-like set could help shock and alarm them, helping to persuade them to accept the health makeover. It also appears that the parents are 'surprised' by what takes place, as one is typically in an intervention. In some episodes, Hark greets the parents and then says, *You must be wondering why I brought you here tonight* (episode 11), which implies that they do not know. In others, she immediately describes what will happen in the encounter, again suggesting that the parents lack awareness (*I brought you here tonight, to offer you a look into the future*; episode 3). And, as discussed in Gordon (2011), the parents produce shocked and surprised reactions to what Hark shows them, including response cries, such as *it's horrible* (father in episode 10), *very-very shocked. Very shocked* (father in episode 12), and *real. rude awakening* (mother in episode 9). They also more directly indicate surprise, such as when the mother in episode 13 reacts to the computer-generated images of her son: *That was scary, not what I expected*. In one case, a mother who had participated in *Honey* reported to the press that she felt 'blindsided' by the images of her children (Owen 2006).

The imposing setting, the ways in which the narrator and Hark talk about the encounter as requiring extra-persuasive efforts, the apparent lack of information the parents have going into the encounter, and Hark's direct statements about the negative consequences if the parents do not reform, all contribute to framing this encounter as an intervention. In this frame, Hark's 'impolite' behaviour serves a meaningful function, and can be interpreted 'politic'. In other words, because the social situation in which Hark's language occurs is discursively defined not only as a health consultation but simultaneously as critical intervention, the term 'impolite' does not fully capture what is going on: While her behaviours may be interpreted as impolite by the participants and/or by the at-home audience, they are in another sense appropriate.

Hark's seeming 'impoliteness' helps motivate parents to take immediate action, which is part of interventions (in successful interventions addicts immediately agree to go to rehab). This surprise and immediate action are lacking in many health consultation frames. In fact, of everyday health communication, physicians' 'zeal to be polite' regarding overweight and obese children leads to lack of recognition of paediatric weight problems by parents, and lack of documentation by physicians (Stephens 2009). This in turn leads to lack of action and hurts children long-term (Stephens 2009). Framing the situation as an intervention sanctions the impoliteness (even if participants or viewers perceive the behaviour as impolite; see Culpeper 2005). Her scare-based tactics are thus 'politic' within an intervention frame. They are also part of what creates that frame. Because the frame is blended, and given the parents' reactions, the 'impolite' reading of her behaviours also remains possible, of course.

Impoliteness (?) in the makeover RTV frame and the RTV discourse system

The blended health consultation/intervention frame is situated within a broader frame: 'Makeover RTV' is continually defining the situation at every moment. For the participants, the cameras are constantly present (though it is possible they sometimes forget them) as they are scrutinized and transformed. Hark's language and behaviours appear highly scripted at times, such as when she offers advice. For the viewing audience (and the analyst), scenes are spliced together and juxtaposed, the narrator constructs a story, and participants' commentaries to the camera are inserted at appropriately dramatic moments to create a plot of health transformation. Thus, even when the frame is a health consultation/intervention, it is more broadly an RTV makeover. Frames are laminated: The health consultation/intervention frame is *embedded* (Gordon 2002, 2009) within the RTV frame. This serves as the 'rim of the frame' that indicates the overall status of the activity (Goffman 1974, p. 82); for instance, while the characters depicted in a novel are engrossed in a card game, the 'rim' is the novel. In *Honey*, Hark's discourse (throughout) is interpreted (or at least is interpretable), by the participants and audience alike, within a definition of the situation that indicates, 'this is makeover RTV'.

Frow (2005) suggests that Goffman's 'rim of the frame' is akin to the notion of genre. The concepts both specify 'which types of meaning are relevant and appropriate in a particular context' (Frow 2005, p. 101). Thus, the generic conventions of makeover RTV must be considered.

These include a specific plot (the transformational narrative; see Weber 2009), as well as the presence of impoliteness – consider for example Stacey London's and Clinton Kelly's teasing criticism of the clothing of participants on *What Not to Wear*, and Chef Gordon Ramsey's abusive berating of restaurant owners attempting to save their businesses on *Kitchen Nightmares*. The behaviour in the blended intervention/medical encounter frames in *Honey* helps assimilate it into the makeover TV genre; in this way the nutritionist's impoliteness is potentially viewable as appropriate (at least for the viewers, if not the participants) and indeed is in some ways obligatory, though the participants may (and do, based on their responses) experience face-threat.

Further, the impoliteness on *Honey* plays a role (along with the computer-generated images) in eliciting emotional responses from the parents, which has a special function on makeover RTV: When participants show negative emotions pre-makeover, it sets the stage for the upcoming transformation. In *Honey*, then, the blended health consultation/intervention frame provides the fundamental first step in the genre's 'move structure' (Garcés-Conejos Blitvich *et al.* 2010, p. 692, following Swales 1990). It initiates the transformation process by establishing that the participants are in need of expert guidance and that 'there is really no choice to make about whether to engage in the transformation' (Weber 2009, p. 7; see also Kendrick 2008). Distressed and/or inadequate parents are confronted; the family's everyday practices, and family members themselves, are subsequently recreated with the help of an expert; and at the end it is clear that the whole family has improved. Thus, Hark's impoliteness contributes to constructing a key move in the unfolding plot of the reality TV makeover genre by creating the intervention frame, while also meeting the norms of the genre.

In addition, RTV in general, as a discourse system, features impoliteness, partly because impoliteness can itself be considered entertaining (see Culpeper 2005). Thus the impoliteness that Hark directs to parents is not only 'for' parents, but also for the audience. Culpeper (2005, p. 45) suggests that impoliteness and entertainment are linked – for instance viewers may derive enjoyment in feeling superior to show participants, and in feeling safe from face-attack themselves. Not only blended frames, but also genre and discourse systems affect interpretations of (im)politeness.

Conclusion

In summary, this study suggests that the notion of 'interactive frame', and especially the idea that frames are layered in RTV discourse in particular ways, lends important insights into the 'impoliteness' used by a RTV show's expert nutritionist. Through various linguistic and visual strategies, the scene in which the 'impoliteness' occurs is constructed as a blended frame: a health consultation and an intervention. In the former frame, the nutritionist's language is readily interpretable as impolite; in the latter, it can be viewed as appropriate. Her language fits in with the norms of the makeover genre, especially regarding the transformation narrative, and within the expectations of the RTV discourse system, again suggesting her behaviour is 'politic'. Audiences may be entertained. Nonetheless, parents respond as if they experience face-threat. This suggests multiple possible readings of her behaviour, not only by role in the encounter (participant vs. viewer), but also by how the encounter itself is socially created and understood at a given moment. The nutrition expert's 'impoliteness' is thus complex and multifunctional, accomplishing identity-work (for herself and the parents), forwarding the transformation narrative, entertaining the at-home audience, and so on.

In conclusion, this study demonstrates how an understanding of RTV based on layered frames is productive for investigating impoliteness in this and arguably other complex, mediated interactions. It complements a related approach underpinned by a psychological understanding of frame proposed by Terkourafi (2002, 2005) which identifies co-occurrences that shape typical interpretations of (im) politeness behaviours in particular kinds of situations. My approach lends insight into how such situations are constructed through discourse, rather than through more general features (such as participants' socio-economic status, or the relationship between them). 'Interactive frame' as a notion also complements the genre approach proposed by Garcés-Conejos Blitvich (2010): It offers a more nuanced, microstructural level of analysis than the concepts of genre and discourse system. Finally, the analysis contributes to the broader ongoing study of impoliteness as a multifaceted, discursive phenomenon that is fundamental to ongoing RTV (and 'reality') and identity construction. An issue that requires further exploration is how such impoliteness affects our understanding of expert–layperson interaction regarding topics such as health, a staple of RTV (e.g., *The Biggest Loser*, *Celebrity Fit Club*). As Goffman (1974, p. 8) notes, 'When individuals attend to any current situation, they face the question: "What is it that's going on here?"' Identifying (im)politeness is thus part of a larger activity – for analysts, participants, and audiences – of making sense of social experience on RTV and beyond.

Notes

1. I thank Najma Al Zidjaly, Alla Tovares, and the volume's reviewers and editors for their constructive comments. I also thank Emily Soule for transcription assistance.
2. Transcription conventions are as follows: Each line represents an intonation unit. A question mark (?) indicates relatively strong rising intonation. A period (.) indicates falling, final intonation. A period between two spaces (.) indicates a micro-pause. A comma (,) indicates continuing intonation. A colon (:) indicates an elongated vowel sound; CAPS, emphatic stress. ((*Italicized material in double parentheses is transcriber commentary.*))

References

Anton, Corey & Valerie Peterson (2003) Who said what: Subject positions, rhetorical strategies and good faith. *Communication Studies,* 54: 403–19.
Bateson, Gregory (1972[1954]) A theory of play and fantasy. In *Steps to an Ecology of Mind* (Chicago: University of Chicago Press), pp. 177–93.
Buttny, Richard (1993) *Social Accountability in Communication* (London: Sage).
Collett, Jessica L. (2005) What kind of mother am I? Impression management and the social construction of motherhood. *Symbolic Interaction,* 28: 327–47.
Culpeper, Jonathan (2005) Impoliteness and entertainment in the television quiz show: *The Weakest Link. Journal of Politeness Research,* 1: 35–72.
Davies, Bronwyn & Rom Harré (1990) Positioning: The discursive production of selves. *Journal for the Theory of Social Behavior,* 20: 43–63.
DeVault, Marjorie L. (1991) *Feeding the Family* (Chicago, IL: University of Chicago Press).
Ferguson, Galit (2010) The family on reality television: Who's shaming whom? *Television & New Media,* 11: 87–104.
Frow, John (2005) *Genre* (Abingdon: Routledge).
Garcés-Conejos Blitvich, Pilar (2009) Impoliteness and identity in the American news media: The 'Culture Wars'. *Journal of Politeness Research,* 5: 273–303.
Garcés-Conejos Blitvich, Pilar (2010) A genre approach to the study of impoliteness. *International Review of Pragmatics,* 2: 46–94.
Garcés-Conejos Blitvich, Pilar (2013) Looking backward, moving forward: From Goffman to practice theory. *Journal of Politeness Research,* 9: 1–33.
Garcés-Conejos Blitvich, Pilar, Nuria Lorenzo-Dus & Patricia Bou-Franch (2010) A genre approach to impoliteness in a Spanish television talk show: Evidence from corpus-based analysis, questionnaires and focus groups. *Intercultural Pragmatics,* 7: 689–723.
Goffman, Erving (1963) *Stigma: Notes on the Management of Spoiled Identity* (New York: Simon & Schuster Inc.).
Goffman, Erving (1974) *Frame Analysis: An Essay on the Organization of Experience* (Boston: Northeastern University Press).
Goffman, Erving (1981[1979]) Footing. In *Forms of Talk* (Philadelphia: University of Pennsylvania Press), pp. 124–57.
Gordon, Cynthia (2002) 'I'm Mommy and you're Natalie': Role-reversal and embedded frames in mother-child discourse. *Language in Society,* 31: 679–720.

Gordon, Cynthia (2008) A(p)parent play: Blending frames and reframing in family talk. *Language in Society*, 37: 319–49.

Gordon, Cynthia (2009) *Making Meanings, Creating Family: Intertextuality and Framing in Family Interaction* (New York: Oxford University Press).

Gordon, Cynthia (2011) Impression management on reality TV: Emotion in parental accounts. *Journal of Pragmatics*, 43: 3551–64.

Gordon, Cynthia (under review) 'We were introduced to foods I never even heard of': Parents as consumers on reality TV. In Anne T. Demo, Jennifer L. Borda & Charlotte H. Krincluding (eds.) *The Motherhood Business: Consumption, Communication and Privilege*. (Tuscaloosa, AL: University of Alabama Press).

Gumperz, John J. (1982) *Discourse Strategies* (Cambridge: Cambridge University Press).

Jackson, Cathy & Carol Gray (2005) The dog's too fat – and so is the client: How to handle delicate consultations. *In Practice*, 27: 219–21.

Karhila, Päivi, Tarja Kettunen, Marita Poskiparta & Leena Liimatainen (2003) Negotiation in type 2 diabetes counseling: From problem recognition to mutual acceptance during lifestyle counseling. *Qualitative Health Research*, 13: 1205–24.

Kendrick, Rachel (2008) 'We can change the face of this future': Television transforming the fat child. *Australian Feminist Studies*, 23: 389–400.

Kosovski, Jason R. & Douglas C. Smith (2011) Everybody hurts: Addiction, drama, and the family in the reality television show *Intervention*. *Substance Use & Misuse*, 46: 852–8).

Lewis, Tania (2008) Changing rooms, biggest losers, and backyard blitzes: A history of makeover television in the United Kingdom, United States and Australia. *Continuum: Journal of Media and Cultural Studies*, 22: 447–58.

Linell, Per & Margaret Bredmar (1996) Reconstructing topical sensitivity: Aspects of face-work in talks between midwives and expectant mothers. *Research on Language and Social Interaction*, 29: 347–79.

Locher, Miriam A. & Richard J. Watts (2005) Politeness theory and relational work. *Journal of Politeness Research*, 1: 9–33.

Lunt, Peter (2008) *Little Angels*: The mediation of parenting. *Continuum: Journal of Media & Cultural Studies*, 22: 537–46.

Lutfey, Karen & Douglas W. Maynard (1998) Bad news in oncology: How physician and patient talk about death and dying without using those words. *Social Psychology Quarterly*, 61: 321–41.

Owen, Rob (2006) Tuned in: Families on TLC diet makeover show report bitter aftertaste. *Pittsburgh Post-Gazette*, http://www.post-gazette.com/pg/06100/680907-114.stm (last accessed 28 May 2012).

Schank, Roger & Robert Abelson (1977) *Scripts, Plans, Goals, and Understanding: An Inquiry into Human Knowledge Structures* (Hillsdale, NJ: Erlbaum).

Scollon, Ron & Suzanne Wong Scollon (2001) *Intercultural Communication: A Discourse approach*, 2nd edn. (Malden, MA: Blackwell).

Skeggs, Beverly & Helen Wood (2011) Introduction: Real class. In Helen Wood & Beverly Skeggs (eds.), *Reality Television and Class* (Basingstoke and New York: Palgrave Macmillan), pp. 1–29.

Stephens, Mark B. (2009) Clinical commentary: Take a direct approach to excess weight. *The Journal of Family Practice*, 58: 431.

Stivers, Tanya (1998) Prediagnostic commentary in veterinarian-client interaction. *Research on Language and Social Interaction*, 31: 241–77.

Swales, John (1990) *Genre Analysis. English in Academic and Research Settings* (Cambridge: Cambridge University Press).

Tannen, Deborah & Cynthia Wallat (1993) Interactive frames and knowledge schemas in interaction: Examples from a medical examination/interview. In Deborah Tannen (ed.), *Framing in Discourse* (New York: Oxford University Press), pp. 57–76.

Terkourafi, Marina (2002) Politeness and formulaicity: Evidence from Cypriot Greek. *Journal of Greek Linguistics*, 3: 179–201.

Terkourafi, Marina (2005) Beyond the micro-level in linguistic politeness research. *Journal of Politeness Research*, 1: 237–62.

TLC (The Learning Channel) press release, www.lisahark.com/presstlc.pdf (last accessed May 29 2012).

van Over, Brion (2009) The 'self' as a culturally constituted discursive resources in interventions. Paper presented at the 59th Annual Conference of the International Communication Association, May, Chicago.

Watts, Richard J. (1989) Relevance and relational work: Linguistic politeness as politic behavior. *Multilingua*, 8: 131–66.

Weber, Brenda R. (2009) *Makeover TV: Selfhood, Citizenship, and Celebrity* (Durham, NC: Duke University Press).

12
Moments of truth: telling it like it is on *The Jeremy Kyle Show*

Andrew Tolson

Introduction: talk shows and 'reality'

As Chapter 1 explains, contributions to this book are interested in exploring a discursive, rather than a generic, approach to understanding reality television. This chapter, which focuses on a UK talk show, is no exception. For if, as was common in its early years, reality TV is analysed generically as 'factual television' (Hill 2005) using 'post-documentary' formats (Corner 2000) to construct dramatic scenarios taken from raw recorded footage (law enforcement, emergency services) or unpredictable interactions in confined situations (*Survivor, Big Brother*), then the talk show, studio-based and substantially pre-scripted, might not fit the bill. In the generic analysis, the emphasis was on new forms of access to 'the real' afforded by new technologies of recording and surveillance. However, if reality TV is defined as an 'order of discourse' (Chapter 1) and if that discourse is understood to produce and not merely reflect the 'reality' it depicts, then perhaps a talk show can be analysed as one particular way of constructing a version of that 'reality'. In Foucaultian terms, reality TV might be understood as a discursive formation; as a set of institutional practices that construct their objects, in relations of power, and according to specific 'regimes of truth' (see Dovey 2000). That is the analytic approach taken in this chapter: it aims to show how one talk show inhabits a broad discursive formation that defines 'reality' on television, and how it reproduces a distinctive version of 'truth'.

The Jeremy Kyle Show (hereafter *Jeremy Kyle*) is currently the most popular talk show on UK national television. It is broadcast each weekday, in a 65-minute slot starting at 9.25am, on the main commercial TV channel ITV 1. In that slot, it replaced a previous daytime talk show

266

Trisha in 2005, and it has achieved audiences of up to one-third (1.5 million) of all viewers at that time. As well as being popular, it has also been controversial. Operating at what might be seen as the 'tabloid' end of the talk show spectrum, it has attracted predictable criticisms from broadsheet columnists for its cynical lack of taste (Vallely 2007) and for its exploitation of vulnerable guests (Cadwalladr 2008). To add weight to these criticisms, the journalists also routinely quote the comments of a judge, Alan Berg, who presided in the trial of a man accused of head-butting a fellow guest on the show:

> It seems to me that the purpose of this show is to effect a morbid and depressing display of dysfunctional people whose lives are in turmoil. It is for no more and no less than titillating members of the public who have nothing better to do with their mornings than sit and watch...a human form of bear baiting which goes under the guise of entertainment. (Cadwalladr 2008, p5)

More broadly however, in terms of discourses of 'reality', *Jeremy Kyle* has similarities with the focus of much reality TV in providing certain representations of social class. As has been demonstrated now in a number of studies (Wood & Skeggs 2008, 2011) social class functions as a key marker of cultural distinction in reality TV, leading to dramatic conflicts, particularly in programmes which contain narratives of transformation. These began with lifestyle makeover shows, initially focusing on consumer taste (Taylor 2005), but later on 'care of the self' – physical appearance, diet, fashion etc. (Palmer 2004). More recent reality programmes have also focused on quasi-educative personal transformations, deemed necessary to pass as 'respectable'. There is a sub-genre of 'social entrepreneurship' which involves 'life-coaching' and/or training in employability skills (Biressi 2011). In all these kinds of programming, it is argued, middle-class taste and respectability is promoted and working-class practices and identities (of a particular sort) are criticized, shown to be lacking and in need of transformation (Couldry 2011).

In the UK context a particularly visible and morally vilified form of social dys-functionality is represented by the so-called 'underclass'. This is a subculture that exists on the fringes of paid employment, is assumed to be dependent on welfare, and yet manages to display conspicuous trappings of consumerism and mass popular culture. It is this 'under-class' that is especially targeted by some reality TV and is also heavily represented on *Jeremy Kyle*. In some accounts (such as that offered by the judge, above) it is suggested that this is for voyeuristic entertainment, akin to that once offered by medieval circuses; but it is undoubtedly also the case that lives lived *in extremis* have the potential for individual disorder and inter-personal conflict on which some TV programmes can thrive. Heather Nunn and Anita Biressi (2008) have identified here a continuation of a familiar (since the nineteenth century) representation of the 'undeserving poor', across a variety of media genres (drama, comedy, documentary, journalism and reality TV):

> This time-hardened category is stereotypically associated with the 'dependencies' of a faltering welfare state and personified in the single Mum, the benefit-rich council estate family, the habitual criminal or the unemployed teenage delinquent; all frequently referenced through notions of fecklessness, indisciplinarity, dependency and moral as well as financial incontinence. (Nunn & Biressi 2008, p.1)

This then begins to sketch the kind of terrain occupied by *Jeremy Kyle*. In terms of discourses of 'reality', and indeed types of talk show, it is at one end of a range of approaches to personal problems and suggested solutions. Here, it differs from its predecessor on ITV 1, for *Trisha* took a more therapeutic approach to talking through problems and making personal commitments to change (Tolson 2006). Shortly I will outline the different approach taken by Kyle, but essentially it seems that his guests are so 'feckless' and 'incontinent' that rather than presenting them with programmes of 'self help' the only option is a form of authoritative 'truth-telling' – a kind of ritual humiliation sometimes ameliorated by 'after-care'.

The show's clientele and its approach seemed to be epitomised by the news in April 2012, that on her release from prison, Karen Matthews was expressing a wish to go on *Jeremy Kyle* to take a lie detector test. Matthews (to whom Nunn and Biressi refer) is one of the most notorious examples of the 'undeserving poor' in recent tabloid history. She was the mother of seven children by five different fathers, living on a council estate in West Yorkshire, who in 2008 organized the 'kidnap' of her own daughter. In fact the daughter had been abducted by the uncle of Matthews' boyfriend in a plot to fraudulently claim a £50,000 reward. For a time in 2008, in the UK national press, Matthews and her 'family' personified the dysfunctional 'underclass' with its 'chav' culture. That she should now, on her release, turn to *Jeremy Kyle* in a bid to prove her innocence is indicative of the kind of 'reality' it constructs, and in particular, its approach to what counts as 'truth'.

Talk shows as broadcast talk

However, from the discourse-analytic perspective that informs this chapter, it is not enough to identify the discursive formations that produce representations of social class. These constitute the historical context and I shall return to the question of their contemporary relevance in my concluding section. But for present purposes it is also necessary to demonstrate how these representations are constructed in specific circumstances. And the specific circumstance of *Jeremy Kyle* is that it functions as broadcast talk where, by virtue of being on television, participants display particular kinds of public identity in a situation defined by 'double articulation' (Scannell 1991). That is, it not only stages interactions between participants on the show; it is also designed, as a product, for consumption by an 'overhearing audience' (see Chapter 2).

To develop this point more precisely, there is general recognition in the literature on reality TV that participants are expected to perform, and so 'performativity' is a key concept. Where social class is at stake, individuals display class membership through what they 'give off' about themselves through language use, mannerisms, deportment and styles of dress (Grindstaff 2011). In the American context, Laura Grindstaff argues that they are encouraged to perform in 'trash-face', a term which also might be applied to *Jeremy Kyle*. However the present analysis seeks to demonstrate precisely how these performances are constructed as 'trashy' in the discourse of the show. No doubt, as Grindstaff (2008) has shown, individuals are selected to appear on such shows because of their pre-existing problems. But the show itself offers the environment in which these are re-enacted, not just as general social identities, but in a forum for the production of broadcast talk.

Accordingly, the key question for this chapter is how is 'trash-face' specifically produced in this context? And the methodology will entail a close analysis of examples of broadcast talk. The discursive formation is therefore made apparent, empirically visible, in transcripts of verbal interactions. As with other talk shows, these consist of (a) interactions between 'guests', (b) interactions between guests and the host, and crucially (c) audible reactions from the studio audience. Here a key feature is audience applause (see Tolson 2006). Of course, the audience routinely applauds when guests are introduced and at the end of each segment of the show. However it also applauds at certain moments in the talk which indicate to the analyst when the show has achieved the key effects it sets out to achieve.

To appreciate the discursive particularities of *Jeremy Kyle* it will be helpful to compare its format with previous talk shows of the 'tabloid' variety. These have been discussed in terms of their production of 'spectacular confrontation', both in *The Jerry Springer Show* (Myers 2001; Lunt & Stenner, 2005) and in *Ricki Lake* (Hutchby 2006). The format of *Jeremy Kyle* has affinities with both these previous shows: it consists of segments, typically three or four but sometimes just two, constructed around ad breaks. Each segment follows the structure of an issue (or complaint) formulated by the first guest, followed sequentially by the introduction of further guest(s) who are required to respond. The segments have titles expressed in the first person, indicating that this is 'first person media' in which ordinary people can 'have their say' (Dovey 2000). Furthermore, as these titles suggest, in the majority of segments the complainants are women, and they are usually making complaints about men. For the purposes of this chapter I recorded a week of shows in June 2011 (to add to previous data randomly recorded as teaching material). Here are the titles of the segments from that week's recording, and I have no reason to doubt that these are typical:

Monday

- Ex-husband you destroyed my life but don't destroy my children's (F)
- I'll prove my grandson stole from me then I'll disown him (F)
- My friend got into our bed and stole my fiancé! (F)
- I told my fiancé a week ago he might not be the dad (F)

Tuesday

- I'll divorce my wife if she's having another affair (M)
- Pregnant and beaten...I won't lose another baby (F)
- My fiancé says he won't marry me if I fail the lie detector (F)

Wednesday

- My boyfriend slept with my best friend and my sister (F)
- Husband, why did you ask another woman to marry you? (F)
- Where does my girlfriend go when I'm asleep at night? (M)

Thursday

- You slept with two of my friends...but which one of us is the dad? (M)
- Is my wife having an affair with her best friend? (M)
- I've finally found you...but are you really my dad? (F)

Friday

- You became a lesbian and started being a bad mum! (M)
- Stop demanding access to a daughter you don't believe is yours! (F)
- Why did you abandon me but look after my daughter? (M)

Overwhelmingly, as this list indicates, the show is about dysfunctional sexual and familial relationships, and about two-thirds of the complaints are from women. In this the show broadly conforms to the 'melodramatic' focus of female-oriented tabloid talk shows (Shattuc 1997) and the 'glamour of misery' promoted by Oprah Winfrey (Illoux 2003). It airs personal problems in public, it stages emotional confrontations, and as such, problems are not just talked about, they are enacted in heightened displays of anger and distress.

However, in another significant way *Jeremy Kyle* differs from its American antecedents. The key factor here is the role of the host, and this can be clearly delineated by comparison with Hutchby's (2006) discussion of *Ricki Lake*. He describes a format where the role of the host is to introduce guests and facilitate their accounts (in a form of interview), but also to react to what they say from the perspective of the audience. The host is positioned in the studio audience to encourage it also to react. At the end of each segment of *Ricki Lake* a 'relationship expert' offers advice; whilst at the end of a *Jerry Springer Show* the host delivers a homily as his 'final thought' (Myers 2001). On *Jeremy Kyle* however the host is much more likely to be on the stage, or just off it, but in front of the studio audience. His role is not so much to orchestrate audience response as to make an active intervention in the proceedings. And there are no relationship experts on *Jeremy Kyle* (there is 'after-care', but it remains off stage). Rather, it is Kyle himself who is the 'expert' on this show, and in this he is supported by another key innovation.

Most of the problems on *Jeremy Kyle* revolve around questions of truth. Relationship problems are to do with whether or not the accused really did cheat on the accuser. Dysfunctional families have issues of parenting which often involve men facing up to the responsibilities of paternity. In these contexts Kyle has access to scientific proof in the form of lie detection and DNA testing. Thus, after a scenario involving accusation and counter-accusation, imagined wrongs and denials, he himself is in a position to deliver an ultimate and unquestionable authoritative judgment. It is how he does this that is the key to understanding the show and specifically how it constructs its guests as undisciplined and feckless representatives of 'trash-face'.

Data analysis: moral judgment as 'harangue'

This section presents four extracts from the data as examples of mediated interaction on *Jeremy Kyle*. These range from the typical to the somewhat exceptional, but nonetheless revealing. Example 1 is a typical complaint made by a woman, Sarah, about her ex-husband Gareth. The issue is that he is not taking responsibility as the father of their children, but there is also a back-story to this. The segment begins, as it always does, with Kyle seated on stage taking the complainant through the back-story in the form of an 'interview' where he prompts her to confirm the details already provided to his researchers. Gareth has a history of drunken violence and he was served with an injunction preventing him from contacting Sarah, though this has now been lifted. He has also been on the show before and has received some 'after-care'. However it is Kyle's conduct of the interview that is interesting. Here is his reaction to Sarah's confession of her previous feelings for Gareth:

```
JK:   I really buy that you know I really buy that 'cos
      some people will watch and go 'why would she be with
      someone like that?' But you do don't you? [S: yeh]
      You say 'I can change him I can be the person' [(...)
S:                                                   [I-I
      was convinced I was the girl for him...
```

Frequently, Kyle personally affiliates with the complainant; there is none of the 'neutralism' of a conventional news interview (Clayman & Heritage 2002). Also however, as this short extract shows, he is in an interesting position with respect to the overhearing audience. He does not orchestrate audience reaction, rather he animates a potential reaction and distances himself from that. Moreover he includes Sarah in his generalized 'you' and with a tag question, prompts her affirmative response. So this is an explicit form of interpersonal alignment, not simply facilitating Sarah's story for the benefit of the audience.

After the basic points of the back-story have been established, the next section brings the accused on stage. Here Kyle vacates the chair on stage and stands directly facing it with his back to the studio audience. It is common for the complainant and the accused at first to engage in direct argument, unmediated by the host, as occurs in Example 1, lines 1–13. At a certain point however Kyle will intervene, and typically what occurs then is a factual interrogation: did the accused do what he is accused of? Here the interrogation discloses Gareth's lack of basic knowledge concerning his children (line 29) and it is this that provokes the next discursive move, into what I will term the 'harangue' (lines 33–44).

Example 1: Ex-husband you destroyed my life but don't destroy my children's.

```
      G:   So if I'm such a bad person why are you trying
           to let me see t'kids then?
      S:   I don't want you to see them kids
      G:   So why did you [come 'ere then?
5     S:                  [They do. They want you. Not me.
           You have supervised contact you can see them.
           You're not having them on your [own.
      G:                                  [You'll put a stop
           to it.
10    S:   I've never stopped you [and I never would. Them boys
           want you.
      G:                         [I'm constantly getting (...)
           [You're messing with me head
      JK:  [Who rang the show? Who rang the show?
15    G:   Obviously she did.
      JK:  Well what the hell does that tell you then that
           she puts the kids before what she might think
           about you and wants to get [this right
      G:                              [She only came 'ere
20         to get her five minutes of fame [S: Oh behave
           yourself] She's seen me on TV so that's what she's
           done.
      JK:  [to S] How old are your kids?
      S:   (.) Five and er (.) six and four.
25    JK:  Right six and four
      G:   She doesn't even know her own kids age
      S:   That's 'cos my youngest one's nearly five
      JK:  [to G] Wh-when are your kids birthdays?
      G:   I'm not sure about that
```

```
30  Aud:  oooooaaaaahhhh
    JK:   [stands] What did you just say?
    G:    Not sure about that
    JK:   DON'T YOU SIT ON MY STAGE AND SAY SHE DOESN'T
          KNOW ABOUT HER KIDS WHEN YOU'VE DONE ZILCH AND
35        YOU CAN'T EVEN GIVE THEIR BIRTHDAYS OUT
    Aud:  eeeeeaaaahhhhxxxxxxxxxxxxxxxx[xxxxxxxxxxxxxxxx
    JK:                               [YOU  DON'T  EVEN
          KNOW YOUR KIDS BIRTHDAYS. THAT IS PATHETIC. SHE
          HAS BROUGHT THEM UP FOR SIX AND FOUR YEARS AND
40        WHERE HAVE YOU BEEN? DRINKING SLEEPING AROUND
          AND LYING. YOU MIGHT HAVE DONE GOOD WORK SINCE
          YOU CAME HERE WITH OUR HELP BUT SHE HAS A VIEW OF
          YOU WHICH YOU NEED CALMLY TO CONVINCE HER IS
          NOT THE RIGHT VIEW. GET IT?
```

The harangue is a very common, distinctive feature of *Jeremy Kyle*. Not all segments involve harangues (because in some segments there are no guilty parties) but of the 16 segments recorded in June 2011, 11 contained this feature. Basically it is a moral judgment delivered by Kyle which involves him shouting at one of his 'guests'. He does this standing in front of them and sometimes leaning forward so that he is literally 'in their face'. Clearly then this is a type of 'impoliteness' which involves an explicit threat to the recipient's 'positive face' (Brown & Levinson 1987) performed in a highly aggressive manner. It can be related to the 'spectacular impoliteness' discussed by Nuria Lorenzo-Dus (2009 and this volume). The harangue also contains discourse features such as colloquial vocabulary (here 'ziltch', line 34) and rhetorical questions which Kyle either answers himself (here lines 40–1) or where an answer cannot be given. In short, the accused does not have a leg to stand on.

The harangue is also notable for the fact that it invariably provokes extensive reaction from the studio audience in the form of cheering and applause. Close observation shows that this reaction is not just a form of response, it is often audience participation which (as here) accompanies the harangue as it is delivered. This seems to indicate that the harangue is, in some sense, the decisive moment or highlight of the show. To be sure, each segment has further business, in the delivery of DNA or lie detector results, or some resolution to the narrative of the complaint (here further after-care for Gareth, to set up an arrangement where he can see his children). But it is the harangue that delivers, if not the narrative denouement, the decisive moral judgment; and it is a signature feature of *Jeremy Kyle* found (to my knowledge) in no other talk shows.

I shall offer some explanations for the use of this feature in my final two subsections. Here I have included examples of two further harangues to illustrate variations in its use. In Examples 2 and 3, it is the complainant not the accused who is the recipient of the harangue, so in these instances it would seem that the moral order is not pre-determined, but rather 'locally occasioned' by what transpires on the show. In Example 2, Adie has been having sexual relations with two boys and requires a DNA test to establish who is the father of her child. She has told the researchers that she would prefer it to be Ashley but it turns out to be Billy, her ex-boyfriend. He reports that he was encouraged to come on the show by Adie's promise that they might be reconciled if the child is his. In the course of these exchanges Kyle seems to form the judgment (i) that Adie is behaving immaturely and (ii) her offer to Billy amounts to a form of 'blackmail' (line 36). This occasions two harangues (the first of which is included in Example 2) directed at Adie even though she is, in a sense, the victim of these circumstances. Note how this harangue utilizes the unanswerable rhetorical question (wh- plus negative interrogative: 'why don't'...) and illustrates another common device – the disingenuous term of endearment: 'sweetheart' (line 59).

Example 2: Ex, our relationship is over...even if you are the dad.

```
    JK:  Thank you very much indeed welcome back just
         before the break I was chatting to Adie can I
         just repeat this right? So you knew Ashley you
         got with Billy you're with Billy two years you
 5       had a break 'cos you had a barney you jump into
         bed with Ashley you don't use contraception with
         either of them you get pregnant you think okay
         that it's Billy's but it might be Ashley's but
         at the moment you're not with either of them
10       although Billy's in love with you and wants you
         back but you're not interested Ashley and you
         apparently are mates although you did say to my
         researchers you know "I would prefer Ashley to
         be the dad and then we'd have to take things
15       slowly and see what happens".
    A:   Yeh like be mates if [you know what I mean
```

JK: [be mates okay fair enough
          okay. And Billy was very upset backstage. He
          says that he loves you er and I think they're
20   both concerned that you'll play God with the
          child's life and not allow them to see the kid.
A: No I'm not going to have that for Preston.
JK: Let's get Billy out ladies and gentlemen.
Aud: xxxxxxxxxxxxxxxxxxxxxxxxxxxxxxx
          [Billy struggles to move chair]
25 Aud: eheheheheheheheh[eheheheheheheh
A: [eheheheheheheh
JK: Do you know what I'm actually going to say to
          you young lady maybe you want to understand
          this is quite serious today [A: I know it is]
30   and not laugh like a little schoolgirl all
          right? **[to Billy]** Why are you so upset? Cos
          this is the baby we're talking about not a
          game.
          . . . .
          **[Billy claims Adie promised to "walk off the
          show" with him if the DNA test proves his
          paternity]**
35 JK: **[sits]** Sit back my friend you're confusing me. I
          understand young lady that you rather blackmailed
          him to come here to this show is that right?
A: Yup
JK: What did you say to him?
40 A: That 'cos obviously I want it sorted okay I
          think erm if Preston's his we'll walk off the
          show together.
JK: So you knew that this man's still in love with
          you so you said if you come to the Jeremy Kyle
45   show and you turn out to be the dad then we
          can leave together just so you can get him here
          and **[stands]** then you come out on stage with me
          and you say "I'd much prefer it to be Ashley".
          Could I be really humble and just suggest some-
50   thing in the nicest possible way? I don't
          condone for one minute the fact that he jumped
          into bed with you and didn't put something on

the end of it <u>and</u> we'll talk about it in a
moment he's allegedly violent. I also don't
55   condone that he too jumped into bed. BUT IT
STRIKES ME THERE'S A LITTLE GIRL IN THE MIDDLE
WHO LOVES ALL THE DRAMA AND LAPS IT UP SO WHY
DON'T YOU GROW UP AND CONCENTRATE ON YOUR KID
SWEETHEART?
Aud: Yeeeaaahxxxxxxxxxxxxxxxxxxxxxxxxxxxxxxxxxxxxxxxxx

Example 3 contains the results of a lie detector test. David is accusing
his wife Yvonne of having an affair, which she denies and passes the
test. It becomes clear however in the second section of this segment,
where the couple engage in extensive direct argument, that this is a
dysfunctional relationship on various grounds and that David is a 'hen-
pecked' husband. After Yvonne has passed the test and demonstrated
suitably emotional reactions (line 28) Kyle turns his attention to David.
Despite the fact that he is the complainant and has, it seems, plenty to
complain about, Kyle's harangue targets his contribution to his wife's
distress. This harangue also contains a disingenuous term of endearment ('my friend' lines 33, 43) and it uses a colloquial expression which
I have to admit was new to me. Apparently 'grow a pair big enough and
walk away' (lines 49) does not refer to his feet but to another part of the
male anatomy more closely associated with his manhood! (I have my
students to thank for this correction).

Example 3: I'll divorce my wife if she's having another affair.
JK: Twelve year relationship. Er last time on the
show you're out here you are sticking up for
her. You're saying I'm with her then you ring
us and you go the relationship is a SHAM [D:
5   yeh] She's a liar she's a cheat she's this
she's that [D: yeh] We asked Yvonne since
she married David eleven years ago have you
had sexual intercourse with any other person she said no (.) Well well well [3 secs]
10   She was telling the truth.
Aud: xxxxxxxyeeeaaaahxxxxxxxxxxxxxxxxxxxxx[xxxxxxxxxxx
JK: [Then we asked
since you married David eleven years ago have
you has sexual contact with any other person

15		that's anything from sex to a kiss she said no and your wife of eleven years my friend was telling the truth.
	Aud:	yeeeeeehhhxxxxxxxxxxxxxxxxxxxxxxxxxxxxxxxxxxxxx xxxxxxxxxxx
20	JK:	Then we asked her since you married David eleven years ago have you passionately kissed any other person she said no er where I come from she passed every question it's called a full house okay **[gives card to Yvonne]**
25		[There you are.
	Aud:	[yeeeeeehhhxxxxxxxxxxxxxxxxxxxxxxxxxxxxxxxxxxxx
	D:	Sorry Yvonne **[stands]**
	Y:	**[teary voice]** You want to be
	D:	Come here **[they embrace]**
30	Aud:	aaaaaaaaaahhhhhhhhhhhhhhh
	JK:	I'm confused [AUD: eheheheh](4 secs) Can I be really honest? If I'm frank don't say (…) my friend don't say another word. It's all well and good to grow a pair isn't it but it is the
35		thing that's a bit confusing. She cheated on me sixteen years ago so we split up she got with another bloke then we got back together. At the exact moment you got back together you had forgiven her for that. This is a classic
40		story of people who do something say they've forgiven it and then it carries on and on and they mither that person. Let me tell you something my friend right? [IF YOU=
	D:	[So why does she
45		treat me like that?
	JK:	=ARE A DOORMAT AND YOU'RE UNHAPPY WITH THE LACK OF SEX THE LACK OF SHARING A BED AND THE FACT YOU GET CHIPS EVERY DAY [D: (…) which I do] GROW A PAIR BIG ENOUGH AND WALK AWAY [DON'T TRY
50		TO BLAME HER FOR YOUR=
	Aud:	[eeeeeehhhhhxxxxxxx xxxxxxxxxxxxxxxxxxxxxxxxx
		=INABILITY TO MAKE THAT DECISION. THAT'S PERFECTLY FAIR IF YOU If you're unhappy in your

55   marriage say "do you know what Yvonne I'm not happy". If it's it's not about her lying if you're unhappy either change it or do one yes?

So as these examples show, the harangue, an aggressive face-threatening moral judgement, is a routine event on *Jeremy Kyle*. It is also apparent that this event generally invokes assumptions about gender. Gender roles are implicated in the construction of moral truths: fathers need to take responsibility for their children, 'hen-pecked' husbands need to assert their masculinity, promiscuous young women need to 'grow up'. But note again that these are not just pre-given assumptions; gender identities are also performed in the host's interactions with his guests, and particularly through the 'terms of endearment'. Thus, Adie is addressed as a 'young lady'/'little schoolgirl' as well as (disingenuously) 'sweetheart'. The advice that David asserts his masculinity is performed as gendered solidarity ('my friend'). A commonsense culture of gender roles and identities encompasses both the host's persona and the performances of his guests, and this is dramatically illustrated by my fourth example – an exception that 'proves the rule'.

In 'My fiancé says he won't marry me if I fail the lie detector', Liam has heard that his girlfriend Chenice has been cheating, but it is she who comes to the show to complain that these are false accusations. She therefore volunteers for the lie detector test which, however, she fails. Something in her demeanour also convinces Kyle that she is lying, but I must say I couldn't see this myself. However Chenice disputes the result, breaks down in tears and walks off the stage (line 13). It is the exchanges that follow that are especially interesting.

Example 4: My fiancé says he won't marry me if I fail the lie detector.

     JK: We asked Chenice since the start of your relationship with Liam apart from the one person you've admitted to have you passionately kissed anybody else? She said no.

5 L: Telling the truth?

     JK: Sorry?

     L: Telling the truth?

     JK: What did I say to you? [L: (…)] **[To Chenice]** You were lying weren't you?

10 Aud: oooooooooooooooooooooooooohhhhhhhhhh

    C: No I wasn't. No I w-wasn't **[starts to cry]**

    JK: Oh we're gonna t- Oh we're gonna cry now are
          we? **[Chenice walks off stage]** Oh we're gonna
          run now **[JK follows her]** That's it we're gonna

15   have a strop. [We're gonna kick something okay.
          It's all going on.

    Aud: [eheheheheh
          **[Chenice   sits   backstage   head   in   hands
          sobbing]**

    JK: Why did you rush off?

    C: **[teary voice]** 'Cos you're making me to look

20   like a fool and I ain't. I haven't hurt him you
          think I want to hurt him I can't hurt him.

    JK: You lied.

    C: No I didn't.

    JK: Yes you did your reaction just told me that you

25   lied and your eyes told me you lied before the
          break and if you don't want to handle that I'm
          sorry but you asked us [to do this test and we
          did=

    C: [I didn't lie I kissed

30   a girl.

    JK: It's not me. You should be going and talking
          to him. Not me. Go and tell him go and tell
          him. You passionately kissed a girl yeh? Did
          you tell him that before?

35 C: Yeh I told him that.

    JK: Go and talk to him.
          [Chenice returns to stage. Audience applauds]
          . . . .

    JK: This test says your girlfriend lied on every
          question.

    C: I didn't

40 JK: I'm paid to read it darling

    C: I haven't lied

    JK: Tell him the truth darling. Your reaction spoke
          volumes. Tell him the truth.

    C: I've told him the truth. I haven't done anything

45   and these lot here **[gestures to audience]** can
          sit here and judge me [but they don't know me

```
JK:                          [I'm not Einstein but I
         could tell as I went to the break you looked
         as dodgy as hell. Tell him the truth.
50  C:   YEH 'COS I LOOK DODGY DON'T I WHAT BECAUSE I
         COME FROM KENT OR I WAS BROUGHT UP IN ESSEX?
         (.) Dodgy yeh
    JK:  [No because you're (.) because
    Aud: [eheheheh
55  C:   Tell you what I aint having this yeh. You're all
         a bunch of [beep] [Chenice storms off stage]
    Aud: ehehehehehehxxxxbooooooooooooooooooooooo
```

There are two points of interest here. The first is that the lie detector test is taken as infallible even though Chenice protests her (partial, because she kissed a girl at a hen-party) innocence, and a disclaimer appears on the screen to the effect that the reliability of such tests is sometimes disputed. However here the test is taken as evidence of an absolute truth to which Chenice needs to confess. There are no grey areas on *Jeremy Kyle*.

Secondly however, as Chenice disputes the result, she also develops a claim that she is being victimized. In this she not only disputes the show's 'truth-claim', she also makes explicit (rather than just suffers) its interactional dynamics: 'you're making me to look like a fool' (line 18). To this, Kyle does not react with a harangue, possibly because she is too stressed; however he does subsequently deliver a face-threatening judgment, in suitably colloquial style: 'you looked as dodgy as hell' (line 49). But how does Chenice respond to this face-threatening act (FTA)? She questions the grounds on which this judgment has been made by explicitly drawing attention to its implicit class and gender stereotyping. In the UK, the term, 'Essex girl' is shorthand, not for an *abject* underclass, but rather for a brash, hedonistic, culturally unsophisticated female working-class lifestyle. In her act of defiance Chenice is accusing *Jeremy Kyle* of visually reproducing class and gender stereotypes as it subjects its victims to its regime of truth. Thus, as the unruly exception, she explicitly names the 'reality' that the harangues deliver.

Positional authority

In the analytic perspective of this chapter, Chenice's outburst offers a clear illustration of a fundamental point. This is that discursive practices do not simply represent pre-existing states of affairs, they also create them; and in *Jeremy Kyle* this is achieved through a process of moral judgment and condemnation. In the examples presented here, an errant ex-husband is judged an inadequate father; a hen-pecked husband needs to show some moral fibre; a 'little girl' needs to grow up; and a woman convicted of lying needs to confess to her partner. However Chenice makes it clear that it is not just prior actions that are being judged; it is also a matter of how participants perform on the show, how they 'come across' in terms of appearance, demeanour and their 'trash-face' – to use Grindstaff's term. Chenice's outburst questions the basis on which such judgments are made, frequently through type-casting social identities.

In three out of four of the extracts above, moral condemnation is delivered in the form of the 'harangue'. What kind of discursive practice, or ritual, is this? In formal terms it might be possible to define this as a 'speech genre', defined by Bakhtin as 'typical forms of utterance' recognized by co-participants (Bakhtin 1986). To be sure the generic form of the harangue is not as tightly structured as other speech genres such as oral narratives and telling jokes. There are repeatable devices such as unanswerable rhetorical questions and disingenuous terms of endearment, but these seem to be used selectively as resources, not structural constraints. There is, however, in Goffman's terminology a recognizable shift of 'frame' (Goffman 1974), a heightened performance characterized by raised pitch and volume and the accompanying audience applause. To qualify as a speech genre it would be helpful if there was a lay term to define such shifts of frame. Perhaps this might be the 'telling off'. Through the harangue participants are told off – and they know this, it shuts them up.

However, in further reflections on this practice I have also been drawn to another argument, of a vintage equal to that of Goffman. Half a century ago, Basil Bernstein was writing an influential series of papers in which he set out his theory of 'sociolinguistic codes' (Bernstein 1971). His basic distinction between 'restricted' and 'elaborated' codes, as linguistic resources differentially distributed among social classes, is widely known and equally widely criticized. However in one paper he also develops a distinction (all his thinking works through binary distinctions) between different ways of expressing authority. Here 'personal' appeals, which work though reasoned argument, are distinguished from 'positional' appeals, which work through imperatives. In 'positional' families and social groups, moral norms are held in common and imposed without question. This is how Bernstein develops the point:

> Where control is positional, the child (the regulated) learns the norms in a social context where the relative statuses are clear-cut and unambiguous. Positional appeals may lead to the formation of shame rather than guilt. In the case of positional appeals, however, certain areas of experience are less verbally differentiated than in the case of personal appeals. Positional appeals transmit the culture or sub-culture in such a way as to increase the similarity of the regulated with others of his social group. They create boundaries. If the child rebels he very soon challenges the bases of the culture and its social organization and this may force the controller (parent/teacher) into the imperative mode. (Bernstein 1971, p. 182)

Clearly *Jeremy Kyle* is not a familial or educative context, though as we have seen he does sometimes address participants as if they were children. However the harangue's reinforcement of 'unambiguous statuses' and its enforcement of clear moral boundaries, does strike a chord. And the point about 'shame' rather than 'guilt' can also be used perhaps to clarify the distinction between *Jeremy Kyle* and other types of talk show. For instance, shows like *Oprah Winfrey* and *Trisha* worked primarily in a therapeutic mode, exhorting individuals to commit to programmes of self-help (Illoux 2003; Tolson 2006). *Trisha's* successor seems more concerned to berate such participants and mutual diagnosis of a problem is replaced by unilateral judgments of inadequacy.

Bernstein also goes on, as we might expect, to link his theory of 'positional' communication to an argument about social class. Here his 'restricted' and 'elaborated' codes come back into view:

> We can now link positional families with closed systems of communication with positional, imperative modes of control. We could, in principle, distinguish between positional families whose preferred mode of control was imperative (the lower working class?) from positional families where the preferred mode was positional appeals with relatively little use of physical coercion. We could distinguish between positional families according to whether the dominant code was elaborated or restricted. (Bernstein 1971, p. 185)

Bernstein is not always as clear as he might be – here the reference to 'physical coercion', in an argument about ways of speaking, seems superfluous. However it is clear where he socially locates his 'positional families' with their 'imperative modes of control' (and 'restricted codes'?). And of course this 'lower working class' is precisely the constituency well represented on *Jeremy Kyle*, and includes the membership category 'Essex girls' to which Chenice lays claim.

Bernstein's general argument, controversial at the time it was made, was that because the education system privileges the 'elaborated code' (and associated forms of authority), some working-class children, socialized in 'restricted codes' would be at a disadvantage. The challenge was for educators to address this 'deficit', to ensure these children's 'educability'. But in that light, fifty years on, it seems odd that a TV programme, on a mainstream channel, should be promoting 'positional' forms of communication. This seems to be accepting that in some cases an educative or therapeutic approach will not work, and the only option is to shame a person into 'after-care'. Without resorting to the position taken by Judge Berg, that this is a form of 'bear-baiting', there is something old-fashioned, perhaps reactionary, about Kyle's resort to a positional authoritarianism, and this warrants further discussion.

Belligerent broadcasting

One way of understanding what is happening here is to see it as an example of 'belligerent broadcasting' (Higgins *et al.* 2011). This is a development in some contemporary reality programming which features presenters acting aggressively towards participants on their shows. To be more precise, this is not just the general preference of much reality TV for 'confrontainment' (Lorenzo-Dus 2009). Nor is this co-participants engaged in heated argument, as is common in reality TV shows like *Wife Swap* (see Wood and Skeggs 2008) or epitomized by talk shows such as *Jerry Springer*. Rather, 'belligerent broadcasting' involves confrontational intervention by a host/presenter, such as Gordon Ramsay in *Ramsay's Kitchen Nightmares*. So whereas Jerry Springer, in a sense, stays 'out of it' (Myers 2001), the belligerence of Jeremy Kyle involves him taking the stage and directly eye-balling his victim as he delivers his harangue. What is going on here?

For one potential answer to this question I want to refer to an article in *The Observer* (Doward 2008). Entitled 'Labour bid to work with Jeremy Kyle', it reported that the Labour government (then under Gordon Brown) was in talks with ITV about developing a programme on the theme of 'welfare to work' using Kyle as its presenter. *The*

Observer article highlighted Kyle's controversial reputation (with the obligatory quotation from Judge Berg); but it is why this idea (to my knowledge a non-starter) should have been considered in the first place that is interesting. It is interesting because it seems that the traditional, authoritarian forms of communication analysed by Bernstein, continue to have a resonance in contemporary British politics.

A helpful perspective on this is provided by Norman Fairclough in his book on the discourses of New Labour (Fairclough 2000). On the theme of 'social exclusion' he lists three discourses in common circulation that might influence government policy. There are: (i) a 'redistribution-ist discourse' that focuses on the eradication of poverty; (ii) a 'social integrationist discourse' which emphasizes getting people off benefits and into work; and (iii) a 'moral underclass discourse' which focuses on deficiencies in the culture of the excluded (ibid., p. 57). Fairclough's argument is that New Labour largely abandoned discourse (i) in favour of a rhetoric combining discourses (ii) and (iii). So in 2008 it was fleet-ingly suggested that Jeremy Kyle might be an appropriate front-man for this approach to social exclusion: a rehabilitative regime rooted in a bedrock of moral vilification of the feckless 'underclass'.

The term 'neo-liberalism' is much bandied about and has been associ-ated with the rise of 'first person media' (Dovey 2000). Here we can see what it means at the level of social policy, and that is precisely a return to pre-social democratic, pre-welfarist and pre-therapeutic approaches to social deprivation. In the neo-liberal world, socially excluded indi-viduals are not encouraged to give voice to their suffering, rather they are required to get off their backsides and take a suitably entrepreneurial approach to work (Ramsay) or they will be shouted at and publicly shamed (Kyle). Accordingly, this neo-liberal regime of truth does not recognize social so much as moral categories of persons and it con-structs interpersonal problems as gendered moral/individual deficien-cies to be both displayed and shamed. Furthermore, it does this through a 'positional' discursive practice that its 'lower working-class' recipients can be presumed to understand! Fifty years ago Bernstein construed this approach to 'imperative modes of control' with their 'formations of shame' as socially problematic. But now it is re-adopted and promoted in the neo-liberal agenda that informs 'belligerent broadcasting'.

References

Bakhtin, M.M. (1986) *Speech Genres and Other Late Essays*, trans. V. W. McGhee (Austin: University of Texas Press).

Bernstein, B. (1971) A socio-linguistic approach to socialization: With some reference to educability. In *Class, Codes and Control, Vol 1* (London: Routledge & Kegan Paul), ch. 8.

Biressi, A. (2011) 'The Virtuous Circle': Social entrepreneurship and welfare programming in the UK. In H.Wood & B.Skeggs (eds.), *Reality Television and Class* (London: BFI/ Palgrave Macmillan), pp. 144–55.

Brown, P. & S. Levinson (1987) *Politeness: Some Universals in Language Use* (Cambridge: Cambridge University Press).

Cadwalladr, C. (2008) When reality bites, it leaves deep scars. *The Observer,* September 7.

Clayman, S. and J. Heritage (2002) *The News Interview. Journalists and Public Figures on the Air* (Cambridge: Cambridge University Press).

Corner, J. (2000) What can we say about 'documentary'? *Media, Culture and Society,* 22: 681–8.

Couldry, N. (2011) Class and contemporary forms of 'reality' production or, hidden injuries of class 2. In H.Wood & B.Skeggs (eds.), *Reality Television and Class* (London: BFI/ Palgrave Macmillan), pp. 33–44.

Dovey, J. (2000) *Freakshow: First Person Media and Factual Television* (London: Pluto Press).

Doward, J. (2008) Labour bid to work with Jeremy Kyle. *The Observer,* September 7.

Fairclough N. (2000) *New Labour, New Language?* (London: Routledge).

Goffman, E. (1974) *Frame Analysis* (New York: Harper & Row).

Grindstaff, L. (2008) Producing trash, class, and the money shot: A behind-the-scnes account of daytime TV talk shows. In A. Biressi & H. Nunn (eds.), *The Tabloid Culture Reader* (New York: McGraw Hill/Open University Press), pp. 259–73.

Grindstaff, L. (2011) From *Jerry Springer* to *Jersey Shore*: The cultural politics of class in/on US reality programming. In H. Wood & B. Skeggs (eds.), *Reality Television and Class* (London: BFI/Palgrave Macmillan), pp. 197–209.

Higgins, M., M. Montgomery, A. Smith & A. Tolson (2011) Belligerent broadcasting and makeover television: Professional incivility in *Ramsay's Kitchen Nightmares. International Journal of Cultural Studies,* 15: 501–18.

Hill, A. (2005) *Reality TV: Audiences and Popular Factual Television* (London: Routledge).

Hutchby, I. (2006) *Media Talk* (Maidenhead: Open University Press), ch. 4.

Illoux, E. (2003) *Oprah Winfrey and the Glamour of Misery* (New York: Columbia University Press.

Lorenzo-Dus, N. (2009) *Television Discourse: Analysing Language in the Media* (Basingstoke: Palgrave Macmillan).

Lunt, P. & P. Stenner (2005) *The Jerry Springer Show* as an emotional public sphere. *Media, Culture and Society,* 27: 59–81.

Myers G. (2001) 'I'm out of it: you guys argue': Making an issue of it on *The Jerry Springer Show.* In A. Tolson (ed.), *Television Talk Shows: Discourse, Performance, Spectacle* (Mahwah, NJ: Lawrence Erlbaum Associates).

Nunn, H. & A. Biressi (2008) Reflections on the 'undeserving poor'. In *Soundings: Class and Culture Debate.* http://www.lwbooks.co.uk/journals/soundings/class_and_culture/nunnbiressi.html

Palmer, G. 'The new you': Class and transformation in lifestyle television. In S. Holmes & D. Jermyn (eds.), *Understanding Reality Television* (London: Routledge), pp. 173–90.

Scannell, P. (ed.) (1991) *Broadcast Talk* (London: Sage Publications).

Shattuc, J. (1997) *The Talking Cure: TV Talk Shows and Women* (New York: Routledge).

Taylor, L. (2005) 'It was beautiful before you changed it all': Class, taste and the transformative aesthetics of the garden lifestyle media. In D. Bell & J. Hollows (eds.), *Ordinary Lifestyles: Popular Media, Consumption and Taste* (Maidenhead: Open University Press), pp. 113–27.

Tolson, A. (2006) *Media Talk: Spoken Discourse on TV and Radio* (Edinburgh: Edinburgh University Press), ch. 7.

Vallely, P. (2007) TV presenter Jeremy Kyle: Meet the ringmaster. *The Independent* September 29.

Wood, H. & B. Skeggs (2008) Spectacular morality: 'Reality' television, individualisation and the re-making of the working class. In D. Hesmondhalgh & J. Toynbee (eds.), *Media and Social Theory* (London: Routledge), pp. 177–93.

Wood, H. & B. Skeggs (2011) *Reality Television and Class* (London: BFI/Palgrave Macmillan).

Index

Printed and bound by CPI Group (UK) Ltd, Croydon, CR0 4YY